The
Woody Allen
Companion

The
Woody Allen
Companion

Stephen J. Spignesi

Andrews and McMeel
A Universal Press Syndicate Company
Kansas City

Library of Congress Cataloging-in-Publication Data

Spignesi, Stephen J.
    The Woody Allen companion / Stephen J. Spignesi,
        p.   cm.
    Includes biographical references.
    ISBN 0-8362-8002-4 (pbk.) : $12.95
    1. Allen. Woody—Criticism and interpretation.   I. Title.
PN1998.3.A45S6   1992   92-31590
791.43′092—dc20   CIP

Book Design: Edward King
Typography: Connell-Zeko Type & Graphics

ATTENTION: SCHOOLS AND BUSINESSES

This book is dedicated
with admiration and thanks
to two men
whose friendship I greatly value,
and whose counsel *is* of great value

John White
and
George Beahm

We shall not cease from exploration
And the end of all our exploring
Will be to arrive where we started
And know the place for the first time.
T. S. Eliot, "Little Gidding"

Probable impossibilities
are to be preferred
to improbable possibilities.
Aristotle, *Poetics*

CONTENTS

III
OUT OF THE WOODWORK . . .
Reflections on the Work of Woody Allen

APPENDICES

ANNOTATED BIBLIOGRAPHY

The Treasure of New York

Nobody expects big box office from Woody Allen. Maybe nobody really wants it. Actors simply die to be handpicked by him to play minor roles in which they invariably don't know what they are doing or what the movie is about. (Or even if their contributions will make it into the final cut.) Woody is an authentic New York City treasure and like New York itself, he may be financially unappealing, but he's got that "certain something" only New York has.

Liz Smith, from her column in the
***New York Post*, February 20, 1991**

Writing comedy for yourself is a fascinating personal confrontation. It contains the ultimately insoluble twin dilemmas of how much do you want your act to be an act, a mask, and how much of your life is itself an act, a mask. And, oh yes, a third dilemma: how relevant they are one to the other.

Dick Cavett, quoted in *Cavett*, by
Dick Cavett and Christopher Porterfield

While other American independent filmmakers have emerged in the eighties . . . Allen's canon remains distinctive for its literate density, diversity and volume. By no one else does the prospect of a new film seem so assuringly yet mysteriously An Event.

Maurice Yacowar, *Loser Take All:*
The Comic Art of Woody Allen

Where art and artist intersect, they reveal the man.

Eric Lax, *Woody Allen: A Biography*

I'm a product of television and psychoanalysis.

Woody Allen

WHILE WRITING *The Woody Allen Companion,* I kept propped up on my desk a black-and-white photograph postcard of Woody Allen taken in 1969. The photo was by Philippe Halsman and showed Woody leaning on an all-white table against an all-white background, wearing a sweater and an open shirt. He had his face propped in his left hand, and a quizzical, befuddled, and, yes, depressed look on his face.

This postcard inspired me.

Whenever I was tired, or frustrated, or bored, I would look at Woody and immediately knew what to do: quit for the day.

But seriously . . .

The Woody Allen Companion is a general-interest book about Woody and his work.

It is in companion format, a style which is very accessible to the average fan, and which serves many purposes, not the least of which is that of offering comprehensive information about an artist's work—information which is not readily available without much time and research.

There have been dozens of interpretive volumes on Woody and his work. These books were, for the most part, very sober and very well done. But they occasionally left the average fan feeling somewhat bewildered by the seriousness of the analysis of a body of work that is essentially *funny.* Woody Allen, you'll recall, is the guy who says he once took a puff on a strange cigarette and broke two teeth trying to give a hickey to the Statue of Liberty. Surely, he's a dramatist too, but he is also one of the world's few living comic geniuses. (That's a fairly grandiose statement, I know, but can you name another living artist, working in as many fields as Woody, whose work will likely be watched, read, and enjoyed a hundred years from now?)

The Woody Allen Companion peers at Woody and his work from a slightly different angle.

For instance, Chapter 12, "Seen Scenes," offers those moments in Woody's films in which his characters watch films, attend plays and concerts, or view TV. This is interesting information because it shows how Woody thinks; how selective he is when choosing the films the characters watch; and how these moments add layers of meaning to the interpretation of his work.

In *Crimes and Misdemeanors,* Cliff and Halley watch *This Gun for Hire* after a scene in which Judah and his brother Jack discussed doing away with Dolores. Thematically, the choice of this film works on two levels: blatantly, since Judah is in fact looking for a "hired gun" to resolve his problem with Dolores; and metaphorically, as Cliff has become a "hired gun" by agreeing to film a biography of Lester. (His role becomes clearer when we see just *how* Cliff planned on presenting the pompous and obnoxious Lester.) Moreover, the choice of *This Gun for Hire* nicely refers back to *Manhattan: Gun* starred Veronica Lake, and in *Manhattan,* Isaac promised he'd take Tracy to see a Veronica Lake movie.

This is interesting information, but not something many fans would recognize. That is the purpose of a "Companion." By seeing all the intricate references and subtextual nuances delineated, we can perhaps get a clearer understanding of Woody Allen and his work.

The primary—and, I think, most important—purpose of *The Woody Allen Companion,* is to assemble, *in one place,* all the information about Woody Allen's work that, until now, has been available, but never really *at hand.*

You, dear reader and Woody fan, will, of course, be the ultimate arbiter of my work, but I send forth this tome believing that it does its job of providing a ready companion and reference to the work of Woody Allen.

I think it's important, for instance, that we have as complete a listing as possible of the cultural references in Woody's work. (See Chapter 10, "Woody Allen, Culture Animal.") I also believe it's important that we have a *complete* listing of Woody's recorded standup comedy routines, as well as a comparison between the original versions and the later, edited versions that appear on his compilation albums. (See Chapter 7, "Woody Allen, Recording Star.")

Woody Allen is too important an artist to just let this information be scattered about—available, yes (even though sometimes only with some serious archaeological work), but always in danger of being lost, or worse, forgotten.

You will not find much here in the way of traditional biographical coverage. For those wanting to know more about Woody's life story, I enthusiastically refer you to Eric Lax's fascinating *Woody Allen: A Biography. The Woody Allen Companion,* instead, focuses mainly on the nuts and bolts of Woody's work, and thus should be read in conjunction with Lax's book for a wide-ranging, comprehensive overview of both Woody and his work.

There is something intangible about the magic of Woody Allen. His sensibility is unique, making it almost impossible to nail down just what it is that makes his work so appealing to so many people.

In 1987, in an interview with William Geist for *Rolling Stone* magazine (the entire interview is reprinted in Chapter 2), Woody Allen described American television as "the height of soulless, plastic, brightly lit, antiseptic . . . stupidity."

Woody's recognition and assessment of the banality of (most of) American TV can help us understand, I think, the genius in Woody's own work. Our culture has become blasé and noncritical, accepting of, on a regular basis, the slightest of works. If you see enough laughtrack-enhanced sitcoms, mawkish made-for-TV movies, and idiotic game shows, it becomes all too easy to lose sight of the fact that you are lowering your artistic standards by allowing yourself to be entertained by these productions. Yes, art should entertain, but it should also make us think, and it should attempt to offer some kind of enlightenment on the human condition. This does not have to be arduous either: *Crimes and Misdemeanors* and "Dynasty" both essentially cover the same turf: difficult relationships, and their attendant intricate problems and moral quandaries. Yet *Crimes and Misdemeanors* is clearly the intellectually—and artistically—superior work. It is also far more entertaining than any ten episodes of "Dynasty."

Perhaps it isn't fair to compare films with television, but I'm doing it to make a simple point: Woody Allen refuses to produce work that would probably be welcomed by a huge number of his fans. Woody probably could have got away with doing *Bananas, Sleeper,* and *Annie Hall* for the rest of his artistic career. Many of his fans would have been happy. Woody himself would not have been. His standards are too high.

His artistic restlessness has resulted in experiments like *A Midsummer Night's Sex Comedy* and *Zelig;* dramas like *Interiors, Another Woman,* and *September;* and "novels on film" like *Hannah and Her Sisters* and *Crimes and Misdemeanors.*

It would be unrealistic not to acknowledge the missteps. And yet, United Artists, Orion, and, now, TriStar Studios are still willing to give carte blanche to Woody Allen. Woody controls it all: the script, the casting, the final cut; hell, even the advertising. And why? Because it is recognized that Woody Allen is probably one of the two or three bona fide "filmmakers for the ages." It is clear and evident that Woody, as an auteur, is in a class by himself. He has a singular vision and artistic voice, and there's no question that his best work will survive. We can legitimately include Woody in the pantheon of great directors where repose Alfred Hitchcock, Orson Welles, Frank Capra, Walt Disney, John Huston, John Ford, Buster Keaton, Charlie Chaplin, D. W. Griffith, Ingmar Bergman, Jean Renoir, Franco Zeffirelli, and Luis Buñuel. (A case can also be made for acknowledging Martin Scorsese in like manner, but that's another book.) And it is because of the obvious major artistic merit of Woody's work that there are almost as many books written—well over two dozen at this writing—*about* Woody and his work as there are works *by* Woody Allen. And Woody does a film a year.

I have tried to include features in *The Woody Allen Companion* that entertain, inform, and enlighten. I hope this book enhances your enjoyment of Woody's work and offers some new insights.

I welcome your thoughts and comments. Fellow Woody fanatics can write to me in care of Andrews and McMeel.

Welcome to the Woodland.

New Haven, Connecticut
December 1, 1991

ACKNOWLEDGMENTS

. . . with a little help from my friends.
John Lennon and Paul McCartney

Thank You

THIS BOOK owes its genesis to one of the men to whom it is dedicated: George Beahm. George didn't have anything to do with the actual construct of this pile of pages. For that I must take blame. But George gave me the idea to do a Woody "companion" after the publication of his own book, *The Stephen King Companion,* another Andrews and McMeel title, and I wanted to publicly express my appreciation to George for the brainstorm.

My appreciation also to . . .

My wife, Pam, for her love and support, and also for keeping track of every "Woody Allen" reference in "Northern Exposure";

My editor, Donna Martin, for allowing me to see my work through her eyes; and also Patty Donnelly and Patty Rice at Andrews and McMeel for all their help and kindness;

My agent, John White, for his years of friendship, support, and invaluable assistance;

The legendary Steve Allen, for his immediate willingness to be a part of this project; the sagacious Douglas Brode, for his interview and his wonderful book; my artist and my brother, David Spignesi; as well as the rest of my always supportive family; Erik Leeming, for help above and beyond;

Roger Ebert; Stephen Farber; Stephen Banker and *Tapes for Readers;* Dan Scapperotti; William Geist; Brian Gerosa and Gerosa Records; that madman across the water, Paddy McKillop; Marge and Steve Rapuano; Laurie and Dave Hinchberger and The Overlook Connection; Tyson Blue; Carolyn Wyman; Tom Schultheiss; Pat Curtis; Mark A. Altman; Katherine Flickinger; Jack Rollins; Lisa Hintelmann at PMK Publicity; Nikki DeGioia at *Rolling Stone;* Melanie Oakes at *Premiere;* Gia Kourlas and John Taylor at *New York;* the madmen at *MAD;* Terry Barbaro at the Mary Ellen Mark Library; Grove Press; Kris and the people at T/Maker Graphics; the *Kenyon Review;* Michael Ochs and the Michael Ochs Archive; Yale University and the staff of the Sterling Memorial Library; the University of New Haven and the staff of the University of New Haven Library, the East Haven Public Library; the

Bridgeport Public Library; *Tikkun;* the *New Yorker* library staff; the staff of the *Playboy* Readers' Service department; Fred Clarke and *Cinefantastique;* Popular Culture, Ink.; Random House; NAL/Signet; the *New York Times;* Liz Smith; Angelyn Spignesi; Dick Baden; Dianne Wiest; Jim Cole; Ted DeMaio; Linda DeLaurentis; the people at Postings; the people at Fotofolio; Bob and Sue Leen and Debbie at Minuteman Press; Linda Zmarthie; Linda Beavis and Tommy K Video; Doug Duve and PrimeTime Video; Dolores and Tony Fantarella; my pal Peppie Perrelli;

Robert Benayoun, Eric Lax, Graham McCann, Thierry de Navacelle, Nancy Pogel, Ralph Rosenblum, and Maurice Yacowar, all for their wonderful "Woody" books;

And most of all, Woody Allen, without whom . . .

PART I

The Woodman
The Life and Times of Woody Allen

CHAPTER 1

The Woody Allen Time Line
A Bio-Bibliographic Chronology

THIS CHRONOLOGY highlights Woody Allen's life and career, and also gives details on ancillary events important to Woody fans.

You will find basic biographical information arranged by year, as well as the dates of important publications by Woody Allen. All of Woody Allen's films, of course, are here, as well as the publication dates of his books.

I decided on this format because I felt it offered much information in an easily obtained manner.

1890
• The Rampone clarinet Woody will later own and play is made in Italy.

1900
• Tuesday, December 25: Martin Konigsberg, Woody Allen's father, is born.

1908
• Friday, November 6: Nettie Cherry, Woody Allen's mother, is born.

1931
• Woody Allen's parents, Martin Konigsberg and Nettie Cherry, are married.

1935
• Sunday, December 1: Allan Stewart Konigsberg (Woody Allen) is born to Martin and Nettie (Cherry) Konigsberg in the Bronx section of New York.

1938 (Age 3)
• Woody Allen sees his first film, Walt Disney's animated *Snow White and the Seven Dwarfs*.

1939 (Age 4)
- Woody Allen sees *Beau Geste* with his mother.
- Louise Lasser is born.

1940 (Age 5)
- According to Woody's mother, this was the year that something happened to Woody that "made [him] turn sour." (Eric Lax, *Woody Allen: A Biography* [New York: Knopf, 1991])
- Woody sees *Pinocchio* with his mother.

1941 (Age 6)
- Woody Allen makes his first trip to Manhattan.

1943 (Age 8)
- Letty Konigsberg Aronson, Woody's only sibling, is born.
- Woody Allen thinks to himself, "Hey, I could do this" (Lax) while watching Tyrone Power in *The Black Swan*.
- In 1943 or 1944 Woody sees his first Marx Brothers movie at the Vogue Theater on Coney Island.

1944 (Age 9)
- The Konigsbergs move to 1216 East Twelfth Street in Brooklyn.

1945 (Age 10)
- Friday, February 9: Mia Farrow is born (Maria de Lourdes Villers Farrow) in Santa Monica, California.

1946 (Age 11)
- Saturday, January 5: Diane Keaton is born in Highland Park, Los Angeles, California.

1947 (Age 12)
- Woody remembers seeing the 1946 film *Dick Tracy Versus Cueball* during the blizzard of 1947 in Manhattan.

1948 (Age 13)
- Woody is bar mitzvahed. (According to Lax, the day before the ceremony, Woody saw *Canon City*.)
- Woody takes up magic as a hobby.

1949 (Age 14)
- Woody graduates from P. S. 99 and enters Midwood High School.

1950 (Age 15)

- The musical cutoff year for Woody Allen's taste in popular music. Woody "has no use for almost any popular song written after about 1950" (Lax).
- Woody begins playing the clarinet.

1951 (Age 16)

- Woody performs at Weinstein's Majestic Bungalow Colony in the Catskills. (Weinstein's is later mentioned in Woody's play *The Floating Light Bulb,* and in his film *Broadway Danny Rose.*)

1952 (Age 17)

- SPRING: "Woody Allen" is born when Allan Konigsberg decides on the name (one he feels is more suited to show business), and begins sending out unsolicited jokes to gossip columnists at New York newspapers.
- Tuesday, November 25: Woody's first published joke appears in Walter Winchell's column: "Woody Allen says he ate at a restaurant that had OPS prices—over people's salaries."
- Woody Allen jokes that appear in Earl Wilson's column include the following:

  - "Taffy Tuttle heard of a man who was a six-footer, and told Woody Allen, 'Gee, it must take him a long time to put his shoes on.'"
  - "Under the heading of 'Wish I'd Said That' was 'It's the fallen women who are usually picked up.'"
  - "Woody Allen reports the latest Tin Pan Alley song hit: 'You Were Meant for Me—Dammit.'"
  - "Woody Allen boasts that he just made a fortune—he was downtown auctioning off his parking space."

- Woody sees his first Ingmar Bergman film, *Summer with Monika.* According to Eric Lax, Woody and his friends considered the film a "mustsee" because they had heard there was a naked woman in it.
- Woody does his first standup routine at a Young Israel social club. He uses his friend Mike Merrick's material.

1953 (Age 18)

- Woody begins working for David Alber, writing jokes after school for twenty dollars a week.
- JUNE: Woody graduates from Midwood High School. His name is misspelled as "Alan Konisberg" on his diploma.
- FALL: Woody enrolls in New York University to study motion picture production. He fails the course. (His term paper was on the importance of music in films. He cited the use of drums in *Stalag 17.*)
- Woody enrolls in City College of New York but drops out there as well.

- Woody signs a five-year 35 percent commission contract with William Morris Agency agent Harvey Meltzer.
- Woody sees *City of Bad Men.*
- Woody first needs glasses. He decides on black horn-rimmed frames in imitation of Mike Merrick.

1954 (Age 19)
- Woody enrolls in a night course in motion picture production at City College of New York. He doesn't last the term.
- Woody takes a class on dramatic writing.
- Woody enrolls in a photography class and never attends.
- Woody attends a New York University summer session. He takes Motion Picture Production and English. He gets a C minus in the film course, and an F in the English course.
- Woody writes bits for Peter Lind Hayes and other radio performers.
- Woody poses in celebrity ads for Parker Brothers.
- Woody meets Harlene Rosen.
- Woody first hears Mort Sahl at the Blue Angel in Manhattan.
- A professor Woody knows recommends therapy.

1955 (Age 20)
- Woody is laid off from David Alber's.
- Woody begins working at NBC for $169 a week as part of its Writer's Development Program.
- Woody moves to Hollywood to write for "The Colgate Comedy Hour."

1956 (Age 21)
- JANUARY: Woody and Harlene Rosen get engaged.
- Thursday, March 15: Woody marries Harlene Rosen at the Hollywood Hawaiian Hotel.
- MAY: "The Colgate Comedy Hour" (now "The Colgate Variety Hour") goes belly up.
- SUMMER: Woody and Harlene, now back in New York, take an apartment at 110 East Sixty-first Street.
- SEPTEMBER: Max Liebman hires Woody to write for "Stanley," a TV sitcom starring Buddy Hackett. ("Stanley" aired from September 24, 1956, through March 11, 1957, and starred Hackett, Paul Lynde, and Carol Burnett.)
- For three summers, beginning in 1956, Woody writes a show a week at Camp Tamiment Resort. He earns $150 a week.

1957 (Age 22)
- SPRING: Woody almost gets hired to write for Sid Caesar's show, "Caesar's Hour," but the show has no budget and the deal falls through.

1958 (Age 23)

- Sid Caesar hires Woody to write for NBC's "Sid Caesar's Chevy Show." The show is aired on November 2, and Woody and Larry Gelbart win a Sylvania Award for their writing on the show.
- Woody works on "The Pat Boone–Chevy Show" for a brief time.
- Woody and Larry Gelbart are nominated for an Emmy Award for the 1958–59 TV season for "Writing on a Single Musical or Variety Program" for their work on "Sid Caesar's Chevy Show" with Shirley MacLaine, Art Carney, and Jo Stafford. They don't win. Bud Yorkin and Herbert Baker win for "An Evening with Fred Astaire."

1959 (Age 24)

- Woody begins analysis.

1960 (Age 25)

- Woody is now earning $1,700 a week as a writer for "The Gary Moore Show."
- Wednesday, April 20: Woody's Broadway debut. The show *From A to Z* opens at the Plymouth Theater, and closes after twenty-one performances. This show contained Woody's skit "Psychological Warfare," and a "Groucho Marx" skit, both from his work at Camp Tamiment.
- OCTOBER: Woody gets a one-night audition at the Blue Angel nightclub.
- Rollins and Joffe put Woody into the Upstairs at the Duplex in Greenwich Village so he can refine his standup act. He does two shows a night, six days a week.
- Woody meets Louise Lasser.

1961 (Age 26)

- Woody moves out of his and Harlene's apartment.
- JUNE: Dick Cavett sees Woody Allen at the Bitter End coffeehouse.
- Woody appears as a guest on "P.M. East–P.M. West," which was hosted by Mike Wallace.

1962 (Age 27)

- Woody appears as a guest on "The Ed Sullivan Show."
- Woody works as a writer on "The Tonight Show," hosted by Jack Paar.
- Woody and Harlene divorce.
- Monday, August 20: An article about Woody titled "Pushing Back" appears in *Newsweek*. It is the first article about Woody to appear in a national news magazine.
- NOVEMBER: Woody returns to Greenwich Village for a four-month booking at the Bitter End.
- NOVEMBER: Woody's standup act is reviewed very positively by Arthur Gelb in the *New York Times*. It his first major review.

1963 (Age 28)

- JULY: Woody appears at Mr. Kelly's in Chicago.
- Friday, November 15: Woody appears on "The Steve Allen Show." [Note: See the feature on Woody's appearance as well as Steve Allen's remembrance of the show in Chapter 30.]
- Sunday, December 22: Woody appears (with Count Basie) at Carnegie Hall. *New York Times* critic John Wilson, in a review of the evening, said that Woody's act rescued an otherwise dull evening.
- Woody appears as a guest on the TV show "Hootenanny." (This is ironic, since at the time "Hootenanny" was still "blacklisting" certain "left-wing" performers (including Pete Seeger and the Weavers). Thirteen years later, Woody would star in *The Front,* a masterful film about the horrors of blacklisting.)
- Woody appears several times as a guest on the TV show "Candid Camera."

1964 (Age 29)

- Midsixties: Woody Allen and Marshall Brickman collaborate on the writing of a screenplay called *The Filmmaker.* It was never produced.
- MARCH: Woody appears at Mr. Kelly's in Chicago. The standup routine he performs that evening is recorded and appears on the record album *Woody Allen.*
- APRIL: Woody is earning $4,000–$5,000 a week doing his standup comedy routine.
- JULY: Woody signs on as the first guest host of Johnny Carson's "Tonight Show," replacing Johnny for a week.
- JULY: Colpix Records releases *Woody Allen,* Woody's first record album. Woody is nominated for a Grammy Award for the album. He loses to Bill Cosby's *I Started Out as a Child.*
- DECEMBER: Woody is earning up to $10,000 for a single personal appearance.
- While performing at the Blue Angel, Woody is approached by agent and producer Charles Feldman, who persuades Woody to take on the scripting chores of the film that was eventually released as *What's New, Pussycat?*

1965 (Age 30)

- APRIL: Woody appears at the Shadows in Washington, D.C. The standup routine he performs that evening is recorded and appears on *Woody Allen, Volume 2.*
- JUNE: *What's New, Pussycat?*, directed by Clive Donner from a screenplay by Woody, is released by Famous Artists.
- FALL: Colpix Records releases *Woody Allen, Volume 2,* Woody's second record album.

• Friday, December 31, New Year's Eve: Woody appears as a guest on "The Tonight Show" with Johnny Carson.

1966 (Age 31)

• Thursday, January 20: Woody's comic short story "The Gossage–Vardebedian Papers" is published in the *New Yorker* magazine. It is Woody's first appearance in the *New Yorker.*
• Wednesday, February 2: Woody marries Louise Lasser. The same night, in the middle of a huge snowstorm, Woody does two shows at the Royal Box at the American Hotel.
• SPRING: Woody completes the writing of his play *Don't Drink the Water.*
• JULY: At the age of twenty-one, Mia Farrow marries Frank Sinatra.
• FALL: *What's Up, Tiger Lily?* an English adaptation of *Kagi No Kagi* (*Key of Keys,* Japan, 1964), is released by American International Pictures. Woody (and others) wrote a new screenplay, which was dubbed in over the original film's soundtrack. Woody was also the film's re-release director.
• Thursday, November 17: Woody's play *Don't Drink the Water* opens on Broadway at the Morosco Theater. It will run for 598 performances.
• Woody performs at the opening of the London Playboy Club.
• Woody appears as guest host of the TV show "Hippodrome."

1967 (Age 32)

• Wednesday, December 27: Woody hosts "The Year 1967 in Review" on "The Kraft Music Hall." (It ran at 9:00 P.M. on NBC.)
• The play *Don't Drink the Water* by Woody Allen is published by Random House.
• *Casino Royale* is released by Columbia Pictures.
• Harlene Rosen sues Woody and NBC for $1 million "for holding her up to scorn and ridicule."

1968 (Age 33)

• AUGUST: Woody appears at Eugene's (a cabaret dedicated to raising money to aid Eugene McCarthy). The standup routine he performs that evening is recorded and appears on *The Third Woody Allen Album.*
• Woody appears at Mr. Kelly's in Chicago. While staying at the Astor Towers hotel, Woody works on the play *Play It Again, Sam.*
• Capitol Records releases *The Third Woody Allen Album,* Woody's third record album.

1969 (Age 34)

• Wednesday, February 12: Woody's play *Play It Again, Sam* opens on Broadway at the Broadhurst Theater. It will run for 453 performances.

- Tuesday, August 19: Woody's first original film, *Take the Money and Run,* is released by Palomar Pictures. It opened at the 68th Street Playhouse on the East Side of Manhattan, Woody and Mickey Rose wrote the screenplay, and Woody directed the film and starred as the hapless crook Virgil Starkwell.
- Sunday, September 21: Woody writes, and appears as the star of, "The Kraft Music Hall: The Woody Allen Special," which also starred Billy Graham, Candice Bergen, and the Fifth Dimension.
- The play *Play It Again, Sam* by Woody Allen is published by Random House.
- The film version of *Don't Drink the Water* is released by Avco Embassy. The screenplay is by R. S. Allen and Harvey Bullock, based on Woody's original stage play.
- Woody and Louise Lasser divorce.
- Woody appears as a guest on "The Merv Griffin Show."

1970 (Age 35)
- Saturday, March 14: Woody's play *Play It Again, Sam* closes at the Broad-hurst Theater.
- Woody Allen buys a duplex penthouse apartment on Fifth Avenue on Central Park East, where he has lived ever since.
- Woody hosts a Saturday morning educational children's program called "Hot Dog."

1971 (Age 36)
- Woody, accompanied by Diane Keaton, attends the New Orleans Jazz and Heritage Festival and sits in on some French Quarter jam sessions. Woody remembers this trip as one of the high points of his life.
- Woody and his New Orleans Funeral and Ragtime Orchestra begin their weekly Monday night stints at Michael's Pub in New York City.
- *Getting Even* by Woody Allen is published in hardcover by Random House.
- *Bananas* is released by United Artists. The screenplay was by Woody and Mickey Rose, and the film was directed by Woody. Woody starred in the film as products tester/revolutionary Fielding Mellish.
- Friday, April 30: Woody appears as a guest on "The Steve Allen Show."
- DECEMBER: The TV special "The Politics of Woody Allen" is filmed for broadcast on PBS. It is never aired because of what the network felt was "too controversial" material. The original title of the special was "The Woody Allen Comedy Special." Woody donated his services to PBS.

1972 (Age 37)
- Friday, May 5: *Play It Again, Sam* is released by Paramount Pictures.
- OCTOBER: Woody writes the play *Death.*

- OCTOBER: Woody does two weeks of standup at Caesar's Palace in Las Vegas. His appearance ended a six-week six-city tour. He earned $85,000 for the two weeks at Caesar's. He was second-billed after Harry Belafonte.
- The film version of *Play It Again, Sam* is released by Paramount Pictures. The screenplay was by Woody and the film was directed by Herbert Ross.
- *Woody Allen's "Play It Again, Sam"* (a frame-by-frame reproduction of the film) is published by Grosset & Dunlap.
- *Everything You Always Wanted to Know About Sex* (*But Were Afraid to Ask)* is released by United Artists. The screenplay is by Woody and is (loosely) based on the book by David Reuben.

1973 (Age 38)
- Tuesday, December 18: *Sleeper* is released by United Artists. The screenplay was by Woody and Marshall Brickman, and Woody directed the film.

1975 (Age 40)
- Wednesday, June 11: *Love and Death* is released by United Artists. Woody wrote the screenplay and directed the film.
- The play *Death* is published by Samuel French, Inc.
- The play *God* is published by Samuel French, Inc.
- *Without Feathers* by Woody Allen is published in hardcover by Random House.

1976 (Age 41)
- United Artists releases *Woody Album: The Night-Club Years, 1964–1968,* a double album comprising material from the albums *Woody Allen, Woody Allen, Volume 2,* and *The Third Woody Allen Album.*
- *Inside Woody Allen,* a comic strip drawn by Stuart Hample, premières in 60 countries, in 180 newspapers. The jokes were by Woody, and the strip would run for eight years, until 1984.
- JUNE: *Without Feathers* is published in paperback by Warner Books.
- *The Front,* directed by Martin Ritt, is released by Columbia Pictures.
- Friday, New Year's Eve: Woody throws a party. Guests include S. J. Perelman, Arthur Miller, Norman Mailer, and his future *Scenes from a Mall* costar, Bette Midler.

1977 (Age 42)
- Thursday, April 21: *Annie Hall* is released by United Artists. Woody and Marshall Brickman wrote the screenplay and the film was directed by Woody.
- Woody appears as a guest on "The Dick Cavett Show." Footage from one of his appearances on the show is used in *Annie Hall.*

- Woody is nominated for an Academy Award for Best Actor for his performance in *Annie Hall.*
- Woody is nominated for Academy Awards for Best Director, Best Picture, and Best Screenplay Written Directly for the Screen (with Marshall Brickman) for *Annie Hall.* (Woody was the first person to be nominated for Director, Picture, and Screenplay since Orson Welles in 1941 for *Citizen Kane.*)
- Woody wins the New York Film Critics Award for Best Director and Best Screenplay for *Annie Hall.*
- Woody wins the National Society of Film Critics Screenwriting Award for *Annie Hall.*
- The thirty-minute documentary *Woody Allen: An American Comedy,* written and directed by Howard Mantell and narrated by Woody, is released by Films for the Humanities, Inc.

1978 (Age 43)

- Orion Pictures is formed by former United Artists executives Arthur Krim and Eric Pleskow.
- Monday, March 27: Woody wins Academy Awards for Best Director, Best Picture, and Best Screenplay Written Directly for the Screen (with Marshall Brickman) for *Annie Hall.*
- Monday, March 27: Diane Keaton wins the Best Actress Academy Award for her performance in *Annie Hall.*
- Monday, March 27: This historic night finds the Woodman playing the clarinet with the New Orleans Funeral and Ragtime Orchestra at Michael's Pub on Manhattan's East Side. He is quoted as saying, "I couldn't let down the guys." Woody returns home at midnight, goes to bed, and doesn't find out until the following morning that he has won the Oscar Triple Crown. He has no comment about his sweep.
- AUGUST: *Getting Even* is published in paperback by Vintage Books.
- Wednesday, August 2: *Interiors* is released by United Artists.
- *Non-Being and Somethingness* by Stuart Hample (a selection of comic strips from the comic strip *Inside Woody Allen*) is published by Random House.
- Woody is nominated for Academy Awards for Best Director and for Best Screenplay Written Directly for the Screen for his 1978 film, *Interiors.*
- Casablanca Record and Filmworks releases *Woody Allen Standup Comic,* a double album composed of material from the albums *Woody Allen, Woody Allen, Volume 2,* and *The Third Woody Allen Album.* The jacket of *Woody Allen Standup Comic* bore this note from producer Steve Tyrell: "This is a unique and historical album, drawn from Woody Allen's formative nightclub years. It embodies his only recordings as a standup comedian. Very little has been lost of the original material. I feel fortunate to have had access to these rare and early live recordings, especially now, knowing the full extent of Woody Allen's comic genius."

1979 (Age 44)

- Monday, April 9: Woody and *Interiors* lose the Best Director Academy Award to Michael Cimino for *The Deer Hunter,* and the Best Screenplay Written Directly for the Screen award to *Coming Home* by Waldo Salt and Robert C. Jones.
- Wednesday, April 25: *Manhattan* is released by United Artists. The screenplay was by Woody and Marshall Brickman and the film was directed by Woody.
- FALL: Woody meets Mia Farrow.
- Woody wins the British Academy Award for *Manhattan.*
- Woody wins the New York Film Critics Award for *Manhattan.*
- Woody and Marshall Brickman are nominated for an Academy Award for Best Screenplay Written Directly for the Screen for *Manhattan.*
- Woody appears in *My Favorite Comedian,* a tribute to Bob Hope, at the New York Film Festival.

1980 (Age 45)

- Monday, April 14: Woody and Marshall Brickman and *Manhattan* lose the Academy Award for Best Screenplay Written Directly for the Screen to *Breaking Away* by Steve Tesich.
- Thursday, April 17: Woody and Mia Farrow meet at Lutèce for lunch, and their long-term relationship begins.
- Woody leaves United Artists and moves to Orion Pictures, where he stays until 1991. (His last picture released by United Artists was *Stardust Memories;* his first by Orion, *A Midsummer Night's Sex Comedy.*)
- *Side Effects* by Woody Allen is published in hardcover by Random House.
- *Stardust Memories* is released by United Artists. Woody wrote the screenplay and directed the film.

1981 (Age 46)

- Monday, April 27: Woody's play *The Floating Light Bulb* opens in New York at the Vivian Beaumont Theater.
- SEPTEMBER: The first printing of the Ballantine Books paperback edition of *Side Effects* is released.

1982 (Age 47)

- *A Midsummer Night's Sex Comedy* is released by Orion Pictures. Woody wrote the screenplay and directed the film.
- The play *The Floating Light Bulb* by Woody Allen is published by Random House.
- *Four Films of Woody Allen* is published by Random House. The book contains exact reconstructions of the scripts of the final screen versions of *Annie Hall, Interiors, Manhattan,* and *Stardust Memories.* Stage directions have been added by the publisher to describe the action.

1983 (Age 48)

- *Zelig* is released by Orion Pictures. Woody wrote the screenplay and directed the film.

1984 (Age 49)

- JANUARY: *Broadway Danny Rose* is released by Orion Pictures. Woody wrote the screenplay and directed the film.
- *Video Review* magazine runs an advertisement for National Video, Inc., featuring Woody Allen look-alike Phil Boroff renting videotapes of *Annie Hall* and *Bananas.* Surveys revealed that many of the people who saw the ad thought it was really Woody Allen. Woody filed suit against actor Phil Boroff, his agent Ron Smith Celebrity Look-a-Likes, and the National Video chain for $10 million, charging the ad was "fraudulent" and embarrassing. (See September 22, 1986.)

1985 (Age 50)

- *The Purple Rose of Cairo* is released by Orion Pictures. Woody wrote the screenplay and directed the film.
- Woody and Mia Farrow adopt a newborn girl from Texas. They name her Dylan O'Sullivan Farrow.
- Tuesday, November 5: Woody and company begin shooting *Radio Days* in and about New York City.
- Monday, December 16: Woody Allen reads two unpublished short stories at a benefit to raise money for the forty-eighth International PEN Congress to be held in January 1986. (Also participating in the benefit was John Updike, who read his poem "Ian Fleming Revisited.") Woody's first story was about a fifty-three-year-old lawyer named Sid Kaplan who has suffered "rejections so numerous they had to be delivered by the Santini Brothers." In the story, Kaplan fantasizes about a gorgeous young woman he saw in the elevator of the Park Avenue building where he lived. The second unpublished story Woody read seemed to be the seminal image for a scene used in *Stardust Memories.* In the story, Phil Feldman's hostility escapes from him (as a hairy black blob with red eyes) and goes on a rampage, attacking Feldman's psychiatrist and his parents as well as feeding a radio to a teenage boy who was playing it too loudly.
- Woody and Mia hire Arthur Miller's daughter Rebecca as an *au pair* girl for baby Dylan. Rebecca will take care of Dylan on the set of *Radio Days* while Mia is working.

1986 (Age 51)

- FEBRUARY: *Hannah and Her Sisters* is released by Orion Pictures. Woody wrote the screenplay and directed the film.
- FEBRUARY: As a protest against apartheid, Woody forbids his films to be shown in South Africa.

- Wednesday, February 19: Woody completes the first shooting of *Radio Days.*
- Friday, April 25: Woody begins the reshoot of *Radio Days.*
- Friday, May 9: Woody completes the reshoot of *Radio Days.*
- Monday, September 22: In Manhattan Federal Court, minutes before a trial was scheduled to begin in the case, Woody Allen settles his $10 million lawsuit against Woody look-alike Phil Boroff, Ron Smith Celebrity Look-a-Likes, and the National Video chain for $425,000. (See 1984.)

1987 (Age 52)
- JANUARY: *Hannah and Her Sisters* is published by Random House (a Vintage original). The book contains an exact reconstruction of the script of the final screen version of *Hannah and Her Sisters.* Stage directions have been added by the publisher to describe the action.
- Friday, January 30: *Radio Days* is released by Orion Pictures. Woody wrote the screenplay and directed the film. He also narrated the film as the adult Little Joe.
- AUGUST: *Three Films of Woody Allen* is published by Random House (a Vintage original). The book contains exact reconstructions of the scripts of the final screen versions of *Zelig, Broadway Danny Rose,* and *The Purple Rose of Cairo.* Stage directions have been added by the publisher to describe the action.
- DECEMBER: *September* is released by Orion Pictures. Woody wrote the screenplay and directed the film.
- Woody is elected one of the ten honorary members of the American Academy and Institute of Arts and Letters. He replaced Orson Welles.
- Mia Farrow gives birth to her and Woody's first child, a boy they name Satchel O'Sullivan Farrow.
- *Hannah and Her Sisters* is nominated for seven Academy Awards.

1988 (Age 53)
- Orion Pictures faces a hostile takeover threat that is averted by an infusion of $250 million in cash from tycoon John Kluge, a friend of founder Arthur Krim. Kluge ends up owning 68 percent of the company.
- SUMMER: Woody works on the first draft of *Crimes and Misdemeanors* in longhand on hotel stationery in Stockholm, Italy, and Copenhagen.
- AUGUST: The *New York Post* reports that Woody's father, Martin Konigsberg, was overheard complaining about Woody's booking ten seats on the Concorde for himself, Mia Farrow, and her eight children. Konigsberg was quoted as saying, "If he keeps spending money like this, he'll end up selling ribbons at Macy's."
- FALL: *Another Woman* is released by Orion Pictures. Woody wrote the screenplay and directed the film.

1989 (Age 54)

- MARCH: The anthology film *New York Stories,* consisting of three separate films by three directors, is released by Touchstone Pictures. The film consisted of *Life Lessons,* directed by Martin Scorsese, *Life Without Zoe,* directed by Francis Ford Coppola, and *Oedipus Wrecks,* written and directed by Woody Allen.
- FALL: *Crimes and Misdemeanors* is released by Orion Pictures. Woody wrote the screenplay and directed the film.

1990 (Age 55)

- *The Big Book of New American Humor,* edited by William Novak and Moshe Waldoks, is published by HarperPerennial Publishers, a division of HarperCollins Publishers. The anthology includes a lengthy excerpt from *Annie Hall,* as well as Woody's essays "Examining Psychic Phenomena," from *Without Feathers,* and "The Kugelmass Episode," from *Side Effects.* The book also included a "quickie" by Woody which consisted of the line "I was the best I ever had." The line was taken from Woody's stand-up routine "Las Vegas," which originally appeared on *The Third Woody Allen Album.* "Las Vegas" was retitled "Vegas" for Woody's two compilation albums, but the "best I ever had" line was edited out.
- Tuesday, May 1: Martin Scorsese, Steven Speilberg, George Lucas, and Sydney Pollack hold a press conference at the Creative Artists Agency in Beverly Hills, California. They announce the formation of the Film Foundation, an organization "dedicated to ensuring the survival of the American film heritage." Woody Allen, Stanley Kubrick, Francis Ford Coppola, and Robert Redford are the other founding members of the organization.
- MAY: Woody finishes editing *Alice.*
- JUNE: Woody finishes the writing of the first draft of *Shadows and Fog.*
- FALL: Woody begins filming *Shadows and Fog.*
- DECEMBER: *Alice* is released by Orion Pictures. The film starred Mia Farrow and Joe Mantegna, and was written and directed by Woody Allen.

1991 (Age 56)

- *Scenes from a Mall* is released by Touchstone Pictures. The film starred Woody Allen and Bette Midler. It was Woody's first appearance in a film solely as an actor since 1976, when he starred as Howard Prince in Martin Ritt's film about blacklisting, *The Front.*
- Friday, February 15: Beth Landman, writing in her "N. Y. Dish" column in the *New York Post* reports, "Columbus, at 69th Street and Columbus Avenue, is hot again now that the cast of Woody Allen's latest film *(Shadows and Fog)* has picked it as their hangout of choice. Madonna, complete with black wig and overalls, Christopher Walken and Danny Aiello are among the stars breaking at the watering hole."
- JULY: Woody flies to Italy to make a series of television commercials for

COOP, Italy's biggest supermarket chain. His fee was $2 million. At a news conference in Rome on Monday, July 8, Woody said that he didn't make enough money from his films, and "I have a big family, and I thought the offer was interesting." In one of the commercials, aliens in a spaceship land and ask what's good to eat on Earth. Other of Woody's commercials were set in a cocktail party, a Soho art gallery, and a psychiatrist's study.

- SEPTEMBER: Woody leaves Orion Pictures to make at least one film for TriStar Pictures. Orion, in financial difficulty, could not come up with the financing for the project Woody wanted to begin after *Shadows and Fog.* Orion stated that it still intended to hold Woody to the three remaining pictures of his contract, but Woody's contract did give him the right to work for another studio if Orion couldn't come up with the money for him to begin filming any of the three remaining films.
- NOVEMBER: Filming begins for *Husbands and Wives,* Woody's first picture with TriStar.
- Sunday, November 10: The *New York Daily News* runs a Woody Allen photo feature on the "People" page titled "Allen the Family." One photo showed Woody on a New York street holding his daughter Dylan's hand; the other photo was of Mia holding Satchel's hand. The caption read: "If Woody Allen looks more harried than usual, it's because Mia Farrow was away for two weeks, reportedly to adopt another child. This left him playing househusband to all the kids, including daughter Dylan. But Mama Mia's back now. With Dylan and son Satchel in tow, they're all off to the set of Woody's new movie."
- Wednesday, December 11: Orion Pictures files for Chapter 11 bankruptcy protection.
- Wednesday, December 11: The *New York Post* runs a story on page 3 headlined, "City Probes Shakedown Attempt on Woody." The story began, "Woody Allen was allegedly threatened in a shakedown attempt by a black activist who said he'd disrupt the filming of Woody's latest movie if he didn't pay a $100,000 'donation,' city officials told the *Post.* The city has launched an investigation into the charges against the activist, Mustafa Majeed." The article included two photos of Majeed, and one of Woody. The article also revealed that "Allen's staff, which hired some of Majeed's people after the filming of *Hannah and Her Sisters* was temporarily halted several years ago, contacted the city to demand an investigation." The article was featured on the front page in a box that read, "City Probes Film Set Shakedown; Woody Allen crews say they had to cough up $100,000."
- Saturday, December 14: The *New York Times* reports that a bankruptcy court judge had cleared the way for Orion Pictures to spend up to $4 million through the end of 1991 for payroll and other expenses. Orion filed for Chapter 11 bankruptcy protection on December 11.

1992 (Age 57)

- Wednesday, February 12: Woody's latest, *Shadows and Fog,* opens in Paris.
- Friday, March 20: *Shadows and Fog* opens in the United States.
- Thursday, August 13: Woody Allen files suit against Mia Farrow for custody of their three children, Moses Amadeus Farrow, 14; Dylan O'Sullivan Farrow, 7; and Satchel O'Sullivan Farrow, 4¹/₂. That evening, Mia Farrow is served with court papers at her Connecticut home regarding the lawsuit. Mia was also served with a temporary restraining order prohibiting her from moving the three children out of the metropolitan area. Mia's sister, Tisa Farrow (who appeared in *Manhattan* as Polly the Party Guest who had the wrong kind of orgasm), told the *New York Post,* "If there's anything that Mia is known for, besides being a wonderful actress, it's being a wonderful mother. I admire her for [having a large family]. All her kids are turning out great."
- Friday, August 14: The *New York Times,* the *New York Daily News,* the *New York Post, USA Today,* and other national newspapers all run stories on Woody and Mia's child-custody battle. When asked to comment on the suit, Leslee Dart, a spokeswoman for Woody, said, "The documents speak for themselves. Mr. Allen has never discussed his private life in public and does not wish to begin doing so now." Ms. Dart also confirmed rumors that Mia would not be starring in Woody's latest film, *Manhattan Murder Mystery,* which begins shooting in September, 1992: "I would think that both would agree that it would be best not to work together on this film." (On Saturday, August 15, the *New York Post* reported that an "intimate" of Mia's said that Mia had a "play or pay" deal for *Manhattan Murder Mystery,* which meant she would receive her starring salary even if she didn't appear in the film.) The *Daily News* reported that a friend of the couple said, "I hadn't realized that it had already come to this, but I must say that it didn't come as a total surprise." The male friend insisted on anonymity.
- Saturday, August 15: The *The New York Daily News* reports that legal heavyweight Alan Dershowitz has been retained to mediate Woody and Mia's child-custody battle. In a unique development, Dershowitz will represent both sides in the dispute.
- Tuesday, August 25: Woody Allen and Mia Farrow meet privately for three hours with Judge Phyllis Gangel-Jacob regarding Woody's suit for custody of the couple's three children.
- SEPTEMBER: Filming begins for Woody's second film for TriStar, *Manhattan Murder Mystery.* The cast includes Woody, Diane Keaton, Alan Alda, and Anjelica Huston.
- Friday, September 18: Woody's first film for TriStar, *Husbands and Wives,* opens in the United States.

CHAPTER 2

Woody Speaks

Interviews with Woody Allen

Nobody likes to write in a vacuum.
Woody Allen

A Conversation with Woody Allen*

A 1973 Interview by Stephen Banker

I have a feeling that everybody feels like a loser.
Automatically. And if they don't, they're wrong.
Woody Allen

THIS never-before-published interview with Woody Allen was conducted by Stephen Banker at the Shady Grove Theater in Shady Grove, Maryland, in 1973, immediately following Woody's concert appearance at the theater. Woody was thirty-eight at the time.

It is a significant interview because Woody is deliberately not "on" during the talk. He is thoughtful, soft-spoken, and serious, and throughout the talk, he doesn't crack a single joke. The interview is also very revealing: Woody talks about sex and death, his two favorite obsessions; he foreshadows his 1983 film *Zelig;* and he gives us a peek at what he's like when he gets up in the morning. (He ain't funny, that's for sure.)

The interview also gives us insight into Woody's ideas about comedy, particularly, standup work. Now that he is a filmmaker, and a filmmaker only, it's interesting to hear his thoughts about essay writing and concert appearances, and what role they played in his early career.

Compare *this* early interview with, say, Woody's 1971 *Rolling Stone* interview, in which almost every one of Woody's answers was either a joke or a non sequitur; or even his 1967 *Playboy* interview, in which he revealed that "everything I've ever written is the result of a sharp, searing blow. I smash my occipital area with a heavy mallet, then write down whatever comes. I do it for the money." (Another notable "restrained" interview is Woody's 1985 talk with Stephen Farber for the now-defunct *Moviegoer* magazine. See that interview in this chapter.)

In this interview with Stephen Banker, which took place after the release of *Everything You Always Wanted to Know About Sex* (*But Were Afraid to Ask)* and *Play It Again, Sam,* but before *Sleeper,* Woody also talks about the failed production of two of his one-act plays that David Merrick was supposed to bring to Broadway. (We also learn about the segment of *Everything You Always Wanted to Know About Sex* that was not included in the final cut—and why it was deleted.)

I asked Stephen to try and encapsulate the essence of Woody's genius. It was a heady task, but he came up with a cogent and perceptive analysis that makes a lot of sense, and also offers us a very good explanation as to just why Woody Allen is *funny.* Here's what Stephen had to say:

> How does Woody Allen makes us laugh? At first, he would appear to be more depressing than humorous since he insists that the world is fragile, dangerous and accidental, governed by entropy. But the care and exactness of his writing, along with his frequent literary allusions, suggest that we exist in a wonderful place, elegantly planned, and that it's fun and even exciting to be alive. The far-flung references add dimension and context—an anchor—to the seeming absurdities of the present. The tension between order and chaos, between entropy and syzygy, is the engine of his comedy. Form pulls the rug out from under content. It's an intellectual pratfall. That's why it's funny.

Here is Stephen's talk with Woody Allen:

SB   Woody Allen, what makes you laugh?
Woody Allen   I'm an easy laugher.

SB   A good audience.
Woody Allen   I'm a good audience, yeah. Now, I don't laugh out loud, you know, but I'm a big enjoyer. I enjoy all the comedy movies . . . all the *old* comedy movies. All the Marx Brothers movies, and all the Chaplin and Keaton films, and Mort Sahl, and Jonathan Winters, and Nichols and May. I'm a very easy laugher.

SB   How about literarily?
Woody Allen   Benchley and Perelman, just about exclusively. I don't think anybody else does it to me at all, in terms of literature.

SB   When did you feel, Woody, that you had made some sort of quantum jump, that you were nationally known, and you had a certain amount of momentum?
Woody Allen   I'm just beginning to feel that. I know people that know me, or that have heard of me, think that I'm much better known than I am. But I'm just beginning. Now with the emergence of my films, I'm just beginning to become nationally known. But there's no reason for me to be really nationally known because I do very little television. I've only appeared on a few shows in the last three years or the last four years. I've been on a half-dozen times, really, and generally it's been late at night.

SB   You doubt—you really seriously doubt—that you're a household word now?
Woody Allen   I do doubt that I am, and I find that when I come out and play concerts, I get very, very small attendance. I'm not a drawing name at all. My movies do very well. But I can't follow the reviews because there's so many hundreds of them in the country. Film reviews are not like theater reviews. In the theater, you pick up the paper, you see three reviews, and

you know what to expect. In films, we open the picture in New York, and you get a good review here and a bad review there. Then you open it in L. A., and you get a good review and a bad review. And then you open it in Utah, and Cleveland, and Cincinnati, and before you know it, there's thousands of film reviews that come in all over the country. So, films are not related to reviews. Films are related to something else entirely, whereas with a play if you don't get perfect reviews, it's a little bit of a struggle.

SB In the one city that you're in with a play, whereas with a movie you're in so many different places . . .

Woody Allen The movie, sure, is an international thing, but even just in the United States, thousands of reviews come in. And I have no idea why one thing does well and another thing doesn't. But I think I'm just beginning to become known to the public.

SB Why do you go on playing concerts then?

Woody Allen Well, I play them very rarely. I'm on a little concert tour at the moment, which is really six weeks long, and it will be the first time in, I'd say, two years, that I've appeared any place live. And I probably won't appear again live for *another* two or three years. So I don't do many concerts.

SB Do you just want to get what President Johnson used to call the "feel of the flesh," or what?

Woody Allen Yeah, I think it's a good thing, because I am basically a comedian. And I don't think it's a good idea to leave it and never do it, you know? So every couple of years I like to appear a little.

SB Can you think of something that you've learned recently in this particular tour? Is that a tough question?

Woody Allen Well, yes I can think of something that I've learned, believe it or not: That I can sustain staying on stage longer than I thought I could. I always had a problem. Owners of clubs always used to ask me if I could please do a little more time, 'cause I have a tendency to get on stage, talk for half an hour, and get off. And that's not long enough for a starring act. And I found on this particular tour, by trying it, because the demands on me were greater, that I could stay on for forty-five minutes and even an hour. And reasonably sustain it.

SB But you're not after the big yuk, the belly laugh, are you? You're after something slightly different, I think.

Woody Allen Oh, no, no, no, no. I'm after the big, big laughs. I mean, I consider it a disaster if I don't get continual big laughter. I think all comedians ultimately have got to go for that.

SB In a way, I'm surprised to hear you say that because I thought of you more as a subtle comedian.

Woody Allen (Laughs) Sometimes it comes out that way, you know, and I don't get the big laughs, but it shouldn't. Hopefully, I would like to get the big laughs.

SB   Can you say why that's so important?

Woody Allen   Because in comedy there's no question about it: When you're standing up there, you get a sense of great tension and frustration when they're not coming. And even if you're getting big laughs for twenty minutes or so, and you reach a low point for maybe, one minute, and you don't get them, you feel it. It's like being suffocated to death. (Laughs) And it's not a pleasant feeling. And it's hard to explain it to someone who hasn't done it. But you get what they call "flopsweat" and it's a very unpleasant feeling not to get the laughs, because that's what a comedian does. I guess it would be like if you were a singer, you know, singing off key or something.

SB   What kind of audiences are the *good* audiences nowadays? Young people, older people, what?

Woody Allen   You know, for me, I can never categorize my audience because I don't think I have a special audience. And I think that's good, but also bad. I see in my audiences, there's young kids, and there's older people. People used to say to me, you'd be a great favorite with colleges. You know, I was *never* a great favorite with colleges. And I was never a great favorite with older people. I always had a smattering of people from each group. But I was *never* a particular favorite with any of those groups.

SB   How about ethnically? How about Jewish people? Do they appreciate you more than other groups do?

Woody Allen   Well, I think Jewish people go out a lot. I think Jewish people form a good part of the audience in the big cities. They have a tendency to like theater and like entertainment, so I'm aware that they're there, and consequently I think they build up a certain sophistication, or a responsiveness to entertainment. And they're good audiences for comedy in particular. So I think that the Jewish audience is a theater- and comedian-oriented audience. So there *is* that. But I've played places where there were practically no Jewish people, and, you know, I mean, they're fine.

SB   Is there such a thing as Jewish humor, Woody?

Woody Allen   I guess there is, sure.

SB   Do you dabble in it?

Woody Allen   Only to the extent that I'm Jewish and that it's with me intrinsically.

SB   It's not planned?

Woody Allen   No, I don't plan to appeal to any group.

SB   Isn't it true that the great comedians have historically been Jewish?

Woody Allen   Most of them, or a good portion of them—a disproportion of them—have been, I think.

SB Let's talk about one or two who have not been. Whom can you think of? The standup comedians?

Woody Allen Well, Bob Hope I can think of who, I think, in his heyday was an absolutely great comedian. I always get a lot of criticism when I say that because in recent years he hasn't been up to par.

SB And also, he has taken very strong political views which in a way has disaffected the other groups.

Woody Allen He was a great comedian. W. C. Fields was not Jewish, and Jonathan Winters is not Jewish. Chaplin and Sellers are both half Jewish. So I don't know where you want to put them.

SB Now we have a new wave of black comedians.

Woody Allen I think that's good. I think that there will never be enough comedians. I don't think that's ever gonna be a worry to comedians that there's too many of them. When you look up and take all the comedians in America—I mean all of them: on television, in nightclubs—you know, what do you have—seventy-five comedians or something, in the whole country? I mean, that's everybody you can think of, that you would know, say. That's not one of the fears, that there's gonna be too many of them. Usually, there's generally about a half-dozen prominent ones, or ten prominent ones, and that's not really enough to cover the enormous amount of demand there is for humor.

SB As an actor (and I've seen you on the stage, as well as on the screen), you seem mostly to portray yourself. And in that respect, you could be compared to Cary Grant, Gary Cooper, or John Wayne.

Woody Allen (Laughs) That's a funny comparison. I think this: that when you go out in films, you have to have some kind of personality, and it's all luck whether you do or you don't. There's nothing you can do about it. So what happens is, you appear in a movie and either the audience responds to you; that is, you have some kind of personality trait that they can identify immediately, or not. And it has nothing to do with talent, and nothing to do with acting, because the guys you mentioned, like Wayne, and Gary Cooper, and Bogart, are not in a class, for instance, not even close to an actor like, say, Paul Muni.

SB Muni is famous for the ability to change himself from role to role.

Woody Allen Exactly. There are certain actors on stage, like Jason Robards and Paul Muni, you know, all these incredible stage actors, and they get on the screen, and something happens, and they don't really score heavily, and yet you get actors that were relatively mediocre, like Bogart, or Clark Gable, and they have that one-dimensional quality that works on the screen, even though they're not good actors. And I fit into that category. I'm not really much of an actor, but I have a personality that is, for better or worse, identifiable to an audience. I mean, they know what it is to expect.

SB Was this a conscious decision that you made where you assessed yourself as an attraction?
Woody Allen Oh, no, it's all luck.

SB It just happened?
Woody Allen Yeah, it's pure luck. You go out and do it, and either you wash off the screen or you don't, you know? There's no way of helping it.

SB Woody, many of the people who have written about the Mafia have been harassed, or in some cases, murdered. I know you haven't been murdered. Have you been harassed by the Mafia? Are they after you?
Woody Allen No, no, not that I know of. I think that they don't take me seriously. (Laughs)

SB Is there a Mafia?
Woody Allen Oh, is there a Mafia? We don't know if there's a Mafia. You know, I'm a big crime fan, and I've read tons of books, and articles and everything, and they're always conflicting. Great experts tell you that there is not, and then experts tell you that there *is* one. So no one has ever been able to determine if there is a Mafia or not.

SB What's your next movie project?
Woody Allen I don't have a movie project. I'm doing a play. I don't want to do a movie so close.

SB Writing a play?
Woody Allen No, I wrote a play. I wrote two one-act plays that David Merrick is producing. And I don't want the movies to come out so close together.

SB Your plays are kind of what they call "talky" rather than moving. Is that a fair observation about them?
Woody Allen I'm not sure exactly what you mean.

SB Well, for instance, it's very important to pay close attention to what the words are. You can't really tell what's going on from watching the way the people or the furniture moves around.
Woody Allen No, I wouldn't say that's true. I would say that the opposite is true. That's why I think *Play It Again, Sam* made a better movie instead of a play. I have a tendency to not really have mastered playwriting too much. I have a tendency to create a lot of problems for the director, and my stuff, I think, is more suited *to* more movement, and a bigger production and more mobility.

SB In one of your films, *Bananas,* you have Howard Cosell reporting from the consummation of a wedding night, and I think from a funeral, and weird other places. That was almost too close to reality. It was funny, yes, but it was very close to the Howard Cosell that we know and the news reportage that we have.

Woody Allen That's why I hired him, because I didn't want an actor doing it, I wanted Cosell doing it. And he was wonderful.

SB Why Cosell?

Woody Allen Because Cosell has some kind of spectacular charisma. Whether you like him or don't like him, you can't deny his enormous uniqueness, and his great stage presence. You're aware of him on stage; his voice has a great journalistic urgency to it; he's got a funny face, and a funny, inquisitive, probing, belligerent attitude. And he's a star. He's the most famous sportscaster in history. And deservedly so.

SB And did you write the part for him?

Woody Allen I wrote it with him in mind. I'd never thought I'd get him, but all we had to do was call him up and he was on the plane the next day.

SB I understand that under his new contract he's not allowed to do commercial ventures anymore.

Woody Allen That I don't know.

SB That would be disappointing to you if true?

Woody Allen Yeah. It would be surprising, too. Because I know one of the things that's of interest to him recently is doing more commercial ventures.

SB Have you ever thought of making the switch the other way, where he has gone from reportage to fiction films. Do you think that you have something to add importantly to documentary techniques?

Woody Allen I like the documentary technique and *Take the Money and Run,* my first film, was a fake documentary. A very broad, pseudo-documentary. But I love that feel very much, and at some point I think I would like to do a comedy, but in a very, very real documentary style, you know? I think that's an interesting form.

SB I think it's fair to say—step on me if I'm wrong—that you have had, in your work that I have read and seen and so on, an obsession with sex. Okay? is it true?

Woody Allen Yes.

SB Talk about it. Why?

Woody Allen Well, it's involuntary. I have an obsession with death and an obsession with sex. Both of those subjects appear in my work all the time, and I don't know why. I just know that if left alone, I write all the time, and then if you look up at the end of the year and see what I've written, and what jokes I tell in my act, and what jokes appear in my movies or plays, an enormous amount of them revolve around sex, and quite a few revolve around death.

SB   Now, in *Everything You Always Wanted to Know About Sex,* were there any sequences or questions in the book, in the Dr. Reuben book, that you left out, that you didn't use? Maybe you can tell us one or two ideas that you had that never were employed in the making of that film?
Woody Allen   Well, I didn't use practically all the questions in the book because there's only, I think, eight . . .

SB   You only used seven, I think.
Woody Allen   Is it seven questions in the movie? We had an idea that we even filmed that didn't work where the girl and I were in it and we played two spiders, and we had elaborate sets.

SB   What was the question? Do you remember?
Woody Allen   Yes. "What makes a man a homosexual?" And I crawl into her web, and we have intercourse, and then she devours me afterward. And we had elaborate costumes made, and a big web made out of steel cable, and it took us weeks to shoot.

SB   It sounds like a ballet.
Woody Allen   Well, it was an interesting idea, but we couldn't have enough mobility on the web to make the thing work. It just didn't work.
     I know that they are two subjects that are very open to comedy, that death is a very rich source of humor. It is to me, anyhow. And sex, too, is something that I could never take seriously. I just think it's one of the silliest things. Enjoyable, but really silly. And wide open for comedy.

SB   No point in analyzing it then?
Woody Allen   I don't think you can analyze humor. It's always a surprise to me. When I'm writing jokes, they come as a big surprise to me. When I'm in the room alone and I'm looking for a joke, and I'm thinking and thinking and suddenly I hear myself say the joke. I'm hearing it for the first time just like anyone else, and it's funny. You don't think of the joke and then say it. You say it, and then you write down what you said.

SB   It's interesting. I've talked to other performers and comedians in the past, and they do have a kind of compulsion to make jokes. Yet you and I have been talking for quite a while and you obviously are free of that. You don't feel that because you're a humorist, you have to be humorous right now.
Woody Allen   No. I'm never on, really, unless they're paying me, you know? I have a really scroungy attitude towards it. It's not even a conscious attitude. I wake up in the morning and I'm generally disgruntled and busy and bored and hostile and I'm never the life of the party or amusing or anything like that. When I get on stage, it's enough of an effort to be.

Sometimes, I can't make it work there either, and it's really embarrassing. But usually I can. I can rise up to the occasion enough to get an audience laughing.

SB Would you be willing to look a little bit ahead? Usually, people's interest in sex decreases; at least according to the charts and graphs from Dr. Kinsey. Tell us, do you suppose this will become a decreasing part of your repertoire?
Woody Allen It wouldn't bother me if it did. I don't care. I think it's so involuntary, that once you're free of the obsession to chase women you can spend a lot more time working.

SB Sophocles said, thank God I'm seventy and sex is behind me. Now I can begin to work!
Woody Allen I know that feeling. When you wake up in the morning and you're sexually obsessed, there is a tendency . . . it distracts you from your work. And it's a shame. It's like being hungry or something. You want to have a meal, and then get to work. Because I have an enormously cold and mechanical view of sex anyhow. (Laughs)

SB Cold and mechanical in what way?
Woody Allen I don't have an enormously romantic view of it.

SB A little known fact is that you were in high school with Erich Segal, the author of *Love Story*. Did you know each other?
Woody Allen No. I think he was one year younger than me. Of course, in high school, I knew nobody. I came to school at the last second; didn't speak to anybody; did the minimal amount of work; and went home afterward.

SB He's also a film writer, I guess, to some extent. *Love Story* was his film as well.
Woody Allen Right.

SB So Midwood High School in Brooklyn, New York, turned out a couple of well-known film writers. Any particular reason?
Woody Allen Pure accident. (Laughs) Just a coincidence. I went to Midwood, but I really had no kind of enriching life there. I wasn't crazy about going there.

SB You are a standup comedian, a writer of essays and humorous pieces, a director, a filmmaker, a musician also. Is there one capacity in which you feel most at home?
Woody Allen Well, it's funny. I enjoy playing music more than anything else, only because I don't do it professionally, and there's no demands on me, and it has the quality of a hobby. But I feel most at home sitting home and writing.

SB Frankly, I think that's what you're very best at. That's the thing I enjoy the most.

Woody Allen That's what I feel the most fun doing. But the trouble is there comes a time when you have to go and put it out. You know what I mean? You have to go and either get it produced, or get it published, or say it to an audience.

SB And you reach so many more people when you *do* it rather than write it.

Woody Allen I think you do. I don't think anybody reads anymore at all. Nobody.

SB Apparently, to judge by what you've written, and some of the things that you've done on stage, you think of yourself as a kind of loser. And yet, you've had the adulation of critics. People have called you the most important humorist of our time. And yet your book is called *Getting Even*. What can Woody Allen be getting even for?

Woody Allen I have a feeling that everybody feels like a loser. Automatically. And if they don't, they're wrong. Because everyone is a loser.

SB Why, Woody?

Woody Allen It's just impossible not to be loser. Just the very facts of life make you one.

SB Can you tell me a sample fact of life or two?

Woody Allen Well, we know that we're mortal. People find themselves living here, and they don't know why they are. And they can't get their human relations straightened out, and before they know it they die and they never knew what anything was all about. And so, you're automatically a loser. There's no question about it. In fact, I don't like people who aren't self-effacing. I take an instant loathing to them. (Laughs) You know, I just can't help it. I just don't like people that are confident, and I don't trust them, and I never have. And I'm always attracted to people, men and women, who are self-effacing.

SB Woody Allen, the comedian, the writer, the practically everything in show business, thanks very much.

This Woody Allen interview can be ordered in audiocassette form from *Tapes for Readers* at 5078 Fulton Street, NW, Washington, D.C. The phone is (202) 362-4585. Order no. L002. The price is $13.95 plus $2.00 for U.S. shipping and handling.

"Human Existence with a Penthouse View"
The Stephen Farber Interview with Woody Allen

[STEPHEN FARBER'S remarkable interview originally appeared in the May 1985 issue of the now-defunct *Moviegoer* magazine.

In it Woody talks to Stephen Farber about many issues of importance, including his feelings about working with Diane Keaton and Mia Farrow, the way he writes, his thoughts about the much-maligned *Stardust Memories*, and his views on the expectations of his audience, and how these expectations sometimes adversely affect the reactions to his films.

Stephen Farber is an astute and intelligent writer and interviewer, and he is is best known for his book (written with Marc Green) about the *Twilight Zone* movie tragedy, *Outrageous Conduct—Art, Ego, and the "Twilight Zone" Case.* He currently writes for *Movieline* magazine.]

Introduction by Stephen Farber

Woody Allen's penthouse apartment, high above Fifth Avenue overlooking Central Park, is *the* place to watch a sunset in Manhattan. On a late winter afternoon, the dying red light adds fiery punctuation to the incomparable city skyline visible from Allen's giant picture window. The image calls to mind the striking tableaux that opened Allen's *Manhattan,* and with good reason: many of those spectacular cityscapes were shot from the director's own terrace. With this privileged view of Manhattan, it's no wonder that Woody Allen is the most diehard and chauvinistic of New Yorkers.

The heavenly view prompts a question, though: what could the occupant of this penthouse possibly have to complain about? Can it be that he isn't happy? Well, yes.

That is the inescapable paradox of Woody Allen: American film's most brilliant comic artist is also a melancholy soul who takes little solace from his own success. Offscreen, Allen is not at all the nervous, self-deprecating jokester one might have expected to meet after seeing his early comedies. On the contrary, he's diffident yet self-possessed, and extremely serious. Instead of regaling a visitor with a stream of uproarious one-liners, the 50-year-old director is more apt to launch into an elegant discourse on the senselessness of human existence. Even human existence with a penthouse view.

Inside his apartment, books and magazines are piled everywhere—on the large coffee table in the middle of the living room, on the floor, on the shelves, in boxes. They run the gamut from *Town & Country* to *The New York Review of Books,* from Rita Mae Brown's *Rubyfruit Jungle* and Melville's *Moby Dick* to philosophical essays by Wittgenstein. And yet, even as he sits among these heaps of literature, Allen says, "I've never enjoyed reading in my life. I read because you can't be a functioning person without reading. I guess my favorite stuff is the heavier stuff."

In his film work, the predilection for weightiness may have been most obvious in the grim, Bergmanesque drama *Interiors* (1978). But it has also colored some of his bittersweet comedies, including *Love and Death* (1975), the Academy Award winner *Annie Hall* (1977), *Manhattan* (1979), and *Broadway Danny Rose,* which earned Allen unexpected Oscar nominations in the screenwriting and directing categories.

A bleak view of reality also underlies his comedy, *The Purple Rose of Cairo,* for which Allen stayed behind the camera to direct Mia Farrow (his constant offscreen companion) and her co-star, Jeff Daniels. Reviewing the film in February 1985, *Newsweek* magazine said that Woody Allen had "come up with a gem, one of the shrewdest, funniest, most plaintive explorations of movies as dream machine and escape mechanism." The *Hollywood Reporter* called the film "an innovative, charming piece" and went on to predict that it "may go beyond attracting the usual Allen devotees, reaching a wider audience simply seeking a romantic comedy."

In *The Purple Rose of Cairo,* set during the Depression, Farrow plays a distaff version of the character Allen himself has embodied in many of his films—a bumbling, helpless waif, unable to hold down a job, browbeaten by her brutal husband, escaping the drudgery of her life only in afternoons at the movies, where she can imagine herself frolicking in the glamorous aristocratic playgrounds that Hollywood conjured up in the 1930s. One day her dream takes on flesh and blood when a handsome playboy (Daniels) in the movie she is watching walks off the screen and into her humdrum world, catapulting both Farrow and the audience into an adventure in which the realms of fantasy and reality, celluloid and soot, keep crisscrossing and colliding with each other.

The movie is packed with vintage Allen wit, but it shows the substructure of thoughtfulness that has been part of the director's films for the last decade. The wacky comedian of *Bananas* and *Sleeper* may be gone forever, replaced by a mature filmmaker who has more on his mind than sight gags and slapstick. Can he still make us laugh? Of course. But that is no longer his only goal.

The implicit warning attached to Woody Allen's recent movies is that audiences should expect the unexpected. Each of his films is a new departure, a surprise—and, so far at least, Allen has maintained a critical and popular following large enough to allow this experimentation. He knows, however, that public support for his movies has been dwindling; *Stardust Memories, A Midsummer Night's Sex Comedy, Zelig,* and *Broadway Danny Rose* drew much smaller audiences than *Annie Hall* and *Manhattan,* his biggest hits of the late 1970s. Allen knows that if he wants to continue working with the same degree of freedom, he has to reach out to a larger public.

One way to do that is to make himself somewhat more visible than he's been for the last couple of years. In any case, Allen insists that his reclusiveness has been "greatly exaggerated" by the press. "Their tendency," he says, "is to want to make me into an eccentric." So if he hasn't exactly jumped onto the publicity circuit with gusto, he is at least resuming relations with the press. While the sunset provides a backdrop to the conversation, Allen talks freely about his latest movie, his leading ladies, his irrepressible pessimism, and his place in the cinema of the 1980s.

SF How did you come up with the idea for *The Purple Rose of Cairo*?
Woody Allen When I'm writing a movie, I walk around the house and think and think. This was just a funny notion that occurred to me one day, and within forty-eight hours all the developments fell into place. Suddenly the story had a tendency to blossom. I got the notion of a character slipping down off the screen, and I thought that was fun to play with. I felt that it could be amusing and romantic, which was good on the entertainment side. I also felt there could be something to say in the picture.

SF There seems to be a strong commentary on fantasy and reality going on in the film.
Woody Allen That's what was interesting to me about doing the script. In life you can't really choose fantasy, because if you do you're very limited. Mia's character can only have a life with this movie hero in a strange, limited way. He only knows certain things, because he's circumscribed by the scriptwriter. And yet for all the limitations of fantasy, it's perfect. They kiss perfectly, they're just great. In real life, people disappoint you. They're cruel, and life is cruel. And if you choose reality over fantasy, which you must, you have to pay the price for it.

SF Why didn't you cast yourself in *The Purple Rose of Cairo*?
Woody Allen I felt that there was no logical part for me. There was the woman, the husband, and the movie character, and I certainly couldn't be a 1930s movie star. It just wouldn't be real. We had huge problems casting that part. The first person cast in it was Michael Keaton, and he worked for about two weeks. Though he was very funny, he was not projecting the 1930s quality. He's just so utterly contemporary. I had to throw that material away. So the people on the production and at the studio were saying, "Well, then, *you* play the role." I was very close to doing that when I met Jeff Daniels. And the minute the screen test was over, we made the deal with him. He didn't know what hit him. He thought that *I* was the star of the movie and that he was just coming in for a small part.

SF The film is set in the thirties. Are you a fan of movie from that era?
Woody Allen The thirties are a little before my moviegoing time. I was brought up in the forties, so to me those films have a more endearing

quality. I'm a big movie fan in general. I see movies all the time, but not necessarily a lot of the contemporary American ones, because I don't think too much of them. My favorite films are almost always foreign. Ever since I was a teenager, I've loved French and Italian and Swedish films. But my own opinion is that a huge number of the movies that have come out over the past few years have not been worth watching.

SF Were there other movie ideas that you played around with before you decided to make *The Purple Rose of Cairo*?

Woody Allen Oh, yes. I write down ideas as they occur to me, and I have a half-dozen things that would make interesting movies. I become very obsessive, because I know I'm going to be spending a full year on whatever project I pick. Then one day, for one reason or another, I go with one of the ideas and start writing the script. It's very rare that I feel secure about it. For the first twenty pages I always think, "I shouldn't have done this one. I should have done the musical or something."

SF You've worked with the same group of actors, actresses, and production people on many of your films. Are you influenced by the people that surround you on a movie set?

Woody Allen Yes. Without knowing Diane Keaton, I would never have been able to write the character of Annie Hall for her. It's a big help to know people so that you can write to their strengths. When I wrote *Broadway Danny Rose,* I was with Mia. We eat in an uptown Italian restaurant very frequently, and the owner is a woman with blond hair and black glasses, constantly smoking a cigarette. She's great. And we'd go there, and Mia would say, "Jeez, someday I would love to play that character." Then I wrote the story. It's funny—when I presented her with the script, she said, "I can't play this!"

SF Was your collaboration with Diane Keaton close?

Woody Allen Diane always had a huge amount of input into everything. It was very important to me for her to read the script and talk to me and comment and all that. Diane could be a fine film director herself.

SF Do you work with Mia Farrow in the same way?

Woody Allen I try to make the pictures as collaborative as possible. Mia's just getting used to that; it's something new in her life. I bother her with it. She helps me as much as she can, but I'm constantly making demands on her, sounding things out.

SF Are you able to remain objective about Mia Farrow's work even though you're romantically involved with her?

Woody Allen I'm told that I err tremendously on the side of being too tough. I do that with myself on the screen and with friends of mine on the screen. I'm very objective, even cruel, in that way. I'm extra strict—the way a parent gets so infuriated with a child.

SF *The Purple Rose of Cairo* is very much the woman's story, and *Interiors* presented the viewpoints of the three sisters. Do you particularly enjoy writing from a woman's perspective?

Woody Allen With the exception of roles written for myself, I feel more comfortable writing female characters. The film I just finished shooting, *Hannah and Her Sisters,* is a three-sister play, having, incidentally, no relation to Chekhov's *Three Sisters.* It could be because I was brought up mostly by women. My father's alive and all that, but otherwise I was the only male in the family. My mother had seven sisters, and all of those sisters had only daughters. I was constantly being ministered to by aunts and female cousins. I would always be playing with girls and going to the movies with girls. So I have a lot of sympathy for them. There are many women in my work situation even now. My editor is a woman, two assistants are women, and our foreign representative is a woman. The people I work with most closely are women.

SF It doesn't seem that all your relations with women work out well. Your movies are filled with unhappy romances.

Woody Allen Right. I find that that mirrors my own observations. I don't mean this happens 100 percent of the time, but I do think that relationships between people are very, very tough. And if I look around at all the people I've known since I was a child, I can find a couple of really delightful relationships. The overwhelming majority have a lot of problems and either break up or stay together for the wrong reasons. It's not easy, but you keep trying and hope that one day there will be an intermeshing of neuroses.

SF The hero of *Stardust Memories* tends to choose his lovers in a self-destructive way. He could have chosen a relationship with a nice, healthy woman, but he is drawn to the darker, more tortured women.

Woody Allen That's a very common problem, the repetitious compulsion to do that. People don't want the healthy relationships, because by choosing trouble they're getting a very significant payoff—emotionally, erotically, or intellectually.

SF Have you done that yourself?

Woody Allen I've done that in my life. I hope I've put it behind me, but I've done it. I could go out tomorrow and do it again.

SF *Stardust Memories* seems to have been the most controversial film you've ever made. Do you have any particular defense of the movie?

Woody Allen I caught a lot of hostile flak on that picture, the most I ever got in my life. But it's my own personal favorite of all my films. I think people made a perceptual error about it when it came out. They thought, "He thinks we're schmucks because we like him and he doesn't return our affection." And I also got, "Why is this malcontent crabbing? He has a Rolls-Royce." But the point of the picture was that there is this character—

not really autobiographical in a significant way—who has wealth, fame, and all that, and he's totally miserable in spite of it. He's unhappy because of the real things: His friend died in the hospital, his girlfriend had a nervous breakdown, he's getting older, and his artistic achievement is not going to put a barrier between him and death. If I hadn't played the lead, it might have been more understandable to people as what I intended.

SF   The relationship between the director and his fans was a particularly unpleasant aspect of the film.
Woody Allen   I said a lot of true things in that picture that people didn't want to hear. One of the most obvious examples is the love-hate relationship that exists between the public and the performer. In the movie, a character comes up to the hero and says, "I love you. You're my favorite thing," and two reels later he tries to kill me. And this is exactly what happened to John Lennon a few months after the film came out. The public didn't want to hear that, but that relationship does exist, that tremendous adulation and adoration of the performer and yet also a tremendous hostility. And it happens the other way around. The performer adores the public and is totally dependent on the public, and also has a hostile feeling, too.

SF   You've been the subject of hostile gossip.
Woody Allen   People thought that I was satirizing *Reds* in *Zelig.* They got into their minds the cheap notion, based on gossip, that I don't like Warren Beatty because I had gone out with Diane Keaton and Warren Beatty came between Diane and myself. You see that in print so many times, but she and I had not been seeing each other for *ten years* before they started seeing each other. But writers will write that he came between us and that there's bad blood. None of that is true but those things are written. When you're younger, you get angry. And then after a while it happens so much, you're accused of so many things, that you just give up on it.

SF   So you're becoming more pessimistic as you grow older?
Woody Allen   I don't believe in suicide or that kind of thing; I don't feel that pessimistic. I see myself in the Sigmund Freud–Eugene O'Neill school of thought. I think life is a definite struggle, and it's hard and tends to be very cruel, and you have to learn to use everything you can to deal with it, whether it takes ducking into the movies or doing charity work or having a couple of drinks now and then. Some people do it with religion, some people do it by watching baseball games with a beer in their hand.

SF   Does negative criticism concern you?
Woody Allen   Well, I like everybody to like my films. That would be my first choice. If I'm in a taxicab and the driver says, "Yeah, I saw your last film. I didn't think it was so great," that bothers me. I would prefer people

to like them, but it can't really influence what movies I make. If I think a film is a good idea, then I'm willing to take the abuse if it should come.

SF   Does it frustrate you that the audience for your films seems to be rather small and specialized?

Woody Allen   It concerns me. No matter how well I do on a film and no matter how well it's received critically, I'm always fighting an uphill battle to break even on it. I have a very small public, and filmmaking is such a gigantic effort. I've done some pictures over the years that have gotten such wonderful reviews, but it's a big fight to break even. One thing that's helped me out enormously is that I have a very solid following in Europe. I do very well in France and Italy, in South America, in England and Germany and Israel. And when I first started, I was unknown there. Now I'm totally dependent on it. Every single picture of mine since *Annie Hall* has made more money abroad than in America.

SF   Would you like to reach a larger audience?

Woody Allen   Yes. It would make life much easier. Not for me; I don't want another penny for myself. But once in a while I'll have an idea for a film that's going to cost significantly more money, and I can't make those films easily. So it would help if just by sheer chance one of my films was a commercial success. It would be comforting creatively.

SF   Would you ever consider changing your style or subject matter to woo a larger audience?

Woody Allen   If I sat down to try to do something popular, I don't think I could. I'm not making films because I want to be in the movie business. I'm making them because I want to say something. And if I had nothing to say tomorrow, I wouldn't hire myself out as a director. I'd write plays or short stories, or retire or something.

SF   Do you think that you were more in sync with the public during the 1960s and 1970s?

Woody Allen   No, I don't think that's what happened. When I first started, I consistently made a certain kind of comedy. We say they're "accessible" now. The funny part of it is that at the time they made no money at all. A picture like *Take the Money and Run* was made for a million dollars and took seven years or something to break even. When everyone thinks of those early films, they think, "Well, the public ate them up." *Bananas* was not eaten up; none of them were. But they were consistent comedies. And then, as I started to feel more secure and steady, I wanted to try different things. In a certain sense, I kind of left my public. I was hoping that they would find these experiments interesting. But they mostly feel apprehensive about them.

SF   How do you react to that?

Woody Allen   I'd prefer that people not be apprehensive when they come into my movies. I would prefer the general image in people's minds to be,

"We don't know what his next film is going to be like. But if we go all the time, we'll be disappointed sometimes, and sometimes we won't." And I think that's a fair deal to make with them. But instead they think, "Gee, let's wait till our friends see it, till we've read the reviews, till we feel on very safe ground with it." This always happens to me when my pictures come out.

SF People prefer to have their expectations fulfilled, rather than subverted.
Woody Allen Right. I adore the Marx Brothers, and they were as funny as can be, but they always made the same film. I think that's one of their problems. You can take eight or ten of their comedies, but then it starts to pall a little bit. Whereas Charlie Chaplin, I feel, was more interesting because he would try different things. And some of them would be terrible. But if he were alive and making films today, you'd want to see what he was doing because it would be more interesting. I prefer that myself.

SF Is Chaplin one of your favorites?
Woody Allen I have been influenced by Chaplin. I like him tremendously. I know it's fashionable at the moment to say that Buster Keaton was better than Chaplin, but I respond more to Chaplin. When he comes down the street with that malice he has, he's funnier and more emotional, and that's important to me.

SF In *Annie Hall* and *Manhattan,* you were dealing with contemporary romantic relationships. I think a lot of younger people passionately identified with those stories. But your more recent films haven't really tapped into those interests and concerns.
Woody Allen Whenever you reinforce the prejudices of the middle class, there's always a pleasant feeling. You know, contemporary relationship pictures like *Annie Hall* and *Manhattan* and *Kramer vs. Kramer* and *Terms of Endearment* always have a built-in commercial guarantee. But I don't want to do those films all the time.

SF Do you see your future films moving in a more serious direction? Would you still consider doing a lightweight comedy?
Woody Allen I wouldn't hesitate to do a lightweight comedy if I had a good notion for one. I'd like very much to do a musical. I have a jazz movie that I've never gotten around to because I've been too lazy to get out of New York; it would require a lot of shooting in Chicago and New Orleans. But I'd like to do many different kinds of things and foist it off on the public as a virtue.

SF Do you ever look back on your old movies and reevaluate them?
Woody Allen No. The truth is that I never, ever see them after they come out. I haven't seen *Take the Money and Run,* my first film, since the day it was released, because I think it would only aggravate my ulcer. I'd look at it

and think, "I've got to get that off the screen, I've got to get into the editing room, and I need two more weeks to shoot!" I'd hate it. I've said this before, and I've never meant it facetiously: To me, they're all failures. When I get the idea for a film and I'm just walking around flushed with the idea, it's magic—it's Renoir and Fellini. It's just great. Then I start to make the film, and the truck rolls in every day with fresh compromises. You can't get the actor you want, and you don't have enough money to do this, and you're not as good as you thought. And by the time the film is finished, it's fifty or sixty percent of what I had envisioned. Of course, I can show it to an audience and they may love it, but they don't know the nuances of what I had in mind. It's very hard on a filmmaker.

SF   Do you have any special affection for *Annie Hall* or *Manhattan*?

Woody Allen   I have nice memories of all my films. Thinking back there were some laughs. . . . It was nice to work with Gordon Willis or Louise Lasser or Diane or Mia. But I don't have any extra regard for those films. I had more fun making *Zelig* and *Take the Money and Run* than I did with *Annie Hall* and *Manhattan*. I like *Love and Death*, but I have some very unpleasant memories of making it—you know, weeks and weeks of being in some field somewhere outside Budapest, freezing and being depressed and alone with the Russian army.

SF   Do you find filmmaking hard work?

Woody Allen   Filmmaking requires a lot of physical stamina, and I'm young enough now to keep doing it. But there will come a time when I want to get up later in the morning, not jump up at 5:30 and run around. You know, Groucho Marx once told me that when he did *A Night in Casablanca,* he and Harpo were running to grab the wing of a plane or something, and Groucho turned to Harpo and said, "Well, have you had enough?" and Harpo said, "Yes." And that was it. They retired after that. I think that will happen to me eventually, because it's hard work making a film. So, if I'm lucky and live reasonably long, I hope I can sit home and write some novels. I'd love to do that.

SF   How would you like members of your audience to think of you?

Woody Allen   I hope that someday it will lock in with them that I never hold them cheaply, that I never write down to them, that I always assume that they're at least as smart as I am if not smarter, and that I try to do films that they will respect. I hope that they'll appreciate that one day, that they'll say, "Gee, this guy is not taking the easy way out." Maybe not. Maybe they'll always say, "Listen, we just want to go see *Ghostbusters.*"

The *Rolling Stone* Interview: Woody Allen*
By William Geist

[WILLIAM GEIST'S interview originally ran in the April 9, 1987, issue of *Rolling Stone* magazine. Woody was on the cover, and the issue also featured an Andy Warhol memoriam, and features on Krishna Killers, U2, and the Beatles on CD.

For several reasons, this is one of the more important interviews Woody has granted. It's lengthy, it's current, and in it, Woody is brutally frank about *everything:* his career, his artistic goals, growing up, and even American television.

The interview took place right after the release of *Radio Days.* Woody had just finished shooting (for the second time) *September,* and was just beginning work on *Another Woman.*

The interview was conducted by William Geist for *Rolling Stone.* Geist also writes for the *New York Times* and *Esquire,* and has done many on-camera pieces for CBS News. He also used to write the "About New York" column in the *Times.* (A collection of his "About New York" columns, *City Slickers,* was published in 1987 by Times Books.)

Woody was obviously very relaxed during this interview, and it's astonishing to read through a seven-thousand-word interview with Woody Allen and not see one joke. We do smile, though, when we read Woody's thoughts about the country and his fear of rabid woodchucks.

Revealing and entertaining, the interview appears here for the first time after its initial appearance.]

Introduction by William Geist

I don't know, Woody Allen seems sane to me. Maybe I've been in New York too long. But it goes further than that: Woody Allen is one of the most well adjusted people I've met in New York.

Could this be one of the seven warning signs that New Yorkers are even more deranged than had previously been imagined? And should the governor place the National Guard on full yellow?

It could also mean that characterizations of Woody Allen have been somewhat extreme over the years. Or maybe Woody Allen has changed some.

On the way to the interview in his film-editing studio in a Park Avenue hotel, I passed a door marked "Service Entrance" and almost went in. I was feeling humble and nervous, about to encounter a man described as a comic genius, a modern existential hero and a filmmaker on the level of Bergman and Fellini.

But Woody Allen put me at ease. He answered the door himself, dressed in a garage-style-sale sweater and a wrinkled shirt. His hair was unmanaged. And he was nice—very casual, not at all condescending, and self-unimportant. He wasn't cynical. He didn't even try to be funny, although his brutal honesty and extraordinary seriousness about the smallest of things made me laugh a lot.

He insisted he was not obsessing over the essential nothingness of the universe at the moment and invited me to sit down. He sat down too, and not at all in the fetal position. It was Saturday. He was working. His newest film, the nostalgic *Radio Days,* was about to open. He had finished shooting another film just the day before and had begun work on yet another.

For a man often depicted as a tormented neurotic, Woody Allen appeared remarkably relaxed, "centered and directed," as pop psychologists say, honest and sincere. And also quite rich. In addition to fortune, he has fame but somehow doesn't get bothered much by fans, while always getting a good table at Elaine's.

True, he is troubled by morbid introspection (he sees the concentration camp as a metaphor for life, a thought you'll never see on a greeting card) and by an inordinate fear of bushes and woodchucks. Yet he *does* have a blonde movie star for a girlfriend.

He loves New York, where he seems to lead a charmed life. In his only brush with crime, burglars broke into his apartment, were scared off before they took anything and left a TV set from a previous break-in.

Born Allan Stewart Konigsberg in the Flatbush section of Brooklyn and raised in a home where, he says, the basic values were "God and carpeting," he is now fifty-one. His appearance hasn't changed in twenty years. Ours has.

He is also more amusing than we are. He began writing jokes for gossip columns at the age of sixteen and barely managed to graduate from high school.

He is at once remarkably productive—he's written and directed fifteen films since 1965 and written or acted in five more—and the only person I have met in New York with Leisure Time. Time for walking around, watching the Knicks, seeing friends and browsing—remember browsing?—in bookstores. He also plays clarinet at Michael's Pub, where he plans to be on Academy Award night, even though his film *Hannah and Her Sisters* has been nominated for seven Oscars.

He has the joy of children—Mia Farrow, the aforementioned star, has eight (five of them adopted)—but he lives across Central Park from her and doesn't have to change diapers.

Unlike most New Yorkers, he recognizes his neuroses, obsessions, phobias (could be the three decades, off and on, of psychoanalysis), and seems to be living comfortably with them now in a large duplex apartment overlooking Central Park.

On this day, Woody Allen seems almost . . . *happy.*

Rolling Stone   You are making a film a year. What drives you?

Woody Allen   It's not a big deal. There have been times when Sidney Lumet or Bergman have done three films in a year. It takes me a couple of months to write a film, several months to shoot and edit it.

A guy who drives a cab or works in an office works more than I do. I have time to practice my clarinet, see films, go out to dinner and see people. And my work doesn't have the sense of labor about it.

But if I worked at a different job, I couldn't wait until I got home to write. I enjoy it. It's like being paid to play baseball or something. It's like I'm on a constant vacation.

Rolling Stone   This doesn't sound like Woody Allen talking at all, actually *enjoying* yourself. Normally you are portrayed as a basically neurotic, workaholic, tormented—shall I go on?—recluse who is incapable of enjoying yourself. Is this something new?

Woody Allen   Probably the truth about me lies somewhere in between. Writers have tended to . . . *emphasize* certain characteristics because it makes good copy.

I'm being paid to do what I like. And that is essentially to write and occasionally to perform. I do have some trouble with my nonwork time, that is true. I'm not a person who gets too much of a kick out of traveling, country houses, boats, vacations or things most people do have a good time with.

Rolling Stone   So you're happier when you're working.

Woody Allen   Yes, it's an important distraction. I've always felt if one can arrange one's life so that one can obsess about small things, it keeps you from obsessing about the really big things. If you obsess about the big things, you are impotent and frightened, because there's nothing you can do about aging and death. But the little things you can spend days obsessing about, such as a good punch line for the third act. And this is a nice problem to obsess over because it's not surgery. . . . I'm a little more morbid than the average person.

Rolling Stone   Do you envy the guy who goes to work and goes out on his boat and drinks beer, and all this stuff never occurs to him?

Woody Allen   No. I do occasionally envy the person who is religious naturally, without being brainwashed into it or suckered into it by all the organized hustles. Just like having an ear for music or something. It would just never occur to such a person for a second that the world isn't about something.

And I wouldn't go out in a boat. I'd hate the boat. I've been out on a boat twice and I got seasick and sunburned and windburned and I was trapped. That would be hell for me.

Rolling Stone Are you agnostic?
Woody Allen Agnostic—I mean, I know as little about it as anyone, you know?

Rolling Stone You seem to be approaching your work in a more relaxed manner.
Woody Allen I think as the years go by, and you gain more confidence, you become more secure about it. My first couple of films, I would have been more frantic and nervous.

Rolling Stone Do you ever worry that you are doing things because they are easier and that the film will suffer a bit?
Woody Allen I'm aware that I'm doing it because it's easy. I mean, I'm completely aware that I'm shooting in New York because it's easy.

Rolling Stone But maybe the finished product is worse because you take it easy. Is that a concern?
Woody Allen Yes, I do think it. And I'm happy to go along with it, even though it's worse. I think, "This may be worse, but it's easy."

Rolling Stone I can't make that—doing things the easy way—fit with your continuing to work so hard and make so many films.
Woody Allen I do say to myself, you know, "This scene would be much better if we went to, say, Philadelphia to shoot it." But I don't really want to go to Philadelphia to shoot it, because it's a two-hour car ride. So let's find a street downtown that we can fob off as Philadelphia, and it won't be as good. I won't have the vista. I won't make a great shot of the Liberty Bell or something.

Rolling Stone But you are trying to make great films, are you not?
Woody Allen I'm trying to make as wonderful a film as I can. But my priorities are always in order, and they're never artistic. Artistic accomplishment is about third or fourth.

Rolling Stone I'm not sure I buy that.
Woody Allen I swear.

Rolling Stone But you are such a perfectionist. You pay such close attention to every detail. There is a story about an extra in *Radio Days* wearing a 1940s-style garter, even though it won't show onscreen.
Woody Allen Still, I wouldn't put making a film above inconveniencing myself where I shot it or an important engagement or appointment.

Rolling Stone What's more important?
Woody Allen Oh, for instance, I've wrapped films early in the day so I

could get home in time to see a Knicks game on television. Sure. They'll say, "But there are two more hours of light."

Rolling Stone   It sounds like the obstetrician who induces labor so he can make tee time on the golf course. Is that an important Knicks game you're talking about or just any Knicks game?
Woody Allen   Important. There have been times when I'd be out with a beautiful woman, and I would think to myself, "Do I really want to stay up all night, till four in the morning?" Because I've got to go in at six o'clock in the morning and shoot the next day.

And I think of my priorities. I think, "What's more important?" The time spent with the beautiful woman is much more important to me than the other time—being on top of it the next day.

Rolling Stone   Is this a new approach?
Woody Allen   It might be. It might be the gruelingness of the filming that has worn me down to a degree. If you were to hang around the set of a picture of mine, you would see that it's all work, even if it happens to be a comedy of the broadest type, whether making *Hannah and Her Sisters* or *Bananas*. It's hard work and has a grim, businesslike quality to it. It's not a gang of guys joking and having a lot of fun. Maybe the films would do better if it was, I don't know.

I want to make more intimate films, which are easier and faster to do, shot indoors, with no bad weather, fewer actors and fewer sets.

Rolling Stone   But *Radio Days* doesn't reflect that approach?
Woody Allen   No, but that was the last straw. That was such a hard job physically for me. It was exhausting to direct. Not all the film made the picture; originally there were 200 speaking parts. You have to do musical numbers and crowd scenes and nightclub scenes.

When I was doing *Hannah,* you know, that was an intimate picture, and I was dealing with small numbers of people, filming in Mia's apartment, and it was a physically easy picture to do. And then I wanted to do a completely different kind of picture. But while I was in the midst of *Radio Days,* I thought, "God, what did I get into?"

I said to myself, "*Forget* it!" I just want to do some nice intimate pictures, a couple of people in a room with some nice personal conflicts.

Rolling Stone   Nice personal conflicts?
Woody Allen   Yeah. Just in terms of sheer physical exhaustion, it's more fun for me to make a small film than a big film. Cecil B. DeMille or Stanley Kubrick or [Franco] Zeffirelli—they love getting a hundred people out there. They love moving them around, and they do it beautifully. But to me, getting two people in a room to talk is more relaxing filmmaking.

Rolling Stone Is the film you just finished shooting like that?
Woody Allen Yes, it's a much-smaller-scale thing, sure. It's a one-set, virtually.

Rolling Stone Can you tell us anything about it?
Woody Allen Well, I can only tell you a couple of things. Mia's in it, of course, and Dianne Wiest. I'm not in it.

Rolling Stone Not even as a narrator, which you are in *Radio Days*?
Woody Allen No, no. And it's a small film, a small idea, a small, intimate kind of film, principally dramatic but hopefully with some laughs in it.

Rolling Stone And you've begun writing another one?
Woody Allen Yes, planning it. That's ninety percent of the work—pacing the floor, thinking it out, the plot and structure. The actual writing just takes two to three weeks. Writing it down for me is the easiest part.

Rolling Stone You use what almost amounts to a repertory company, with many of the same actors—many of them close friends of yours, such as Mia, Diane Keaton, Dianne Wiest and Tony Roberts—in each film.
Woody Allen It's much easier to work with my own friends and acquaintances because if I'm shooting with Michael Caine [who was in *Hannah*], when I finish, he goes to India or England to do another picture. But Mia or Dianne Wiest or Tony Roberts, I can call them up on a moment's notice and say, "Listen, I've got a great idea for a new scene, let's meet and shoot it."

Rolling Stone Does that really happen?
Woody Allen All the time, on every picture, constantly on *Hannah*. In the original version of *Hannah*, there was only one Thanksgiving party, at the beginning of the picture. And when I saw the picture and started to get ideas about how it could be developed and amplified in a good way, I thought, you know, "Let's make it end with Thanksgiving too. That would be a nice thing." I did that. And I said, "You know what would be really great too? If we had one more Thanksgiving party in the middle of the picture."

Rolling Stone So you just all gathered back at Mia's apartment?
Woody Allen Right. Shooting at her apartment made things easier, too.

Rolling Stone Also, you sometimes use friends of yours who aren't even actors.
Woody Allen Yes, because I'm aware of them as good types. In a relatively minor acting part, it's not so risky.

Rolling Stone Are you more contented too in your personal life?
Woody Allen Well, for the last seven years I've been seeing Mia, and

things have been stable. And I've been introduced through her to a lot of children and all the activities with them.

Rolling Stone   How do you get along with them?
Woody Allen   Fine, fine.

Rolling Stone   Well, you are also portrayed as someone who probably wouldn't get along with pets and children.
Woody Allen   Oh, pets I hate. Mia has many pets. I hate them. I do everything I can to avoid them. She has a dog and cats and fish and a parrot and hamsters. She's really got the full complement of creatures. But I've never had problems with children.

Rolling Stone   Are you ever sorry you don't have children of your own?
Woody Allen   Well, as it's turned out, I'm so involved with all of hers, as a group and individually. Individual ones prevail upon me to take them places or to hang out with me.

   If you spend time with Mia, you automatically spend time with a lot of children because that's a huge part of her life.

Rolling Stone   What is the latest count of her children?
Woody Allen   Eight.

Rolling Stone   And you think that children have had an effect on you?
Woody Allen   It's, it's a . . . pleasurable dimension. And it's extra pleasurable for me because she has always done the hard work, and I sort of live across the park and get to have the fun of the kids without having to raise them and do all of that stuff.

Rolling Stone   Do you function okay when you leave the city to visit Mia's country home in Connecticut?
Woody Allen   No, I don't function okay. I'm like a fish out of water. I'm just not comfortable. When the evening comes, it gets dark and there's no place to go. A walk in the woods at night or something is not very appealing to me.

Rolling Stone   Why not?
Woody Allen   There's nothing to do or feel or see. I'm definitely a child of the city streets, and I feel at home on my own two feet, you know, not in a car or train or anything like that.

   In Manhattan, I know the town. I know how to get places. I know where to get cabs. I know where to duck in and go to the bathroom if I have to. And what restaurants to eat at and which ones to avoid. I just feel at home in the city.

   I don't go swimming in her pond because I've seen snakes in the water.

Rolling Stone   You know how to swim?
Woody Allen   I was always a good swimmer, a good athlete.

Rolling Stone Really?
Woody Allen I really was, in many sports. Baseball and basketball and track.

Rolling Stone That's something a lot of people wouldn't guess.
Woody Allen But I never know what to do in the country. I like to be able to be in a place where, if I want to, I can go downstairs and there's stores and people around. I like to look at people. I like to watch people. I like to look at stores.

Rolling Stone You can go around in New York and do that fairly easily without being bothered, can't you?
Woody Allen I can do it because I'll wear a hat, and that will cut down hugely on my recognition. I enjoy it, but as soon as I go to the country, I find it so quiet.

Rolling Stone What is it you don't like about the quiet?
Woody Allen I don't find there's a lot of things to do. I'm there and, yeah, sure, I can read a book for a while. But I can read a book in my apartment, too. Mia and I are always arguing about this. I don't mind on a given day—let's say a beautiful fall day or something—I can see getting into the car and driving up to the country and getting out and walking around and looking at the lake and leaves and that kind of thing and then getting back in the car and coming home. That I can see. To go and spend two hours, five hours in the country, something like that. I can't see bedding down in the country overnight. I see nothing in that.

I like to know, although I've never done it, I like to know that if at two o'clock in the morning I get a sudden urge for duck wonton soup, that I can go downstairs, find a taxicab, go to Chinatown, get it and come back home. This is important to me.

Rolling Stone You're not telling a joke here, are you?
Woody Allen No, I mean it sincerely.

Rolling Stone Why would that be important to you?
Woody Allen It makes me feel comfortable to know I'm in that atmosphere. You know, after dinner if I want to take a walk, for instance, and go look in the bookstores and maybe drop into the Regency Theatre or go up to Elaine's or something, I know that I have the options. I eat dinner out 360 nights a year.

I like the idea that it's a live active city. I don't like to know that if I go outside, it's all trees and bushes and paths.

Rolling Stone Just because it's dull, not because it's threatening.
Woody Allen Both. I find it threatening, too. I find that while it may be true statistically that the city is more dangerous, I feel less endangered in the city. This may be a false feeling of security, but it's still psychologically

helpful to me. I feel that in a crisis situation I'd at least have a chance. I know where to go and how to avoid certain things and where to seek refuge.

In the country, as I said in *Annie Hall,* if Dick and Perry—you know, the guys in *In Cold Blood*—if they show up at the house at night, I mean, you've had it. That's the end of it.

Rolling Stone   So you aren't just afraid that a woodchuck might come at you?

Woody Allen   I wouldn't like that either. I would not like to be in the country and come face to face with a rabid possum or rabid woodchuck. I don't appreciate that stuff.

Rolling Stone   When was the last time you were outside New York City?

Woody Allen   Except for Mia's place in Connecticut? A few years ago, when Mia and I went to Paris and Rome for a week.

Rolling Stone   You don't go out of New York to America?

Woody Allen   Sometimes I get to thinking New York is America, but that is wrong. Once I was in the suburbs, and I drove by one of those theaters with about eight movies playing at once, and I almost couldn't imagine one of my films playing there.

Rolling Stone   You could almost be a target for the House Committee on Un-American Activities. Do you have a valid driver's license?

Woody Allen   I do, but I haven't driven a car in many years.

Rolling Stone   In how long?

Woody Allen   Oh, I'd say twenty-five years.

Rolling Stone   *Twenty-five?*

Woody Allen   With the exception of once I had to make a shot in *Annie Hall,* so I drove . . .

Rolling Stone   Not very well.

Woody Allen   That's why I don't drive in real life.

Rolling Stone   Do you watch television? Do you own a television?

Woody Allen   I watch sports and films and news.

Rolling Stone   Do you ever watch your own films on TV?

Woody Allen   No, I never watch my films, anyplace, ever. They disappoint me.

Rolling Stone   Do you watch "The Love Boat?"

Woody Allen   No.

Rolling Stone   "Dallas?"

Woody Allen   No, I don't watch what is purported entertainment. Not that I watch highbrow stuff . . . I watch baseball and basketball.

But I don't watch the junk stuff. I don't find it even *remotely* reward-ing, on any level. It seems to me if I happen to see it while dialing through on the way somewhere, it just looks like elevator music, the height of soulless, plastic, brightly lit, antiseptic, you know . . . stupidity. I don't think it's worth anybody's time.

Rolling Stone Have you ever been in a shopping mall?
Woody Allen I don't know that I've ever been on a shopping mall.

Rolling Stone You said *"on* a shopping mall." Shopping malls are en-closed, you know.
Woody Allen Oh, are they? Then I've never been in one, no. Then what am I thinking of? When I visit Mia in Connecticut, sometimes she'll go to buy something, and I'll be in the car with her, and I'll get off, and that's where I think I've been on a mall.

Rolling Stone And you don't get *off* a car either. You get *out of* a car.
Woody Allen Okay.

Rolling Stone At the opening of your film *Manhattan,* there is a state-ment that the lead character loves New York, even though he views it as a metaphor for the decay of civilization. Is this your view?
Woody Allen Yes. But I think of it often as it used to be. When I was growing up and could ride the subways with impunity at age ten . . . it was coming to the end of the really golden age. My guess is that in the twenties and thirties there was probably nothing to equal Manhattan ever in the history of the world. When you think that there would be a hundred plays at once, you just can't get your mind around that. And the movie houses and nightclubs and speakeasies.

Rolling Stone Is it depressing for you to look at some of it now?
Woody Allen It's crushing to me. I speak to people that were in Broad-way shows, older actresses, and I was speaking to one woman who was saying to me she and her girlfriend would do a show, and the curtain would come down at 11:15, and they would get dressed and go out for dinner in Times Square—two girls about nineteen years old, totally unescorted—and then go to a movie house on Forty-second Street after dinner and see a Katharine Hepburn or Spencer Tracy picture. And then walk home through Central Park. I wish I could have lived in New York in a different period.

Rolling Stone Other directors say there are problems to shooting a film in New York, such as traffic and people walking through scenes. Norman Jewison said he just had a guy walk into a bakery where he was shooting, which was full of lights and sound technicians and actors. The guy said he didn't care, he wanted four loaves of bread. He picked them up, and Jew-ison told him to pay the lady at the counter, who was Cher. He did.
Woody Allen Gee, I haven't had too many problems. There is a lack of

studio space, and the seasons can be merciless. But in the spring or fall, there are no drawbacks at all.

Rolling Stone   Is the film you just shot set in New York?
Woody Allen   Well, no, it's set in Vermont. But I shot it in New York.

Rolling Stone   How do you make New York look like Vermont?
Woody Allen   It all takes place in one house.

Rolling Stone   What do you enjoy about filmmaking?
Woody Allen   I enjoy the writing most. It always seems great in the writing. You're at home alone in your apartment and you know it's just wonderful. Then reality suddenly starts to creep in. You start to realize that this actor is unavailable, so you're going to have to settle for that actor, and you really can't afford $200,000 for a set, you're going to have to get one for $15,000. Gradually the compromises come in. And those lines are not so funny that you thought were so great back in your apartment.

Rolling Stone   Or too funny? Too funny can obliterate all else.
Woody Allen   Or it's too funny, yeah, although too funny is usually one of those problems like too rich.

Rolling Stone   Do you enjoy the directing?
Woody Allen   No. I would like to conceive of the film and then press a button and have the film master. Directing is enervating, and very often you're standing around on freezing-cold street corners at six in the morning, and I don't think anyone would find that much fun. And it's long hours, and often the results are very disappointing when you see them the next day in the screening room, in terms of lighting and acting and that your idea was not so good. And you directed it too slow or too fast and you're going to have to go back the next day and do it again.

Rolling Stone   *Radio Days* was warm and funny, but it didn't seem as ambitious as some of your others.
Woody Allen   Well, I don't want to do a series of films that always seems to make profound statements. That would be really limiting. You want to do a certain number of films and try to do that, and I would like, in the course of my life, to do some broad comedies and a musical. You want to mix it up.

When I did *Annie Hall*, everyone wanted *Annie Hall II*, and the same with *Hannah*. But it's very important for me not to do that. After *Annie Hall*, I made *Interiors*, and after *Hannah*, I made a completely different kind of film, because it's important not to get suckered into the success syndrome because the public likes something.

Rolling Stone   Why this picture, *Radio Days*, at this time?
Woody Allen   I spend almost a year on a film, and by the time you've

lived with something for a year, you want to get on. You get bored with that subject matter and that style of film, so you want to get into something different.

Hannah was a living-room picture. It becomes dull, so you look for something different to do, just to break the monotony. And so I thought it would be fun to do something that was episodic and full of music and cartoonlike and nostalgic.

Rolling Stone Why do you do so many films? Couldn't you do fewer and make them all great, important works that would go down in film history?
Woody Allen No. I wouldn't want to make those kinds of films. They'd be expensive and they'd be hard work and you'd have to emotionally commit yourself for years to the same project.

I'd much rather make small pictures and just make many of them. I don't find any correlation between size and greatness. You take some of those Bergman films that are enormously complex, enormously complex. He shoots those things quickly, like in four weeks', five weeks' time. They're the best films in the world, I think.

I just do as many films as I have ideas for, just as fast as I can. And when I'm finished making films in my life, I will have made whatever number of films, and some of them, if I'm lucky, will be very good films, and some of them won't be good films, and some will be entertaining.

Rolling Stone Something people always want to know: How much of *Radio Days* is autobiographical?
Woody Allen Some of it is loosely autobiographical, but very loosely. The radio programs, such as "The Masked Avenger," were generic because it would be such a nuisance to get clearance on actual radio shows.

Rolling Stone The sports program was hysterical, the inspirational story about the pitcher who loses his leg, then his arm, then his eyesight, but goes on pitching.
Woody Allen The man who played the role of the sportscaster for me, Guy Le Bow [a real-life veteran sportscaster], was fondly remembering off camera that radio show and was saying one story he had heard on it was Abraham Lincoln on his deathbed saying to Abner Doubleday, you know, go out there and don't give up on baseball.

Rolling Stone Abner was at his bedside after the shooting?
Woody Allen Sure. He had heard that for real on that show.

Rolling Stone The film painted a grim picture of Hebrew school.
Woody Allen Public school was equally bad. I went to both. Double horror.

Rolling Stone Were you funny in school? Did they send you out in the hall a lot?
Woody Allen There'd be periods when I was really quiet and never said

anything and other periods when I was amusing and we'd get into trouble constantly. But it was never a pleasurable experience. It was a spectacular treat to be sick because you could avoid school, which was the blessing of all times.

Rolling Stone What was so awful about school?
Woody Allen Everything. First of all, there were the natural things that kids would not like: sitting still, being disciplined, not being able to talk and not being able to have fun. It was a loathsome thing. The teachers were backward and anti-Semitic.

Rolling Stone In your neighborhood in Flatbush? There weren't a lot of Jewish kids in school?
Woody Allen Almost all.

Rolling Stone But the teachers were just anti-Semitic anyway?
Woody Allen Uh-huh. And they were stupid and mean. They were unpleasant people, and one never wanted to go to school.

Rolling Stone Did you write in high school?
Woody Allen Yes.

Rolling Stone Things that were not always appreciated by teachers?
Woody Allen I used to write things that they thought were dirty.

Rolling Stone Were they?
Woody Allen No, they were dirty by the backward, ignorant standards of my teachers. My mother was called so often because of that and other problems.

Rolling Stone Like what?
Woody Allen Truancy, bad marks, causing disturbances. She was called to school so frequently that into her sixties, when my mother was still in the old neighborhood, kids who went to school with me would recognize her and say hello to her because she was such a frequent figure.

My mother's eighty now. My father's eighty-six. They live just a couple of blocks from me. My sister lives ten blocks from me.

Rolling Stone Has any of the stuff that borders on the autobiographical ever bothered them?
Woody Allen No, because the stuff that people insist is autobiographical is almost invariably not, and it's so exaggerated that it's virtually meaningless to the people upon whom these little nuances are based. People got it into their heads that *Annie Hall* was autobiographical, and I couldn't convince them that it wasn't. And they thought *Manhattan* was autobiography. Because I make the lead character a comic or a writer, I play it myself. I'm not going to make the lead a mechanic. I know the language of certain people.

Rolling Stone   Although you say you were never the schlemiel you have made yourself out to be, does it feel good to make films where you get the girl and all of that?

Woody Allen   I've had a certain amount of successes and failures in every aspect of life. My life where I grew up in Brooklyn and in Long Beach was completely average. I was a perfectly good schoolyard athlete. And I had friends and dated some girls and was rejected by others.

Rolling Stone   Do you ever reflect on your situation now and say, "Wow, I'm having relationships with movie stars?"

Woody Allen   I've been in the movie business the last twenty years. So it's logical that I would be seeing an actress or screenwriter or someone in my related field.

My life began being special when I was sixteen and got a job writing comedy. But even then I went to school in the daytime. I had lower-than-average marks and only went to NYU for a very short time to please my parents.

I was dropped by NYU after less than one year because of bad marks. I was a film major at NYU but couldn't even pass my major. I took what was called the limited program—three subjects.

Rolling Stone   You failed the limited program?

Woody Allen   And I couldn't care less, because I'd ride the train to NYU from Brooklyn and I'd think to myself, "Don't get off here. Keep going." And I'd go right up to Forty-second Street, cutting school to go to the movies, hang out at the automat, buy the newspapers, and go to the Paramount—and then go in to work in the afternoon.

Rolling Stone   By then you had a job and an inkling you might do well.

Woody Allen   I felt very confident. . . . And again, to please my parents, who were so crushed by this because all of my friends were becoming lawyers and doctors and going to college and doing well, I also went for a very, very short time up to City College.

Rolling Stone   Have you changed along with your films?

Woody Allen   I don't know that *I* have changed. The films have. I've become more interested in doing what for me is intellectually more difficult and more challenging.

Rolling Stone   How do you respond when people ask you, in effect, "Why don't you cut the crap and just be funny?"

Woody Allen   Well, it has never really meant a thing to me what anyone said. I'm just sort of going the route I've chosen to go. If people like it, they like it, and if they don't, they don't. Crowd pleasing just never interested me.

Rolling Stone   This kind of goes back to your school days, when what teachers said apparently didn't mean anything to you. What then do you tell the youth of America? Is it okay for them to goof off and just do what interests them?

Woody Allen   It's hard to give advice, in that sense. You see, I was lucky. I don't think you can count on being lucky. I was lucky in that I had a talent to be amusing. If I didn't have that talent, I would have been in great peril. You can only be independent that way if you luck out. But you can't count on it.

But people have always told me what to do. And I always listened politely and I'm always nice to them, but I always do what I want to do.

The world is full of people who are quick to tell you films you should be doing and what to cut out and what to put in. There is an old proverb: "He can't think, but he knows all about it."

Rolling Stone   Or, in more recent history, as you said on film, "Those who can't do, teach, and those who can't teach, teach gym."

Woody Allen   Yes, that was in *Annie Hall,* and I always felt people are very quick with advice, fast advice from the man on the street and profound advice from your peers. You read your books and you live your life and you see your friends and make your own evaluation as to what you want to do.

People are forever telling me, well, don't do this joke, or don't dress that way, or don't do this subject matter, or don't do that kind of film. You don't want to do *Take the Money and Run.* You want to do a different kind of film. You don't want to do *Annie Hall,* you know, because it's really less funny than *Bananas.* You don't want to do *Interiors* because of this and that. And I always listen politely, because they are nice people, but, you know, I do what I want to do, because your *body* demands it. You feel it. It's not so much a conscious decision. You go your route.

Rolling Stone   Have you ever thought afterward that those people were right?

Woody Allen   That could never be, because I've always done what I wanted to do at the time. This doesn't square itself, necessarily, with commercial success. But who cares about that?

I've done films that were not commercial successes that I think were much better than ones I've done that were tremendous commercial successes.

Rolling Stone   For example?

Woody Allen   I think *The Purple Rose of Cairo* was a much better film than *Hannah and Her Sisters.* Much better. Much more imaginative. It's just a better film.

Rolling Stone   How about *Radio Days*?

Woody Allen   It was the best I could do at that time. As with all my films, you know, when I see it I always feel disappointed, because I have such grandiose notions at first. But when you get into the very, very difficult world of having to translate those grandiose fantasies from a piece of paper and your mind to reality, and it requires props and people and huge crews and music and everything, it's very hard to transfer it with the same perfection that you conceive it in your mind, where everything moves beautifully. So, I'm always disappointed.

Rolling Stone   How did *Radio Days* fall short?
Woody Allen   Well, the concept in my mind was more glorious, was grander and more beautiful and funnier and more profound and more moving. It fell short in every important way. But this is not infrequent for me. It is quite usual.

And when you say this, you are not being falsely modest. The fact of the matter is that when you approach something, its potential is very often tremendous. And it's not an easy job to milk the potential from something, to realize that potential. And the more challenging a project is, a movie like *Zelig,* the harder it is to get the potential out of it.

Rolling Stone   As one who thinks about mortality, have you ever thought in terms of perhaps only living long enough to do ten or fifteen or twenty more films, and that they'd better be good and they'd better be this kind or that?
Woody Allen   No, only because it really doesn't matter to me. It wouldn't matter to me if I stopped making films tomorrow. I'd be just as happy to write books.

Rolling Stone   Do you get any enjoyment from fame?
Woody Allen   No, I'll tell you what I do like. The perks of being well known are very good, because I can always get a hotel room or a plane reservation or a table in a restaurant. And you do get good service.

Rolling Stone   That's it? You know, you really don't have to keep doing a film a year and be compared to Bergman to get a good table.
Woody Allen   Yeah. One of the reasons I don't travel more is because I'm bothered by the *paparazzi*. That's one of the drawbacks of being well known.

Rolling Stone   You're really more free to walk around New York than you are in Rome?
Woody Allen   Yes, or Paris, absolutely. There's no satisfaction in the fame. When you're a kid, you think there would be. But as soon as you become an adult you see that there's nothing outside of these practical purposes like . . .

Rolling Stone   Getting a table.
Woody Allen   And good theater tickets.

Rolling Stone   Is there some way you want to be remembered?
Woody Allen   No. Someone once asked me if my dream was to live on in

the hearts of my people, and I said I would like to live on in my apartment. And that's really what I would prefer.

Rolling Stone   Forever.
Woody Allen   Exactly. Nothing short of changing the human condition would be worth it. You drop dead one day, and it means less than nothing if billions of people are singing your praises every day, all day long.

Rolling Stone   Oh, come on.
Woody Allen   You wouldn't know it. It would mean less than nothing.

Rolling Stone   You wouldn't like it if once a year there was a Woody Allen ticker-tape parade up Broadway?
Woody Allen   You'd be better off with a couple of years extension.

Film Clip: Woody Allen*

[ROGER EBERT'S interview is the latest of his yearly talks with Woody Allen, and it is a particularly amusing one.

We get a look at Woody's hypochondria, and observe how a phobia can manifest itself in a work of art, transmuted from the chaotic worries of the hypochondriac into a narrative both entertaining and penetrating.]

New York, December 19, 1990—Woody Allen found the first ticklings of inspiration for *Alice,* his new movie, by getting a sty in his eye. One of those annoying little bumps by the tear ducts. That was why he went to the acupuncturist. And then the incident began to grow in his imagination, flowering and folding in upon itself, and finally it became a story about Mia Farrow as a rich New York trophy wife who is compelled to evaluate every aspect of her life after a strange old man in Chinatown gives her special herbs for her tea.

"When you get a sty they're very annoying," Allen was explaining to me the other afternoon. We were sitting in a corner of his living room on Fifth Avenue, and the winter sun was hanging low over Central Park. He sounded like someone for whom the very memory of a sty was painful.

"They're not fatal, but you have to have them lanced, and it's a very unpleasant thing, and when you get one, you tend to get a wave of them. I tried everything, and then someone told me that she was seeing this tremendous acupuncturist downtown at this dingy little place. He was giving

---

*From *Roger Ebert's Movie Home Companion* (1992 Edition; Andrews and McMeel). © 1990 Roger Ebert. All rights reserved.

her herbs every week in little bags, and I'd notice she'd go into the kitchen sometimes and pour these things together and drink them before going out to dinner, and I figured, gee, this guy's making a fortune!"

"A friend of mine went down there and said all these rich women come in to see this man. They think it's for their skin, their hair, their youth, and I was completely skeptical about it. I thought it was a total fraud. And she said, 'Why don't you try and have him cure your sties? You've been going to a Western doctor now for years, and you still keep getting them. Give this guy a chance.'"

"I said, 'I'll bet anything that there's no chance in the world that this guy can ever cure my sties. I think this guy's a total fraud.' So he came over to this apartment, and he read my pulse to diagnose me, which was just nonsense I thought, and told me to stop eating shellfish, and then he said, 'The way I think you can get rid of them is with a cat's whisker.'"

Woody looked up at the ceiling, as if appealing to reason and sanity. "He kept saying, 'Whisker of cat, whisker of cat! I take care of this with whisker of cat!' I was totally skeptical. The next week the guy came back with his niece and a little silver box, and in it were these little cat's whiskers. She held my arms down, and he got over me, and he started manipulating a cat's whisker in the tear duct, and I'm thinking if this works, it's going to be the miracle of all time."

But, of course, we are inhabitants of the New Age, and so we know how the story ended. The agnostic Woody was completely and miraculously cured, and has not had a sty in his eye ever since. Right?

"It didn't work at all. It was a totally meaningless thing, and when I told my eye doctor about it, he said, 'Jeez, don't let this guy poke cat's whiskers in your tear ducts because it's not going to help any, and it could create a problem.' The guy was totally fraudulent, but it stayed with me, because it was such a funny story. The guy was here, my friends were here, and they were laughing hysterically, but to the best of my knowledge he still runs an incredibly thriving business in a dive in Chinatown, and rich women still go up the rickety stairs to see him."

And he is probably famous as the guy that Woody Allen always uses.

Woody laughed. "I don't think he needs me."

In a lot of your movies, I said, you like to write in wise people who are supposed to have the answers. Shrinks or rabbis or priests or philosophers. Even magicians.

"It doesn't hurt. Everybody, including me, is always searching for something, but nobody ever helps you—that's the problem."

He thought for a moment about the meaning of the Chinese acupuncturist and magician.

"One could make the case," he said, "that in a certain sense what he does isn't that different from a psychoanalytic experience. You wish your analyst could perform magic, but he can't, so in a very slow, tedious way you start to find out about yourself, and this takes years, if it happens at all, and finally you change your life. In the movie, she goes and she gets a very fast, much more colorful version of it, but she's really doing the same thing, working with her creative impulses, her dreams, past memories of relationships. I didn't intend it that way when I wrote the movie, but now I can see that possibility."

And in *Alice*, which is a whimsical comedy with an undercurrent as dark as dread, after the mysterious magician does help the Mia Farrow character, her life is never the same again. The film opens with a virtuoso scene at breakneck pace, establishing Alice as the rich and pampered wife of an incredibly wealthy investment professional—a cool, detached man (played by William Hurt) who deflects all possible arguments with vague reassurances and slippery compliments. They live in a hermetic womb of creature comfort, with a cook who buys only free-range chickens, and a nanny who attends to the children so efficiently that the parents barely even need to talk to the little darlings.

One day, after sixteen years of marriage, like a thunderbolt, the notion of an affair strikes Alice. Dropping her kids off at private school, she drops a book on the stair. A dark, handsome stranger (Joe Mantegna) returns it to her, and soon she can think of no one else. She's so worked up, she develops back pains, and so she has the limousine drive her down to Chinatown, where the fabled Dr. Yang (Keye Luke) occupies a shadowy office filled with strange props, like a revolving pinwheel that hypnotizes her.

He thinks her problem is not her back, but her marriage. He supplies Alice with various herbs and potions that liberate her so completely that for the rest of the movie she's on an inspection tour of her own life, re-evaluating her husband, her mother, her sister, her purpose for living. At times she even flies above the spires of Manhattan, held safely by the ghost of a former lover—or is that a dream, inspired by the herbs Dr. Yang asked her to burn in a teacup?

The world of *Alice* is the world of wealthy New York, of men who make money and women who spend it with skill and grace. It is a New York of elegant brownstones, exclusive high-rises, private schools, expensive shops, and little private parks with quaint benches lining the paths. The end credits thank Cartier, Ben Kahn, Valentino, and the New York Zoological Society. The musical score is lush with Erroll Garner, Paul Weston, and those romantic big-band arrangements Jackie Gleason was famous for. This is a New York that exists only in ads in *Architectural Digest* and *Town & Country,* and in this movie.

"It's the rich New York," Allen said. "If you have as much money as these people did, you can live pretty well. If you live on upper Fifth Avenue or Park Avenue, and you shop on Madison, and you have all the charge accounts, and you have a car and a driver, and nannies, and maids, and you live in a building that's heavily door-manned, and you know the city well enough so that you eat at Le Cirque and the Russian Tea Room, and you know certain parts of the park that are beautiful and quite safe—you can live a perfectly fine life. But if you're not in that fortunate group, then you have to take public transportation, and you've got to be in neighborhoods that aren't safe, and your hours are not your own, so you've got to travel in traffic, and in the park where it's not so safe . . . and it's not so good. What's killing the city is that it has no middle class."

The other New York, of the people who have to take public transportation, is nowhere on display in *Alice*, at least not until the very end, when Alice sees spiritual inspiration in a most unlikely quarter. At the beginning, she is a woman so elevated above the daily inconveniences of life that she hardly has responsibilities even to her children—except to bear them, of course, as a gesture to her husband. You have to listen carefully to even catch her speaking to the children, who are ignored most of the time and are backdrops the rest of the time.

"That's a phenomenon that I have observed," Allen said. "Not with Mia, because she's the opposite, but I've seen it when I used to go pick up my kid from school. I'd see nannies doing everything. I'm not blaming the parents necessarily, because probably a number of them are working, but it is an amazing thing how people delegate that responsibility."

Allen himself became a parent only in his fifties—he and Farrow adopted one child and conceived another—and these days he gets up early, at five, so he can be across the park to her apartment by six to spend time with the kids before they go to school and go to work. And in the afternoon, after his clarinet practice, he's there for dinner and story time. "They are the absolutely central fact of my life," he said, shaking his head wonderingly, this man who never saw himself as a father.

But Alice, I said, only goes to school to pick up her kids because she wants to run into this guy she has a crush on. Otherwise she wouldn't even be there.

"Yeah. You see that frequently at the schools. The nannies do it all. I'll take the kids to school, and it will be a dreary, cold winter morning, and it will be some nannies and a half a dozen mothers, and I'll be surrounded by all these floor-length mink coats. They're from around the corner on Fifth Avenue, with no makeup on, almost with their hair in curlers, wearing whatever house clothes they threw on, with their floor-length mink coats thrown on top, to take the kid to school. It looks a little like a mink farm."

Although many of Allen's movies use Judaism as either a background or a comic foil, the religion of choice in *Alice* is Catholicism. The character was raised as a Catholic, went through a "religious phase," and now considers herself culturally Catholic but nonpracticing. This arouses the considerable amusement of Dr. Yang, who makes a couple of jokes at her expense, but it also inspires a fantasy scene in which Alice revisits her childhood home and finds a priest and a confessional installed in the front yard.

"Mia has had a very Catholic background," Allen said, "and I drew on some of it for the screenplay. She was going to be a nun for a long time. Mother Teresa has been a major icon in her life. She was raised Catholic, and it was always interesting to me to hear about it. I've always been interested in the aesthetics of Catholicism. It's such a lovely religion to an outsider from an aesthetic point of view. Remember, I was contemplating becoming Catholic in *Hannah and Her Sisters,* because it's so filled with beauty and ritual. I got that all from Mia. When she was a little girl she used to pray with her arms outstretched so it would be more uncomfortable.

"I remember when I was very young, I went on a trip to a monastery outside of Washington. It was very quiet and peaceful. There were very few people there. Just the thought that the monks would wake up in the morning, and they would tread those paths, and they were not afraid of dying, and they didn't want anything—I loved that. It was a stoic life. They had no great desires. They just trod, and sat, and thought, and prayed. I guess there were ones like Mendel who wanted to fool around with pea pods and cross-pollinate and do their little hobbies. It is seductive, there is no question. But on the surface, I don't believe in any of this."

You've often said, when life is over, it's over.

"It certainly seems that way."

And yet you're afraid to sleep in a graveyard, or spend the night in a haunted castle. Why should *your* life be over for good, when all of these other lucky people get to be ghosts and hang around to frighten you?

"You just can't know for sure. So, while I'm totally skeptical, and I believe that of course you can walk under a ladder, and there's nothing more to life than what you see, there's always that element of doubt. When I go to Mia's house in Connecticut, it's not that I'm afraid that two guys are gonna pull up like Dick and Perry in *In Cold Blood.* It's more that I'm gonna see two eyes at the window, or I'm going to be walking along the shore and a hand is going to come up out of the lake. Or if I'm home alone, and the city is very black, and it's a big house, eleven rooms, and you hear a little noise, and you get a slightly creepy feeling. It isn't that a mugger is in the house. That's not frightening. That you can deal with. If it's a mugger you can scream, pick up the phone, pick up the fireplace poker. It's that there might be . . . something else."

And because there might be something else, we should lead good lives.

"Well, we should not waste time. That's what I was always told as a child: Don't waste time! And so I have this movie coming out, and I'm shooting another one right now, and I'm working on the screenplay for the next one, and I would enjoy nothing more than writing and directing a really good detective movie, because I'd enjoy that more than anything, but I never will—because I would be afraid of wasting my time."

CHAPTER 3

Regarding Woody

I give as much contact as is required professionally.
Socially is a whole other world . . .
Woody Allen

Chips

Insiders Talk About Woody Allen

Woody Allen, Conundrum

Woody Allen is perceived as a mysterious, enigmatic ascetic.

It is generally assumed that he is a reclusive, private man, and in some ways, he is. But the media often make him sound like Howard Hughes and J. D. Salinger rolled into one. The truth is, of course, always different. Woody Allen does not do many interviews, but he *does* grant them. He has been far from as taciturn as some pundits would have you believe. The reality is that the man is busy. World-class busy. He is, at any given moment, shooting one film, editing another, and writing yet another. And you wonder why he stopped writing essays for the *New Yorker*?

But what I have found fascinating over the couple of years it took me to research and write *The Woody Allen Companion,* is how every now and then a little anecdote about Woody would be made public, usually from someone who worked on a Woody film (but not always).

This section takes a look at a few of those moments, with the intention of perhaps illuminating some of the facets of Woody's personality not normally seen or made available to his public and fans. (Also included are a few off-the-cuff remarks about Woody, as well as some completely fictitious stories about Woody. Woody's role as a popular culture icon is such a given (and his public persona so identifiable) that writers often write about the *image* in lieu of the *reality.*)

Dick Cavett and Woody Allen: A Special Friendship*

Dick Cavett and Woody Allen have been close friends for almost thirty years now, and Cavett can justifiably be considered one of the truly scarce genuine "Woody Allen Insiders."

There are some interesting "Woody" anecdotes in *Cavett,* and this sampling offers rare insight into Woody's thoughts. (All page references are to the Bantam paperback edition.)

• Page 135: Christopher Porterfield relates that Woody Allen once told Dick Cavett that he (Woody) never in his life had to earn a living.

• Pages 165–66: *Dick Cavett on first meeting Woody during one of Woody's appearances at the Blue Angel*:

> [T]here was this newcomer named Woody Allen playing there, and everything I had heard about him sounded good. I was dazzled by his credits,

*Quotations from *Cavett,* by Dick Cavett and Christopher Porterfield (New York: Bantam, 1975).

which included writing for Sid Caesar while still a teenager, and I had the feeling this was someone I would like to get to know, even though I had neither seen him nor met him. His sounded like one of the lives I would like to lead.

I got there just as the lights went down and he came on. His opening jokes were marvelous. They were not formula; they showed complex intelligence and genuine wit. It was marvelous just to see this high level sustained throughout his act, instead of the intermittent gems of good but lesser comics. Yet about a third of the way through the audience began to murmur and talk. Woody plowed on, his face largely concealed by the mike, and ended, more by excusing himself than finishing, and left the stage to polite applause. Somehow I felt there had been a kind of arc traveling from him, on the stage, to me, standing there in the back. I recognized immediately that there was no young comedian in the country who was in the same class with him for sheer brilliance of jokes, and I resented the fact that the audience was too dumb to realize what they were getting. They were mildly appreciative, but they would have preferred a folk singer, which they soon got. Woody had been casting pearls over the heads of swine.

While the folk singer was on, I sought him out, and we sat down in the pink light of one of the lounge booths of the Angel, hit it off immediately . . . and have been close friends ever since. A few days after he met me, incidentally, he got a divorce. None of the rumors, I might add, are true.

• Page 167: *Dick Cavett on Woody's writing and work habits*:

Woody is much closer to being an intellectual than I am, and if he wanted to he could conduct a seminar on writing and comedy at any major university. He once threatened to publish a series of essays on comedy, and I hope he gets around to it. It's about the only form of writing he hasn't turned his hand to, except the novel. I wouldn't be surprised if he had two or three of them in a trunk somewhere—novels, I mean—and an epic poem or two that he isn't telling anyone about. I think too he would like to write and act in a serious film, but his comic image is so strong in people's minds that he has held off. I hope he does it anyway.

The only discomfort I felt in getting to know Woody was how ashamed of myself I would get when I saw how disciplined he was. He can go to the typewriter after breakfast and sit there until the sun sets and his head is pounding, interrupting work only for coffee or a brief walk, and then spend the whole evening working. I had the feeling that one day like that represented more work than I had done in my life. But even this discomfort proved to be a good thing, since exposure to Woody was what finally prodded me into getting an act together for myself.

• Page 191: *Dick Cavett on Woody's neuroses*:

Woody used to talk about what a backbreaking job it was for him to sit down and write his own jokes. . . . I really envy Woody. He has great concentration. He's supposed to be neurotic; *he* goes to an analyst. But he functions. I'm supposed not to be neurotic. But I have all the symptoms.

• Pages 192–93: *Dick Cavett on Woody's advice to him about his own writing*:

> [W]hen I was faced with writing for me I had no known quantity to imitate. What . . . was my *voice*? . . . Woody's advice was, don't get paralyzed with this thought, but go to the typewriter whenever possible and put down anything I thought was funny. This unblocked me. . . . Woody based a lot of his humor on his unheroic appearance, on his looking like a victim, but I found I couldn't make my appearance the basis for jokes. [So] a Nebraska Yankee at Yale and in New York became my comic persona. . . . When Woody had told me that he sometimes spent a day getting a joke right, I couldn't imagine what he was talking about. He said you can't just accept the first thing that comes into your head; you have to keep thinking until you know you've got the best possible joke on the subject at hand. Woody certainly put this principle into practice. I think his albums show the finest sustained level of joke-writing genius in the history of standup comedy. But to me, at the time, this was a discouragement. After a couple of weeks, I had about nine jokes I felt were worth using. When I realized how hard Woody worked, how disciplined he was, and how many brilliant jokes he had already and many more he intended to have, I had to lie down with an ice bag on my forehead.

• Page 219: *Woody's advice to Cavett about being introduced at comedy clubs*:

> I called Woody [and] he pointed out that you have to insist on an intro that makes two things clear: That you are a comedian, and that the audience is expected to laugh. His other advice was to do another show soon, which I did, and which worked out well.

• Page 227: *Woody Allen's views on other comics' stealing his jokes*:

> Sometimes I would call Woody to report the latest theft of one of his jokes. He finally asked me to stop, because, number one, it pained him and if he didn't know about it he would feel better, and, number two, it didn't matter because the crap comics would always be crap comics, and although it hurts to have your jokes stolen, something about you puts you forever in another category and world from them, or at least that is what you tell yourself. He was right.

The Woodman in Idaho

Mariel Hemingway, granddaughter of Ernest Hemingway, overwhelmed people with her performance as Tracy, the seventeen-year-old girlfriend of Isaac Davis (Woody) in *Manhattan*. After the film was finished, Mariel invited Woody to her parents' place in Idaho—and he went. The quintessential Manhattanite got on a plane to go commune with nature. The mind boggles.

Mariel Hemingway was a guest on "Late Night with David Letterman" on Friday, August 2, 1991, and she told Dave the story:

David Letterman I didn't realize this and I still don't believe it. . . . After you had done *Manhattan,* you invited Woody Allen to come visit you in Montana . . . or Idaho?

Mariel Hemingway Idaho. Yes, I did. He came out there and it was an experience. . . . Getting off the plane, he said, "I think we just landed on the moon." (Laughs) He had never been in any environment like that ever before. I took him on a huge hike the next day thinking, God, this'll be great. We'll get him in the outdoors, [but] there was . . . snow up to his waist. And he had to eat dinner that my father had just shot. He was perplexed. And at eight o'clock, we all went to bed. And [you could see] he was [thinking], "What do they do here?" I mean . . . he doesn't wake up till then.

David Letterman But how did you even get him out of Manhattan, out of New York? . . . I was under the impression that he certainly didn't go anywhere if he didn't have to.

Mariel Hemingway I have no idea, and I think that he would never go back. (Laughs) He's never left [New York] since!

David Letterman Are you folks still friendly?

Mariel Hemingway Yeah. I mean, I see him occasionally, but not often.

David Letterman He doesn't come up to [your] restaurant?

Mariel Hemingway (Petulant and fake-pouting) No.

David Letterman (Laughing) Well, that's too bad.

Woody the Director

Joe Mantegna got invisible with Mia Farrow in *Alice,* and used the opportunity to watch model Elle Macpherson undress.

When talking to David Letterman about working with Woody, he didn't mention that particular moment, but did offer a glimpse into what it's like to be directed by Woody Allen:

David Letterman [Y]ou were in these two movies that were produced about the same time. *Alice,* with Woody Allen . . .

Joe Mantegna Right. *Alice* and *Godfather III.*

David Letterman Yeah. Now how was that possible from a production standpoint . . . your personal time?

Joe Mantegna It was difficult, it was difficult. 'Cause I was here doing *Alice* for a couple of months, and then I remember, on a Friday night . . Woody shook my hand and said, "Well, have a nice trip to Italy." And I go on the plane. The next day I went to Rome for a month, worked on *Godfather [III],* came back, worked on Woody's film for two more months, and then worked on *Godfather* again.

David Letterman Tell me about your relationship, with Woody Allen . . . on this movie, *Alice*. You've known him for a long time, haven't you?

Joe Mantegna No, actually not. I met him for the first time when I did the film. (Audience laughter)

David Letterman (Laughing) Yeah, that would have been my second guess.

Joe Mantegna Woody's great. He's kind of a quiet, low-key kind of guy. I remember once he was talking to his daughter on the set. She plays a role in the film as Alice's daughter. And I remember he was talking to her in his . . . in Woody's indim, inim . . . whatever that word is . . . way.

David Letterman Did you say "dimwitted way"?

Joe Mantegna (Laughing) No, no, I think you know what I mean. Anyway, he was talking to her . . . and he wasn't aware, I'm sure, that I was listening because I just happened to be behind him. And he was explaining to her how she would have to watch the action of the circus. And she was saying, "Oh, well, can I have a hot dog?" and he said, "Oh, sure, that's the prop man's job. If you want a hot dog, he'll bring you a hot dog. If you want cotton candy, he'll bring you cotton candy. If you want a Ferrari, he'll bring you cotton candy." (Audience laughter) And he said it just for her benefit, you know. She didn't laugh, she's four years old. But it was a great "Woody Allenism."

David Letterman And when he's directing you, does he say much to you?

Joe Mantegna No, he doesn't say much, and I think what you learn is that when he says nothing, everything is fine. So in other words, if you're looking for somebody to say, yeah, great, this is not [that type of situation].

David Letterman And were you comfortable with that relationship?

Joe Mantegna Yeah, very much. I mean, you get to be. He does re-shoot a lot, and your first impulse is, "I did it, I ruined it, I'm gone." But then you'll say, "Woody, what would you like me to do different in the re-shoot? And he says, "Nothing, [it was] fine, just do it [the same way]."

David Letterman Well, that's good.

Woody and Diane's Cab Ride

The July 10, 1991, edition of CBS-TV's "48 Hours" was about traffic in New York City. The reporter covering the story interviewed a cab driver who had a "Woody Allen" story.

With all the crime in New York (and especially with all the crime directed against cab drivers) the reporter was surprised to see that this cabbie had no partition in his cab separating the front seat from the back.

The cabbie explained that it was because of a ride he once gave to Woody Allen and Diane Keaton.

One day he picked up Woody and Diane at the Eagle Tavern in Manhattan. Woody had on his "camouflage" army hat, and as soon as they got into the back seat, Woody began whispering something to Diane. Diane started laughing, and said, "Oh, that's so funny! Put that in your next picture." The cabbie said he kept trying to hear because he didn't want to miss what he called "a private performance by Woody Allen." The only problem was the partition. He couldn't hear through the glass.

The cabbie took down the partition that very day. He told the reporter, "I don't care if they kill me, but I don't want to miss any more private performances by Woody Allen."

Spike Lee Talks About Woody Allen*

Talking to Jay Leno, Spike Lee had the following comment on Woody and his films:

> I enjoy his films but there's certain things [aimed at] his audience—intellectual, Jewish, upper West Side New York—that I don't get. But it doesn't deter me from enjoying the film overall. But there are [those] little inside things.

Jeff Daniels on Woody on Showtime

During a Showtime interview, Jeff Daniels talked about auditioning for *The Purple Rose of Cairo*:

> I went in there . . . and here comes Woody Allen, walking out of the cutting room. . . . I was amazing . . . I did everything I could to not get the part. He said, "What have you done?" And I said, "Oh, not much. Some Broadway, and some theater, and some TV. And that's about it." I completely forget the fact that I had just done *Terms of Endearment*, that everyone was standing up and cheering about. But he, I think, out of more of a favor to Juliet [Taylor], who was pushing me, said, all right, we'll give you a screen test. And that afternoon, I got a screen test, and apparently the test was pretty good, because . . . he called, and he said, well, we want him. . . . And so I did a somersault. That's what I always do when I get a role I wanted. I just stop everything and do a quiet somersault on the floor.

Bette Midler in *Movieline* Magazine

In an interview ("Playing to Win") with Lawrence Grobel in the December 1991 issue of *Movieline,* the conversation turned to Woody Allen, and the following exchange took place:

*From "The Tonight Show"; Tuesday, June 11, 1991.

Movieline   Would you do a Woody Allen film if he asked you?
Bette Midler   Absolutely.

Movieline   Would you rather be directed by Woody Allen than have starred with him in *Scenes from a Mall*?
Bette Midler   Well, I've been around for twenty years and he's never asked me to be in one of his movies, so I figure I was lucky to get what I got. You know? I had a wonderful experience. In fact, I still to this day think that picture was unfairly maligned. I loved the picture. I don't think anybody saw it, otherwise they couldn't have said those horrible things about it.

Movieline   How do you know what they said if you don't read the reviews?
Bette Midler   I heard.

Movieline   Did you say to Woody, "You going to ask me to be in your next picture?"
Bette Midler   Well, you know, he never calls, he never writes . . . I dropped a few hints but I don't know. I thought he liked me. I thought he enjoyed it. [Woody's agent] Sam Cohn called me and said he thought *Scenes from a Mall* was the best thing he'd ever seen me do and he was sure it would be a big hit, and he sounded genuine. He had no reason to lie. He thought we were fabulous together. And I thought, "Gol-ly, I hope I get to do it again."

Movieline   Which of Woody Allen's films are your favorites?
Bette Midler   I love his *Alice.* I thought it was brilliant. I've seen them all. Oh, *Broadway Danny Rose,* that's a big favorite of mine. I identify with that end of the business.

Bette Midler in *US* Magazine

In an interview titled "Bawdy Soul," conducted by Jerry Lazar for the December 1991 issue of *US* magazine, Bette Midler had the following to say about Woody when asked for a "quick description" of her costars:

> My dream date. I just never laughed like that on a set. I couldn't wait to get into my makeup and costume every day because I knew I was going to get out there and he was going to say something that was going to make me fall down. The people that work with him always told me that he usually isn't as much fun. He was probably trying to keep me in good spirits. But I had a ball.

Woody Allen in *Spy High: Spy* Magazine's "Make-Believe Yearbook of the Rich & Famous"

The always irreverent but scathingly funny *Spy* magazine published in 1991 what it styled a "make-believe yearbook of the rich & famous." And that's exactly what it was. If everyone famous you've ever heard of went to the same high school, its yearbook would doubtless look like *Spy*'s. Woody Allen was included as a member of the student body.

Woody was a senior, along with Robert De Niro, Michael Jackson, David Letterman, Roseanne Barr, Sandra Bernhard, Mario Cuomo, John Gotti, Fran Lebowitz, Stephen King, Jack Nicholson, Yoko Ono, and many others. And for each "student," the magazine's writers supplied one of those obnoxious little "mini-bios" that appear in every yearbook.

For Woody, they published a photo taken by Marina Garnier, beneath which was the following quotation by Dostoevski. "Man is sometimes extraordinarily, passionately in love with suffering and that is a fact."

Woody's bio read:

> "The Woodman" . . . Freshman-year nebbish, senior-year brain . . . *His latest projects show he's no dummy/But we liked him better when he was funny.* Just kidding . . . Why so secretive? . . . DK *and* MF? Who woulda thunk? . . . Goal: work in Sweden.

According to the yearbook, Woody's high school "activities" were: "Cinephiles 2,3,4; Calliope 2; National Honor Society; Jazz Band 2,3,4."

Woody is also pictured on the yearbook's "National Honor Society" page. He appears in a photo with Norman Mailer and John Updike, and the caption reads: "Please someone tell us—what do these eggheads know about girls that we don't? Left to right: senior Norman Mailer, junior John Updike, senior Woody Allen."

Woody was also featured on the "Senior Superlatives" page. He was given the "Got Most Wedgies" award. (Don ["Stinky"] Trump got the "Gave Most Wedgies" award, Stephen King captured the "Creepiest" award, Marilyn Quayle garnered the "Most Likely to Experience a Stress-Related Disorder" award, and Madonna received the "First to Make a Million" award.)

Woody's New Year's Resolution*

In *Playboy*'s January 1991 issue, writer Robert Wieder offered a very funny look at the ersatz "New Year's Resolutions of the Rich and Famous," and one of Woody's pledges was included.

The Woodster's resolution was simple and to the point: "I will make a movie about people who live in New York City. I won't enjoy it, but I'll do it."

Kathy Bates and Jay Leno Talk About *Shadows and Fog*

Kathy Bates won an Academy Award for her role as Annie Wilkes in Rob Reiner's adaptation of Stephen King's novel *Misery,* and before she moved on to *At Play in the Fields of the Lord,* she flew to New York to play a

---

*From *Playboy* magazine, January 1991.

role in Woody Allen's 1992 film, *Shadows and Fog.* Kathy appeared on "The Tonight Show" on December 17, 1991, to promote *Fried Green Tomatoes* and *At Play in the Fields of the Lord,* and talk soon turned to her participation in Woody's film. Bates told Jay Leno what she knew about the film: hardly anything. And Leno revealed that, while he may enjoy the Woodster's stuff, he is really not a Woody fan. He was surprised about Bates's revelation that cast members never get the entire script, nor do they ever know what the movie is about, a factoid most fans are aware of. Here is their conversation about *Shadows and Fog* (Leno's "donut" remark is a reference to the donuts Kathy ate while filming *Fried Green Tomatoes*):

Jay Leno   You did a Woody Allen film, too?
Kathy Bates   Yep. I did. I actually spent a week in a corset with Woody Allen.

Jay Leno   A week in a corset . . . well, you were not both in the corset . . . *you* were in the corset and Woody was . . .
Kathy Bates   I was in the corset.

Jay Leno   What movie is that?
Kathy Bates   It's called *Shadows and Fog,* but I don't know anything about this movie. All that I know is that I was in a scene with Jodie Foster and Lily Tomlin, and it was great fun, but I have *no* idea what it's about. It's at the turn of the century, and I had to be in a corset, but I don't have any idea what it's about.

Jay Leno   Don't they send you the script and you read it and you just . . .
Kathy Bates   No. They don't want you to know anything about it. So, I don't know . . .

Jay Leno   Did they promise you a lot of donuts? I mean, why did you take this job? I mean . . . I don't understand. They say to you, fly to New York, be in this movie . . . This could be a porno film! You don't even know what it is? How can you not know what it is?
Kathy Bates   Well, you kind of go on blind faith because it's Woody.

Jay Leno   'Cause it's Woody Allen. Oh, I see.
Kathy Bates   It's Woody Allen. So you say, well, I'm gonna go do a Woody. So, I did a Woody.

Jay Leno   So, if this was, like, Allen Funt, you would not do this?
Kathy Bates   (Laughs)

Allen on Allen: One Comic Genius Talks About Another

An Interview with Steve Allen

THE "SHORT" version of Steve Allen's official biography reads as follows:

> Andy Williams once said, "Steve Allen does so many things, he's the only man I know who's listed on every one of the Yellow Pages." It is, in fact, difficult to believe there is only one Steve Allen. Not only is he the only TV comedian from the Golden Age of Comedy of the 1950s still appearing frequently on TV, but he has:
> - Created and hosted "The Tonight Show";
> - Authored 36 published books;
> - Starred on Broadway in *The Pink Elephant*;
> - Starred in motion pictures, most notably Universal's *The Benny Goodman Story*;
> - Written over 4,000 songs, including "This Could Be the Start of Something Big," "Picnic," "Impossible," "Gravy Waltz," and "South Rampart Street Parade";
> - Written the score for several musicals, including the Broadway production of *Sophie* and the CBS-TV version of *Alice in Wonderland*;
> - Made some 40 record albums;
> - Written the stirring Irish drama, *The Wake,* which won an L.A. drama critics' nomination as best play of 1977;
> - Starred in the critically-acclaimed NBC series "The Steve Allen Comedy Hour";
> - Created, written, and hosted the Emmy Award-winning PBS-TV series "Meeting of Minds";
> - And been inducted into the TV Academy's Hall of Fame.

Allen is married to actress-comedienne Jayne Meadows.

In addition to the accomplishments listed above, Steve has also hosted "I've Got a Secret," won a Grammy Award for his song "Gravy Waltz," and written his autobiography, the 1960 volume *Mark It and Strike It.*

It's obvious from Steve Allen's credits why I wanted to speak with him about Woody Allen. In the world of criticism, there are opinions, and then there are informed opinions. Steve Allen's thoughts unquestionably fall into the category of "informed," and it would not be overstating it to say that his opinions are knowledgeable, perceptive, and downright smart.

I was impressed with Steve's cogent analysis and appreciation of Woody in a chapter of his 1981 book *Funny People,* and thought that since it had been a decade since he wrote the chapter, *The Woody Allen Companion* might offer a good opportunity for him to update his thoughts on the Woodman and the Woodwork.

The following interview* is the result.

[I'd like to extend my sincerest thanks to Mr. Allen for his generosity with his time, his help with the reprinting of his chapter, and the video of Woody's appearance on his TV show. His assistance was greatly appreciated.]

SS   In your 1987 book *How to Be Funny* (and elsewhere), you are quoted as saying that tragedy plus time equals comedy. Now even though Woody Allen had the character he didn't like (Alan Alda's obnoxious TV producer Lester) in *Crimes and Misdemeanors* use the line, it's obvious it meant, and said, something to Woody. How do you feel about being quoted in a Woody Allen film?

Steve Allen   I'm very honored. I like my material to be kept in circulation. (Laughs) Actually, that observation is sort of "Scotch-taped" to one that would come prior to it, and that is that comedy is *about* tragedy. Most people's eyebrows pop up when I say that to them, or when they consider it for the first time, because there's a tendency to think of anything comic as being in the same category as red balloons and cotton candy and children giggling at the beach, while the raw material of comedy is likely to be death, cancer, divorce, adultery, or venereal disease.

SS   Woody has been extremely productive in many areas of the creative arts. He wears lots of hats. What particular area of his work do you find most interesting and appealing?

Steve Allen   My interest in Woody has chiefly been in what he doesn't even do anymore: perform comedy. I think he's one of the giants. First of all, the material was always powerhouse, and even though it took the original audiences a few minutes to get used to seeing this mousy little character mumbling softly on stage, he still, I thought, was a major talent right from the start.

SS   What do you think is the essence of Woody Allen's comic genius?

Steve Allen   Marvelous question. The answer to it has several components.

The first is that judged as a joke writer, a gag writer, he's one of the very best. His joke lines are always strong. And that, of course, was the first way he communicated with the world when nobody knew who he was. Back in high school he was submitting jokes that were published in New York columns, and then he went from that to writing for other entertainers for a brief period, including his work on the Sid Caesar show, which I still think is the best example ever of television comedy. Sometimes when I say that in the context of an interview, someone will say, "You mean, even better than your own show?" And I say, "Yeah!" and our own show was sensational.

I'm not talking about just comparing Sid to Steve. That's not the point. Sid's my favorite television comedian, so I couldn't care more about his work than I already do. But when you review that list of writers on "Your

Show of Shows": Woody, Neil Simon, Larry Gelbart, Mel Brooks, and all the others who didn't become as famous but were equally funny on paper, it was natural and inevitable that it would still be considered the peak of achievement.

Excellence, once it's achieved in any of the arts, no longer seems "comparable" to me. You may prefer Van Gogh to Da Vinci, but that's your preference. I don't think it's possible to say in any quantifiable sense that one guy is *better* than the other. You *can* say that a great artist is better than your nephew, who also paints. I'm not talking about that. My point is that once you reach the Olympian peaks, it all seems to me to be of the same general level of achievement.

I've thought of that before in the context of evaluating the classic popular music, the best work of Irving Berlin, Cole Porter, Jerome Kern, Richard Rodgers. The best song of each man is just about as good as the best song of any of the others. They're all nudging up against perfection. So Woody's excellence as a joke writer is point number one.

Point number two is related more to Woody's comic character. His school, the 1960s school of monologists, had in common a seeming amateurishness. The old school—the Bob Hopes, the George Burnses, the Danny Thomases—they had a great air of authority on stage. As soon as Bob Hope walks on stage—whether you think he's funny or not—it's clear he has an authority, a stage presence. And that was typical of the old-timers: Milton Berle, for instance, and whomever else you want to add to the list. Practically all of them had that air of professionalism, and being in charge.

But then in the sixties, and come to think of it, starting in the fifties, too, there were people like Woody, Mort Sahl; types that are now fairly common, but that were almost shocking then because they *seemed* unprofessional. They were actually superior in their mentality, their comic perceptions and the strength of their jokes, but judged purely as performers, they were very unfinished, and that eventually did not work to their disadvantage. But initially it did. I understand that Woody was petrified during his early experiences with standup. And that sounds odd to me because I never have been. It's always been kind of relaxed and fun for me, but apparently he suffered on stage, brilliant as he was.

His character was naturally comic. First of all, he looked funny. And that's an advantage. I do not, as a standup comedian, look funny. I was saying to somebody recently that I look as if I teach history at a small Catholic college in the Midwest. And there's nothing whatever even remotely comic about my persona, or my face, or my attire. Whereas Woody looked a little nebbish. He looked a little bit as if he came to deliver the sandwiches from the delicatessen. And that very fact we interpret as funny. We may interpret it as forty-seven other things, too, but funny is one of them. Contrary to that, Johnny Carson doesn't look funny, I don't look funny, Jack Paar didn't look funny. So Woody's visual effect was a refreshing note.

This is not to say that funny-looking people had never before got laughs. In fact, that was typical of the character comedians in those old marvelous 1930s and 1940s comedies. They often *looked* funny, whereas the star looked like Cary Grant or Jimmy Stewart—because they usually *were* Cary Grant or Jimmy Stewart!

But in the field of standup, there weren't that many people who had that sort of "unfinished" look. A possible relevant case would be Professor Irwin Corey, who *did* look funny, but he looked funny on purpose. On the street he was neither funny nor unfunny. He just looked like any guy walking past you on Forty-seventh Street. But he would wear the goofy black sneakers, and the goofy swallowtail coat, and make his hair silly on stage. So his case was different from Woody's. In Woody's case, that was the *real* Woody Allen whose looks we were laughing at. So that's the second point.

The third factor which contributes to the essence of Woody's genius (and I touch on this in the chapter you're reprinting in the book) is that Woody was an average guy who fell into, say, the Don Knotts or Wally Cox category—a little bit of a wimp. (And I'm only talking about appearances, here, not the reality of these people.) If any of these guys talked about love, or romance, or sex, they would usually put themselves down, the gist of their message being, "I have a lot of trouble getting any." (Laughs)

But Woody—in his jokes and the references to his love life—always acted like a Jewish Errol Flynn. He had this supreme confidence as a lover. And it was the contrast between his appearance and this almost braggadocio that was one more element of his funniness.

SS What is your most vivid memory of Woody's appearance on your television show?

Steve Allen I had never seen Woody work until that night. I had heard about him, but I knew practically nothing about him.

One interesting story I do remember is the time Woody applied for work on my staff and was turned down because I had got some terrible material from someone with the same name about three years earlier.

When I was in Los Angeles back in 1948 to 1950, I was doing radio comedy and was apparently perceived as a "comer." In my own mind I was just working day by day and having a lot of fun, but as I look back, I see how I might have been perceived.

Because of this, comedy material was occasionally submitted to me— and most of it was not very good. (Parenthetically, I will say that one of the writers who submitted to me—a guy named Bill Larkin—was *very* good. Bill ended up becoming my first writer when I finally made enough money where I could get a little writing help. Before that I'd written everything myself or ad-libbed it. Bill worked with me for years, and then later spent about twenty with Bob Hope.)

There was this one guy who submitted material whose name I remember as "Woody Allen." I'm 100 percent certain the first name was Woody, but if God said to me, "Listen, the guy's name was Woody *Arnold,* and you just forgot a little bit of it," I would say, "Okay, thank you. I'm not too sure about that."

Now we jump ahead to 1956 or so, and the *real* Woody Allen applies for work on my staff. Leonard Stern, who was then head of my writing staff, came to me and said, "There's a writer named Woody Allen who would like to work for you." And I said, "Unfortunately, that's not going to work out." And he said, "Really? Why? I hear he's good." And I said, "He sent me some stuff in Los Angeles a few years ago, and it was literally the worst I had ever read."

Now obviously that was not *the* Woody Allen, because Woody never wrote a bad joke in his life. But from such little tragic mistakes, bad stuff flows. I ended up deprived of the services of a marvelous writer. Who the hell knows how either of our fates might have changed if we had had the pleasure of working together?

Now we fast-forward to 1963.

I was doing a late-night show that David Letterman used to watch every night. (He's been trying to do my show for years now, but he still doesn't do it right.) (Laughs)

Anyway, we had a lot of funny people and a lot of craziness going on every night. We had a great location. It was a funky, broken-down theater at the corner of Vine Street and La Mirada in Hollywood right across the street from an all-night place called the Hollywood Ranch Market. And it was a real wild, wacko, very funny show.

So one Friday night they hand me a little card to introduce this fellow whom I'd never seen. And the card said something like, "This man writes seven hundred jokes a day," and I remember holding up the card so people would know I was just reading this information. Then I jokingly said, "Well, I doubt that, but I understand that he's very funny, so who cares how many jokes he writes every day. Let's give him a big hand, Woody Allen." Just a standard intro of a talk show host to a comic.

And Woody came out and he did this marvelous bit for which, I understand, he later got sued. It was the joke about his ex-wife being "violated," but Woody was sure it wasn't "a moving violation." [Note: See the transcription of Woody's monologue in Steve Allen's article "Woody Allen," reprinted in this chapter. You'll note (and Steve acknowledges) that the "moving violation" joke was not included when the show aired.]

By the time the show was off the air, Woody was gone. I don't remember that we ever did sit down and talk. I later met him at a couple of social events, but we never really got to hang around.

Recalling that evening, I was impressed by the kind of tentative way he spoke, and apparently it's really him. Now since I've never spent an evening with him, I cannot comment on the degree, if any, between the real Woody Allen that you have dinner with, and that character he plays. It seems to me that there isn't much difference, but I may be wrong.

SS Have you seen any of his dramatic work?

Steve Allen I've seen *Interiors,* which I thought was great.

SS Why do you think a *comic* genius like Woody would deliberately eliminate any and all humor from a creative project?

Steve Allen I think that maybe because I'm a comic I can understand that (although I think a streetcar conductor could probably come up with a theory about it too).

Comedy is, among other things, playful, and thus the critical community sometimes, perhaps unconsciously, interprets the work as therefore light, inconsequential, and not truly an art form—in the sense that serious drama is an art form.

There seems to be a perception that comedy is something almost anybody can do, and that it's not that tough to get laughs.

The reality, however, is quite different.

There are thousands of actors on the earth, but the number of professional comedians (although the ranks have mushroomed in the last few years) has always been small.

I did a piece for *Atlantic* at the end of the 1950s that reported on the state of American comedy, and I remember making the casual observation that at that time there were only about fifty comedians in show business. Hearing that today, that sounds like either a mistake, or an astonishing fact. But fact it was. The shakeout of vaudeville had taken place, and some of the hundreds of old vaudeville comedians had died, or got work as something other than a comic, so that by the time the fifties came along, there were only about fifty comedians in the business.

Now we have thousands.

So on the one hand, you write the number 50, and then opposite that, you write that there are maybe 20,000 actors, and it's clear that the arithmetic of comedy *alone* establishes its rarity as an art.

To get back to Woody, I think he wanted to show that there was much more to him than "the little funny fellow" who had been so successful at the box office.

I personally don't think this is typical of comedians. It may be typical of only those who are highly intelligent and can do other things than get laughs. I don't think Jerry Lewis, or Red Skelton, or Milton Berle, just to pick three names out of the blue, ever had any intellectual or artistic pretensions. It simply had no more to do with them than baseball has to do with them. Or lung surgery. It's just outside their scope. But in the case of rare individuals such as Woody, he is capable of doing more, and therefore it was perfectly reasonable of him to do it.

However, if Woody had ever said to the world, "You know, I've just thought it over, and I've decided never to be funny again and never to do another funny film," then perhaps people would have tried to get him to a treatment center. But he never said that. What he was saying in effect was, "I can be serious . . . and damn talented, too."

SS Is there any way to articulate the spirit and essence of the "Woody Allen Experience"?

Steven Allen Probably not. I tend to think of dozens of reactions to that type of question, rather than some deathless epigram. I think there's really too much to Woody to do him justice with some "in a nutshell" evaluation.

I think he's a great "mine" of comic consciousness. As you say, he was greatly influenced—and thank God he was—by Benchley and Perelman, and some of the other giants of that period. As you'll recall, when I reviewed *Without Feathers,* I put Woody right up there on the same level with those people—who are my gods in funniness. It wasn't, "I think this young man will one day be perceived as . . ." or "I predict . . ." No, Woody is there right now. His stuff is just as funny as Perelman's or Benchley's.

But, really, there's no way you can pin down *all* that Woody is.

To clarify by analogy, I'll say that there was more to Benchley, too. Benchley was not only one of the funniest people on paper, but he had the gift, as does Woody, of acting in a natural way. Most professional actors do not have that gift. Most of them talk like asses. To me, Robert De Niro is how people should act. You should sound like you're not acting. Doing Shakespeare is a whole other thing. I'm not talking about that. But if somebody writes a line in a script like "Hey, Charlie, where's the salt?" it should be said the way you would in real life.

We could all name dozens of professional actors who have never been able to do that. They may sound rather marvelous, or sexy, or dashing, or cute, or they may have other things going for them, but talking like a human being is not one of them. Benchley just naturally had that ability.

Another great humorist, Will Rogers, had that ability. Rogers was a damned good actor. He only did that one character, himself, but he had naturalness. Woody has that naturalness as an actor. He doesn't sound phony or stilted.

SS Mr. Allen, I thank you for your visit to *The Woody Allen Companion.*

Steve Allen My pleasure, Steve, and good luck with the book.

"Woody Allen"*
by Steve Allen

[STEVE ALLEN *really* knows comedy, and his following essay is a perceptive and knowledgeable look at the humor—and genius—of Woody Allen.

Steve does us all a favor here. He tells (and shows) us *why* Woody is funny, and by thus shining a light on Woody's particular (some would say peculiar) comedic prowess, he enhances our appreciation and enjoyment of the Woodman's work.

This essay is an important one, and I am honored to reprint it in *The Woody Allen Companion.*]

I start this appreciation of Woody Allen by considering S. J. Perelman and his *The Road to Miltown*. Reading Perelman, the professional humorist is apt to experience sensations similar to those known to pianists who listen to an Art Tatum recording. One feels like giving up.

Perelman was simply too good. The suspicion arose finally that there was no real Perelman, but that some ingenious technician had succeeded in equipping a UNIVAC machine with a complete supply of the world's literary clichés, a vocabulary ranging from Chaucer to Madison Avenuese, the British gift for understatement, counterbalanced by consummate mastery of the American gift for overstatement, a jolt of Groucho Marx lunacy (Perelman wrote for Marx), and the perception of a philosopher, and that this fantastic device simply kept Simon and Schuster supplied with an endless stack of funny essays, constructed along certain predictable but always eminently successful lines.

The machine never faltered. Year after year it hewed to the formula. The writing style was basically tongue-in-cheek turn-of-the-century, studded with jewels of contemporary phraseology that consistently caught the reader by surprise. Color was added by profligate use of words that could be in no real human's vocabulary, unless they were used by that old British colonel, the late C. Aubrey Smith.

The machine isolates a phenomenon of our culture (an intrinsically silly one, but few besides Perelman would perceive the silliness) and then extends it to the ultimate degree of absurdity. Witness the chapter in which the author encounters an actual printed message attached to a boned veal steak, stated in the first person and purporting to be the steak's own address to the chef. This is the sort of thing with which advertising people confront us at every turn, but to Perelman it suggested that before long he might receive written messages from *all* the foods in his icebox.

Another example: I recall being amused years ago by an article in *Glamour* that I found charmingly and a little pathetically asinine. It consisted of a list of twenty-five things a girl might do to relieve boredom within her four walls, and included such suggestions as: "Partition a room with fishnet running on a ceiling track . . . Paint a gaily fringed rug on a wooden floor . . . Give houseroom to a tree in a big wooden tub," and so forth. Imagine my pleasure to find that Perelman, too, had come across this gem. For the details see his chapter titles, "De Gustibus Ain't What Dey Used To Be."

It must not be assumed that the late S. J. was "only" the perceptive philosophical humorist laying about with iconoclastic glee. He was also an ace Broadway-TV-type jokesmith. When one of his characters promised to pay a bill "just as soon as my ship comes in," it was not surprising that her calculating debtee responded, "I'll be studying the *Maritime News.*"

The three funniest men writing in English in our time have been Thurber, Benchley, and Perelman. Each was supreme in his own area; I think it inconceivable that any of them could be surpassed. But Woody Allen, in my view, may be mentioned in the same breath, so much is his literary style like Perelman's.

When—was it in the 1950s?—a number of our most able novelists affirmed their Jewishness and—the result must have surprised them—achieved even greater popularity by doing so, a fresh and vigorous strain was introduced into modern American literature. Bellow, Roth, Herzog, et al. (I particularly like Al), wrote not merely as sensitive observers of our culture but rather out of the distillation of their own ethnic experiences. But so unique a style of literary expression must, of course, inevitably attract the attention of satirists. (See, in Woody's *Without Feathers,* "No Kaddish for Weinstein.")

Some forms of humor give pleasure out of their very airiness. Light verse, casual autobiographical reminiscence, frothy spoofing of various kinds can succeed without having an overwhelming impact on the reader. Satire, on the other hand, has to be funny as hell or it falls on its face. The satirist, after all, lives on *chutzpah* and effrontery. He brazenly attacks a popular target and, at least momentarily, strips the mask of seriousness from it. Satire is, therefore, a risky business. But when it is pulled off successfully, as it is in *Without Feathers,* it is one of the few forms of humor guaranteed to make the reader literally laugh aloud.

Allen, of course, developed gradually to his present level of achievement.

He worked for Garry Moore early in his career. Moore's recollections of him are surprisingly vague. "He did indeed work on our variety show," Garry wrote me, "but we rarely saw anything of him. Both his contributions and personal appearances were—well, random. As I recall we fired him eventually, for nonfeasance, which resulted in some kind of brouhaha with the writer's union. Our viewpoint was upheld. I also recall that one late afternoon when Woody was discovered ambling through, on his way to God wot, the other writers tried literally to tie him into his office chair for the night to assure his presence at the next day's meeting. I was pretty close to the rest of the writing staff, but not with Woody. He is will-o'-the-wisp in my memory and it wasn't until I saw him in *Play It Again, Sam* that I got a real good look at him. He seemed fine."

Pat Boone, for whom Allen wrote in 1958, sent the following recollection in response to a letter asking if Woody had been on his staff, as reported.

Hi Steve!

Yes, Woody Allen was one of my writers—though I hardly ever hear him mention it. You would think this would be a very important item on his list of credits, wouldn't you? I guess he doesn't like to brag.

Actually, the probable reason is that we scarcely ever used any of his material. He was attending some kind of classes, at NYU or someplace, and spending only a couple of hours a day at our offices. As I remember, our head writer at the time was Larry Gelbart, and we also had a fellow named Tony Webster on our staff. No wonder I was so funny.

I think it was for a part of one season only, and I believe that was 1958. I was doing my weekly show, taking a full load of courses at Columbia University (I graduated in '58), making records, doing all kinds of personal appearances on the weekends—and having a baby a year with Shirley. So Woody and I didn't spend much time together. I really don't know how much he contributed to the overall scripts, but I do have one very vivid memory.

I remember Woody and me standing in the hallway of our offices, on a number of different occasions, while he outlined some outlandish routine or sketch that he thought I ought to do. He was always pretty deadpan, so I was never sure if he was serious or not. Anyway, he would set up this crazy premise, pepper it with a lot of little jokes, and lead up to some preposterous payoff that obviously I couldn't use on the show. I would dissolve laughing, sometimes sliding down the wall to a sitting position on the floor. Woody would be quite animated and really get into the whole caper, acting it out for me. Finally, when he had presented the whole thing, he would stand there with an expectant look on his face, waiting for me to stop laughing and tell him whether to write it up for the show or not.

The answer was always "no," accompanied by a lot of laughs.

As I think back, I realize Woody was actually polishing his own routines for what would become his standup comedy act. I'm probably responsible for his whole career as a comedian and solo performer, because I guarantee he never had a better audience than I was. I probably misled him into thinking he could be successful.

Whatever happened to him, anyway?

Warm good wishes,
Pat Boone

In his early work *Without Feathers,* Allen coolly took aim at a wide variety of targets: literary diaries, psychic phenomenalists, the ballet, the Dead Sea Scrolls, Scandinavian playwrights and their critical apologists, tough-private-eye fiction, intellectual pretension, Civil Disobedience, Irish poetry, the Theater of Obscurity, Greek drama, mythology, and critics of the Shakespeare-didn't-write-his-plays school, among others. Nothing, not to coin a phrase, is sacred.

Other iconoclasts, perhaps, have attacked as many temples. But for general effectiveness Allen takes all honors during National Havoc-Wreaking Week. It would be marvelous if the millions of young people who enjoy Woody Allen films could be Pied Pipered into bookstores, where they would find a Woody Allen richer, deeper, wider, and—most importantly—even funnier than that available on screen. For Allen is essentially a writer. His true comic gift is literary. He is amusing in films, obviously, but his physical image is not that of the true clown, the true entertainer. If he were not brilliantly gifted as a humorist, if—let's say—he were not a writer at all, he would have had considerable difficulty even getting work as a standup comic. Becoming a serious actor would have been out of the question altogether. But the flame of comic genius has burned brightly enough somehow to light up this plain-looking little man. Despite his unpretentious, almost amateurish attitude and manner, his image glows with a fierce, bizarre brightness.

The naturalness Woody Allen brings to acting is lacking, oddly enough, in the dramatic performances of most professional comedians. Fred Allen, Jack Benny, Bob Hope, George Jessel, Eddie Cantor, Groucho—most comedians, in fact—have had no discernible qualifications judged purely as actors, for all their talents at making us laugh. There are a few exceptions. Will Rogers and Robert Benchley were fine naturalistic actors, entirely believable even in noncomic scenes or moments. Jackie Gleason and Art Carney, too, have the actor's gift. And Woody at least has the knack of believability, but again it is on paper that his true gift shines.

One characteristic of Allen's style is the creation of dazzling incongruities of almost a surrealistic nature. In "The Stolen Gem," a satire on that sort of detective fiction totally out of touch with reality, a character says "The sapphire was originally owned by a sultan who died under mysterious circumstances when a hand reached out of a bowl of soup he was eating and strangled him."

Come to think of it, we staged just that bit of business as a "Crazy Shot" on one of my early shows, but Woody is still a master of the specific art form.

An abductee in "The Bizarre Kidnapping" described how the crime occurred. "I was on my way downtown to have my hat blocked when a sedan pulled up and two men asked me if I wanted to go see a horse that could recite the Gettysburg Address. I said sure and got in."

Woody appeared on my late-night syndicated comedy-talk show on Friday, November 15th, 1963. Oddly enough, we did not actually meet on that occasion. Talk show hosts ordinarily don't have time to see their guests before a program starts, and some actually prefer not to. The freshness of the moment of the encounter might be lost if it took place in a hallway or dressing room rather than on stage. In any event, Woody made one of his first television appearances. One of the lines was the by-now-well-known reference to Woody's ex-wife: "She was coming home late at night and she was violated. That's how they put it in the New York papers: She was violated. And they asked me to comment on it. I said, 'Knowing my ex-wife, it probably was not a moving violation.'"

I recently went to the trouble of having a typed transcript made of Woody's monologue. Consequently, the refreshment of my recollection makes it possible to recall that the "moving violation" joke was not included, probably at the request of our producers. Our society has changed so much since the early 1960s that the monologue, which then seemed daring, and undoubtedly offended a few of our viewers, now seems very tame.

His monologue, which is transcribed here, is brilliantly funny, a perfect gem of comic construction.

(Music, whistling and applause)

Woody:
    Thank you. Thank you.
    Actually on television around three weeks ago now, I mentioned that I was married . . . had been married and that I had had a bad marriage. That's what I mentioned. I mentioned that I had married one of the few white Muslims in New York, actually . . .
(laughter)
    . . . and too young. And I also want to elaborate on it. I had a bad marriage and it was partially my fault. For the first year of marriage, I would say, I had a bad basic attitude toward my wife. I tended to place my wife underneath a pedestal all the time, and we used to argue and fight, and we finally decided that we would either take a vacation in Bermuda or get a divorce, one of the two things.
    We discussed it very maturely and we decided finally on the divorce, 'cause we felt we had a limited amount of money to spend on something and that a vacation in Bermuda is over in two weeks but a divorce is something you will always have.
(laughter)
    It seemed good. I saw myself as a bachelor again, living in the Village in a bachelor apartment with a wood-burning fireplace and a shaggy rug, you know, and on the walls some of those great Picassos by Van Gogh, and just great Swede airline hostesses running amok in the apartment, you know?
    And I got very excited and I ran into my wife; she was in the next room at the time listening to Conelrad on the radio . . .
(laughter)

. . . a very nervous woman. I laid it right on the line with her. I came right to the point. I said, "Quasimodo, I want a divorce."
(laughter)

No mincing words. And she said, "Great, get the divorce."

But it turns out in New York State they have a very funny law that says you can't get a divorce unless you can prove adultery, and that's very strange because the Ten Commandments say "Thou Shalt Not Commit Adultery."

So New York State says you have to.
(laughter and applause)

It's like a toss-up between the Bible and Rockefeller, you know? You don't know which way to go. So I figured that one of us has got to commit adultery to get the divorce. I volunteered for it.
(laughter)

'Cause I thought it would be a very simple matter for me, and I am a very sexy man.
(laughter)

It so happened . . . did you whistle at me? Not long ago, I sold my memoirs of my love life to Parker Brothers and they're going to make it into a game.
(laughter and applause)

I'm thin but fun.

When you're married and out of circulation there are not that many women that you know that you can actually call, and the only woman I knew was my wife's best friend, Nancy. So, I called up Nancy on the phone and I asked her if she would have adultery with me. She said, "Not even if it would help the space program."
(laughter)

Which I took as a negative, at the time. There's a bar in my neighborhood, an agnostic bagel shop that traffics in professional-type women that earn their living through advanced fondling.
(laughter)

There was at the bar a professional-type lady, really great hair and mascara on the lips . . . and I explained my situation to her and she was very willing—but too expensive.

The plan was that if I could convince her that I was still attending New York University, I qualified for a student discount.
(laughter and applause)

So what finally happened, my wife committed adultery for me, rather well.

She's always been more mechanically inclined than I have.

Well, I guess I'm going to go now . . . I've told you about my love life . . . I married a very immature woman and it didn't work out.

See if this isn't immature to you. I'd be home in the bathroom, taking a bath, and my wife would walk right in whenever she felt like and sink my boats.
(laughter)

I sound bitter now . . . She has all the charm of a Southern sheriff.

Anyhow, I'd better go 'cause I said my thing. You should see this while I have it out. *(pocket watch)* Actually, I was checking my timing, about five minutes. This speaks for breeding and it's mine. It's an antique gold heirloom—*(laughter)*. Actually my grandfather on his deathbed sold me this watch.
(enormous laughter)
(applause and music)

Note that the jokes are all personal. They relate to what Woody alleges to have been his actual experience. And yet, by this means, he does make philosophical comment on the reality of his society. The lines about New York divorce laws, for example, are in the Lenny Bruce tradition.

The monologue was not only early and original, it also became influential. Allen depends on the incongruity between two factors: his alleged prowess as a lover and his mousy physical appearance. This appearance makes it possible for him to say certain things without offending. The same lines would be objectionable from a good-looking comedian such as Bob Hope or Johnny Carson. The image of Woody Allen as a "great lover" is funny for the same reason that a Tim Conway or Don Knotts in boxing trunks is funny before anything is said or done. A Steve Martin or Fred Willard in boxing trunks would not be funny at all until some uniquely comic action had taken place.

Needless to say in making these observations I make no reference whatever to the reality of Woody Allen's sexual or romantic experience.

Woody is not only a master of joke invention; he also has consummate control of his formulas. The toy-boats-in-the-tub formula is one he has frequently employed. Another instance would be the joke in which he refers, as if contemptuously, to the idea that someone has accused him of practically thinking he is God. With an attitude of "isn't that ridiculous?" he then adds, "So I said unto her . . ."

Woody's talent continued to blossom throughout the early and mid-1960s, until he began to establish a formidable reputation as a comedian. The "moose" story is a classic example of his early monologue form. Consider its structure and style.

"Here's a story you're not going to believe," he begins. "I shot a moose once. I was hunting in upstate New York and I shot a moose."

This is funny at once because Woody is so poorly cast in the role of hunter.

And I strap him onto the fender of my car, and I'm driving along the West Side Highway. But what I didn't realize was that the bullet did not penetrate the moose. It just creased his scalp, knocking him unconscious. And I'm driving through the Holland Tunnel and the moose woke up.

The absurd, cartoon-like imagery of the account begins to impress itself on the listener's imagination.

So I'm driving with a live moose on my fender and the moose is signalling for a turn. And there's a law in New York State against driving with a conscious moose on your fender, Tuesdays, Thursdays, and Saturdays. And I'm very panicky. And then it hits me—some friends of mine are having a costume party. I'll go. I'll take the moose. I'll ditch him at the party. It won't be my responsibility. So I drive up to the party and I knock on the door and the moose is next to me. My host comes to the door. I say, "Hello, you know the Solomons." We enter. The moose mingles. Did very well. Scored. Some guy was trying to sell him insurance for an hour and a half.

Twelve o'clock comes, they give out prizes for the best costume of the night. First prize goes to the Berkowitzes, a married couple dressed as a moose. The moose comes in second. The moose is furious. He and the Berkowitzes lock antlers in the living room. They knock each other unconscious. Now, I figure, here's my chance. I grab the moose, strap him on my fender, and shoot back to the woods. But I've got the Berkowitzes.

So I'm driving along with two Jewish people on my fender. And there's a law in New York State. Tuesdays, Thursdays, and especially Saturday.

The following morning, the Berkowitzes wake up in the woods in a moose suit. Mr. Berkowitz is shot, stuffed, and mounted at the New York Athletic Club. And the joke is on them, 'cause it's restricted.

The moose story begins with an air of unbelievable believability. Woody alleges that he was hunting in upstate New York, shot a moose, and strapped him onto the fender of his car. To this point the account could be right out of *Field and Stream,* assuming there are any wild moose in upstate New York. The first hint of real exaggeration comes with the line, ". . . and I'm driving home along the West Side Highway. . . ."

It would be totally absurd for a man to take a dead moose to his home, his actual dwelling place, so some members of the audience presumably laugh at that absurdity perceived. But others might interpret the word "home" as simply New York City and therefore still believe, or pretend to believe, in the story to this point.

Now Allen introduces the first plot twist. The moose had not been killed by the bullet; it had merely creased his scalp, knocking him unconscious.

"And I'm driving through the Holland Tunnel and the moose woke up."

The image is instantly hilarious. Allen ably employs the specific rather than generic illustration. Driving through a tunnel when the moose wakes up is already amusing, but the specificity of the *Holland* Tunnel, the reality and familiarity of that particular tunnel brings the comic image into much sharper focus.

"So I'm driving with a live moose on my fender, and the moose is signalling for a turn."

A moose trying to release himself from straps and ropes, waving his legs in such a way that the movements could be interpreted as signalling for a turn, is incongruous, unexpected, and hence funny.

"There's a law in New York State against driving with a conscious moose on your fender . . ."

Absurd, hilarious, but still a line that other jokesmiths might have created. Only Woody, however, is likely to have added the phrase, "Tuesdays, Thursdays, and Saturdays," to the joke, thus appealing to a frustrated familiarity with New York's traffic and parking.

The narrator tells us that he is "very panicky." So we are presented with the classic dimensions of a good story. A protagonist is faced with a problem, a dilemma. How shall he solve it?

"And then it hits me—some friends of mine are having a costume party. I'll go."

The audience at this point begins to anticipate what is coming and sure enough, the narrator adds, "I'll take the moose. I'll ditch him at the party. It won't be my responsibility."

Allen is digging into a vein that is almost his exclusive domain among American humorists and comedians; middle-class New York Jewish cultural experience, with its million-and-one emotional and psychological nuances.

"I'll ditch him at the party. It won't be my responsibility."

The word "responsibility," too, means something special in the context of Jewishness.

"So I drive up to the party and I knock on the door and the moose is next to me . . ."

At this point, while the bounds of credulity have certainly been badly stretched, they have not been totally transgressed beyond the possibility of misunderstanding. But at this stage of his narration Woody ascends to quite a separate level, *the level of the animated cartoon world* in which, while physical laws operate, they can be broken at the clown's whim.

"The moose is next to me. My host comes to the door. I say, 'Hello, you know the Solomons.' "

An ingenious conversational ploy, passing the moose off as a couple in a moose suit.

"We enter. The moose mingles."

Mingles! Incredible word. So conversational. So right.

"Did very well."

At this point Allen is again speaking the language of New York middleclass Jewish culture. A German, a black, a Swede, a Chinese referring to a successful party, would report simply that he had a good time. This is something quite different from "doing very well," which can be interpreted either in the broad social sense—making "contacts"—or sexually. Woody clarifies that he is covering both ends of the spectrum by use of the one word, "scored." Not *he* scored, or *the moose* scored, but simply the one syllable, far preferable because it is authentic, conversational, true in its mindless bourgeois vulgarity.

The line is funny to men because—at least until recently—it is recognizable as private man-talk language. It's funny to women because of their being permitted to hear what was—at least in the 1960s—usually a bit of personal male sex-lingo. Obviously enough, the idea that a moose could have sexual contact with a human female has its own insane absurdity. It is not as logically outrageous but almost as funny as the image that follows: an earnest Republican dolt trying to sell the moose insurance, not for a few seconds until he notices his mistake, but for a full "hour and a half." At this point, if the narration were cinematic rather than verbal, we would fade out of the scene and fade in again at 12:00, the hour that "they give out the prizes for the best costume of the night." Again the audience begins to anticipate generally what sort of thing is coming. If they could anticipate it precisely they could finish the story for Woody. "The first prize goes to the Berkowitzes, a married couple dressed in a moose costume."

There are apparently no gentile characters at all in Woody Allen's jokes. Why is it funnier that the Berkowitzes won first prize rather than the Randolphs, the O'Briens, or the D'Antonios? The simple name, "the Berkowitzes," suggests a couple in their late thirties or early forties. Berkowitz is perhaps a dentist, a schoolteacher, or a pharmacist. He is a serious fellow but—as the Jewish equivalent of a Rotarian or a Shriner—is not above going to a costume party and trying to have a little desperate fun once in a while. If the name "Berkowitz" suggested a jazz musician, a marijuana user, or anything the least bit hip, the name would not be so funny in this story, nor would the other straight-faced Jewish names in so many other Woody Allen sketches, monologues, and films.

In a more or less conventional comedy switch, Woody reports that "the moose came in second." Most competent joke writers dealing with this kind of story material would have come up with the same plot twist. They could not, however, have written the following line, "The moose is furious." That statement is not the simple playing with logic that "the moose comes in second" is.

The Berkowitzes and the moose now lock antlers, knock each other unconscious, and the moose—as the narrator believes—ends up back on his fender, presumably on his way to the woods upstate. But in a predictable enough plot device it turns out to be the Berkowitzes rather than the moose on the fender. Woody does not just employ this comic moment and then step away from it; he relishes it. "I'm driving along with two Jewish people on my fender. There's a law in New York State. Tuesdays, Thursdays, and especially Saturday."

Part of the element of the Jewish experience is humiliation. This comes through, but to hilarious effect. When the echo of anti-Semitism ("There's a law in New York State"), a somber subject matter, is juxtaposed against the zany context of this story, the comic-tragic mix makes us laugh until we cry.

The ending of the story is Thurberesque. Berkowitz is shot, stuffed, and mounted in the New York Athletic Club and the joke is on them because the New York A.C. is notorious, in New York and liberal circles, for its long-standing policy of refusing membership to Jews. So Woody, with mad confidence, finishes an insane story with a neat, seemingly rational social moral.

A bravura performance.

Although Woody pretends to talk about reality, he rarely does. Certain of my own nightclub routines are literally the truth or—like some of Buddy Hackett's monologues—an exaggerated version of incidents that have really happened. Woody's natural and sincere manner of speaking keeps pulling audiences off guard. They feel that here at last he's going to relate something literally autobiographical. It rarely happens.

Consider another of his early classics, the "kidnapping" story.

I have made separate paragraphs of the individual, component building blocks of the story, to enable the reader better to see precisely where it is that the laughs fall, as they invariably do.

Note that Woody deliberately builds the story around the standard clichés of kidnappings: abduction in a car, the sending of a ransom note to distraught parents, instructions on where to leave the money, the last-minute dramatic involvement of the police or FBI, confrontation between the FBI and the kidnappers, the use of tear gas.

All of this is familiar to us from a thousand-and-one instances in the worlds of printed news, fiction, radio, television, or films. Allen's humor utilizes the tension between familiar and realistic dramatic elements and absurd switches or twists.

Observe, too, how—like Bill Cosby—he makes frequent references to childish things, as in the mention of comic books, chocolate buttons, and wax lips. The childish element will apparently always be crucial to Woody's humor, if he lives to be a hundred. Although he is now in his late forties, those who know his age literally do not have the factor in realistic focus. He always somehow seems about twenty-seven, and a rather childish, klutzy twenty-seven at that. He seems like a fellow who not terribly long before in his life's experience has actually hung around New York streets, or a middle-class candy store.

The bizarre elements in the kidnapping story are reminiscent, in mood and color, of Perelman and Benchley at their best, which is intended as the highest sort of compliment.

The monologue is also a masterpiece of economy, consisting of just fourteen separate laughs perfectly strung together by a gossamer thread of craziness. It is crucial to appreciate that the routine would work so well only for Woody Allen. When rereading the lines, imagine for a moment that they are being recited by Dick Cavett, Milton Berle, Bob Hope, or almost any other comedian. The routine would not, in such an event, be nearly as funny.

> I was kidnapped once. I was standing in front of my school yard and a black sedan pulls up and two guys get out and they say to me, do I want to go away with them to a land where everybody is fairies and elves and I can have all the comic books I want, and chocolate buttons and wax lips, you know.
>
> And I said, yes.
>
> And I got into the car with them, 'cause I figured, what the hell, I was home anyhow that weekend from college.
>
> And they drive me off and they send a ransom note to my parents. And my father has bad reading habits.
>
> So he got into bed that night with the ransom note and he read half of it and he got drowsy and he fell asleep.
>
> Meanwhile they take me to New Jersey bound and gagged. And my parents finally realize that I'm kidnapped and they snap into action immediately: They rent out my room.
>
> The ransom note says for my father to leave a thousand dollars in a hollow tree in New Jersey. He has no trouble raising the thousand dollars, but he gets a hernia carrying the hollow tree.
>
> The FBI surround the house. "Throw the kid out," they say, "give us your guns and come out with your hands up." The kidnappers say, "We'll throw the kid out, but let us keep our guns and get to our car."
>
> The FBI says, "Throw the kid out, we'll let you get to your car, but give us your guns."
>
> The kidnappers say, "We'll throw the kid out, but let us keep our guns; we don't have to get to our car."
>
> The FBI says, "Keep the kid."
>
> The FBI decides to lob in tear gas. But they don't have tear gas.
>
> So several of the agents put on the death scene from *Camille*. Tear-stricken, my abductors give themselves up.
>
> They're sentenced to fifteen years on a chain gang and they escape, twelve of them chained together at the ankle, getting by the guards posing as an immense charm bracelet.

About eighty percent of American comedians are Jewish. To me the Jews are funnier, as a people, than any other group. Why? Because they have had more trouble. And trouble is often the heart of humor. "I laugh," said Abraham Lincoln, paraphrasing Byron, "because I must not cry." "Everything human is pathetic," said Mark Twain. "The secret source of humor itself is not joy but sorrow. There is no humor in Heaven." This attitude is particularly representative of Jewish humor.

Traditional Jewish humor often converts a joke into a form of social comment or criticism. It must not be supposed, however, that the humor of the Jews is only a weapon with which they subtly strike back at a bullying world. A great deal of their laughter is directed at themselves. Self-criticism is one of the earmarks of Jewish comedy.

Humorists are forever being asked if we don't think that the grimness of the times will somehow shrink the boundaries of comedy. The reverse, of course, is true. The more difficult the human predicament the more man needs laughter. For thousands of years the Jews have had to laugh off their troubles because they were rarely powerful enough to control the circumstances that produced them. That is the reason why even today in the United States, where Jews are no longer forced to live in ghettos, there is still a tradition of humor that produces hundreds of professional funny men and women.

The following list of Jewish comedians makes the point clear.

Don Adams; Dayton Allen; Marty Allen; Woody Allen; Morey Amsterdam; Joe Baum; Gene Baylos; Jack Benny; Gertrude Berg; Milton Berle; Shelley Berman; Joey Bishop; Mel Blanc; Ben Blue; Victor Borge; David Brenner; Fanny Brice; Albert Brooks; Mel Brooks; Lenny Bruce; George Burns; Abe Burrows; Red Buttons; Sid Caesar; Eddie Cantor; Jean Carroll; Jack Carter; Charlie Chaplin; Myron Cohen; Irwin Corey; Billy Crystal; Bill Dana; Rodney Dangerfield; Gabe Dell; Bob Einstein; Marty Feldman; Totie Fields; Phil Foster; David Frye; Alan Gale; Leo Gorcey; Sid Gould; Shecky Greene; Buddy Hackett; Stanley Myron Handleman; Harry Hershfield; Lou Holtz; Marty Ingles; Gabe Kaplan; Andy Kaufman; Danny Kaye; Alan King; Robert Klein; Bert Lahr; Steve Landesberg; Pinky Lee; Jack E. Leonard; Jerry Lester; Sam Levenson; Jerry Lewis; Joe E. Lewis; Groucho Marx; Jackie Mason; Elaine May; Henry Morgan; Zero Mostel; Jules Munshin; Jan Murray; Louis Nye; Gilda Radner; Carl Reiner; Don Rickles; The Ritz Brothers; Joan Rivers; Mort Sahl; Soupy Sales; Avery Schreiber; Peter Sellers; Dick Shawn; Allan Sherman; Lonnie Shorr; Phil Silvers; David Steinberg; Jerry Stiller; Larry Storch; Paul Winchell; Henny Youngman.

Behind these entertainers stand, in addition, hundreds of comedy writers and humorists of Jewish extraction, such as S. J. Perelman, Max Shulman, A. J. Liebling, Milt Gross, Rube Goldberg, Bennett Cerf, George Kaufman, Moss Hart, Dorothy Parker, Leonard Q. Ross, Arthur Kober, Neil Simon, Ira Wallach, Al Capp, Ben Hecht, Harry Kurnitz, Marvin Kitman, and Art Buchwald.

The world owes a great debt to the Jewish humorists.

A musician friend of mine once made an interesting observation. "You rarely," he said, "find a square Jew or a square black man, but when you do they're the squarest."

The opposite of square, in this connection, is *hip*. What my friend was saying about Jews and blacks is that adversity has taught them to roll with the punches, has made them philosophers and poets. It has sent them to the stage, the typewriter, the microphone. It has made them funny.

Jewish comedy is almost inevitably concerned with things gastronomical. The Jews enjoy talking about food more than any other people. Through many centuries they lived in enforced poverty. If they could not invent food out of thin air, they could at least invent stories and jokes about it to take their minds off their misery.

In this connection critic Richard Schickel correctly identifies one of Allen's basic obsessions as food and eating. But he fails to perceive that this concern grows, at least in part, out of Allen's Jewishness.

Why is it that words like *lox, herring, chopped liver, chicken soup,* and *matzoh* are inherently more amusing than *trout, bass, lamb stew, vegetable soup,* and *whole wheat bread*? The words have a strong associative power. They immediately bring to mind a whole ethnic aura that is powerful raw material for a joke.

By simply adding a Jewish component to a sentence, even in the absence of any other comic device, Woody Allen amuses. In his film *Sleeper,* for example, a character explains that the United States of 1973 was destroyed "when a man named Albert Shanker got hold of an H-bomb." Why is this funny? Albert Shanker is president of the United Federation of Teachers. He led the famous teacher's strike in the sixties, and is known as a very explosive man. In political terms, it would be like giving Quadaffi an H-bomb. Moreover, the words "got hold" suggest the casual nature of an accident, of a chance event. Albert Shanker's apparent lack of intention leads to the destruction of the United States. In the film's context of absurdity, this is funny. But there is another level of humor. The Jews have finally bombed back. When we laugh at Albert Shanker we are in part releasing through laughter our own angers (if we are Jewish) and fears (if we are not).

Imagine that same sentence rendered as follows: ". . . when a man named Tom Montgomery got hold of an H-bomb." With an Anglo-Saxon name the humor totally disappears.

In *Getting Even,* Allen refers to "taking a whitefish across the state line for immoral purposes." Again the Jewishness of "whitefish" provides much of the humor. The sentence would be considerably less amusing if the word "trout" replaced whitefish.

Audiences are more than willing to go along with Woody's flights of absurd fancy—as in the moose story—simply because Woody projects, on stage, a natural, non-show-biz aura. He has none of the dynamic self-confidence of those professional comedians who work in nightclubs. Don Rickles,

Milton Berle, Henny Youngman, Jack Carter, Alan King, Jan Murray, Buddy Hackett, Shecky Greene—all not only amuse an audience, they control it by an act of almost aggressive dominance. Woody does not have that shiny-tuxedo expertise. He literally could not have functioned as a professional comedian at all in the days of vaudeville; he speaks so softly he could not be heard beyond the tenth row. Even those vaudeville comedians who seemed to work in a naturalistic manner, such as Jack Benny and Will Rogers, projected to the back wall of the theater. In this surface lack of professional confidence, Woody *is* like the young college men, graduate students, young doctors, lawyers, businessmen, and semi-hipsters who see him as one of their own. As regards his true gift—the ability consistently to write the funniest jokes in the business—he is a rare bird indeed.

In my view, Allen is primarily a writer, and only secondarily a comedian, though certainly a marvelously funny and successful one. Quite obviously he has a personality more typical of the writer than of the performer. He is not a social extrovert and, in fact, sometimes seems scarcely to be social at all.

It's interesting that Woody considers Mort Sahl one of the primary creative influences on his own work. The differences between the two are enormous. Nevertheless the slender factors the two share seem important in Woody's mind. Pre-Sahl nightclub comics include high-powered performers like Milton Berle, Buddy Hackett, Jan Murray, Shecky Greene, Jack Carter, Myron Cohen, Jerry Lewis, and others of that school. They walk on stage with the confidence of a General MacArthur and prowl about like aggressive tigers, for all their smiling. Their stage manner is part of the poor or lower-middle-class urban Jewish milieu from which they sprung, and they have had to emphasize the already aggressive components of their personalities in order to survive. A delicate comedian—a Wally Cox, a Bob Newhart—trying to perform at a Jewish hotel in the Catskill Mountains or a Vinnie-and-Vito type club in Brooklyn or New Jersey is simply an absurdity. The gentle comedians would not be hired for such duty in the first place.

But finally Mort Sahl appeared on the scene. He did not wear a tuxedo; he wore a comfortable-looking sweater. He did not come on with a lot of Morey Amsterdam–Henny Youngman one-liners, but seemed rather a sort of urban Jewish Will Rogers commenting on the news of the day. Everything about him was "unprofessional." He didn't smile much, he neglected to finish sentences, he rambled, he seemed personally self-effacing, although philosophically gutsy. His general image was more or less like that of a left-wing college professor of sociology.

I would assume that this was the style that suddenly made Woody Allen realize—back in 1954 when he first saw Mort in action—that he, too, could possibly become more than a joke writer, could get up on a stage and deliver his own material rather than simply submitting it to other comedians for the rest of his life. He knew he could not compete in precisely the same ball game played by the Youngmans and the Berles, but he was at least able to *identify* with a comedy performer. Woody, like Mort Sahl, was also personally an intellectual of sorts, not physically attractive, not conventionally charming. He spoke in a tentative, nonglib, realistic manner and seemed like a funny guy one might meet or know instead of a funny performer.

But that is as far as the similarities with Mort Sahl could go. As for the differences:

Mort deals with everyday reality, social and political. As a comic, Woody usually does not. He specializes in absurd fantasy.

Mort rarely talks about himself—at least on stage. Woody talks about very little else.

Mort takes a political stand. Woody does not.

There is a strong philosophical component to Sahl's monologues. There is none to Woody's, though there are certain nuances in some of his writing for motion pictures.

Mort's audiences, his constituency, is appreciative, responsive, but statistically quite small—rather like the audience for progressive jazz or modern painting. Woody's audience—although by no means universal—is much wider.

Mort, even on his most successful night, always gives the impression of being to a certain degree uncomfortable in front of an audience. Woody appears more relaxed, though he was not always so.

A portion of Sahl's nightclub act is spontaneous and free flowing. Woody ordinarily wouldn't change a syllable of one of his standard routines.

There is a sprinkling of bitterness, of sarcasm, sometimes even of paranoia in Sahl's monologues. This is not so with Woody's.

One of the oddest things I discovered in doing research on Woody was that he has twice been quoted as saying that of all the comedians in the world his favorite was Bob Hope. I find this an absolutely stupefying assertion. In fact it struck me as so odd that when I first read it I wrote a letter to Woody asking whether his answer was like that of the late Louis Armstrong. Louis, whenever asked who his favorite orchestra leader was, avoided an answer by saying, "Guy Lombardo." Louis, one of the great jazz artists himself, could not possibly have meant that Lombardo was better than Duke Ellington, Lionel Hampton, Benny Goodman, Fletcher Henderson, Jimmy Lunceford, Tommy Dorsey, or any other great orchestra leader.

If Woody were entirely serious in feeling that Bob Hope is funnier than Sid Caesar, Jonathan Winters, or W. C. Fields—to name only a few great comics—his high opinion might grow out of the fact that Hope does have the one factor that Woody lacks as a performer: a brash, totally-in-control manner of walking on stage and taking charge of a show. Meaning no disrespect to either Woody or Bob, Woody's stage manner is (successfully) at the opposite pole. He enters with a tentative, ill-at-ease air, speaks in a natural manner, and seems to fear, especially during the first few minutes of a performance, that he is imposing on an audience.

In his answer of July 5, 1979, Woody specifically excluded such hypotheses.

> Dear Steve,
> I'm not kidding when I say that Bob Hope is my favorite comedian, and it has nothing to do with his authoritative quality, or adult, masterful assurance on stage. None of that means anything to me at all. I find him very funny in every way, and it's important for a comedian to be funny.
> Whether he's funnier than Sid Caesar, or W. C. Fields, or all the other people you name is impossible to answer. At times he is, and at times any one of them can be. When you're talking about that level it's very difficult to compare an intangible like funniness, but I find him as funny and consistent as any of those others, and in certain ways, particularly personal to myself, I often prefer him.
> Good luck with your book.
> > Woody.

A number of comedy writers to whom I have shown copies of this letter suggested that the letter itself is a continuation of the put-on.

There is no way to resolve the conundrum, so the reader may make up his own mind.

Comedians as a class are quite inept at straight acting. Is Woody Allen the exception—or do audiences simply respond favorably to him because they like the image he projects?

Answer: both.

Allen has the ability to do what it would seem all actors ought to be able to do—though in fact many do not—and that is to speak in a natural and unstilted way. The average man speaks in a natural manner his entire life, but if asked to do precisely the same thing in a school play or amateur theatrical, he simply loses his everyday ability and can be counted upon to sound like something of a jerk. Comedians are fairly adept at performing in roles much like their actual images. But one cannot imagine Bob Hope convincingly playing Hamlet, Milton Berle as Henry the Eighth, Don Rickles as Abraham Lincoln, or Steve Martin in a Humphrey Bogart role.

There has always been a small number of comedians, however, who are able to do the remarkable thing that is beyond the competence of even a good many professional actors: read a line naturally.

The point has nothing whatever to do with comedy talent. Groucho Marx was a master comedian, but possibly the worst actor in the history of the trade.

Part of the trick involves still being *something* even when one is not funny. Most comedians tend to turn into an odd sort of nothing when they're not funny. Woody Allen succeeds as a film comedian partly because the character he projects is so real, so believable, and hence so vulnerable. As an actor he communicates with a minimum of effort and gesture. His various roles of the past fifteen years have presented precisely the same disheveled-looking expressionless young fellow.

Most professional actors, by way of contrast, do considerable work with their faces to convey fury, anger, depression, puzzlement, ease, guilt. But almost none of these occurs on Allen's face except in the subtlest of ways. But the very blankness of his features gives the audience the freedom *to make its own interpretation.*

A story about Greta Garbo illustrates the efficacy of a blank expression. In *Queen Christina* she is standing on the deck of a ship, about to be separated, for all time, from the man she loves. The camera holds on a tight and heartbreaking close-up of her for quite a while. By what *means* is the audience made to empathize? As Garbo later conceded, she was thinking of the discomfort of the pair of shoes she happened to be wearing at the moment. The blankness of her face became a screen upon which the emotions of the audience could play. It was the *story line,* the situation, the music, the lighting, the camera work, and other elements that combined to convey the proper message to the audience.

Woody, too, communicates with a minimum of visible effort.

I am deliberately saying little or nothing about Allen as a film director. He's a very good one, indeed, whether handling comic or serious material; his achievements are not only worthwhile, but important. But so much has already been written about his directing that I choose not to enter upon that particular digression here.

As a writer of films, however, Allen calls for at least passing attention here because he has usually written for himself, building stories around a character that is not only consistent but is not terribly far from the actual Woody Allen. The primary difference between the on-screen, imaginary Woody and the millions of real-life Woody Allens—which is to say the unhandsome, short, shy, socially unpolished klutzes, who far outnumber the Robert Redfords or Cary Grants of this world—is that such nebbish characters in film fiction often have surprisingly little difficulty in attracting particularly beautiful or glamorous women. Woody's popularity as a screen figure is in part due to his real-life counterparts, who can enjoy Walter Mittyish fantasies while watching his movies.

Woody's development as a joke writer was not, it seems to me, the long slow process, whereby the initial creations are rather weak and polish comes only after long experience, that most professionals experience. In 1956, when he was still in high school, New York columnist Earl Wilson printed the following joke of Woody's: "A hangover is when you don't want to come out of your room because you think your head won't fit through the door." That sounds like a line from one of Kaufman and Hart's best Broadway comedies, a story by Ring Lardner, a comic essay by Robert Benchley, a high-quality radio script by Fred Allen, a monologue by W. C. Fields. It was written by an unknown schoolboy. The gift obviously appeared very early.

As a seventeen-year-old at Brooklyn's Midwood High School, Allen began selling jokes to New York newspaper columnists. On the basis of this modest credit he was able to sell some lines to the Peter Lind Hayes radio show and use that achievement as a stepping stone to joke sales to Herb Shriner and Sid Caesar.

Although some people imagine that jokes about religion are off limits, with the single exception of the St. Peter-at-the-Pearly-Gates sort, this is not the case. Everything depends on the finesse with which jokes are constructed. Woody has long seemed fascinated by religious and other serious philosophical questions. But precisely those Christian and Jewish theologians who, it might seem, would be most offended by his religious jokes are, in fact, usually amused.

One of the reasons that Allen's marvelous jokes about religion are *perceived* as marvelous (the connection is not always guaranteed) is that the philosophical distance between the two components of the joke—the straight line and the punch line—is enormous. Woody's line starts out by introducing a profoundly serious philosophical or religious concept. It is the very incongruity, the shocking difference between the often somber beginning and the comic conclusion that makes the laughter all the more intense. "Not only is there no God"—one of Allen's jokes starts—"but try getting a plumber on weekends."

Or: "The universe is merely a fleeting idea in God's mind"—one of those depressing, disturbing philosophical reflections that has a sort of nineteenth-century Germanic tinge to it, but Woody concludes—". . . a pretty uncomfortable thought, particularly if you've just made a down payment on a house."

Consider the following exchange from *Love and Death*, between Allen and Diane Keaton as Boris Grushenko and Sonia:

Boris   What if there is no God? What if we're just a bunch of absurd people who are running around with no rhyme or reason?
Sonia   If there is no God, then life has no meaning. Why go on living? Why not just commit suicide?
Boris   (Disconcerted) Well, let's not get hysterical. I could be wrong. I'd hate to blow my brains out and then read in the papers they found something.

In a later scene in the film, Boris, dead, but still talking, says, "If it turns out there is a God, I don't think He is evil. I think that the worst thing that you can say about Him is that He is an underachiever."

John Dart, religion editor of the *Los Angeles Times,* singles out Woody's attention to a philosophical cliché—though a profound one—that crosses every thoughtful person's mind at least at some point in his life, the question as to why, if God really exists, he doesn't give clearer demonstrations of the fact. "If only God would give me some clear sign," Woody's joke goes, "like making a large deposit in my name at a Swiss bank."

Boris Grushenko returns again and again to the same theme, yearning for even the slightest signal from God that He exists. "If He would speak just once—if He would just cough." He also says to Sonia, "If I could just see a miracle. Just one miracle. If I could see a burning bush, or the seas part, or my Uncle Sasha pick up a check."

Comedy—as I have observed earlier—is about tragedy, or at least about largely serious subject matter. Of all writers of comic prose, Woody Allen seems to have the best understanding of this. In 1974, the *Wittenberg Door,* a magazine published by evangelical Protestants, named Woody "Theologian of the Year," and ran one of his articles, "The Scrolls," a wild religious satire in which it is suggested that the prophet Abraham is convinced of the authenticity of the divine instruction to kill his own son because the voice's orders were delivered in a "resonant, well-modulated voice."

From the beginning of his career Allen has dealt with religious philosophy and biblical themes. David Steinberg, too, has done monologues based on biblical material but has frequently been roundly criticized for doing so. For some reason, Christians and Jews do not seem to protest Allen's experiments of the same sort.

Referring to *Love and Death,* in an article in *Esquire,* Woody concedes that the film could be construed as anti-God. "It implies that he doesn't exist, or—if He does—He really can't be trusted. Since coming to this conclusion I have twice been struck by lightning and once forced to engage in conversation with a theatrical agent."

Religion writer Martin Marty has observed that if young seminarians could be as interested about life as Allen is about death, it might lead to "a new generation of theological winners." Marty referred to Allen's saying, "Death is one of the few things that can be done as easily lying down." And also, "I do not believe in an afterlife, although I am bringing a change of underwear." John Dart did a wonderfully perceptive study called "Woody Allen, Theologian" in the June 22–29, 1977, issue of the *Christian Century* in which he said:

> A character in Allen's "Notes from the Overfed," an essay in *Getting Even,*
> observes that some people teach that God is in all creation. The Allenian
> character draws a calorific conclusion from that teaching. "If God is every-
> where, I had concluded, then He is in food," he said. "Therefore, the more I
> ate the godlier I would become. Impelled by this new religious fervor, I
> glutted myself like a fanatic. In six months I was the holiest of holies, with
> a heart entirely devoted to my prayers and a stomach that crossed the state
> line by itself. To reduce would have been folly—even a sin."

As might be guessed the Konigsberg Kid (Allen's real name is Konigsberg) was submerged in religious imagery in his Brooklyn childhood, which included eight years of Hebrew school. He once wrote that he was "raised in the Jewish tradition, taught never to marry a gentile woman, shave on Saturday, and, most especially, never to shave a gentile woman on Saturday."

Eric Lax, in his well-written *On Being Funny: Woody Allen and Comedy,* makes an interesting reference to the fact that Woody does not ad-lib when doing his standard routines.

A little more than halfway through the act, he stops for a moment and pulls out a pocket watch. "Pardon me for a moment while I check the time," he says. "They're very punctilious about time here and I can hear the band padding in behind me." He looks at the watch and holds it up, as if all 1,200 people could see it. "I don't know if you can see this, but it's a very handsome watch." He brings his hand down and looks closely at the watch. "Has marble inlay. It makes me look Italian. My grandfather, on his deathbed, sold me this watch." If the audience believed for a moment that he really did have to check the time, they know now they've been had. What they don't know is that the line gives him a chance to see how he really is doing against time. He is supposed to do forty-five minutes; that joke should come at about twenty-eight minutes into the act. If it comes before that, he'll have to stretch the rest of the material as much as he can while protecting the laughs. Unlike most comedians, he cannot just go on and on; he feels obliged to do material he has worked out and which he knows is good.

Again, however, Woody—being a brilliant and original humorist—can ad-lib when the occasion requires. He sometimes accepts questions from his audience, to which he gives what are, for the most part, spontaneous answers.

Because Woody is not primarily an ad-lib comedian on stage, he tends—not too generously—to deprecate the art. "I put no premium on improvising," he says. "It's nice if you feel in the mood, but it's not a big deal."

On the contrary, true comic ad-libbing is a remarkably big deal, if only because of its rarity. There are perhaps only five men on earth who can, by ad-libbing, convulse an audience with laughter for an entire show. Woody naturally has a rationalization for his view, from the picture *Don't We All?* "But I do improvise when I write the act. I don't want to improvise in front of an audience because I feel they should have the benefit of perfected material."

Actually, Allen is quite good at making audiences laugh with spontaneous answers to questions. These answers are not usually jokes. Rather they are bizarre, surrealistic verbal images that induce laughter because of their strangeness. Eric Lax quotes Woody's answer to the question, "What is one of your biggest thrills in life?"

"Jumping naked into a vat of cold Roosevelt dimes," Woody said.

This, although I find it amusing, is not by any stretch of definition a joke, nor is his answer to the question as to what his greatest sin was: "Having impure thoughts about Art Linkletter!" One can imagine certain people hearing that and literally not being able to perceive what its humorous component was—remarkable in the case of any professional comedian but even more striking in the case of Woody Allen, because he is nothing less than a superb writer of jokes.

A good working illustration of his ability to ad-lib answers amusingly to random questions is given by Mel Gussow, writing in the *New York Times* for Sunday, August 6, 1972, and quoting Woody's answers to his questions.

Mel Gussow What kind of woman *don't* you find sexy?
Woody Allen Martha Raye. She's not my idea of someone enormously sexy. And Nina Khrushchev.
Mel Gussow What can a woman do to initiate sexual intercourse?
Woody Allen She has to show up. That does it for me.

Note that the questions—themselves obviously silly—naturally call for silly answers.

Mel Gussow What are sex perverts?
Woody Allen Sex perverts are the most wonderful people in the world. They're a much-maligned minority group.
Mel Gussow Have you known many?
Woody Allen Just family. Immediate family.
Mel Gussow You don't consider yourself a sex pervert?
Woody Allen I consider myself the zenith of sexual perversion.
Mel Gussow What is a fetish?
Woody Allen A fetish is when you're sexually aroused by some individual part or object rather than by the whole person. An obsession with a girl's nostril would be a fetish.
Mel Gussow Do you have a fetish?
Woody Allen I like a *big* vaccination.
Mel Gussow In his films, Buñuel often has foot fetishes. That doesn't stimulate you at all?
Woody Allen No, not Buñuel's feet.
Mel Gussow How do children get sexually well-educated?
Woody Allen Only on their own.
Mel Gussow On street corners?
Woody Allen Yes, that's where all the good stuff is learned.
Mel Gussow Where did you learn about sex?
Woody Allen I'm self-taught—like my clarinet playing. I'm still learning. I just manage to have the fundamentals down pat.
Mel Gussow Did your parents ever take you aside and explain anything to you?
Woody Allen I wouldn't go aside with my parents. I didn't trust them.

Mel Gussow   As a child, how did you feel about women?
Woody Allen   I was always crazy about them. Planning attacks on girls at seven years old.
Mel Gussow   You at seven, or they at seven?
Woody Allen   Me at seven, they at nineteen.

Allen has an odd effect on journalists. They seem to be torn between the honest urge to say straight out that they find him the funniest man in the world, that they laugh themselves silly every time he opens his mouth on or off the screen, and, on the the other hand, a tendency—which I consider rather stupid—to avoid giving themselves up body and soul to Woody on the first date. There's nothing sexual about this: The point applies to both men and women. But many journalists—and critics—seem too unsure of their own judgments to say plainly that something, or some-body, is terrific. They will compliment talent, when they're sensitive enough to perceive it, but they seem more comfortable if they can withhold at least some small part of their approval, in the *Time* magazine manner.

For example, Gail Rock, writing of Woody in *W* says, *"Play It Again, Sam* is another dose of Woody Allen's silliness, for which I am grateful, because I find Allen irresistibly funny. *Even when the dialogue is so predict-able that I can whisper it along with him, and even when the jokes are terrible groaners, I still laugh."* (Italics added)

This is bullshit of the worst sort, though of a very common sort. If Ms. Rock is literally able to whisper Woody Allen's dialogue along with him, logic forces us to the conclusion that her abilities as a humorist closely approach those of Woody himself. If that is the case she is in the wrong business. She must get herself to Hollywood immediately; her services are badly needed and there are wheelbarrows full of money ready to be dumped all over her.

If she also feels qualified, and superior enough to Woody on the sub-ject of jokes, to advise him as to just which of his funny lines are "terrible groaners" she can also find immediate employment as script editor or writer in television, Broadway, or films.

But I am being smart alecky here at Ms. Rock's expense. The truth is she isn't able to whisper a syllable of Woody Allen dialogue along with him, just perhaps half a second *after* him, thus deluding herself about the factor of timing. And Woody Allen has yet to write a "terrible groaner" of a joke.

He happens, quite simply, to be the best joke writer in the business. This is not to say that every one of his witticisms is as good as the best of Mark Twain or Robert Benchley, but he is the present champ nevertheless and is constitutionally incapable of writing a "groaner."

Published accounts of interviews with Woody bear out an observation based on my own early experience in New York after CBS had given me a nightly TV comedy program. The network publicity people at once set up an almost endless series of press interviews. Half of the subsequently published accounts described me as witty, quick-minded, a true humorist. The other half described me as deadly serious, humorless, dull, and inhibited. When I tell you that some of these stories were based on the same group interview, you'll perceive the point. The writers were describing their own reactions to me, not my essential reality, whatever that might be.

This is true of all reality, of course. We're almost always describing our impressions, rarely the objective materiality. Some journalists describe the Woody Allen we know and love; others paint him as morose, serious, and not in the least interested in joking banter.

He's at his best in those situations when, perhaps despairing of being intelligently questioned, he permits the joke-making part of his mental computer to turn on, after which no one can get a straight answer out of him. The incredible thing is that it sometimes takes journalists a few minutes to perceive that they are being put on. A good instance is related by Robert Greenfield in the *Rolling Stone* of November 30, 1971, in which he describes a press session in London during which the following exchange takes place.

"Woody Allen," a radio interviewer says into his microphone, "you're a film director, a musician, a scriptwriter, an actor, and a comedian. Which of these roles do you prefer?"

"Yes," Woody says succinctly.

"Yes, which?" the interviewer asks, eyeing his precious tape time rolling away.

"Yes, all of them. Whichever one I'm not doing."

"I—ah—see. And how do you get your ideas?"

"They come to me all at once," Woody says, completely deadpan, like a highly intelligent mouse talking to the cat in a Disney cartoon. "I see the opening credits unfold and then the first scene . . . and then the rest of it."

"You mean you see all of it at once?"

"Yes."

"How long does that take?"

"In the case of *Bananas,* eighty-two minutes."

"All of it at once?" the interviewer asks, incredulous.

"Yes," Woody says.

"You're not sending me up, are you?"

"No," Woody says seriously, "not at all."

Later that same day, Greenfield relates, Woody was in his suite at London's Dorchester Hotel.

"You're often portrayed as a loser in your films, Woody. Are you?"

"I was. Now I'm a winner."

"What happened?"

"It's a strange story," Woody says, shifting into total fiction. "I was originally the son of a Presbyterian minister. Then I became an atheist. It might seem strange, but two years ago I found religion again . . . Judaism."

"How did that come about?"

"Well, it's a difficult story to tell, I ran into some Jews . . . and they seemed happy . . . So I took on a Hebrew name, Yitshak."

"And how do you spell that exactly?"

"Y-i-t—shak."

"Seriously, Mr. Allen, how do you get your ideas?"

"I have a Negro gentleman in my apartment. In my closet. And whenever I need an idea, he gives me one."

"And do you pay him?"

"Well, I sing the blues for him now and then."

"And that's sufficient?"

"He seems happy."

"So you . . . you keep a colored man in your closet to give you ideas . . . who you don't pay . . . Is there no organization in the United States to protect him?"

"None at all. Every American has one."

"What is *Bananas* about, Woody?"

"The film is about the lack of substance in my movie."

"You mean in America?"

"No, there's lots of substance in my America. The theme is that the film is empty. The lack of substance puts you to sleep. It's an hour-and-a-half nap."

"Why have you made it then?"

"To confuse my enemies, who are legion."

"And what do they want?"

"To make me think like them."

"Which is what, exactly?"

"Numerically."

"And you think?"

"In letters, usually."

"Are you in analysis?"

"Yes, I have been for the past thirteen years."

"And what has the analyst done for you?"

"He's agreed with me that I need treatment. He also feels the fee is correct."

"How about your parents?"

"My mother speaks to me once every two years and asks me when I'm going to open a drugstore. My father is on my payroll."

"Were they always like this?"

"Yes, but younger."

"And you're an only child?"

"I am an only child. I have one sister."

"And she's not connected to your life?"

"Not in any way. She's just someone I know as a person my mother gave birth to some years ago."

Allen has yet another unfortunate effect on people who interview him. After what is perhaps a heady experience, they return to their typewriters and, far from being content merely to report accurately the amusing things Woody has said, attempt rather to become humorists themselves. The results are frequently painful, as witness the following paragraph introducing *Time*'s July 3, 1972, cover story on Woody.

> His deciduous mud-red hair has been dried in a wind tunnel. His posture would be unsatisfactory for a question mark. His adenoidal diction suggests that he learned English from records—played at the wrong speed. He has the kind of profile that should not be painted but wallpapered.

Now, really.

Such embarrassments come, perhaps, because Woody, like many artists, makes his tricks look easy. One hears a record by Bing Crosby and foolishly assumes one can do his thing. One laughs at Woody Allen and foolishly tries to be funny when writing about him. Terrible.

I return again to the point that one of the reasons for Woody's success is that a whole generation, whatever that means, identified with him in a way that it could not with Bob Hope, Milton Berle, Jackie Gleason, or Sid Caesar. Nor is age the separating factor. The same generation might laugh uproariously at John Byner or Jackie Mason but, again, would not see in those richly amusing gentlemen a reflection of themselves, which is what they imagine they see when they watch a performance by Woody Allen.

The key word in the preceding sentence is *imagine,* for in reality Woody is remarkably unlike the average thoughtful, young, well-educated American chap between, say, twenty and forty.

David Steinberg's best monologues would actually work better if delivered by Woody Allen. Woody would get the larger laughs, even in front of separate audiences, neither of which had ever heard of either man. The reason is, simply, that Woody looks silly whereas David looks serious. Even though David smiles a great deal whereas Woody rarely does, looking silly has nothing whatever to do with smiling. It is in the context of comic show-business that the seemingly ordinary Allen looks so peculiar. As a clarinetist, for example, he seems perfectly natural.

Seeing Woody perform as a clarinetist is a rather uncanny experience. He is definitely a professional, and is—most interestingly—deadly serious about playing the clarinet. I happened to be at Michael's Pub one evening when Woody played. If anyone had come hoping to see Woody Allen the comedian, the film zany, he would have been disappointed, but I suppose everyone in the room had learned what to expect. Woody not only did not entertain the audience, he did not even look at it. He addressed his attention entirely to his colleagues and to the music. He took no bows, said not a word.

When interviewed on the subject of music, he seems invariably to give answers so straightforward they might have come from any dentist, stockbroker, or high school football coach. "I got to play with Pops Foster and Wild Bill Davidson and other good musicians," Allen recalled in an interview with John S. Wilson of the *New York Times.* "Then, in New Orleans, they let me play in a street parade with Percy Humphries' band and I played in Congo Square with Punch Miller, C. I. E. Frazier, Chester Zardis—all the people I'd heard about. I was awestruck meeting them when I sat in—with (Albert Burbank) in New Orleans—he intimidated me. He's got the most unearthly beautiful sound. The thing that always gets me the most about a clarinetist is the tone."

As a bandleader, Wilson reported, Allen gave no indication of his reputation as a comedian. "I just come in and play and leave," he explained. *"I'm not too funny normally anyhow.* That's a distinct Kafkaesque quality about me." (Italics supplied)

So serious is Allen about his music, in fact, that he devotes two full hours daily to practicing the clarinet, an obligation he will vary only for the most pressing of reasons.

Although the fact does not seem to be generally recognized within the entertainment industry, Woody Allen is not a particular darling of the under-thirty audience. I did not arrive at this knowledge by deduction but was simply told it by a bright twenty-one-year-old of my acquaintance.

But Woody's gifts are such that, like all true artists, he does make certain demands on his audience. He is now a filmmaker who creates movies for bright people and even a twenty-year-old with a high I.Q. is simply not worldly-wise enough to appreciate many of his nuances.

I take it as inarguable that Woody's films mean little to small-town or rural audiences, to born-again conservative Christians, to people over sixty-five, to anti-Semites, and to perhaps a few other pockets of American society. As for the passionate tastes of the young, in the field of comedy they run—as of 1981—more to Steve Martin, John Belushi, Dan Aykroyd, Bill Murray, Robin Williams, Gilda Radner, and a few others. I do not suggest the young are not amused by the older comedians; they often demonstrably are. But there is a wide difference between simply enjoying a given artist's performance and having an emotional and even personal investment in him.

But the popularity of some young comedians may not persist, for whatever reasons. Woody's stature, by way of contrast, is secure. He is a true artist, and one of lasting importance.

An Interview with Douglas Brode

DOUGLAS BRODE is the author of the book that I consider to be among the best (if not *the* best) of the critical studies of Woody Allen's work. Called *Woody Allen: His Films and Career,* it was originally published as a hardcover in 1985 by Citadel Press. The book was reissued in an expanded edition as an oversized trade paperback in 1991 as *The Films of Woody Allen.*

I review Professor Brode's volume and its main thesis, the "paradox principle," in the Annotated Bibliography and refer you there for details.

Douglas lives near Syracuse, New York, and teaches film studies at Onondaga Community College.

He has my sincerest appreciation for his participation in this project.

Here's my talk with Douglas Brode:

SS Let's start off with this: Can the essence of Woody Allen's genius be defined, and if so, what do you think it is?

Douglas Brode Woody's genius, in essence, is the ability to find the perfect form to express his own unique content. In *Manhattan,* it is not only the film's sentiment that makes this such a masterpiece, but also Allen's formulating the perfect style to express what he has to say. The black and white is no mere affectation, but the necessary means to convey the central character's insistence on seeing the world as filtered through old *films noir;* the widescreen is there for a purpose, as it allows Allen to place characters who seemingly have a relationship but are actually far apart (emotionally and intellectually) at the far ends of the screen, so we see the truth of their relationship while they engage in small talk. The meaning of any one scene is in the way it is shot, not in the dialogue itself; that means Allen has mastered the concept of "pure cinema," expressing ideas cinematically. And that is true of every great filmmaker.

SS What are your *personal* favorite Woody Allen films, and why?

Douglas Brode My personal favorites among Allen's films are *Manhattan* and *The Purple Rose of Cairo,* because they contain a warmth and debonair sense of whimsy that mark the truly sophisticated artist—something Allen, the one-time gag man, has always wanted to be. *Manhattan* captures a sense of New York City as filtered through the unique consciousness of old movies. It is 1979 New York viewed, thanks to the glorious black-and-white cinematography and accompanying Gershwin music, by the last man who refuses to admit that the 1940s era is long gone. *The Purple Rose of Cairo* is Allen's impressive improvement on his own earlier play *Play It Again, Sam.* His love of old movies is the source of a bittersweet character study here, one of the saddest comedies of all time. For Allen's fellow devotees of

Manhattan and old movies, these two films automatically qualify as personal favorites.

SS On the other hand, which films do you consider Woody's *best* work, and why?

Douglas Brode In my opinion, the very best Woody Allen films are *Hannah and Her Sisters* and *Crimes and Misdemeanors*. What I most admire about them is the perfect balance achieved between Allen's own introspective need to consider existential themes and weighty social issues, and the lingering need of his audience to be entertained by clever comedy. Each of these films is "serious" in intent and ambition; each is highly entertaining to watch. Woody wants to make *Another Woman* and *September;* audiences want to watch *Sleeper* and *Bananas. Hannah* and *Crimes* brilliantly manage to have it both ways.

SS What *don't* you like about Woody's work?

Douglas Brode What I like least about Allen's work is his tendency toward pretension and his inability to grasp where emulation leaves off and imitation begins. His *Stardust Memories* is insufferable because it's the film that contains both of his worst qualities in mammoth proportions. That film is unrelentingly pretentious, announcing all its big themes humorlessly; the film is self-congratulating whereas Allen's best work is self-critical. And rather than be influenced by Fellini in a positive way (every artist has a right to pick up pointers from a previous artist), the movie is an outright carbon copy of $8^1/_2$. It's as if Woody's secret fantasy were to be in the movie $8^1/_2$ and, when he made *Stardust Memories,* he not only lived out that fantasy but expected us to pay for his "trip" through ticket purchases.

SS How, specifically, has Woody's work moved you personally? Particular scenes and/or moments would be of interest.

Douglas Brode Woody's work moved me personally by showing us that a New York Jewish neurotic can, if he only believes in himself, become a kind of latter-day Great Gatsby. In my book *Woody Allen: His Films and Career* (a.k.a. *The Films of Woody Allen*), I pointed out that Woody, like his idol F. Scott Fitzgerald, is a misplaced Romantic, not in the common sense of that word—meaning a guy who wants to kiss the pretty girl—but in the more philosophical sense. Allen's hero wants the woman he can't have because the very impossibility of his obsession ensures that it will not be soiled by reality. So the scenes that touch me most deeply are those in which Allen's character momentarily brushes against the perfection he's always searching for: sitting by the bridge with Diane Keaton in *Manhattan;* watching Mariel Hemingway's hair suddenly fall into her face, making her look momentarily like Veronica Lake; and a great moment in my least favorite film *Stardust Memories*—when near the end—on a flashback to a Sunday afternoon listening to great jazz, reading through the *Times,* and gazing at a beautiful woman as a wonderful breeze passed over everything. Perfection can be achieved, but only fleetingly—making the mundane everyday life all the more difficult to bear.

SS It has always been my feeling that the volume of books about a subject usually is a good indication of the significance of that subject to popular culture. With the publication of my book, *The Woody Allen Companion,* there will be close to forty books that have been written about Woody Allen and his work. What do you think this says about Woody's long-range, overall importance as a creative artist and filmmaker?
Douglas Brode Any filmmaker who inspires forty books has got to be important, whether one likes him or not. And Woody Allen is just that—important. The irony, of course, is that his comedic films will outlast his supposedly serious ones like *September* and *Another Woman*—those two being the films he would most like to be remembered for.

SS Of all the books written about Woody and his work, how many have you read, and of those that you have seen, which do you think are the best?
Douglas Brode I've only read three books on Allen:
  1. The Eric Lax biography, *Woody Allen: A Biography* (1991), which I found embarrassingly self-serving. It was as if control-freak Allen wrote the book himself, presenting himself as he wishes to be seen by the public, and invented Eric Lax so he'd have a byline.
  2. . . . *but we need the eggs* (1982), Diane Jacobs's occasionally overly academic work that makes a very interesting point about the significance of magic in Allen's films; too bad her work was written before the release of *A Midsummer Night's Sex Comedy,* which would have been the perfect film to end her thesis-book on.
  3. *Loser Take All* (1979) by Maurice Yacowar, which had some very good observations on Allen's films, though it was marred by the author's faulty notion that if one's words are very big, they make the ideas even bigger.

SS Based on your knowledge of Woody Allen and his work, how do you think he feels about this unrelenting dissection—in print—of his creative output?
Douglas Brode Allen is flattered by the academic-level criticism of his work, since he aspires to be a literary artist worthy of such debate, like Bergman, Fellini, or Chekhov (and, at his best, is indeed in their league). However, he is also a control freak, and getting worse all the time; so he would like to control the image of himself as presented through the media, and his allowing Eric Lax to write an "authorized biography"—filled only with laudatory comments—is the ultimate example of this.

SS Has Woody seen or read your book, and if so, what did he think?
Douglas Brode Though Woody has never attempted to communicate any reaction to me about my book, I'm told that an English interviewer

asked him about it and that he had indeed read it, and had been fascinated by some of my points, especially the concept that food, sex, and death become linked in his movies—something that has always seemed very obvious to me, but has never been pointed out by any other critic.

SS Even though he's an avowed agnostic/atheist, it's obvious (and another example of your "paradox principle"?) that Woody has a real heartfelt fascination with religious thought, imagery, and ritual. How do you think Woody's artistic vision has been affected by his inability to believe in a personal God?

Douglas Brode I find a fallacy in your question owing to the next-to-the-last word. I'm not altogether sure that Woody is unable to believe in a personal God. He may doubt, but that's not the same thing as saying he's unable to believe. What he clearly has not accepted is any shared, mass-conceived vision of God as Judaism, Christianity, or an Eastern religion would present Him. But that is merely another indication of Allen's strong individuality. However, like other artists—even the most radical ones in their youth—Allen is growing far more conservative in his later years; in *Hannah* and *Alice,* he flirts with becoming a Catholic, the Western religion that would seem least appropriate for him. Essentially, Allen's doubts about the existence of God affect his artistic vision by giving him a theme, which has also been the key twentieth-century theme for all serious writers—a search for some proof of God (and, therefore, proof that life has a meaning) in a world that exists on the edge of ruination.

SS What thematic concerns do you think will interest Woody artistically as he gets older and closer to death?

Douglas Brode He has already indicated his upcoming thematic concerns with recent films that have demonstrated his growing conservatism (in a philosophic, not social, sense). The attraction toward Catholicism in several recent movies is no gag and no coincidence. Watch for Allen to share, in his upcoming films, an appreciation—even awe—for simple, structured, family life.

SS Professor Brode, I thank you for your thoughts and participation.
Douglas Brode You're very welcome.

"Henna and Her Sickos"
(or "Play Annie Hall's Manhattan Memories Again, Sam!")

A PARODY of *Hannah and Her Sisters* called "Henna and Her Sickos" appeared in the September 1986 issue of *MAD* magazine. The piece was written by Debbee Ovitz and illustrated by artist Mort Drucker.

"Henna and Her Sickos" appeared in the "Knock on Woody Dept." and was introduced by a guy named "Woody Alien":

> I'm Woody Alien! I'd like to introduce you to my latest film! I'm very proud of it—it's new, it's different! Like for instance, even though it's the 14th consecutive film in which I've played a total neurotic, this is the first time there are other neurotics in even worse shape than me, mainly . . . Henna and Her Sickos.

In *MAD*'s inimitable style, the film was hilariously lambasted from front to back, beginning with the character's names. Hannah was "Henna"; Holly was "Hollow"; and Lee was "Loose" (a.k.a. "Leah"). Mickey was "Murky"; Elliot was "Elliyup"; and Frederick was "Heimlich."

The piece opened with a two-page Thanksgiving dinner spread attended by not only Henna and her family, but also Ed Koch, Gene Siskel and Roger Ebert, Gene Shalit, Louise Lasser, and a pilgrim.

At one point, Henna's father says "Grace":

> Thank you for the blessings we're about to receive—the turkey, the stuffing, the cranberries, and the one-liners about Franz Kafka, Nazis, and psychoanalysis!

At one end of the table, Siskel and Ebert discuss Woody's filmmaking:

> **Ebert**   This is a veritable masterpiece! Woody has certainly grown as a filmmaker!
> **Siskel**   What brilliant touches! Instead of Gershwin music, he's using Rodgers and Hart! And instead of Diane Keaton talking in overlapping dialogue, he has Mia Farrow doing it!

When Gene Shalit is told that Woody "shows real maturity as a Director since 'Manhattan' and 'Stardust Memories,' " he replies, "Right! Woody's finally learned where to buy color film!"

Here is a look at some of the more memorable satirical backhands in "Henna and Her Sickos":

• Heimlich tells Loose that he's "entered in the All-City Brooding Tournament," and that he's "seeded third."

• Murky goes to the doctor because he thinks he has a brain tumor, and the doctor tells him it's just a minor hearing loss, and asks if he's banged his ear lately? Murky tells him that he did bang his ear against the side of the oven: He was attempting suicide because he was sure he had a brain tumor!

• David takes Hollow and April for a tour of his favorite architectural sights. When the girls complain, "We're two horny gals and you take us on a 'Wide World of Concrete' Tour?" David responds, "Hey, don't blame me, I didn't write this scene! Woody is horny for anything and everything about New York City!"

• When Murky finds out that he doesn't have a brain tumor, he says, "My brush with death gives me a chance to do a 'search for the meaning of life' segment . . . complete with a voice-over monologue that enable me to use leftover gags from my other films, since they're all so easily interchangeable . . . I can pick on Socrates, homosexuals, Ice Capades, boiled chicken and deal with some major questions that have been plaguing mankind, like 'Does God exist?' 'Is there life after death?' and 'Will I ever be able to top "Annie Hall"?' "

• The satire ends with Hollow and Murky getting together and having this conversation:

> **Murky** Sitting in that movie house has turned my life around! I've made a major, mind-blowing discovery! The Marx Brothers made movies just to be funny! They never felt they had to hide from the press or fear their fans . . . never felt the need to drop the names of pseudo-intellectuals in their movies . . . never became obsessed about secrecy over their next film! They never took themselves seriously and today, they're considered great artists!
>
> **Hollow** And I'll bet no one ever told Groucho that they liked his earlier films better!

"Henna and Her Sickos" is a hilarious but affectionate look at Woody and his work. The *MAD* artwork, as usual, is superb, and the writing is even funnier because it's clear that Ovitz and Drucker are fans of Woody too.

(Special thanks to the "Usual Gang of Idiots" at *MAD* for their help with this piece.)

CHAPTER 4

Louise Lasser, Diane Keaton, and Mia Farrow

The Women in Woody's Life—and Films

I really do get hooked into bright, highly educated girls.
It must be some carryover from my teen years.
Woody Allen

Playboy   What kind of girls turn you on?
Woody Allen   Oh, tall, gelid, aloof Teutonic-Prussian girls. I
adore Villagey-looking blondes. I like a girl who's arrogant,
spoiled and dirty, but brilliant and beautiful.
          "The Playboy Interview," *Playboy,* **May 1967**

FOR ALL HIS seemingly voracious carnal and romantic proclivities, Woody
Allen has been remarkably "nonpromiscuous" in his own personal relationships.

To date he seems to have had four serious relationships. Two he cod-
ified by marriage, and two he did not. The latter were long term. Woody
also has very serious long-term nonromantic relationships with a few
other women in his life, most notably his sister Letty Aronson, his secretary for the past twenty-five years, Norma Lee Clark; and his closest woman
friend, Jean Doumanian. (Woody and Jean share an answering service.)

This chapter peeks at the important women in Woody's life, all (except
for Harlene Rosen) of whom he has worked with in his films.

Harlene Rosen

Playboy   Are you still paying alimony on your first
marriage?
Woody Allen   We've an arrangement. We alternate. I pay
her for a year; then she pays me for a year. The unfair thing is
I'm paying for child support and we had no children.
Playboy

WOODY'S first serious relationship was with his first wife, Harlene Rosen,
whom he met in late 1954.

Harlene played piano in a trio at a Young Israel social club where the
nineteen-year-old Allan Konigsberg would do some of his early standup
routines (many of which utilized comedy material written by Mike Merrick). They were engaged in January 1956, married on March 15, 1956, at
the Hollywood Hawaiian Motel in Hollywood, and divorced in 1962.

Other than musically, Harlene and Woody never really "worked" together. According to Eric Lax, in *Woody Allen: A Biography,* the coda to their
marriage was in 1967 when Harlene sued Woody and NBC for $1 million
"for holding her up to scorn and ridicule." She didn't like many of Woody's
"ex-wife" jokes. In favor of her, it must be acknowledged Woody did often
hold her up to "scorn and ridicule," and not a few of his jokes about her in
his standup routines were quite nasty.

Here is a sampling of Woody's "ex-wife" jokes from his three comedy
albums, *Woody Allen, Woody Allen, Volume 2,* and *The Third Woody Allen
Album*:

> • I ran into my ex-wife . . . who I did not recognize with her wrists
> closed.
> • . . . she was one of the few white Muslims in New York.
> • The Museum of Natural History found her shoe and, based on the
> measurements, they reconstructed a dinosaur.
>> From "Private Life," on *Woody Allen*

> • . . . the dread Mrs. Allen.
>> From "Brooklyn," on *Woody Allen*

> • I wanted to discuss my marriage . . . or as it was known, "The Ox-
> Bow Incident."
>> From "My Marriage," on *Woody Allen*

> • [R]ight after the wedding my wife started getting weird. . . . [S]he
> pierced her ears one day with a conductor's punch.
> • I kid my ex-wife all the time, but she was animal. . . . She was not

technically animal, officially. Officially, she was reptile.
From "What's New, Pussycat?", on *Woody Allen, Volume 2*

- My wife divorced me 'cause she thought I was weird.
- It was my wife's birthday . . . so I bought her . . . an electric chair. Told her it was a hairdryer.
- She divorced me. . . . She got the house, car, bank account, Rotissemat. In the event that I remarry and have children, she gets them.
From "Reminiscences," on *Woody Allen, Volume 2*

- I should have known something was wrong with my first wife when I brought her home to meet my parents, they approved of her. [But] my dog died.
From "Second Marriage," on *The Third Woody Allen Album*

Rather caustic, eh?

Regarding their marriage, Woody Allen told Eric Lax, "Today, we would have just lived together. We were both young." According to Lax, Woody "places the blame for the lawsuit on a lawyer he feels talked her into it as a way to make money for himself." Harlene and Woody settled the lawsuit out of court and Lax reports that they have not seen each other in over twenty-five years.

Louise Lasser

I became a human being with Louise. She made a major, lasting
contribution to my life. The years with her were the time I
made the transition from writer to comedian. Before that
I was just someone who lived in Brooklyn and moved
into New York and didn't know anybody besides
my wife. With Louise I assumed
citizenship of Manhattan.
From Eric Lax's *Woody Allen: A Biography* (1991)

WOODY'S second important relationship was with Louise Lasser.

Woody had met Louise sometime in 1960 and they were married on February 2 (Groundhog Day), 1966.

Through 1969, the year she and Woody were divorced, Louise appeared in *What's New, Pussycat?*, dubbed dialogue in *What's Up, Tiger Lily?*, and appeared in *Take the Money and Run*. Even after they divorced they remained close friends, and Louise went on to appear in *Bananas* and *Everything You Always Wanted to Know About Sex* (in the segment "Why Do

Some Women Have Trouble Reaching Orgasm?" and a segment that was cut from the final film, "What Makes a Man a Homosexual?"). She also appeared in Woody's 1980 release, *Stardust Memories* (in an uncredited role as a secretary.) (Woody has remarked that Louise Lasser is the only person who can actually—if you can believe it—cheer him up.)

Diane Keaton

Tony Roberts used to feel that [Diane] was the type that would wake up in the morning and immediately start apologizing.
Woody Allen, in *Rolling Stone*, June 30, 1977

I have not been a crutch for her at all. It's been absolutely above-board.
You could reverse that and think that she's been a crutch
to me in many ways, I mean, she's been an enormously
supportive person to *me* on projects. . . . [Diane is] the
best person in the world to let read a script, because
she's totally ingenuous. She's not trying to be
impressive, she doesn't care if it was written
by Chekhov. She's perfectly willing to pick
it up, read it and say, "I think it's boring,"
or "I think it's wonderful." I feel secure
working with her. If she tells me
something is creepy, I reexamine it.
Woody Allen, in *Rolling Stone*, June 30, 1977

IMPORTANT Relationship Number 3 for Woody was the one that many of his fans consider to be Woody's archetypal 1970s relationship.

In 1968 Diane Keaton (whom Woody calls Keaton) showed up for an audition for Woody's soon-to-be produced play *Play It Again, Sam.* She got the part of Linda Christie, and this was the beginning of a relationship that spanned seven films (from *Sam* through *Radio Days*) and more than twenty years of friendship.

Diane Keaton has the singular notoriety of being the quintessential Woody Allen female character, Annie Hall, in the film of the same name. (Diane Keaton's real name is Diane Hall.) Her mannish wardrobe became trendy, and her nervousness and trepidation about romantic relationships coalesced the fears of a postsixties generation that was slowly awakening to the fact that there was no such thing as "free love" and that relationships came with a price, even if that price was only heartbreak and loss.

During her time with Woody, Diane Keaton played five memorable female characters: Luna in *Sleeper,* Sonia in *Love and Death,* the title character in *Annie Hall,* Renata in *Interiors,* and Mary Wilke in *Manhattan.* Woody's predictions for Diane came true in 1987 when she released her pseudodocumentary *Heaven,* which marked her directorial debut. And in the fall of 1991, a film directed by Diane called *Wildflower* appeared on the Lifetime cable TV network. She also starred with Steve Martin in a remake of *Father of the Bride,* which was released in December 1991.

Mia Farrow

Woody is secure enough not to need that legal piece of paper. We're one family but we don't live together. It would be too disruptive because we both need time alone. I like the idea of seeing one another in our prime time—when we want to.
Mia Farrow, in an interview with Glenn Plaskin,
New York Post, **January 7, 1991**

ON SUNDAY, April 22, 1979, the *New York Times Magazine* ran a cover story on Woody Allen by Natalie Gittelson titled "The Maturing of Woody Allen," which began:

> The only time Woody Allen rises from his chair is to change the background music in his duplex penthouse living room: He switches records from Mozart to Beethoven, from Beethoven to Schumann. On the coffee table beside him, crowned with fresh spring flowers in perfect esthetic array, bowls of nuts and fruits—arranged with Cézanne-like care—look almost too good to eat. He doesn't eat. He doesn't peel a banana or nibble an almond. He doesn't smoke and he doesn't drink— not even a glass of water. He hardly even gestures. Not to put too fine a point on it, he hardly even moves.

The magazine's cover photograph showed Woody holding an open umbrella over one shoulder. Typically, it wasn't raining. Mia Farrow noticed the picture, read the article, and tore the photo off and saved it. At this point, she had seen two of Woody's films, *Annie Hall* and *Manhattan.* Now, twelve years later, she has starred in twelve of Woody's films, and it is assumed she has seen the ones she hasn't appeared in.

Woody Allen and Mia Farrow have been together since April 17, 1980, the day they first had lunch together at Lutéce. (Mia commemorated the date on a needlepoint sampler which Woody now has hanging on the wall outside his bedroom.) Mia's first Woody Allen film was *A Midsummer*

Night's Sex Comedy in 1982. She played Ariel, and from there went on to appear as Eudora Fletcher in *Zelig*, Tina Vitale in *Broadway Danny Rose* (in a role specifically written for Mia), Cecilia in *The Purple Rose of Cairo*, Hannah in *Hannah and Her Sisters* (much of which was filmed in Mia's New York apartment), Sally White in *Radio Days*, Lane in *September*, Hope in *Another Woman*, Halley Reed in *Crimes and Misdemeanors*, Lisa in Woody's *Oedipus Wrecks* segment of *New York Stories*, Alice Tait in *Alice*, and Irmy in *Shadows and Fog*. (After the beginning of her relationship with Woody, she has appeared in only one "non-Woody" film, as Alura in 1984's *Supergirl*.)

Mia Farrow is also the mother of Woody Allen's only child. There are eleven children in the Woody Allen and/or Mia Farrow family: fraternal twins (by André Previn) Matthew and Sascha Previn, Fletcher Previn, Lark and Daisy Previn (Vietnamese orphan girls adopted by Mia and Previn), Soon-Yi Previn (a Korean orphan adopted by Mia and Previn), Misha (Moses) Amadeus Farrow (an orphaned Korean boy with cerebral palsy adopted by Mia and whom Woody has adopted), Dylan O'Sullivan Farrow (a newborn American girl adopted by Woody and Mia), Satchel O'Sullivan Farrow (a son born to Woody and Mia and named for Satchel Paige), Isaiah, an 8-month-old African-American cocaine-addicted baby, and Tam, a 12-year-old blind Vietnamese girl.

Woody Allen himself has remarked upon the dissimilarities between himself and Mia. In Eric Lax's *Woody Allen: A Biography*, Woody tells Lax:

> I could go on about our differences forever: She doesn't like the city and I adore it. She loves the country and I don't like it. She doesn't like sports at all and I like sports. She loves to eat in, early—five-thirty, six—and I love to eat out, late. She likes simple, unpretentious restaurants, I like fancy places. She can't sleep with an air conditioner on, I can only sleep with an air conditioner on. She loves pets and animals, I hate pets and animals. She likes to spend tons of time with kids, I like to spend my time with work and only a limited time with kids. She would love to take a boat down the Amazon or go up Mount Kilimanjaro, I never want to go near those places. She has an optimistic, yea-saying feeling toward life itself, and I have a totally pessimistic, negative feeling. She likes the West Side of New York, I like the East Side of New York. She has raised nine children now with no trauma and has never owned a thermometer. I take my temperature every two hours in the course of the day.

Thierry de Navacelle, in his book *Woody Allen on Location*, describes Woody and Mia's interaction on the set of *Radio Days*:

> Woody looks at her, taking her by the hand. They have a sort of removed attitude with each other, but with a lot of attention given on both sides. You have a feeling that Woody is proud of her, and impressed by her, too. [P. 148]

> Woody is very considerate with [Mia], completely different than with [Dianne Wiest]. With [Dianne], it is more of a game, a pal rela-

tionship. He just looks at [Mia], stares at her, touches her as if she were not real. There is respect and admiration in his behavior—at least that is how it seems at first glance. [P. 153]

And according to Fern Buchner, the makeup woman on Woody's films, "[Woody] likes [Mia] with no makeup, like she is when she gets out of the shower." (Navacelle, *Woody Allen on Location,* p. 157.)

As of this writing, Woody and Mia's romantic relationship seems to be over. [See the "1992" section in Chapter 1.] Woody and Mia were not only lovers and co-workers, but they were also deeply committed to each other as friends. Because of Mia's reported withdrawal from the cast of *Manhattan Murder Mystery,* it appears that *Husbands and Wives* may very well be the final "Woody Allen/Mia Farrow" film. Mia Farrow's years with Woody resulted in thirteen films, one son, and the adoption of two other children.

Louise Lasser, Diane Keaton & Mia Farrow "Woody Allen" Filmography

The following filmography provides a chronological overview of these three fine actresses' work with Woody Allen.

1965: *What's New, Pussycat?* (Lasser)
1966: *What's Up, Tiger Lily?* (Lasser)
1969: *Take the Money and Run* (Lasser)
1971: *Bananas* (Lasser)
1972: *Play It Again, Sam* (Keaton)
1972: *Everything You Always Wanted to Know About Sex* (*But Were Afraid to Ask)* (Lasser)
1973: *Sleeper* (Keaton)
1975: *Love and Death* (Keaton)
1977: *Annie Hall* (Keaton)
1978: *Interiors* (Keaton)
1979: *Manhattan* (Keaton)
1980: *Stardust Memories* (Lasser)
1982: *A Midsummer Night's Sex Comedy* (Farrow)
1983: *Zelig* (Farrow)
1984: *Broadway Danny Rose* (Farrow)
1985: *The Purple Rose of Cairo* (Farrow)
1986: *Hannah and Her Sisters* (Farrow)

1987: *Radio Days* (Keaton, Farrow)
1987: *September* (Farrow)
1988: *Another Woman* (Farrow)
1989: *Oedipus Wrecks* (in *New York Stories*) (Farrow)
1989: *Crimes and Misdemeanors* (Farrow)
1990: *Alice* (Farrow)
1992: *Shadows and Fog* (Farrow)
1992: *Husbands and Wives* (Farrow)
1993: *Manhattan Murder Mystery* (Keaton)

PART II

Enter These Enchanted Woods...

The Work of Woody Allen

CHAPTER 5

Woody Allen, Auteur
The Films

I hope that someday it will lock in with them that I never hold them
cheaply, that I never write down to them, that I always assume that
they're at least as smart as I am if not smarter, and that I
try to do films that they will respect.

When I'm finished making films in my life . . .
some of them, if I'm lucky, will be very good films . . .
and some will be entertaining.

There's never been a film of mine
that I've really been satisfied with.
Woody Allen

1.
What's New, Pussycat?
(Famous Artists, 1965); Running Time: 110 minutes; Unrated; Color.

I wrote an offbeat script about a hypersexual guy living in Paris and afraid to get married. Establishment people poured money into it. While they managed to retain some of the jokes, they lost fifty percent of them.
Woody Allen, in *Seventeen* magazine, 1972

What's New, Pussycat? is the story of the love "lives" of a satyrical "allergic-to-marriage" Parisian fashion magazine editor named Michael James (Peter O'Toole).

Even though Woody loathes the movie and considers the final version not what he originally wrote, there are still lines and moments in the film that are quintessential Woody.

Overall, the film is a bore, and it is easy to understand Woody's abhorrence for the final screen version. However, it is clear that there was a "Woody Allen" script buried somewhere in this mess.

What's New, Pussycat? made loads of money and established Woody Allen as a screenwriter. Because of that, the film cannot be completely dismissed, although it would have been nice to see a film that was true to Woody's script. (See in this chapter Woody's *Playboy* article, "What's Nude, Pussycat?" for Woody's spin on the making of the film, and a look at his original story.)

Some of the more amusing gags include Fritz Fassbender (Peter Sellers) asking James if he can tell him what he once did in a Latvian brothel, and Fassbender's reply to a romantic speech by James: "I like thighs. Do you like thighs?" And when Fassbender telephones his lover, Zsa Zsa, he begins the conversation, "Hello, my little laxative."

The very first time we see Woody on screen, his character Victor Shakapopolis is playing chess at an outdoor café with a beautiful Parisian girl named Tempest O'Brien (Nicole Karen). He distracts her, grabs a chess piece off the board, and throws it over his shoulder. Victor tells Michael James, "We played strip chess. She had me down to my shorts and I fainted from tension."

Victor works at a striptease club, helping the girls dress and undress for twenty francs a week. When Michael remarks that that's not very much, Victor says, "It's all I can afford."

Another funny moment occurs later, during a group therapy session. The talk turns to a patient's dream about a train going into the tunnel. Fassbender remarks, "Dat vas a good one." And during this session a fat patient attacks Michael James and Fritz scolds him and calls him "Nail-biter!" (In Woody's standup routine "Private Life," which appears on his first album, *Woody Allen,* Woody talked about being captain of the Latent Paranoid Softball Team: The Nailbiters against the Bedwetters.)

The story revolves around the romantic chaos caused by everyone wanting someone else and no one wanting the one he's with, and the film concludes with an "orgy" of confusion, chase scenes, a bomb-waving radical, fights, and bad one-liners. When the police arrive at the hotel where everyone has gathered for the weekend, the entire cast flees in go-carts, and there is another "orgy" of ridiculous slapstick crashes and sight gags.

What's New, Pussycat? was a huge financial success: It ended up grossing $17 million. Woody reportedly earned $50,000 for the script, in addition to a salary for appearing in the film.

Look for . . .

• Henri de Toulouse-Lautrec and Vincent van Gogh (complete with bandaged ear) sitting at the table next to Victor and Tempest in the outdoor café scene early in the film.

• Richard Burton's cameo appearance in the Crazy Horse Saloon. As he's leaving, Michael James says, "Give my regards to what's-her-name."

• Peter O'Toole playing his drunk scenes similar to the way he played swashbuckling hero Alan Swann in his 1982 film, *My Favorite Year.*

• The scene where Victor tells Carol (Romy Schneider) he's got some salmon salad that he made in April, but that "if you smother it in pepper, it's fine." (In *Manhattan* Ike reminds Mary that in her refrigerator is "a corned beef sandwich . . . from nineteen fifty-one.")

• The scene where Michael bursts in on Carol while she's teaching a class. This foreshadows the scene in *Manhattan* where Ike calls Yale out of a class to confront him about Mary.

• The scene where Victor has dinner by the side of the river as Fritz prepares to kill himself Viking-style by dousing himself with kerosene, wrapping himself in a flag, and setting himself ablaze in a boat that will then drift out to sea. Victor tells Fritz it's his twenty-ninth birthday, and this scene was actually shot on December 1, 1964—Woody's twenty-ninth birthday.

A Few Words from Woody . . .

• In a 1970 interview in *Boston After Dark,* Woody said, "I loathe everyone and everything concerned with it and they all loathe me. . . . They butchered my script. They wrenched it into a commercial package. . . . It ended up in the hands of establishment people who were hep, not hip. I couldn't go to see it for a year."

• In a 1972 interview with *Cinema* magazine, Woody said, "I fought with everybody all the time. I hated everyone, and everyone hated me. When that picture was over, I decided I would never do another film unless I had complete control of it." . . . I saw the picture once, fleetingly, years ago. I don't remember much about it at all. I certainly don't remember any of the dialogue. A lot of ad-libbing went on, which I like in the films I direct, but there was nobody on *Pussycat* to control the ad-libbing. They just slopped it all on the screen."

Woody's *Playboy* Article
"What's Nude, Pussycat?"

The August 1965 issue of *Playboy* magazine featured an article by Woody Allen about the making of *What's New, Pussycat?* accompanied by photos from the film, as well as photos definitely *not* seen in the film. It is fascinating to read Woody's comments about a film we later learn he loathed, and wished to disassociate from. Were some of the jokes in the piece *really* jokes? You be the judge.

In the opening paragraph of the piece, Woody wrote:

> *What's New, Pussycat?* marks my filmic debut—both as an actor and screenwriter—so I suppose I shouldn't admit that I wrote the whole thing as a joke, never once believing that the Charles K. Feldman who commissioned me to do the script was actually *the* Charles K. Feldman, or that anyone in their right mind would ever produce such a film. The final version of *Pussycat* is the result of a 200-page filmscript that blew out of a taxicab window and was never put back in its original order after its retrieval from a passing chestnut vendor's pushcart, my typist having forgotten to number the pages. That Peters O'Toole and Sellers agreed to play the lead roles in the film is a miracle, and I'm certain that neither would have touched it in its original form. Therefore, credit must be given to the cabdriver who helped me put the script into its present order—especially since the loss of certain pages provided the plot with just the proper shade of incoherence. My initial story described the search of a psychotic gynecologist and a Lithuanian jockey for stable values in a world threatened by the influx of bad singing groups—with Romy Schneider, Capucine, Paula Prentiss and Ursula Andress cast as the 1936 Notre Dame backfield. United Artists felt this was a little too "offbeat," and made a few subtle changes. The present plot involves a Paris fashion editor (O'Toole) and a horny Viennese psychiatrist (Sellers) in search of Romy, Capucine, Paula, Ursula, and a clutch of strippers from the Crazy Horse Saloon—with a special role written in for me to give the film an earthy appeal.

Woody's essay was accompanied by forty photos, all of which had captions by Woody. Here is a sampling of the pictures and Woody's comments:

• Page 100: The photo accompanying Woody's text was a black-and-white shot of the final orgy scene. The caption said, "This scene . . . is based on a real incident from my own life and shows . . . me with a copy of

Heidi—a book that has sustained me in my darkest moments. As you can see, I'm no fun at orgies."

• Page 101: One black-and-white picture shows Ursula combing her hair while an assistant holds a mirror in front of her. Her right breast is completely exposed in the photograph. As a caption, Woody wrote, "Here we see Sellers in one of his incredible make-up jobs. . . ."

• Pages 102–3: A series of twelve color photos spotlights Paula Prentiss. Woody wrote, "Paula is so beautiful that I pulled a muscle in my hip just watching her rehearse this number. She's the kind of tall, violently sexual woman that I knock off every day by the carload—in daydreams. In real life, she could turn me into a lamp base."

The bottom photo spread was of Woody and Paula rehearsing a love scene that was cut from the film. Woody wrote, "Incidentally, during rehearsals I had to be hosed down several times by the studio's volunteer fire department to prevent an ugly scene. That I'm an animal soon became apparent to everyone who played love scenes with me."

• Page 105: Six color photos display real strippers backstage at the Crazy Horse. Woody wrote, "During this phase of my research I tried to follow one simple rule at all times: If it moves, fondle it!" He also admitted, "I had hoped to sit out front and lend the girls moral support, but during their acts I was backstage getting my insulin shots."

• Pages 106–7: The final six photos of the section had Woody playing football with topless strippers from the Crazy Horse Saloon. Woody is *also* topless for the photos, and of the experience he wrote, "Fondling the back of a French stripper is the greatest tactile sensation I've had since jumping naked into a vat of cold Roosevelt dimes."

2.
What's Up, Tiger Lily?

(American International Pictures, 1966); Running Time: 79 minutes; Color. (Originally produced and released in Japan as *Kagi No Kagi* [*Key of Keys*] in 1964.)

All we did was put five people in a room and keep them there improvising as the film ran. It was a nuisance but OK. We still haven't seen any money from it though.
Woody Allen, in *Rolling Stone*, September 30, 1971

This is a weird one.

What's Up, Tiger Lily? is the story of a James Bondian Japanese spy on the trail of a secret recipe for the world's best egg salad.

When Woody Allen and his cohorts "revamped" the Japanese spy movie *Kagi No Kagi* (*Key of Keys*) into this "new and improved" version, they gave birth to a certifiable lunatic of a movie, a movie which snares the viewer immediately in a web of insanity.

Tiger Lily begins with scenes from *Kagi No Kagi,* still with the original Japanese dialogue. After a chase scene and a fight scene we . . . FREEZE FRAME.

Cut to Woody Allen and an interviewer in a well-appointed study.

Interviewer   Ladies and Gentlemen, what you have just seen is an excerpt from a motion picture that was made in Japan. I am sitting here chatting with Woody Allen, the author of this film. Woody, is the word "author" quite the correct word to use? I mean, exactly what did you do with that film?

Woody Allen   Well, let me see if I can explain this to you accurately. They wanted, in Hollywood, to make the definitive spy picture. And they came to me to supervise the project, you know, because I think that if you know me at all, you know that death is my bread, and danger my butter. Or danger's my bread, and death is my butter. No, no, wait. Danger's my bread, death . . . no, death . . . I'm sorry . . . death is my . . . death and danger are my various breads and various butters. So we took a Japanese film, made in Japan by Japanese actors and actresses; we bought it. And it's a great film; beautiful color, and there's raping, and looting, and killing in it. And I took out all the soundtrack. I knocked out all their voices, and I wrote a comedy. And I got together with some actors and actresses and we put our comedy in where they were formerly raping and looting. And the result is a movie where people are running around killing one another and, you know, doing all those James Bondian things; but what's coming out of their mouth is something wholly other.

Interviewer   I see. To my recollection, I've never heard of that being done before, where the actors would be acting one story and saying another.

Woody Allen   It was, actually. It was done in *Gone With the Wind*. Not many people know that. That was . . . those are Japanese people, actually, and we dubbed in American voices on that . . . Southern voices.

Interviewer   Really?

Woody Allen   Oh, yes.

Interviewer   Oh.

Woody Allen   That was years ago during the war, though, and there had been many naval bases and things, so it was kept quiet.

Interviewer   Yeah, well, be that as it may, do you think we could run this film now?

Woody Allen   Sure. Watch this.

A projector is started, the Lovin' Spoonful begin singing on the soundtrack, and the credits are run against a background of scantily clad or nude Oriental girls (à la every James Bond movie) as an animated lascivious "Woody" character frolics all over the girls.

There are some funny lines in *Tiger Lily,* and much of the entertainment value of the film comes from the incongruity of hearing wisecracking one-liners issuing from the mouths of so-serious Japanese actors.

For instance, our hero, Phil Moskowitz, has gone to a hotel room with a girl. We see her undressing behind a screen. She comes out in a towel and says to Phil, "Name three Presidents." Phil replies, "Roosevelt, McKinley . . ."; he opens her towel, looks down, and asks, "Lincoln?"

A running gag throughout the film is the use of clichéd epithets that the various characters hurl at one another during fight scenes. Thugs and heroes alike are repeatedly called "Saracen pig," "Spartan dog," "Roman cow," "Spanish fly," and "Anglo-Saxon Hun."

Woody and company also have fun with the visual nature of the film. In one scene outside a prison, a guy waiting for an escaping con says to another chap, "This thing has got to go off like clockwork. I want you to follow every move I make. When I take a step, you take a step." He then takes a couple of steps and his colleague makes the exact same moves. On the soundtrack Woody says, "Excellent."

Another funny moment is when one of the girls tells Phil that she thinks he's cute. Phil tells her, "Meet me in the bedroom in five minutes and bring a cattle prod."

At another point, Terry tells Phil that she'd like to tear off his clothes and make violent love to him. He says, "I'll go along with that," moves to kiss her, and she rebuffs him. (This is very similar to a scene Woody would use in his play, *Play It Again, Sam* six years later, in which scene Vanessa tells Allan Felix that "my life was a continual round of orgies" and that she "took on the entire Tau Epsilon Phi Fraternity at Yale." Then when Allan lunges for her, she jumps up and says, "What did you take me for?" A bewildered Allan asks himself, "How did I misread those signs?" See the section on *Play It Again, Sam* in this chapter.)

There is also some blatant sexism in the new dialogue. In one scene, Shepherd Wong surveys a bevy of beautiful babes in their underwear. As he peruses them, he says, "Loin, shank, sirloin . . . why, this is the best shipment of meat we've had this year." One of his thugs says, "Now, boss, aren't you glad you gave up being a vegetarian?"

The plot becomes convoluted to the nth degree as we follow Phil and company to Raspur, "a nonexistent but real-sounding country." (They're waiting for an opening on the map.)

Woody and company also have fun with the terrible performances delivered by the Japanese actors. Phil asks, "Wing, do you think I'll win an award for my acting in this picture?" Wing Fat then beats Phil with a pipe: "You are the worst actor I've ever seen. This is for Sonny Tufts; this is for John Wayne; this is for the Flying Wallendas." A thug says, "Gee, boss, you really know how to hurt a guy."

After a shipboard fight scene set to "The Man on the Flying Trapeze," the original version of the film ends.

The film then cuts to Woody lying on a sofa, eating an apple. Standing in front of the sofa, the Chinese stripper, China Lee, does a sensuous strip-tease as the following message—complete with eye chart—scrolls up the screen:

> The characters and events depicted in this photoplay are fictitious. Any similarities to persons living or dead is purely coincidental. And if you have been reading this instead of looking at the girl, then see your psychiatrist, or go to a good eye doctor.

When China Lee is down to nothing but her underwear, Woody Allen leans up on one elbow, looks into the camera, and says, "I promised I'd put her in the film. Somewhere."

Look for . . .

• The Yokohama Harbor scene. Phil and Terry are looking out the window of an observation tower and Phil says, "This is the obligatory scene. The director always has to walk through with his wife." A Caucasian couple then walks through the scene and Phil mutters, "Egomaniac."

• Midway through the movie the film stops and a hand begins to do shadow puppets against the light of the projector. It's Woody Allen and Louise Lasser fooling around in the projection room. First they both do shadow puppets, then Woody kisses her hand; then they both kiss in front of the light and we hear:

Max Dolores, we can't keep meeting here like this. My wife is getting suspicious.
Dolores But Max, I love you.
Max Yes, but not in the projection room. It's against union rules.

• Woody's second "study" scene:

Interviewer Woody, because the story is a little bit difficult to follow, would you give the audience and myself a brief rundown on what's gone on so far?
Woody Allen No.

• The loose hair waving in one of the film's frames. A silhouetted hand appears in the frame and tries to catch the loose hair.

A Few Words from Woody . . .

In the May 1967 issue of *Playboy* magazine, Woody observed, "It's an experimental film. Originally it was a Japanese espionage vehicle. What I did was to cut out the Japanese dialogue, write new dialogue and put it into the mouths of the actors. What I wrote is completely contrary to what they're doing at the same time on the screen, so it comes off funny. Matter of fact, *Tiger Lily* was just voted one of the ten most Japanese pictures of the year."

3.
Casino Royale
(A Famous Artists Production, released by Columbia Pictures, 1967); Running Time: 131 minutes; Color.

In *Casino Royale,* the *real* James Bond comes out of retirement to take on the evil Dr. Noah and his criminal organization SMERSH.

Casino Royale tries way too hard. Just the fact that five directors were used should have been a good sign that there was a hole in the boat, and the vessel was filling up fast.

Apparently, producer Charles K. Feldman wanted to emulate the style—and successes—of his earlier screwball comedy, *What's New, Pussycat?* This time he decided on *Casino Royale*—the only James Bond title not owned by the Harry Saltzman–Cubby Broccoli team. Feldman saw *Casino Royale* as an opportunity to reunite select members of the *Pussycat* cast and create a clever, wacky, lucrative James Bond parody. (It didn't work: *Casino Royale* was a box-office bomb.) To do so, he felt he needed five directors and eight writers. (Ben Hecht, Terry Southern, Billy Wilder, Frank Buxton, Mickey Rose, Peter Sellers, Val Guest, John Huston, and Joseph Heller all contributed [uncredited] to the screenplay.)

The film is a disaster. It is not funny, not entertaining, and actually quite sad to watch. The phrase "exquisitely boring" captures the essence of this film. It tries so hard to be clever and wry, and yet nothing works—not the script, not the sets, not the performances. (Sheridan Morley, in his book *The Other Side of the Moon: A Biography of David Niven,* called *Casino Royale* "a shameful travesty of [Ian] Fleming's original novel.")

Woody Allen flew to London in the spring of 1966 for what was supposed to be six weeks of shooting that turned into six months. He played poker (and usually won), hunted for rare jazz recordings, and bought German expressionist paintings with his gambling winnings.

In the film, Woody played Jimmy Bond, James Bond's nephew, a lecher who was really "Dr. Noah," head of the crime organization SMERSH. His plan was to release his bacillus germ into the atmosphere. The germ would make all women beautiful . . . and destroy all men over four feet six inches tall.

Dr. Noah ends up swallowing explosive "tiny time pills" and expiring during an overblown finale which includes cowboys and Indians, the Keystone Kops, a monkey in a wig, girls painted gold, bubbles, a seal, paratroopers, and the French foreign legion.

Look for . . .

• Woody's first scene in the film. He's being brought before a firing squad and Woody's dialogue is looped (rerecorded) so badly, it's easy to understand why Woody refuses now to use anything but production sound on his films.

• A quintessential "Woody Allen" plea to the firing squad:

> Listen, you can't shoot me. I have a very low threshold of death. My doctor said I can't have bullets enter my body at any time. What if I said I was pregnant? Could I have a last cigarette? I'm gonna give it up any day now. . . . You realize this means an angry letter to the *Times*?

• Woody's use of physical humor during the scenes at SMERSH headquarters, including climbing onto—and falling off—a mechanical bull.

• Another classic "Woody" line: The Detainer agrees to be Noah's co-ruler, and so he agrees to unstrap her from a table where he had bound her. He tells her he'll release her and they'll run amuck. But if she's too tired, they can walk amuck.

• Dr. Noah's speech on the airplane. (During which the platform he's on rises up out of the floor.) As Noah is speaking and the floor is rising, we hear a choir humming "Mine Eyes Have Seen the Glory." As the platform rises, we see that there is actually a choir of men beneath the floor. This device would be used by Woody in *Bananas,* in the scene where he checks into his hotel room and hears harp music, and there is an actual harpist in his closet. And also in the "What Happens During Ejaculation?" segment of *Everything You Always Wanted to Know About Sex;* there the gonad workers hum "Mine Eyes Have Seen the Glory" as they crank up Sidney's erection.

A Few Words from Woody . . .

• During a discussion of *Casino Royale* with Harold Mantell for the 1977 documentary *Woody Allen: An American Comedy,* Woody called the film "an unredeemingly moronic enterprise."

• Woody Allen, in a letter to Richard O'Brien, reprinted in Eric Lax's *Woody Allen: A Biography,* said, "*Casino* is a madhouse. I haven't begun filming yet but saw the sets for my scenes. They are the height of bad pop art expensive vulgarity. Saw rushes and am dubious to put it mildly, but probably film will coin a mint. (Not money, just a single peppermint.)"

Woody's *Playboy* Article
"The Girls of *Casino Royale*"

The February 1967 issue of *Playboy* magazine featured an article by Woody Allen about *Casino Royale*. There were fifty photos in the feature, and Woody introduced the spread with the following remarks:

Last winter, producer Charles K. Feldman approached me to appear in his new James Bond extravaganza, *Casino Royale*—not, as I had expected, as James Bond, but as 007's nephew, Little Jimmy Bond, who eventually is unmasked as the evil Dr. Noah. We dickered for a few days, until I asked him if there were going to be any girls in the picture. He started listing them, and three hours later I interrupted to accept his original cash offer of three dollars. Armed with assorted aphrodisiacs and my fatal good looks, I quickly embarked for London. Soon I was submerged in more flesh than Flo Ziegfeld ever imagined in his wildest fantasies, with Ursula Andress on my right, Joanna Pettet on my left, Barbara Bouchet on top of me and 24 girls beneath me, making the world's most electrifying blanket. . . . Imperfect . . . I dare say, are the *Playboy* editors, who begged me to act as an editorial consultant for the captions accompanying these 13 pages of pictures of my conquests—the girls of *Casino Royale.* You'll notice a certain flippancy in their treatment of my inside revelations, which they've subverted with a host of irrelevancies they call facts. There's only one reason I'm letting them get away with it: They're giving me a free copy of the issue.

Here's a sampling of Woody's captioning contributions:

Page 110—Joanna Pettet: Two photos show Pettet standing in front of a giant statue of Buddha. Woody wrote, "I'd hate to tell you where that Buddha has his hands, but you'll notice he's smiling."

Page 111—Ursula Andress: Woody wrote, "If Botticelli were alive today, he'd probably want to jump on Ursula like the rest of us."

Page 112 (top)—Fang Girls: A series of nude photos expose the "Fang Girls," Ursula Andress and Fiona Lewis. Of the three photos, Woody said, "[These photos] provide the framework of a brilliant new panel show, in which blindfolded contestants would have to figure out by touch which girl is Ursula."

Page 113—Barbara Bouchet: A photo shows Bouchet standing with her hands on her hips and wearing nothing but a short skirt. The caption read, "Woody insists that Barbara's 'proud, defiant look,' in the shot above, is a result of the fact that she had just had the privilege of sampling the Allen body—'I fell on her when somebody ripped off my pasties. Barbara later confessed to me that the incident filled her with precisely the same animal excitement one feels when shuffling a deck of cards.'"

Pages 116–17—Orgy Girls: Eight stills display an orgy sequence that was shown only briefly as background stills. Regarding the orgy itself, Woody wrote, "I was technical director for the whole sequence, calling on my vast experience as idea man in a French brothel. I contained myself magnificently during the shooting, although I must admit I still have a fair amount of Max Factor on my hands."

Page 119—Goldfinger Girls: Three photos exhibit girls painted gold for the fight scene at the end of the film for the *Goldfinger* reference. In one of his rarer JFK/assassination references, Woody wrote of a painted girl, "The girl in the photo below . . . is not a professional actress but one of the witnesses before the Warren Commission. This is how she appeared after the hearing—obviously having been finger-painted. The fact that she is not mentioned in the Report is the real factor in the drive to reopen the investigation."

4.
Don't Drink the Water
(Avco Embassy, 1969); Running Time: 98 minutes; Rating: G; Color.

Don't Drink the Water is about an American caterer and his family who are inadvertently trapped behind the Iron Curtain while on a European vacation. The film was directed by Howard Morris (the legendary Ernest T. Bass on "The Andy Griffith Show") and based on Woody's stageplay of the same name.

Overall *Water* is a bland and mildly pleasant viewing experience, although the final third of the film does bog down thanks to a somewhat convoluted plot that *has* to get the Hollanders out of Vulgaria, but doesn't quite know how to go about it.

Jackie Gleason sparkles as usual, but Estelle Parsons really overplays her role as the daffy wife. Joan Delaney is good as the horny daughter (Delaney later appeared in *Scenes from a Mall* as a woman interviewer), and Ted Bessell, Phil Leeds, Michael Constantine, and Richard Libertini all turn in well-honed performances. (Bessell, in particular, is quite good as the ambassador's "loser" son, as is Leeds as Walter's "idiot" partner, Sam.)

Woody has said that *Don't Drink the Water* was his spin on what would happen if his family went on a European trip together.

Jackie Gleason plays Walter Hollander, a caterer from Jersey who gets "persuaded" by his family into taking a European vacation. While innocently taking a snapshot in the Iron Curtain country of Vulgaria, Walter and his family are mistaken for spies and end up prisoners in the American embassy.

The remainder of the film focuses on Axel's attempts to win their release, and on the blossoming romance between Hollander's daughter and Axel.

There are some funny lines in the film. On their way to Athens, Marian says to Susan, "Even your father will get something out of Greece." Walter replies, "Four more days of uninterrupted diarrhea." At one point Axel Magee reminds his politically minded father that his "broad outlook will appeal to psychotic liberals as well as militant fascists. Something for everybody." There is also a political gag in the script: Axel's father scolds Axel, "It would have been nice, when Vice President Agnew dropped by, if somebody had recognized him." Axel replies, "Yeah, but, dad, nobody recognizes him in America either."

Howard Morris's direction is very cartoonish in this film. He uses many exaggerated closeups, and directs the cast to play *very* broadly.

The film deteriorates into a typical, lame, wacky sixties comedy/ chase/costume movie for the last fifteen minutes.

Look for . . .

• The film's two "Fruit Cart!" scenes. (Roger Ebert defines this particular type of scene in his 1991 *Movie Home Companion:* " 'Fruit Cart!' [is] an expletive used by knowledgeable film buffs during any chase scene involving a foreign or ethnic locale, reflecting their certainty that a fruit cart will be overturned during the chase, and an angry peddler will run into the middle of the street to shake his fist at the departing Porsche.") Magee's limo crashes into a fruit cart the first time the Hollanders flee to the embassy; and the secret police's truck crashes into the same vendor's cart the second time the Hollanders have to abscond to the embassy.

A Few Words from Woody . . .

• Asked if the negative comments about the film version of *Don't Drink the Water* bothered him, Woody replied, "As long as they pay, it doesn't bother me for a second."

5.
Take the Money and Run
(Palomar Pictures, 1969); Running Time: 85 minutes; Rating: M; Color.

[*Take the Money and Run*] has a sort of loose-leaf form. You have a feeling that scenes, perhaps entire reels could be taken out and rearranged without making much difference in total impact, which is good because it all looks so effortless.
Vincent Canby, in a review of *Take the Money and Run*,
***New York Times*, August 24, 1969**

Take the Money and Run tells the story (in documentary form) of ill-fated crook Virgil Starkwell. Virgil turns to crime as a child, ends up in trouble, falls in love, ends up in trouble, marries, tries to go straight, ends up in trouble, has a child, gets in trouble, ultimately ends up in prison, and again courts trouble by trying to fashion a gun from a bar of soap.

Take the Money and Run was dubbed the first unadulterated "Woody" movie because it was the first film which he wrote, directed, and starred in, and it gave American cinephiles ample evidence of Woody Allen's "talent to amuse." The film is a mock documentary that foreshadows Woody's more sophisticated 1983 fake documentary *Zelig. Take the Money* was the first real indication that we were dealing with a comic genius of the first order. It has a rough-and-tumble feel to it that carries you along from one gag to the next. And because of the documentary parody format, you sense that you've seen and heard this before (and in a way you have—the narration for the film was supplied by noted documentary narrator Jackson Beck) but something's different, for sure. It is very funny, very well written, and a wonderful comedy.

Take the Money is loaded with gags, visual and verbal. Some of the funniest sight gags include Virgil's cello flying out a second-story window of his house; Virgil trying to play the cello in a marching band; Virgil's parents being interviewed wearing fake noses and mustaches; Virgil carving a gun from a bar of soap in prison and when it begins to rain during his escape, left holding a handful of suds; Virgil volunteering for an experimental vaccination and, for several hours, being turned into a rabbi; Virgil tipping a maître d' with dozens of coins he just stole from a gumball machine; and Virgil finding a brassiere in the prison laundry.

The verbal jokes are even funnier. Some of Woody's most hilarious lines include Virgil's remark about the navy inkblot test: "That looks to me like two elephants making love to a men's glee club"; and his observation that Louise's mother, a religious fanatic, had "conversations with God in which they discussed salvation and interior decorating." (This refers back to Woody's standup one-liner about his parents, whose values were "God and carpeting.") Another witticism has Virgil and Louise naming their first child "Jonathan Ralph," after Virgil's mother. And of course, the most oft-quoted scene from the film—Virgil robbing a bank:

> **Teller** What does *this* say?
> **Virgil** Can't you read that?
> **Teller** I can't read this. What's this? "Act natural"?
> **Virgil** No. (reading the note) It says, "Please put $50,000 into this bag and act natural."
> **Teller** Oh, it does say "act natural."
> **Virgil** (still reading) "Because I am pointing a gun at you."
> **Teller** That looks like "gub." That doesn't look like "gun."
> **Virgil** No, it's "gun."
> **Teller** No, that's "gub." With a "b."
> **Virgil** No, see, that's an "n." It's "g-u-n." That's "gun."

Teller   George, would you step over here a moment, please? (George walks over) What does this say?
George   "Please put $50,000 into this bag and abt natural." What's "abt"?
Virgil   "Act! Act!"
Teller   Does this look like "gub" or "gun"?
George   "Gun."
Virgil   See?
George   But what's "abt" mean?
Virgil   "Act. A-C-T. Act natural. Please put $50,000 into this bag and act natural."
Teller   Oh, I see. This is a holdup.
Virgil   Yes.
Teller   May I see your gun?
Virgil   Oh. (lifts his jacket to reveal a revolver)
Teller   Well, you'll have to have this note initialled by one of our vice presidents before I can give you any money.
Virgil   You see, I'm in a rush.
Teller   What?
Virgil   I'm in a rush.
Teller   I'm sorry, but that's our policy. See the gentleman in the grey suit.

Other funny verbal gags include one about Virgil's robbery of a butcher shop: "[Virgil gets] away with 116 veal cutlets" and then "had to go out and rob a tremendous amount of breading." And when in prison, Virgil was tortured by being "locked in a sweat box with an insurance salesman." (An insurance salesman joke is also used in *Love and Death*.)

An interesting anecdote about the music in the film comes from Eric Lax's book, *Woody Allen: A Biography*. The music for the scene where Virgil gets ready for his first date with Louise originally had a "dreary, dirgelike piece of music" behind it. "[Ralph] Rosenblum replaced it with a piece of Eubie Blake ragtime and said, 'Look. Look what happens when you put a piece of lively music behind it.'" Woody's reaction? "The whole thing came to life. I was suddenly just bouncing along. It made all the difference in the world."

There's also a reference to Woody's second marriage (to *Louise* Lasser) in the film. Virgil and Louise marry in a simple ceremony following what Virgil later described as "a deeply moving blood test." Virgil says of the day, "This was the happiest moment of my life. I just wish my parents could have been there." (When Woody and Lasser were married at the Lasser home on Groundhog Day, February 2, 1966, Woody's parents were not present for the ceremony. The only people there besides Woody and Louise were Louise's parents, Mickey Rose, Judy Rose, and Jean Doumanian.)

The original ending of *Take the Money and Run* was what editor Rosenblum called "grotesque and offensive": "[L]eading his gang out of a bank after a holdup, Woody is gunned down by the police in a hideous death scene reminiscent of *Bonnie and Clyde*. The last shot in the movie has the camera pulling away from Starkwell's blood-drenched, bullet-ridden body. It was very chilling. I thought, *Holy Cow*."

Look for . . .

• Janet Margolin's dialogue flub. After Virgil and five other cons escape, they go to Louise, who wants to discuss Virgil's robbing of banks—while Virgil is still chained to the other five inmates. Virgil says he wants to wait until they're alone. And then, in a gaffe that was not edited out, Louise replies, "All right, you don't want to discuss it alone? Okay. I'm going in the next room and I want to talk about it right now." Janet Margolin probably should have said, "You *want* to discuss it alone?"

• Louise Lasser appearing as an old friend of Virgil's who, when interviewed about him, says she thought he did a great acting job: she really believed he was an idiot.

• *Take the Money and Run*'s assistant director, Stanley Ackerman, appearing as the photographer who filmed Virgil's final arrest.

A Few Words from Woody . . .

• Woody Allen told biographer Eric Lax, "Pictures like *Take the Money and Run* and *Bananas* were forerunners of movies like *Airplane!*—although they didn't make a fiftieth of what *Airplane!* made." Woody also said that they are "funny in a sort of infantile or youthful way" and that "they trade on what Noël Coward called the talent to amuse."

6.

Bananas

(United Artists, 1971); Running Time: 81 minutes; Rating: PG; Color.

Bananas is the story of a schlemiel of a products tester (Woody as Fielding Mellish) who falls in love with a political activist (Louise Lasser as Nancy) who dumps him because she wants a leader. He then joins a band of rebels in a country in turmoil called San Marcos (thinking he'll win her heart if he shows he's brave), becomes its president, travels back to the United States in disguise, gets arrested for conspiracy, receives a suspended sentence, and ends up winning back—and marrying—Nancy.

Bananas is the type of "Woody Allen" film many critics of his later works pine for: wacky, irreverent, absurd, surrealistic, and riotously funny.

It belongs in the basket holding *Take the Money and Run, Play It Again, Sam, Everything You Always Wanted to Know About Sex, Sleeper,* and *Love and Death.*

Bananas has it all: the Woody Allen persona, the unbelievable sight gags, the references to big breasts and analysis, the pseudoautobiographical one-liners, and memorable jokes. (Such as: "I'm not suited to this job. Where do I come off testing products? Machines hate me. I should be working at a job that I have some kind of aptitude for—like donating sperm at an artificial insemination lab." And, "Why did I quit college? I could have been something today. I was in the black studies program. By now I could have been black.")

Bananas is, in its own ragged way, brilliant. The humor is a coalescence of the influences on Woody Allen, including the Marx Brothers, Charlie Chaplin, bad movies, Sergei Eisenstein, American television, and sixties and seventies psychobabble.

Bananas contains classic bits of funny business, and a few lines ("Hey, Ralph! How much is a copy of *Orgasm?*" for one) that will definitely be included when the *Big Book O' Comedy from the Twentieth Century* is finally written.

Some of the funniest scenes in the film take place when Fielding is in San Marcos. We get to see a rebel soldier being tortured by having the entire score of *The Naughty Marionette* played for him. And there are several very funny sight gags during the rebel camp training scenes, including Fielding mistakenly throwing the pin and holding the grenade, which then blows up in his hand; and Fielding getting urinated on behind his newly built camouflage screen. In one humorous sequence a first-aid instructor tells the rebels that if someone is bitten by a snake, he must immediately suck out the poison. A topless woman then runs through the camp holding her bare breast and yelling that she was bitten by a snake. Every male in the camp—including, of course, Fielding—begins to chase her.

As noted, Woody's influences are very evident in *Bananas*. When Fielding acts as his own lawyer during his conspiracy trial, he says, "I object, your honor. This trial is a travesty. It's a travesty of a mockery of a sham of a mockery of a travesty of two mockeries of a sham"—a blatant reference to similar outpourings of Groucho Marx.

The film ends with Howard Cosell's live wedding night coverage of the consummation of Fielding and Nancy's marriage.

Look for . . .

• Rocky himself, Sylvester Stallone, as a hood in the subway scene.

• The Execusizer scene, a very funny sequence that many critics and film scholars (most notably, Douglas Brode) assert owes its genesis to the assembly line sequence in Charlie Chaplin's *Modern Times.*

• The seemingly ad-libbed dialogue between Woody Allen and Louise Lasser in one of the park scenes. Nancy has to tell Fielding something but doesn't know how to break it. He then asks, "Why? Have you seen the X-rays of me?" Lasser cracks up. Her laughter seems to be a genuine response to Woody's apparently ad-libbed joke. She replies, "I've seen X-rays of you" (which doesn't sound like a scripted line), and he says, "I fail to see the humor in this," and she responds, "You didn't see the X-rays," which cracks Woody up. She then tells him she doesn't want to see him anymore, which appears to be where the written dialogue takes over.

• Woody completely immersing himself in a river to evade mercenary soldiers. It seems that as Woody's fame and power grew, his willingness to do personally distasteful stunts such as this diminished. Here we have him hiding underwater for the scene, and yet in 1982's *A Midsummer Night's Sex Comedy*, when he and Ariel (Mia Farrow) crash into the pond on Andrew's flying bicycle, Woody had a stunt double go into the water for him. For the next scene, he doused himself with Evian to appear wet, rather than set foot in the pond.

• The "take-out for an army" ordering gaffe. Fielding has to feed the army and so orders 1,000 grilled cheese sandwiches to go: 490 on rye, 110 on whole wheat, 300 on white bread, and 1 on a roll. This adds up to 901.

• The reference to Sergei Eisenstein. When an army of rabbis and Hassidic Jews arrives to help defend the capital city of San Marcos (because the president hired the UJA [United Jewish Appeal] instead of the American CIA), a baby carriage rolls down the steps of the municipal building, as in a scene in Eisenstein's 1925 silent classic, *Battleship Potemkin*.

• Woody's blatantly autobiographical college joke. He says to the rebels, "What is this with my education? I had two days of college. I need three years and 363 days to get a degree." Woody dropped out of college after a very brief stint.

A Few Words from Woody . . .

When asked why his film was called *Bananas,* Woody replied, "Because there are no bananas in it."

7.
Play It Again, Sam

(An Apjac Picture, released by Paramount Pictures, 1972); Running Time:
85 minutes; Rating: PG; Color.

Since Woody Allen writes, directs, and stars in so many of his own
movies, a lot of people accuse him of being an egocentric moviemaker.
But somehow, he's never been afraid of working with talented women and
carrying that close relationship over into his personal life. First there were
movies where he starred with Louise Lasser. Then along came Diane
Keaton. And these days, he seems to be in the Mia Farrow era.
Tonight's film comes from his Diane Keaton period and it's
full of the kind of romantic comedy that made them
both famous. He plays your basic Woody Allen
nebbish—now don't ask me to sign for that word—
with an imaginary Humphrey Bogart alter ego.
Here's this week's Hollywood classic, directed
by Herbert Ross—*Play It Again, Sam*—
rated PG—with closed captions for the
first time on TV. Enjoy yourself.
**Marlee Matlin's signed introduction to the Movie Channel's first-ever
broadcast of *Play It Again, Sam* with closed captions.**

Play It Again, Sam is about a film reviewer with a Bogart fixation who is
divorced by his wife and while trying to find a meaningful relationship,
ends up having an affair with his best friend's wife.

Play It Again, Sam holds up remarkably well after twenty years and it is
because of Woody's excellent screenplay (and earlier stageplay). *Sam* is
witty, touching, and intelligent, and while a few period references are
somewhat dated (Polaroid at $8^1/_2$, for instance, or the cab filled with pot-
smoking hippies), overall the film is still timely, entertaining, and *very*
funny.

The integration of Bogart into the life of Woody's neurotic film
reviewer Allan Felix works: the interaction between the characters is seamless, and this device was equally effective on the stage.

Classic Woody Allen one-liners mark the film, as well as delightful
performances by Woody, Diane Keaton, and Tony Roberts. Remarkable
also is Jennifer Salt's interpretation of Sharon, Allan's blind date. She was
very natural, and gave a confident performance.

Play It Again, Sam can justifiably be considered a "Woody Allen Classic." It is a quintessential Woody Allen film, and is better than many "comedies" of today.

There's much to like in *Sam*.

The films opens with the last scene of *Casablanca*, and Woody superbly communicates the disappointment and depression that occur when a film ends and the lights go on. The move from the dark womb of cinematic fantasy into the cold harsh light of reality is something he's often talked about. (We were supposed to get this same feeling in the scene in *Crimes and Misdemeanors* where Cliff and his niece Jenny exit a movie theater. In Eric Lax's biography, he reveals that the scene in the original script called for Cliff to say, "Oh, God, sunlight—traffic—" as he and Jenny left the theater, but the lighting didn't work, so they canned it.)

Sam takes place in San Francisco, but there isn't the negative tone to Woody's writing about the West Coast that would mark his later references to California. The film is a very clever romantic comedy, and one can almost call it the first real Woody Allen film—if you're one of those fans who consider *Annie Hall* and *Manhattan* the *real* Woody Allen movies, and all the others experiments.

Allan is an aspirin junkie, and one of life's "great watchers." When thinking about "stepping out" a little after his divorce, he says he'll bring "broads" up to his apartment: "swingers, freaks, nymphomaniacs, dental hygienists."

In a funny sight gag, Bogey suggests a little bourbon and soda to Allan, but Allan tells him, "My body will not tolerate alcohol." He sips the drink anyway, does a spit take, coughs and gags, and then collapses on the bar.

Some of the verbal gags work very well, too. At one point, Allan tells Dick and Linda he doesn't cook his TV dinners: he sucks them frozen.

Allan and Linda end up having a brief but sincere love affair and when faced with choosing her husband or Allan, she elects to save her marriage and the film ends with Allan walking off into the fog to "As Time Goes By" on the soundtrack and while the credits roll.

Look for . . .

• Woody's disguise. In the scene where Allan Felix walks to the laundry lamenting that his analyst is gone for the month of August, Woody is wearing the rain hat that he often uses in real life to avoid recognition.

• Dick Christie's very funny, obsessive call-forwarding fixation. Throughout the film, he calls his office *nine times* to tell them where he'll be so they can forward his calls.

• An early Woody Allen Nazi reference. After Allan fantasizes about his ex-wife Nancy dating a tall blond biker, he says, "We're divorced two weeks, she's dating a Nazi."

• Another Philharmonic reference. Jennifer tells Allan that she once slept with the string section of the New York Philharmonic. In *Take the Money and Run* Virgil told Louise that he played cello with the Philharmonic, and in *Stardust Memories* Daisy is a cellist with the Philharmonic.

• Diane Keaton and Woody Allen's first walk through a museum. They will do the same later in *Manhattan*.

• Woody's first use of his spider motif. On the way to the beach house, Allan asks Dick and Linda if there are spiders at the beach. This foreshadows the spider scene in Woody's 1977 film, *Annie Hall*.

• Woody's use of standup routines in the film. At one point, he tells Dick and Linda he shouldn't be in the sun: "I'm red-headed, I'm fairskinned. I don't tan, I stroke." This is a line from Woody's early standup comedy routine, "Private Life," from his first album, *Woody Allen*. And after Allan and Linda make love, Linda asks Allan what he was thinking about as they were doing it. He tells her baseball players, because it keeps him going. She says she couldn't figure out why he kept yelling "slide." This is from another early Woody Allen standup routine called "Second Marriage," from *The Third Woody Allen Album*.

• Diane Keaton's laughter "problems." In the scene where Allan tells Dick and Linda about getting into a fight with the bikers, Woody/Allan describes the scenario as only Woody Allen can, and Diane Keaton/Linda cracks up as he's relating what happened. It seems as though Woody is *genuinely* cracking her up—not just laughing because the script calls for it.

• Woody's Midwood High reference. At one point, Allan calls up "Marilyn Perry" from Midwood High School. Woody Allen actually went to Midwood High School.

A Few Words from Woody . . .

In his article titled "How Bogart Made Me the Superb Lover I Am Today," in the March 1969 issue of *Life* magazine, Woody remarked on the writing of the stage version of *Play It Again, Sam*:

> The first Humphrey Bogart movie I saw was *The Maltese Falcon*. I was 10 years old and I identified immediately with Peter Lorre. The impulse to be a sniveling, effeminate, greasy little weasel appealed to me enormously and, setting my sights on a life of mealymouthed degradation and crime, I rapidly achieved a reputation that caused neighboring parents to appear at my doorstep carrying torches, a large rope and bags of quicklime. . . . I wrote *Play It Again, Sam* to honor Bogart for at least giving me a few months of smooth sailing, and also to get even with a certain girl (or a particular sex that gives me trouble, to tell the truth).

8.
*Everything You Always Wanted to Know About Sex**
*(*But Were Afraid to Ask)*

(United Artists, 1972); Running Time: 87 minutes; Rating: R; Color.

Working with Woody is what it must be like to work with Ingmar
Bergman. It's all very hushed. . . . He said three things to me while
we were shooting—"You know where to get tea and coffee?" and
"You know where to get lunch?" and "Shall I see you tomorrow?"
Oh, and there was one other thing—"If you don't like
any of these lines, change them."

**Gene Wilder, on working on the set of *Everything You Always
Wanted to Know About Sex*, from an interview with Kenneth Tynan
in *New Yorker*, October 30, 1978**

Everything You Always Wanted to Know About Sex (*But Were Afraid to
Ask)*, was (*very* loosely) based on the David Reuben bestseller of the same
name, and consisted of seven vignettes. The following takes a peek at the
seven skits, and also offers details on an eliminated segment.

• In Segment 1, "Do Aphrodisiacs Work?" a court jester slips an aphro-
disiac to the Queen, gets caught, and is beheaded. The skit was very funny,
and perfectly executed (no pun intended). Woody played the Fool, who
told jokes about the King of France, the Black Plague, and taxing the poor,
and carried a bell dummy that had horn-rimmed glasses painted on it. The
puns flew fast and furious in this segment, some of which were such
groaners that you just know that Woody's tongue was firmly embedded
within his diminutive cheek when he wrote them. For instance, after the
Queen knocks him to the ground and he falls on his "bells," the Fool
ponders, "TB or not TB. That is the congestion. Consumption be done
about it? Of cough, of cough." Or this one: Just before the Queen drinks
the love potion, she turns to the Fool and says, "Cheerst." He replies, "And
Roebuck." But the best line in the segment must be this: As the Fool is
trying to unlock the Queen's chastity belt, he says, "I must think of something quickly because before you know it, the Renaissance will be here and
we'll all be painting." "Do Aphrodisiacs Work?" is one of the funniest skits
in the film.

• In Segment 2, "What is Sodomy?" a doctor falls in love with a sheep.
Gene Wilder plays the doctor who is visited by a shepherd who has fallen
in love with one of his flock. The doctor ends up falling for the sheep
(named Daisy) and enters into a passionate love affair which ends in disas-

ter. After losing his wife, his savings, his medical license, *and* Daisy, he is left alone and helpless, drinking Woolite straight from the bottle. This segment is only partially successful. It's played a bit too straight, and thus, the laughs are lost. One humorous line comes from the doctor's wife. While the doctor is in the middle of his affair with Daisy, his wife catches him fondling his lamb's wool sweater and tells him that lately he always smells "from lamb chops." However, "What is Sodomy?" misses more than hits.

• In Segment 3, "Why Do Some Women Have Trouble Reaching an Orgasm?" a newlywed Italian couple discovers that the wife can only have an orgasm if they have sex in public. This is a clever vignette, which is beautifully photographed in the style of Italian director Michelangelo Antonioni, yet it's slow-paced at times. The funniest moments are when Woody plays Woody: when the vibrator explodes, and when he tries to stimulate his wife "by the book." (Woody and Louise Lasser speak perfect Italian—with English subtitles—in this segment.)

• In Segment 4, "Are Transvestites Homosexuals?" a man gets caught in public wearing a dress belonging to his daughter's future mother-in-law. This segment isn't bad, but its weaknesses lie in the fact that the story-line is not fully developed, nor is it resolved properly. One of the funniest scenes is Lou Jacobi prancing around the bedroom fully dressed in a woman's outfit—with a mustache.

• In Segment 5, "What Are Sex Perverts?" we watch an episode of "What's My Perversion?" which includes a man who exposes himself on subways and a rabbi with a silk stocking and domination fetish. This segment is humorous because it is played so straight that it's believable. You feel as if you're watching an episode of a real TV show. For instance, Regis Philbin's straight-faced question is, "When you're doing your perversion, do you have any need for props? You know, whips, or leather boots?" The winner of the "act out your fantasy" award on the show is Rabbi Chaim Baumel. His fetish is silk stockings, and his fantasy is to be tied up. After he's bound, a model from the Lucy Jones Modeling Agency pretends that she's the rabbi's governess and spanks him. While this is going on, his wife sits at his feet and eats pork.

• In Segment 6, "Are the Findings of Doctors and Clinics Who Do Sexual Research and Experiments Accurate?" a gigantic breast escapes from a sex researcher's lab and terrorizes the countryside. Woody plays a writer named Victor Shakapopolis (the same name as the character he played in his 1965 film *What's New, Pussycat?*) who, with reporter Helen Lacy, visits a sexual research scientist named Dr. Bernardo. (Victor's latest book was called *Advanced Sexual Positions—How to Achieve Them Without Laughing.*)

Dr. Bernardo lives in a classic Gothic castle, complete with a hunchback assistant named Igor and innumerable chambers of horrors—only in Woody's hands the "horrors" are the most hilarious, sexually bizarre experiments you could imagine.

Dr. Bernardo had been thrown out of the Masters & Johnson clinic, with no severance pay, for building a four-hundred-foot diaphragm. His goal was "birth control for an entire nation at once!"

Dr. Bernardo has a somewhat notorious reputation in the sexual research field. He believes that the average length of a man's penis should be nineteen inches; he is the first scientist to have discovered how to make a man impotent by hiding his hat; he is the first one to explain the connection between excessive masturbation and entering politics; and he is the first one to assert that clitoral orgasm should not be only for women.

Dr. Bernardo's experiments have included removing the brain from a lesbian and putting it into the body of a man who works for the telephone company.

It now turns out that Dr. Bernardo wants to use Helen in one of his experiments and so she and Victor flee his lab. As they dash across the countryside, there's a huge explosion and a gigantic female breast (an experiment gone awry) bursts out of Dr. Bernardo's house and begins pursuing Victor and Helen across the field. Victor thinks "it looks angry. The nipple's getting erect." As Helen urges Victor to flee the approaching tit, Victor says, "Not so quickly; there are all boys in my family."

Victor and Helen report the giant breast to the Sheriff, who puts out an APB: Be on the lookout for a large female breast. Victor assists by describing the menace: "About a 4,000 with an X cup."

They decide on a plan. Victor takes charge and lures the breast into a large open field where the breast attacks him by squirting milk at him. (The breast had already killed one guy: he slipped in the cream and drowned in the milk. Victor noted, "We're up against a very clever tit. It shoots half and half." When Helen expresses concern that Victor might be in danger when he goes after the escaped breast, he says, "Don't worry. I know how to handle tits.")

Victor defends himself against the breast by holding up a crucifix and then lures it towards a camouflage net behind which is a gigantic bra. The breast falls for it and is captured.

All's well that ends well, and the vignette ends with Victor revealing to Helen that as a child he was "breast-fed from falsies." (This gag is from Woody's early standup routine "The Vodka Ad," which is on *The Third Woody Allen Album.* In that routine, however, Woody says, "I was breast-fed *through* falsies.")

The segment ends with Victor musing that this incident has taught him a lesson: "[W]hen it comes to sex, there are certain things that should be always left unknown. And with my luck, they probably will be."

• In Segment 7, "What Happens During Ejaculation?" we are witness to a hilarious, *Fantastic Voyage*-ish demonstration of the functioning of a man's body during sex.

The fantasy here is that the human body is a giant technologically sophisticated machine, and that a computerized "Brain Room" ("Mission Control") controls all bodily functions, including sight and sound, digestion, erections, and all humor and pleasure responses. The stomach is a huge chamber where white-suited workers with bulldozers process all incoming food and drink; the Pleasure Center is a moaning guy in a plastic bubble; and the reproductive center is a steam-filled room where gonad workers raise erections manually with a crane.

The plot revolves around Sidney's attempts to score with his date. He has been having erection problems and the Operator can't figure out why. Everything works fine; all bodily functions are normal, and yet the gonad room can't keep Sidney's erection up without more help from the Brain Room. The problem is solved when Security finds a priest tampering with the Cerebral Cortex. The clergyman had tied the Conscience to a chair and turned up Sidney's Guilt Reflex.

Woody plays a reluctant sperm (complete with tail and horn-rimmed glasses) who is petrified at the idea of being shot out into who knows what. He's afraid of the pill, and he's also heard about guys who slammed into a hard wall of rubber. He's also concerned that Sidney's tryst might be a homosexual encounter, and even wonders aloud, "What if he's masturbating? I'm liable to wind up on the ceiling!"

When Sidney's date reveals that she's a graduate of New York University, the Operator exclaims joyfully, "We're gonna make it!"

After the rebel religious element is discovered, intercourse proceeds apace, and Woody and his fellow sperm (including a black sperm who keeps asking, "What am I doing here?) prepare to do the job they trained for in Sperm Training School.

As the erection workers keep winding the crane that keeps Sidney's erection up, they sing "Mine eyes have seen the glory of the coming of the Lord."

Sidney reaches his orgasm, and the sperm run down and leap out a long tunnel. As Woody reaches the end of the tunnel, he looks around before he leaps and remarks, "Well, at least he's Jewish."

• In the eliminated segment, "What Makes a Man a Homosexual?" two spiders make love after which the female eats the male.

This unreleased vignette had Woody Allen playing a spider named Sheldon Wexler who is made love to, and then eaten, by a female spider named Lisa, played by Louise Lasser. (Seventeen years later Woody used "Sheldon" and "Lisa" as the names of the two main characters in *Oedipus Wrecks*.)

Sheldon tries to seduce Lisa (who is a black widow) with a mating dance that Lisa says looked as if he were having a convulsion. The tables turn on Sheldon, though, when Lisa begins to come on to him. He responds, and when their lovemaking is over, she informs him that she is now going to devour him. As he tries to escape, but can't, the scene pulls back to a laboratory where Woody is now a professor who has been watching the goings-on of the spiders through a microscope.

His secretary—Louise Lasser—enters and asks if she can leave; she and her husband have theater tickets. Woody responds in a stereotypical homosexual lisp, and the point of the piece seems to be that men become homosexuals because they're afraid of women.

Two years after the piece was filmed, Woody told Eric Lax:

> It never had an ending and it never went anyplace. The thing that was wrong with it in the first five seconds that I thought of it remained wrong right through. You think you'd be able to get a three-minute sequence out of that. It was one of the most hateful experiences of my life. If I could have gotten any kind of ending I would have left it in.

Look for . . .

• Woody's *Play It Again, Sam* reference. In Segment 1, the ghost of the Fool's father appears by calling him "Felix." Nowhere else in this segment is the Fool's name given, and it is obviously a nod to Woody's character, Allan Felix, in *Sam*.

• Woody's Armenian reference. In Segment 2, Stavros Milos, Daisy's owner, is Armenian. Woody will use Armenians for comic effect again three years later in *Love and Death*. In that film, Boris Grushenko contemplates suicide by inhaling next to an Armenian.

• Woody's missing black horn-rims. In Segment 3, Woody wears stylish gold eyeglasses or wraparound sunglasses—one of the few times he's ever been seen without his trademark black frames.

• Another park scene. In Segment 4, the final pastoral scene where Victor and Helen walk in silhouette reminds us of the park scene in *Take the Money and Run.*

• Woody's baseball reference. In Segment 5, the Operator tells the memory to think of baseball players to prevent premature launching (ejaculation). (On *The Third Woody Allen Album*, Woody does a standup routine called "Second Marriage," in which he talks about thinking of baseball players to prevent premature ejaculation.)

A Few Words from Woody . . .

Just before *Sex* opened, Woody Allen told Mel Gussow, "I don't think everybody conceives of sex the way I do—surrealistic and rich with humor . . . I've treated it as if I were making a movie about cattle ranching."

Woody's *Playboy* Article
"Everything You Always Wanted to Know About Sex . . .
You'll Find in My New Movie—Plus a Couple of Things
You Never Bargained For"

The September 1972 issue of *Playboy* magazine featured a rare nonfiction appearance by Woody Allen. The piece was accompanied by eight photographs from the film.

The article began:

> What you'll find on these pages are some stills from my new movie, *Everything You Always Wanted to Know About Sex . . . But Were Afraid to Ask.* I had a choice of filming this or the Old Testament and chose the former because it made more sense.

Woody continues:

> The picture expresses my feelings about sex: that it is good in moderation and should be confined to one's lifetime. I have tried to remain faithful to the book, which is more than I did with my wife, and have attempted to delineate for all time the various perversions, along with tips on what to wear.

Woody wrote the captions for the eight stills that accompanied the article, and here is a look at what photos ran, and what Woody had to say about them:

- 1. Title page photo (from Segment 6): The giant breast squirting milk at a crucifix-wielding Victor Shakapopolis.
- 2. Pages 116–17 (from Segment 6): A two-page spread of Victor standing in front of the giant breast. Woody wrote, "We obtained the tit from a famous Hollywood actress who shall remain anonymous; she was between movies and willing to rent us one."
- 3. Page 117, top left (from Segment 7): Woody as a sperm.
- 4. Page 117, top right (from Segment 7): A shot of all the sperm seated on benches along the penis walls. Woody wrote, "A sperm's life . . . isn't bad; of course, it depends a great deal on who your landlord is balling."
- 5. Page 118, top (from Segment 3): Fabrizio (Woody) standing next to a bed holding a vibrator while his wife looks on apprehensively. Woody wrote, "To prove how I can really hold a grudge, the girl playing the part [of my wife] is my ex-wife, Louise Lasser, who was not frigid when we were married and could come at the drop of a hat—the big problem was that I rebelled against wearing a hat to bed, although I didn't mind earmuffs."
- 6. Page 118, center (from Segment 2): Dr. Doug Ross (Gene Wilder) in bed with Daisy the Sheep (Daisy the Sheep). Woody wrote, "Let me make it perfectly clear that I abhor sodomy as much as the next man; however, I would enjoy being beaten with live eels if the girl doing it were Presbyterian."

• 7. Page 118, bottom (from Segment 4): Sam Waterman (Lou Jacobi) lying on a bed in bra and underwear. Woody wrote, "Please understand that [Lou] is not a fag but a transvestite; the latter requires a college degree."

• 8. Page 119 (from the eliminated segment): Two spiders making love. Woody wrote, "To the right are two spiders having intercourse. This is not as easy as it sounds and in order to find the number of possible positions, one must take the square root of her eight legs and my eight and multiply them by the number of positions in the *Kama Sutra*. This gives you some idea of how much fun these little creatures have and why they always look so tired." (Interestingly, as of the time this article was prepared (March or April of 1972?), Woody still planned on using the ultimately eliminated segment, "What Makes a Man a Homosexual?")

9.

Sleeper

(United Artists, 1973); Running Time: 88 minutes; Rating: PG; Color.

I'm always joking. It's a defense mechanism.
Miles Monroe in *Sleeper*

In *Sleeper,* a health-food restaurant owner cryogenically frozen in 1973 during routine surgery is defrosted two hundred years later and becomes part of a future underground revolutionary movement.

Sleeper—a *very* amusing film that has held up remarkably well over the past two decades—is a hilarious stew made from a recipe that includes slapstick, one-liners, romance, science fiction, social satire, and a quintessential Woody Allen persona. It is wonderful entertainment for everyone: the people who don't get all the references (verbal and visual) can sit back and enjoy the physical humor. The viewers who pick up on all the little asides and references Woody and company make will easily find a deeper, more satirical humor running throughout the film.

Shooting for *Sleeper* began on April 30, 1973, with a $2 million budget, and parts of the film were shot on the Selznick set where *Gone With the Wind* was made.

The slapstick in *Sleeper* includes Miles eating a rubber glove upon being defrosted; Miles slapping a dish of blue food in a guard's face; Miles slipping on a giant banana peel (you *know* it's coming, but you laugh anyway); Miles shaving in a mirror that shows someone else; Miles in a HydroVac suit rocketing across a pond with Luna on his back; Miles spinning around in a tree after his propeller-driven flying pack gets stuck in a branch; and Miles dangling from a government building wrapped in recording tape after Luna hits the fast-forward button.

There are some wonderful verbal gags in *Sleeper.* For instance, Miles says that his brain is his "second favorite organ." And his commentary on "ancient twentieth-century artifacts" is hilarious: Joseph Stalin (a Communist he was "not too crazy about"); Bela Lugosi (he identified him as the mayor of New York City); Charles de Gaulle (a "fantastic French chef"); F. Scott Fitzgerald (a romantic writer who was very big with "college girls, English majors, and nymphomaniacs"); Chiang Kai-shek (he was "not too crazy" about him either); Billy Graham ("he knew God personally"); girls burning a brassiere (notice that it's a "very small fire"); Norman Mailer (a very great writer who "donated his ego to the Harvard Medical School"); and a *Playboy* centerfold (he told the doctor that these girls didn't actually exist—they were rubberized and you had to blow them up. Miles put the picture in his pocket). Miles was also shown Chattering Teeth (he tried to explain the joke—they didn't get it); a Richard Nixon videotape (he told the doctors that Nixon was an American president and that when he left the White House the Secret Service counted the silverware); and a videotape of Howard Cosell (the doctors hypothesized that citizens guilty of a crime were forced to sit and watch Cosell. Miles said yes, that was correct). Miles also tells the doctors that he wasn't the heroic type: he was once beaten up by Quakers.

Miles hooks up with Luna, a poet influenced by Rod McKuen. Luna went to the university and there majored in "Cosmetic Sexual Technique and Poetry." (She had a Ph.D. in Oral Sex. Miles told her he was an English major with a minor in Foreplay.)

Food—a crucial thematic element in all of Woody's films—plays a big role in one of the funniest scenes Woody Allen has ever written and/or directed. It seems that in the future, farmers have perfected agricultural technology, thereby allowing them to breed giant animals and grow giant food. When Miles first stumbles upon a giant fruit and vegetable farm, he thinks, "I'd hate to see what they use for fertilizer." And in a perfect slapstick moment, after Miles peels a ten-foot-long banana, he—of course—slips on the banana peel. While trying to escape with the stolen food, he spots a guy walking a ten-foot-tall chicken. His reaction? "That's a big chicken."

After seeing the chicken, Miles asks Luna if 2173 has any weird futuristic animals—"like something with the body of a crab and the head of a social worker."

Miles and Luna also discuss God: Miles describes himself as a "teleological existential atheist." He believes there is an intelligence to the universe, "with the exception of certain parts of New Jersey."

Sleeper ends with Woody's famous "sex and death" line: Miles and

Luna end up together and Miles tells Luna that he doesn't believe in science, that it's "an intellectual dead end." When asked what he does believe in, Miles replies, "Sex and death—two things that come once in my life, but at least after death, you're not nauseous."

Look for . . .

• The work of costume designer Joel Schumacher, who went on to direct *Flatliners, The Lost Boys,* and *St. Elmo's Fire.*

• The music. Miles played clarinet with a band called The Ragtime Rascals, and the music for *Sleeper* was performed by Woody Allen, with the Preservation Hall Jazz Band and the New Orleans Funeral Ragtime Orchestra.

• Miles's flying pack. It had a propeller on top, similar to the flying bicycle in *A Midsummer Night's Sex Comedy.*

• Woody's hair length. Most of the time his hair is *really* long in this film, but the length changes noticeably throughout the film.

• Woody's "first wife" reference. When Luna and Erno make Miles relive traumatic events of his childhood, one of the incidents they reenact is a Sunday dinner at his parent's home on K Avenue in Brooklyn during which Miles tells his parents that Arlene and he are getting a divorce. ("She thinks I'm a pervert because I drank our waterbed.") Woody's first wife's name was "Harlene" and he once lived on K Avenue in Brooklyn.

The Lost Scenes . . .

• In his 1979 book *Loser Take All,* Maurice Yacowar notes, "In the French print [of *Sleeper*], *Woody et Les Robots,* there is an intervening scene that I have not noticed in any English print. At dinner with Luna, Miles eats quickly, in time to the music. Then he does his Suave Lover act, which concludes with him eating the candle and napkin. He then does several magic tricks that charm Luna out of her earlier dislike for him."

• In his 1975 book on Woody Allen, *On Being Funny,* Eric Lax details a dream sequence that was cut from *Sleeper.* The scene was shot in the Mojave Desert and since it was part of Woody's "fantastic vision" for *Sleeper,* it is worth a look. In the script, two doctors involved in Miles Monroe's care hook him up to a machine that allows them to see what Miles is dreaming. From the script:

> They are standing over Miles who is in a restive sleep, his head hooked into a device that produces his dream on a large wall screen. He tosses and turns and moans and finally, after some abstractions, we see forms corresponding to his moaning. Gradually a dream appears. It is an enormous chess board and Miles is a white pawn.
> White is obviously losing, and as he stands erect on his square, he is surrounded by incredibly powerful and hostile black pieces, knights on horse-

*back, bishops hostilely brandishing heavy crucifixes like policemen's billies
ready to smash his head in. On the square next to Miles is another feeble white
pawn. Suddenly the black knight moves, leaping from his position to the
square occupied by the pawn next to Miles. The knight falls upon the pawn
and destroys him brutally with something like a mace and chain and then
runs him through with a long sword until he's dead. Miles is quaking in his
boots, naturally unable to move and at the mercy of the man playing the
game, whom we don't see of course because he'd be too enormous in scale.*

Knight (*now looking viciously down right next to Miles*) You're next . . .
Black Bishop (*several squares away, tapping a crucifix menacingly*) Leave
him to me, I'll take care of him.
Miles It's a nice board, isn't it?
Man's Voice (*playing*) I think my best move is to sacrifice that second
pawn.
Miles I'm fine here. Hey . . . that's me. I'm happy right where I am.
Man's Voice If I move my pawn the knight'll take him but I'll get his
rook. I'll sacrifice a stupid pawn and win a rook.
Miles No . . .

*Suddenly he is moved forward into the midst of a knight, bishop, and
queen. He is face to face with a menacing black pawn.*
Ad-lib fear business and chatter . . .

Miles (*continuing*) Hey, fellas . . . it's only a game. We'll all be together
later in the box.
Knight I'm going to cut you in two . . .
Opponent's Voice Look where he moved that pawn . . . Should I take
him with my bishop or knight? . . . Let's see . . . On the other hand, why
does he want me to take it? . . . Maybe I should wait a move . . . No, what
the hell, I'll take the pawn . . .

*The knight charges for the pawn. Miles, breaking the laws of chess, starts
running in the awkward way a chess piece might. (Miles cops a feel on the
queen before running away.) The knight chases Miles off into the distance,
then into a corridor. Suddenly Miles runs through a doorway and emerges on
the other side in white tie and tails on stage at the opera house. Miles acknowledges applause, bows, and gestures to stage right where the second member of
his musical group comes out, a man in a cello suit, giving the appearance of a
cello with legs. The cello walks out on stage and squats, ready to play himself.*
*Another man, the next member, enters in white tie and tails, but instead
of a head coming out of his collar is an enormous light bulb. Miles pulls a
chain hanging from the man's arm and the bulb goes on.*
*Miles lifts his violin and bows majestically, but just before he plays the
bow suddenly sags limp like a noodle. He is terribly embarrassed by this
obviously sexual symbolism and the audience laughs but he cannot make the
bow erect enough to play.*

10.
Love and Death

(United Artists, June 11, 1975); Running Time: 85 minutes;
Rating: PG; Color.

When Woody Allen makes a movie, it's a very different ball game from
the usual procedure where script approval by the studio is an absolute
must for any other filmmaker. Allen's producers rarely know
anything about the films they're spending several million
dollars on. Even the actors don't get to read the whole
script. Each person gets the pages in which he has lines,
but is not permitted to see the rest of the screenplay.
It's a unique method but it works as we'll see when
Woody Allen and Diane Keaton star
in the PG-rated *Love and Death.*
Sally Kellerman's introduction to a Woody Allen doubleheader
(*Love and Death* and *Manhattan*) on the Movie Channel

Love and Death is an unqualified success.

The film is about Boris Dmitrivich Grushenko, a Russian pacifist, who
ends up being executed for assassinating Napoleon's double.

The story is told by Boris on the eve of his execution. Boris didn't kill
the man, but was captured with a gun in his hand standing over the dead
body.

The writing is first-rate, the jokes are funny and intelligent, and
Woody and company's performances are clearly the work of people having
a good time.

The film opens with Boris's voice-over expressing Woody Allen's teleological existential atheistic philosophy: "How I got into this predicament, I'll never know. Absolutely incredible. To be executed for a crime I
never committed. Of course, isn't all mankind in the same boat? Isn't all
mankind ultimately executed for a crime it never committed? The difference is that all men go eventually, but I go six o'clock tomorrow morning. I was supposed to go at five o'clock but I have got a smart lawyer. Got
leniency."

Love and Death contains Woody's famous "enormous restaurant" theory. Boris and his cousin Sonia discuss nature:

Sonia I definitely think that this is the best of all possible worlds.
Boris It's certainly the most expensive.
Sonia Isn't nature incredible?
Boris To me nature is spiders and bugs and big fish eating little fish and
plants eating plants and animals eating . . . it's like an enormous restau-
rant. That's the way I see it.

There are religious jokes aplenty in *Love and Death*. Boris, who didn't believe there was a God, said he would accept the following miracles as proof of a Deity: a burning bush, the seas parting, or seeing his Uncle Sasha pick up a check.

When Boris expresses his doubt about the existence of God to Sonia, the following exchange takes place, included here for its shameless absurdity: The dialogue is so existentially precise and yet so patently incongruous that the conversation enters the realm of the fantastic (while still concluding with a very funny one-liner from Woody):

Sonia Boris, let me show you how absurd your position is. All right, let's say that there is no God and each man is free to do exactly as he chooses. Well, what prevents you from murdering somebody?
Boris Murder's immoral.
Sonia Immorality is subjective.
Boris Yes, but subjectivity is objective.
Sonia Not in any rational scheme of perception.
Boris Perception is irrational. It implies imminence.
Sonia But judgement of any system or *a priori* relation of phenomena exists in any rational or metaphysical or at least epistemological contradiction to an abstract and empirical concept such as being, or to be, or to occur in the thing itself, or of the thing itself.
Boris I've said that many times.

After Boris is sentenced to death, Sonia agrees to marry him out of pity. She tells him that since it's his last night on earth, she'll make love to him. Boris responds, "Nice idea. I'll bring the soy sauce." The film then cut to them in bed. Boris surfaces from beneath the covers, puts on oven mitts and dives back under.

Discussing marriage, Boris says he has some eccentricities. He "won't eat any food that begins with the letter 'F'—like chicken."

After he's dead, Boris addresses the audience. He tells us there are worse things than death: "If you've ever spent the night with an insurance salesman you know what I mean."

The film ends with Boris and death dancing away as Prokofiev's music plays on the soundtrack.

Look for . . .

• Woody's "old Gregor/young Gregor" gaffe. As part of Boris's introductory narration, he tells us about people from his town. He says, "There was old Gregor and his son young Gregor. Oddly enough, young Gregor's son was older than old Gregor." Doesn't he mean (for the purposes of the joke) that *young* Gregor was older than *old* Gregor? Later in the film, there seems to be another gaffe: During his final speech to the audience, Boris says, "If [the world] were logical, how would Old Nehamkin be younger than young Nehamkin?" This would seem to be a reference to the young Gregor/old Gregor joke earlier on, but here he says "Nehamkin" instead.

• Boris's "review" of the military "Hygiene" play. "It was weak. I was never interested, although the part of the doctor was played with gusto and verve and the girl had a delightful cameo role. A puckish satire of contemporary mores, a droll spoof aimed more at the heart than the head."

• Another of Woody's standup comedy references. Boris tells the countess's lover, "Nice seeing you, Quasimodo." In one of Woody's early standup routines, he talks about his divorce from his first wife. One of the lines was, "I laid it right on the line with her. I came right to the point. I said, 'Quasimodo, I want a divorce.' "

• Woody's use of his masturbation motif. After the Countess tells Boris that he was the greatest lover she ever had, he says, "I practice a lot when I'm alone." (See the sections on *Stardust Memories, Zelig,* and *Hannah and Her Sisters* for other uses of this "motif.")

• An essay reference. During their "pre-assassination attempt" rendezvous, Napoleon toasts Sonia with "To your eyes." She counters with "To the bridge of your nose." In Woody's 1970 *Getting Even* essay, "A Look at Organized Crime," we learn that "[Irish Larry] Doyle was killed when the Squillante Construction Company decided to erect their new offices on the bridge of his nose."

• Woody's nod to Ingmar Bergman. One of the last scenes in the film is of Diane Keaton and Jessica Harper's faces seen at right angles to each other, as in a similar scene from Bergman's *Persona.*

A Few Words from Woody . . .

• In a 1978 interview with Robert Benayoun, Woody Allen said, "(*Love and Death*) is my favorite film. Even *Annie Hall,* which gave me real success . . . isn't as dear to me." (He later added *The Purple Rose of Cairo* to his list of his personal favorite films, but in 1978, three years after *Love and Death* was released, it was his favorite of the eleven films he had written or directed up to that point.)

• In Eric Lax's *Woody Allen: A Biography,* Woody is quoted as saying that *Love and Death* was "my funniest picture to that time, but its approach to the audience is on a kidding-around level."

11.
The Front
(Columbia Pictures, 1976); Running Time: 94 minutes; Rating: R; Color.

These are the tranquillized Fifties . . .
Robert Lowell, from "Memories of West Street and Lepke"

The water is full of sharks.
Hecky Brown

In the 1950s a cashier and part-time bookie named Howard Prince puts his names on scripts written by writer friends who have been blacklisted.

The Front may be the most important movie Woody Allen has made.

One comes away from this brilliant film angry. Angry and outraged that the abhorrent and disgraceful scurrility known as "blacklisting" actually took place in a country that prides itself on freedom of speech, personal liberties, and the rights of the individual.

The Front is Walter Bernstein's and Martin Ritt's actual story. They were among the cadre of entertainment professionals in the fifties who were accused of being either Communist sympathizers or outright Reds, and were thus put on the blacklist: a corrupt and malevolent, never-acknowledged underground of innuendo and discrimination that put them out of work.

Many people who were in their teens and twenties in the fifties look back to those years as the "good old days." A valid response to that kind of thinking might be: What was so great about a time when so many peoples' lives were ruined because of whispered accusations and Big Brother–like governmental subterfuge and spying?

The Front should be must-viewing in every high school in the land. The film is important for one critical reason: It lays bare a malignant time in our history that should embarrass every American. It tells the story of a time when America forgot what it meant.

The Front begins with Frank Sinatra singing "Young at Heart" and a montage of scenes from the 1950s, including the thirty-eighth parallel in Korea; an American family excitedly entering their cozy little bomb shelter; Marilyn Monroe (looking awfully like Madonna); Jake LaMotta (looking awfully like Robert De Niro); and Julius and Ethel Rosenberg.

The story revolves around Howard's fronting of his blacklisted friends' "Grand Central" TV scripts (and his romantic involvement with one of the show's producers) and the show's star Hecky Brown's problems with the Freedom Information Board. Hecky, you see, once marched in a May Day

Parade. Why? Because he "wanted to get laid." He "had the hots for a Communist girl with a big ass."

His story (which happens to be true) doesn't sway the Fascist-like Freedom Information agent. Hecky is fired, and then is given a choice: spy on Howard Prince and find out why he's hanging around blacklisted writers, or remain on the blacklist, unable to work.

Hecky chooses to spy. And when Howard is called before the House Committee on Un-American Activities, Hecky is so distraught over his betrayal of Howard, he commits suicide by jumping out a window. (In *Crimes and Misdemeanors,* Professor Louis Levy also commits suicide and leaves a note that says, "I've gone out the window.")

Hennessey, the Freedom Information guy, is written as an extremely sleazy character, and rightly so. Walter Bernstein and Martin Ritt paint a vivid picture of the "Communist conspiracy" paranoia of that period. At one point, Hennessey says, "We're in a war against a ruthless and tricky enemy . . . who will stop at nothing to destroy our way of life. To be a spy on the side of freedom is an honor." He says his job is to advise on "Americanism."

After Hecky's death, Howard is forced to testify before an Un-American Activities subcommittee. This is a transcript of the questioning and his testimony:

> **Committee Counselor**   Just a few questions, Mr. Prince. We know you're a busy man. Mr. Prince, do you happen to know an Alfred Miller?
> **Howard**   Who?
> **Committee Counselor**   Alfred Miller.
> **Howard**   Why?
> **Committee Counselor**   If you'd just tell the committee . . .
> **Howard**   I can't know why?
> **Committee Chairman**   Mr. Prince, you don't have to worry. Anyone that comes here and tells the truth has got nothing to worry about.
> **Howard**   Which Alfred Miller?
> **Committee Counselor**   Do you know Alfred Miller, the writer?
> **Howard**   When you say know . . . I mean . . . what do you . . . can you ever really know a person? I think . . . I grew up with an Alfred Miller, but . . . do I know him? Would you say . . . do I know him . . . can you know . . . in a biblical sense . . . know him? Am I right?
> **Committee Counselor**   Would that be the same Alfred Miller you met with several times in Hammer's Dairy Restaurant?
> **Howard**   Who says I did?
> **Committee Counselor**   Is it or is it not true?
> **Howard**   No, I asked you first.
> **Committee Counselor**   Is it true?
> **Howard**   I don't understand . . . is anybody accusing me of anything?
> **Committee Counselor**   If you would answer the question.
> **Howard**   Well, which question? You asked one question and then I answer that question and then you . . .

Committee Counselor   Do you know Alfred Miller?

Howard   You already asked that question.

Committee Counselor   Do you know Alfred Miller?

Howard   Are you guys aware that every week busloads of Communists are coming in over the border? I mean, is anybody doing anything about that?

Committee Counselor   We are not concerned at this time with anything other than the communist conspiracy in the entertainment world.

Howard   But how come? I mean, why aren't we doing something about it? I mean, why isn't everybody armed? Everyone should learn how to use a gun, I think. I think it's a big mistake that anyone goes to military school is only . . . you send them there when they're bad.

Committee Chairman   Mr. Prince, this committee is just as concerned about the threat of communism as you are.

Committee Counselor   Since your memory is unclear about Alfred Miller, do you know any of these other people? William Phelps? Herbert Delaney? Florence Barrett? Herschel Brownstein—also known as Hecky Brown?

Howard   (Quietly) He's dead.

Committee Counselor   Did you know him?

Committee Chairman   Mr. Prince. Now, you came here to cooperate, did you not?

Committee Counselor   Mr. Prince, let me ask you another question. Do you know Patrick Callahan?

Howard   Who?

Committee Counselor   The bartender at the Friendly Tavern where I believe you once worked as a night cashier.

Howard   I did?

Committee Counselor   Do you know Daniel LaGattuta?

Howard   Doesn't he sell fruit?

Committee Counselor   You placed bets for Mr. Callahan and Mr. LaGattuta, did you not?

Howard   In a strictly friendly way.

Committee Chairman   I remind you that placing bets is a crime.

> (*Howard's attorney speaks with the chairman. They'll make a deal—but they want names from Howard*)

Committee Counselor   Mr. Prince, I ask you for the record. Did you know Herschel Brownstein? Also known as Hecky Brown? Did you know this man as either Brown or Brownstein?

Committee Chairman   Either name will do, Mr. Prince.

Committee Counselor   Brown or Brownstein?

Committee Chairman   Just the name.

Committee Counselor   Are you refusing to answer?

Howard   (Rising from the table and walking toward the door) Fellas, I don't recognize the right of this committee to ask me these kind of questions. (He reaches the door) And, furthermore, you can all go fuck yourselves.

The film ends with Howard kissing Florence and being taken away to jail for contempt.

In *The Front,* Woody Allen proves that he can bring to life characters not of his own creation, and that he can bring them to life believably and realistically. He would wait fifteen years before tackling his next non-Woody role, that of Nick Fifer, in Paul Mazursky's *Scenes from a Mall.*

Look for . . .

• Danny Aiello in his first professional collaboration with Woody Allen. Danny would go on to play Monk in *The Purple Rose of Cairo;* Rocco in *Radio Days;* and Max Pollack in Woody's Broadway play *The Floating Light Bulb.* In *The Front* Danny plays a fruit-stand owner to whom Howard owes gambling winnings.

• The final credits, in which many of the cast and crew—including director Martin Ritt, writer Walter Bernstein, and star Zero Mostel—reveal that they were themselves blacklisted in the fifties.

• The occasional Woody Allen one-liner, including his remark to Andrea Marcovicci's character, Florence, that in his family "the biggest sin was to buy retail," and that swimming is not a sport, "swimming is something you do so you shouldn't drown."

A Few Words from Woody . . .

In a 1976 *Rolling Stone* interview with Ken Kelley just before *The Front* came out, Woody said, "I remember hearing about blacklisting when I was in public school, not really understanding the implications of it all. But in retrospect, what I know now historically, it was a horrible time. The script expresses me politically, even though I didn't write it. . . . It was fun to try and act in something serious."

12.
Annie Hall

(United Artists, April 21, 1977); Running Time: 93 minutes;
Rating: PG; Color.

Woody's had a very positive influence on her, very much like *Annie Hall.*
Diane Keaton's mother, Dorothy Hall

It's eighty-five percent true—even to Dorothy and my mother!
Diane Keaton's father, Jack Hall

You know, I have a hyperactive imagination. My mind tends to jump around a little, and I have some trouble between fantasy and reality.
Alvy Singer in *Annie Hall*

Annie Hall is the story of the love affair between a comic and a singer in New York City in the late seventies, and it is the film that most critics feel is a quintessential Woody Allen movie. It is the perfect blend of comedy, nostalgia, sentimentality, psychosexual angst, brilliant dialogue, and characterization.

It was also a groundbreaking film. Woody consciously and determinedly used disparate filmmaking techniques (animation, breaking the fourth wall, stepping into flashbacks, subtitles, and absurdism) in a contemporary romantic comedy set in New York City. He had skimmed the surface of these techniques with his ghostly Bogart in *Play It Again, Sam,* and an occasional remark to the camera in *Love and Death,* but *Annie Hall* marked the first time he went after a particular cinematic style with a vengeance.

Annie Hall won four Academy Awards: Best Picture, Best Actress (Diane Keaton), Best Director (Woody Allen), and Best Screenplay Written Directly for the Screen (Woody Allen and Marshall Brickman).

It's fairly easy to understand the uproar over *Annie Hall.* There really had never been anything like it to date. In 1977 *Annie Hall* opened in theaters as a film which pulled the rug out from under us with the very first scene. The opening credits end and suddenly there's Woody Allen, speaking directly into the camera. Is he speaking to the audience as Woody? Is this part of the film? Is he supposed to be a character speaking to the audience? Let's face it, we were instantly and irrevocably hooked. This was different.

And it got only better. Virtually every line in *Annie Hall* is quotable. And Woody used the aforementioned techniques and devices to take the traditional narrative form of the contemporary romantic comedy and stand it on its head.

Annie Hall did not do enormous box office, but it was definitely an "also-ran." (The biggest-grossing film of that year was *Star Wars,* with a current box-office total of $322 million.)

[Note: The final version of *Annie Hall* that we have all come to know and love bears little resemblance to the original draft. Many, many scenes, sketches, flashbacks, and lines of dialogue were cut in the editing room. For complete details on these "lost scenes," see the article "*Annie Hall:* It Wasn't the Film He Set Out to Make" in editor Ralph Rosenblum's 1979 book, *When the Shooting Stops . . . the Cutting Begins.* Try your library or used-book dealers.]

Annie Hall opens with the previously mentioned shot of Woody, in character as Alvy Singer, talking to the audience. His now-classic monologue ran thus:

> There's an old joke. Two elderly women are at a Catskills mountain resort, and one of 'em says, "Boy, the food at this place is really terrible." The other one says, "Yeah, I know. And such small portions."

Well, that's essentially how I feel about life. Full of loneliness and misery and suffering and unhappiness, and it's all over much too quickly.

The other important joke for me is one that's usually attributed to Groucho Marx, but I think it appears originally in Freud's *Wit and Its Relation to the Unconscious.* And it goes like this (I'm paraphrasing): "I would never want to belong to any club that would have someone like me for a member." That's the key joke of my adult life when it comes to women.

You know, lately the strangest things have been going through my mind, 'cause I turned forty, and I guess I'm going through a life crisis or something, I don't know. And I'm not worried about aging. I'm not one of those characters, you know. Although I'm balding slightly on top, that's about the worst you can say about me. I think I'm gonna get better as I get older, you know? I think I'm gonna be the balding, virile type, you know, as opposed to, say, the distinguished gray, for instance, you know? 'Less I'm neither of those two. Unless I'm one of those guys with saliva dribbling out of his mouth who wanders into a cafeteria with a shopping bag screaming about socialism.

Annie and I broke up and I still can't get my mind around that. You know, I keep sifting the pieces of the relationship through my mind and examining my life and trying to figure out where did the screw-up come, you know, and a year ago, we were in love, you know. And it's funny, I'm not a morose type. I'm not a depressive character. You know, I was a reasonably happy kid, I guess. I was brought up in Brooklyn during World War II.

During several flashbacks, we meet Alvy's two wives, Allison Portchnik, (". . . New York, Jewish, Left-Wing, Liberal, Intellectual, Central Park West, Brandeis University, the Socialist summer camps, and the father with the Ben Shahn drawings . . ."), and Robin, a liberal intellectual who can't (or won't) make love to Alvy. (Alvy tries seducing Robin at a party loaded with people from the *New Yorker* magazine. "All those Ph.D.s are in there . . . discussing modes of alienation and we'll be in here quietly humping.") (Woody, of course, wrote for the *New Yorker.*)

Alvy performs standup comedy at a pro–Adlai Stevenson rally, and jokes: "I, interestingly, had dated a woman in the Eisenhower Administration, briefly, and it was ironic to me 'cause, I was trying to do to her what Eisenhower has been doing to the country for the last eight years."

During their marriage, Robin and Alvy are at odds because Robin's analyst wants her to live in the country but Alvy wants nothing to do with rural surroundings. Alvy tells her:

> The country makes me nervous. You got crickets, and it's quiet; there's no place to walk after dinner, and there's the screens with the dead moths behind them, and you got the Manson family possibly; you got Dick and Perry . . .

It's fascinating (and yet another example of Woody's imagistic genius) what he was able to do with that "I hate the country" speech. Notice how his list of negative elements about the country begins with innocuous things like crickets and no place to walk and sets you up to shrug this off as just another overreaction by this archetypal Woody character. After all, who gets nervous about crickets except total paranoids? But then the list grows darker as he mentions screens with "dead moths" behind them, and then suddenly we're into some macabre and horrible place where we're isolated and stranded and liable to be victims of the Manson family and the *In Cold Blood* killers. Very funny, very well written, and very accurate in showing just how paranoid obsessive-compulsives think. (See also the *Rolling Stone* interview with Woody in Chapter 2 for Woody's thoughts about the time he spends at Mia Farrow's country place in Connecticut.)

When we first meet Annie, she is wearing baggy pants, a man's shirt, a necktie, a vest, and a bowler hat. In a June 30, 1977, *Rolling Stone* interview with Ben Fong-Torres, Diane Keaton admitted that this outfit came out of her own closet. "Mainly, I like that kind of clothing," she said.

After a relationship that ends when Annie moves to California and refuses Alvy's proposal of marriage, Alvy writes a play about their time together, only this time the ending is different: they get back together.

After a time, Alvy sees Annie again, and he reminisces to us in this final speech from the film:

> [I]t was great seeing Annie again . . . I realized what a terrific person she was and how much fun it was just knowing her and I thought of that old joke, you know, this guy goes to a psychiatrist and says, "Doc, my brother's crazy. He thinks he's a chicken." And the doctor says, "Well, why don't you turn him in?" And the guys says, "I would, but I need the eggs."
>
> Well, I guess that's pretty much how I feel about relationships. You know, they're totally irrational and crazy and absurd . . . but I guess we keep goin' through it because, most of us need the eggs.

Look for . . .

• Alvy's childhood home underneath a roller coaster. This was a real house that burned down on Wednesday, May 15, 1991. The house was situated under the old Coney Island Thunderbolt roller coaster.

• Woody's birthday. As the camera pans past three of Alvy's childhood teachers, we see things written on the blackboard behind them. The first teacher the camera passes has "Tuesday—Dec. 1—" written on the board behind her. Woody Allen was born on Sunday, December 1, 1935.

• Alvy's appearance on Dick Cavett's talk show. This is actual footage of Woody Allen on TV. He does the following joke, which was from his standup routine, "The Army," off his first album, *Woody Allen*:

> They did not take me in the army. Interestingly enough, I was four-P. [beat] In the event of war, I'm a hostage.

(On *Woody Allen,* the lines were, "I was not in the regular army. I was classified four-P by the draft board. In the event of war, I'm a hostage.")

• The real Marshall McLuhan. At the New Yorker theater, Alvy and Annie are in front of a guy who is pompously lecturing his date on the work of Marshall McLuhan and the Italian director Federico Fellini. Alvy gets more and more agitated by the guy's overbearing commentary and then, in a brilliantly surrealistic moment, Alvy pulls McLuhan out from behind a poster, and McLuhan castigates the guy, telling him he knows nothing about his work. The scene ends with Alvy again speaking to the audience, saying, "Boy, if life were only like this!"

• The unplanned laughter of Woody Allen and Diane Keaton in the famous "lobster scene"—actually the first scene shot for the film. In a discussion of extraneous laughter in the play *Play It Again, Sam,* Eric Lax (in *Woody Allen: A Biography*) talks about this scene from *Annie Hall*:

> An example of this [unplanned, unscripted laughter] on film is the scene in *Annie Hall* where Alvie [*sic*] and Annie, both squeamish in the face of crawling crustaceans, attempt to prepare a lobster dinner at a beach house. It was the first scene shot for the movie and neither Woody nor Diane was acting. Their laughter was completely spontaneous, and it gives the scene a vitality that cannot be planned.

The entire scene takes place in the kitchen, and (except for being broadly sketched out) seems to be unscripted, and ad-libbed. Being aware of Woody's personal aversion to all things creeping and crawling, a viewer easily believes the genuine fear (and resultant humor) from his encounters with the lobsters. A particularly funny line in the scene comes when Woody realizes there's a lobster behind the refrigerator and says, "Maybe if I put a little dish of butter sauce here with a nutcracker, it will run out the other side?"

• The foreskin reference. There seem to be two foreskin references in Woody's work and reported remarks. The first is in *Annie Hall.* In a scene set in the Wall Street Tennis Club locker room, Alvy whines to Rob about his Jewish paranoia, and remarks, "[T]he failure of the country to get behind New York City is anti-Semitism. . . . I'm not discussing politics or economics. This is foreskin." The second reference is a remark by Woody quoted in Eric Lax's *Woody Allen: A Biography:* "While a scene for *Oedipus Wrecks* was being readied in the apartment of the quintessential Jewish mother being visited by her son and his quintessential Wasp girlfriend, . . . Woody turned to [costume designer Jeff Kurland and said], 'Is there something we can put on the bureau that she can pick up and look at, something alien to her? Like a foreskin, something she wouldn't see where she comes from?'" (p. 45).

• The subtitle scene. On the balcony off Annie's apartment, Alvy and Annie's words belie their real thoughts:

Alvy   So, did you do those photographs in there or what?
Annie   Yeah, yeah, I sorta dabble around, you know.
Annie's Thoughts   *I dabble? Listen to me—what a jerk.*
Alvy   They're wonderful, you know. They have a quality.
Alvy's Thoughts   *You are a great-looking girl.*
Annie   Well, I would like to take a serious photography course soon.
Annie's Thoughts   *He probably thinks I'm a yo-yo.*
Alvy   Photography's interesting, 'cause, you know, it's a new art form, and a set of aesthetic criteria have not emerged yet.
Alvy's Thoughts   *I wonder what she looks like naked?*
Annie   Aesthetic criteria? You mean, whether it's a good photo or not?
Annie's Thoughts   *I'm not smart enough for him. Hang in there.*
Alvy   The medium enters in as a condition of the art form itself.
Alvy's Thoughts   *I don't know what I'm saying—she senses I'm shallow.*
Annie   Well, to me, I mean, it's all instinctive, you know? I mean, I just try to feel it, you know? I try to get a sense of it and not think about it so much.
Annie's Thoughts   *God, I hope he doesn't turn out to be a schmuck like the others.*
Alvy   Still, you need a set of aesthetic guidelines to put it in a social perspective, I think.
Alvy's Thoughts   *Christ, I sound like FM radio. Relax.*

• Truman Capote. While ranking on people in Central Park, Alvy calls one passerby the "winner of the Truman Capote look-alike contest." The passerby is really Truman Capote.

• The Norman Mailer reference. At one point, Alvy tells Annie she's extremely sexy, and that because she feels sexual arousal in every part of her body, he considers her "polymorphously perverse." Woody may have got the term "polymorphously perverse" from Norman Mailer. The opening line of Mailer's 1971 book *The Prisoner of Sex* is "Near the end of the Year of the Polymorphous Perverse (which is to say in the fall of '69) there were rumors he would win the Nobel." And in *Hannah and Her Sisters,* Woody's character Mickey Sachs describes Dianne Wiest's character as "polymorphously insensitive."

• Woody's use of three jokes from his early standup material. While performing at the University of Wisconsin, Alvy uses the following jokes:

> I was thrown out of NYU my freshman year for cheating on my metaphysics final. I looked within the soul of the boy sitting next to me. [From the routine "Private Life" on his first album, *Woody Allen.*]

> When I was thrown out, my mother, who's an emotionally high-strung woman, locked herself in the bathroom and took an overdose of Mah-Jongg tiles. [From "Private Life."]

> I was suicidal. As a matter of fact, I would have killed myself but I was in analysis with a strict Freudian and if you kill yourself they make you

pay for the sessions you miss. [From the routine "Second Marriage" on *The Third Woody Allen Album*.]

(In his *Woody Allen on Location*, Thierry de Navacelle revealed that this "performance" scene was shot in an empty room. "And when the audience was finally filmed, they didn't know what they were laughing at." This may be true, but there *is* one scene that shows Alvy *and* the audience at the same time.)

• Woody's use of the "Snow White" story. Annie, Rob, and Alvy appear as animated characters in a "remake" of *Snow White and the Seven Dwarfs*. The first film Woody remembers seeing was *Snow White and the Seven Dwarfs*. He saw it in 1938, at the age of three.

• The visible spectators. During the scene where Alvy stops passersby on the street to ask about their love lives (the "love fades" scene), spectators can be seen at the end of the block watching the filming of the scene. They were being held back behind a police barricade.

• Woody's unplanned sneeze. Alvy's sneeze during the "cocaine" scene was an accident which everyone decided to leave in the final cut of the film. Editor Ralph Rosenblum had to add extra "dead" footage to the scene because audiences laughed so long after the sneeze that they lost some of the dialogue from the next scene. (Watch Diane Keaton after the sneeze: she had to cover her face with her hand to keep from cracking up on camera.)

• The Warren Beatty reference. Annie eventually moves to California and lives with record producer Tony Lacey, a thinly disguised satirical depiction of Warren Beatty.

• Early appearances of Shelly Hack, Jeff Goldblum, Beverly D'Angelo, Christopher Walken, and Sigourney Weaver.

A Few Words from Woody . . .

• In a 1987 *Rolling Stone* interview with William Geist, when asked if any of his films that bordered on the autobiographical ever bothered his family, Woody replied, "No, because the stuff that people insist is autobiographical is almost invariably not, and it's so exaggerated that it's virtually meaningless to the people upon whom these little nuances are based. People got it into their heads that *Annie Hall* was autobiographical, and I couldn't convince them that it wasn't. And they thought *Manhattan* was autobiography. Because I make the lead character a comic or a writer, I play it myself. I can't play an atomic scientist. I'm not going to make the lead a mechanic. I know the language of certain people."

• Woody also had this to say about *Annie Hall:* "I wanted [the film] to be about . . . real people, real problems besetting some fairly neurotic characters trying to exist in male-female relationships in America in 1977. So it turns out to be more serious than anything I've ever tried before."

13.
Interiors

(United Artists, August 2, 1978); Running Time: 93 minutes;
Rating: PG; Color.

They hold their hands over their mouths
And stare at the stretch of water.
from "The Poets Agree to Be Quiet by the Swamp,"
in 1966 collection *Staying Alive* by David Waggoner

Interiors could justifiably be called *Hannah and Her Sisters: The Dark Side*. It is the story of a family in trouble, and shows how three complex and disparate women try to cope with their obsessive, suicidal mother.

Woody Allen's first foray into serious drama was met with praise, derision, admiration, and ridicule. He was accused of being an Ingmar Bergman "mimic," and, by totally eliminating any humor at all from the story, of creating a dark, brooding piece that betrayed the purported purpose of honest cinema: to document one particular vision of reality. Even with as somber a personal situation as these characters were experiencing, the rationale went, in real life, somebody would have at least cracked a joke once in a while!

Perhaps.

But *Interiors* works.

The performances are spectacular, especially those of Geraldine Page, Maureen Stapleton, and Mary Beth Hurt; the cinematography is stunning; and the story is important, told with fervor, and in a clear and consciously honest manner. At one point during the film, Renata describes Frederick's latest novel as "precise, sparing, gripping, meaning." That is also an accurate way of describing *Interiors*. It is dark, yes. It is brooding, yes. But it is also a scathingly credible cognitive study of a disintegrating family. It is a "slice" of the emotional life of eight intricately put-together people; a snapshot taken (for all its many summer beach-house scenes) during the sadness of these characters' psychological winter.

Interiors (whose title was suggested by Diane Keaton) begins with a stunning montage of still-life scenes. We hear Arthur describe his wife Eve as "very pale and cool . . . and distant. She'd created a world around us . . . where everything had its place . . ." (According to Eric Lax, the character of Eve was modeled on Louise Lasser's late mother.)

The first time we see Eve is after her separation from Arthur and after a stint in the sanitarium where she had electric shock therapy. She is obviously obsessive; fixating on minor, insignificant details of decorating and design.

Early in the film, Joey acknowledges her mother's problem by telling Mike, "Stop picking on her. . . . She's a sick woman." But in her final speech to her mother, she commutes that defense. (See the excerpt below.)

Joey tries to be honest with her mother and force her to accept the reality of the collapse of her marriage. But Renata counteracts Joey's sometimes harsh treatment of Eve by encouraging and coddling her mother.

Renata, an established and respected poet (her poems have been published in the *New Yorker*), is married to Frederick, a disgruntled and confused novelist who resents the critical acclaim Renata receives for her poetry. (See *Hannah and Her Sisters* for another disgruntled artist named Frederick.)

Joey is frustrated because she feels the need to "say something," but doesn't seem to have the talent or focus to "turn things out." Renata describes her sister to Frederick as "[having] all the anguish and anxiety, the artistic personality, without any of the talent."

The character Flyn is essentially a cipher in this family. She's distant (both physically and emotionally), and she works in the "lightweight" medium of television, while Renata and Joey attempt to do more "important" work. At one point, Frederick tries to purge his rage and feelings of impotence by forcing himself on Flyn, but she rebuffs him, and he is left humiliated and hollow.

Arthur, who favors Joey (but subsidizes Renata so she can write), obviously loves Eve as the mother of his children and a lifelong friend, but has essentially had it with her emotional instability. He wants to get on with and enjoy his life, and Eve doesn't have a role in his new plans. Arthur marries Pearl, whom Joey describes as "a vulgarian," but who is everything Arthur wanted from Eve, but couldn't have. Pearl is funny, earthy, and a genuine lover of life. (She dresses in bright colors, particularly red, in marked contrast to Eve's "beiges and earth tones.") Pearl eats what she wants, drinks, dances, does card tricks, tells fortunes, has buried two husbands, and gives Arthur the time of his life. Joey, who admits that her whole life she has wanted only to be her mother, loathes Pearl and accuses her of wanting Arthur for his money.

Arthur marries Pearl at the beach house, and later that evening, Eve shows up. Joey speaks to her, and consistent with her frank approach to her mother, tells her, "I think you're really too perfect to live in this world. . . . All the beautifully furnished rooms, carefully designed interiors . . . everything so controlled. There wasn't any room for any real feeling. . . . You're not just a sick woman. That would be too easy. The truth is there's been perverseness—and willfulness of attitude—in many of the things you've done. At the center of a sick psyche, there is a sick spirit."

After Joey's speech to her mother, Eve walks into the ocean and commits suicide. Joey tries to rescue her, and nearly drowns. She is saved by Pearl, who resuscitates her on the beach.

After her mother's death, Joey begins to write in a journal, obviously freed from her creative block, and now ready to speak honestly from her soul.

The final scene of the film shows the three sisters, all dressed in black, standing at a window in the beach house, staring at the ocean. Joey says, "The water's so calm." Renata replies, "Yes. It's very peaceful." And the film fades to the credits.

Look for . . .

• Renata's Woody Allen-ish existential angst. "Increasing thoughts about death just seemed to come over me. . . . Just what am I striving to create anyway? I mean, to what end? For what purpose? . . . Do I really care if . . . my poems are read after I'm gone forever? Is that supposed to be some sort of compensation? I used to think it was. But now . . . I can't seem to shake . . . the real implication of dying. It's terrifying. The intimacy of it embarrasses me."

• A clean image. According to Pauline Kael, writing in the *New Yorker,* "The prints of *Interiors* were processed on a new film stock, and during the showings for the press and people in the industry in Los Angeles, Allen had the print returned to the lab after every screening to be washed." (Video versions may not be as pristine as theatrical showings.)

• The silence. *Interiors* has no musical soundtrack. The only music heard in the film is recorded.

A Few Words from Woody . . .

• In the September 22, 1979, issue of the British music magazine *New Musical Express,* interviewer Marc Didden asked Woody Allen, "With *Interiors,* was there any conscious intention to 'do an Ingmar Bergman,' to prove that Woody Allen could make a serious movie?" Woody replied, "*Interiors* is a story that came to me in different parts. Some characters came to me years ago, some parts of the story, too, but none of it materialized. As a matter of fact I have always wanted to make serious films—in addition to comic films—and when I got the opportunity and I felt the time was right, *Interiors* happened to be the first one that I made. I would like to think it was successful enough so I can make more of them, which would mean that I would just have to make [more] amusing films. I simply think that I have enough ideas in my head to make a serious film now and then. I was not trying to prove anything. And when I say 'serious,' I only mean a film that is not primarily intended to make the audience laugh."

• In an interview with Tom Shales that appeared in the April 1987 issue of *Esquire,* Woody Allen said, "*Interiors* was my first attempt at a serious film, and I plunged right in there. I think I made a number of mistakes in it, as I did, though they're less apparent, in my comic films. A serious film won't tolerate mistakes so easily, whereas with a comic film you can get away with a rougher kind of situation."

14.
Manhattan

(United Artists, April 25, 1979); Running Time: 96 minutes; Rating: R; Black and White.

A . . . story about people in Manhattan who are constantly
creating these real, unnecessary neurotic problems for
themselves 'cause it keeps them from dealing with
more unsolvable, terrifying problems
about the universe.
Short-story idea by Isaac Davis

Woody Allen has always tried to recapture the past.

In his 1979 masterpiece *Manhattan,* Woody tried for an archetypal *New York City,* a city that "existed in black and white and pulsated to the great tunes of George Gershwin," a town that he saw as "a metaphor for the decay of contemporary culture" but that he still "adored."

Eight years later, in 1987, Woody would try to snare his childhood with *Radio Days,* but here, at the end of the seventies, it was time for a different sort of assessment. By focusing on the vagaries of interpersonal relationships in an age of divorce, crime, and the death of the nuclear family, Woody attempted to elucidate the ludicrous roles we are willing to play in our lives, and he used New York as a symbol of the decay (personal and societal) that comes with the dishonesty those roles demand.

Manhattan is a twisted love story, but a love story nonetheless.

It is the story of Ike's self-centered love for Tracy, Yale's blasé love for Mary, Emily's steadfast love for Yale, Mary's destructive love for Yale, and Ike's ardent love for New York.

These people dwell in a world of books, writing, teaching, the arts, concerts, and all the extraneous niceties that go with the lives of highly educated, fairly well-to-do people living in the most important city in the world.

Yes, these people are very well educated, but they are also neurotic. Textbook neurotic.

Ike loves Tracy, but, like Alvy Singer, won't commit.

Yale loves Mary, but won't make the commitment to leave his wife.

We get to know all of these people's "quirks and mannerisms" intimately by the end of the film.

Manhattan is Woody at his best: penetrating, touching, human, and, of course, enormously funny.

Manhattan opens with Isaac Davis dictating the opening lines to a new novel into a tape recorder. His first try (aside from the almost perfect first paragraph, the "black-and-white/Gershwin" lines), he decides is too corny. His second, too preachy. His third, too angry. And then finally, when he comes up with the line about the main character's black-rimmed glasses and coiled "jungle cat" sexual power, he decides that it's perfect.

Throughout Ike's writing, we are treated to sights of New York City that conclude with a dazzling display of fireworks that seems to be timed to explode to the final strains of George Gershwin's "Rhapsody in Blue." (The closing montage of fireworks was filmed from the bathroom window of the Central Park West apartment that belonged to the parents of one of the production staff. According to Eric Lax, the cameraman hung out the window to film the pyrotechnics.)

The film gracefully guides us through the relationships and lives of these Manhattanites, focusing on Ike's attempts to rid himself of Tracy and somehow find a way to have a relationship with Mary, with whom his best friend Yale is also having an affair. (There does seem to be *some* loyalty among these two male philanderers.)

As Ike tells Yale, "When it comes to relationships with women, I'm the winner of the August Strindberg Award." And his actions confirm his words. When Tracy tells Ike that she thinks she's in love with him, Ike, unwilling to commit, tells her not to get carried away, and to get dressed because he doesn't want her to stay over. (This is similar to the response of Woody's character Alvy Singer in *Annie Hall* when Annie suggested they share an apartment. In *Manhattan,* Ike verbalizes the same feelings: "I don't want you to get in the habit, because the first thing you know you stay over one night and then two nights and then, you know, you're living here.")

While walking through Manhattan after the two couples bump into each other at the Guggenheim Museum, Mary and Yale share their invention, the Academy of the Overrated, with a not-too-thrilled-to-hear-about-it Ike and Tracy. Mary and Yale have determined that the following artists are overrated: Sol LeWitt, Gustav Mahler, Isak Dinesen, Carl Jung, Scott Fitzgerald (the "F" pretentiously ignored), Lenny Bruce, Norman Mailer, Walt Whitman, Heinrich Böll, Vincent van Gogh, and Ingmar Bergman. Ike asks them why they left out Mozart as they were "trashing" people, and then gets his dander up when Mary includes Bergman, whom Ike considers "the only genius in cinema today."

Ike muses to Tracy that Yale was always a sucker for brainy women like Mary, and he imagines that they sit around on the floor with wine and cheese and mispronounce "allegorical" and "didacticism." Ike thinks people should mate for life, "like pigeons or Catholics."

Ike eventually breaks up with Tracy for Mary, Tracy decides to move to London for six months, Mary ends up back with Yale, and Ike regrets letting Tracy go. The film ends with Ike's jog all the way from Second Avenue in the Yorkville section of Manhattan, past Gramercy Park, to Tracy's apartment building, hoping to catch her before she leaves for London. Tracy won't change her mind about leaving, and ironically tells Ike (who has seen a lot of deceitful and faithless behavior in the recent weeks), "Not everybody gets corrupted. Look, you have to have a little faith in people."

Look for . . .

• The blocked camera shot. In Elaine's, when Tracy comes back from the bathroom and tells Ike they should leave because she's got an exam tomorrow, just as Ike is getting ready to respond, a couple walks in front of the camera, blocking the shot, and Woody and company laugh as Woody postpones his line. He recovers quickly, though, and then says, "She's got homework. I'm dating a girl who does homework." (It's interesting that Woody decided to leave that foulup in.)

• Karen Allen as the catatonic Mrs. Payne Whitney-Smith on Ike's TV show, "Human Beings, Wow!"

• Mia Farrow's sister, Tisa Farrow, as Polly, the girl who finally had an orgasm, but the wrong kind. Ike responds to this with, "I've never had the wrong kind. My worst one was right on the money."

• The paper towel gaffe. When Mary goes to Ike's place to tell him about breaking up with Yale, an amusing gaffe occurs when *Ike* brings Mary a huge piece of paper towel to blow her nose, and then when Mary is leaving with the giant wad, Ike says, "That's a nice healthy piece of towel paper you got." The tone in his voice makes you think Mary had gotten the paper herself. Ike's line sounds ad-libbed.

A Few Words from Woody . . .

Regarding his wardrobe in *Manhattan*, Woody Allen said in 1979, "Mariel Hemingway . . . saw *Annie Hall* again and called me up, amazed that I wore the same clothes she sees me in all the time. Actually I wear some of the same clothes in both *Annie Hall* and *Manhattan*. I'm still wearing a shirt I wore in *Play It Again, Sam* on Broadway in 1969."

15.
Stardust Memories
(United Artists, 1980); Running Time: 89 minutes; Rating: PG;
Black and White.

Stardust Memories is about Sandy Bates, a successful filmmaker with a popular *and* cult following, who attends a weekend arts seminar in his honor, and during the retrospective of his films, reevaluates his work, his romantic relationships, and his life.

Fans and critics alike were not too happy with Woody after the release of *Stardust Memories.*

The film seemed to be perceived as a "whine" heard round the world.

No matter that Woody has denied that it is an autobiographical statement (even though there are certain elements in the film that clearly emanated from Woody's life and career). And no matter that he has publicly denied that he has any animosity toward his fans.

What people picked up on was the "fan-specific" misogynist tone of the film. The fans in *Stardust Memories* are grotesque, literally and figuratively. But as Woody has often said, the point (and the theme) of the film was that of a director reevaluating his world and coming to the realization that one, he was not happy, and two, his art would not save him from death.

Stardust Memories—utilizing a disquieting mix of flashbacks, daydreams, memory flashes, and fantasy montages—is a brilliant exploration of the overwhelming power the artistic sensibility has on the artist. It gives us a look at the heady complacency (and arrogance) the creation of art can generate in the artist. The film perfectly illustrates the compelling danger inherent in becoming an Artist/God: After all, man as artist creates something from nothing (like God), and the resultant notion of the ego is that such creation necessarily brings with it an immortality. *Stardust Memories* shows us what happens when the artist confuses *artistic* immortality with *personal* immortality. The result is despair, confusion, ennui, and existential trauma.

A writer or director can insert elements from his or her life into the work, and yet exaggerate them (or change them, for that matter) so that they are not literally true. The point is, artists can "use" their own reality—for their own artistic means—without having to be a slave to the facts.

Stardust Memories opens with scenes from Sandy's new film, which has visions of sea gulls and dead cars. The film is not well received by the studio weasels watching it. When Sandy meets with his lawyer, manager, accountant, and doctor, he tells them, "I don't want to make funny movies anymore. They can't force me to. I don't feel funny. I look around the world, and all I see is human suffering."

But human suffering aside, *Stardust Memories* has some hilarious lines. At one point, Dorrie (who was supposedly based on Woody's real-life second wife, Louise Lasser) tells Sandy he smells nice. She says, "That aftershave. It just made my whole childhood come back in a sudden Proustian rush." Sandy tells her, "That's 'cause I'm wearing Proustian Rush by Chanel. It's reduced. I got a vat of it." (Maybe/maybe not department: Diane Keaton has a sister named Dorrie who graduated from college with a degree in art.) Later, Sandy meets an old friend from the neighborhood where he grew up, and tells the guy, "It's all luck. . . . [I]f I had been born in Poland . . . I'd be a lampshade today, right?" And later, Daisy tells Sandy, "You know, for a guy who makes a lot of funny movies, you're kind of a depressive, you know? He defends himself and says that he does a lot of things for laughs, like . . . "get undressed and perform the Heimlich Maneuver on a loved one." And when asked if he studied philosophy at school, Sandy replies, "I took one course in existential philosophy at New York University, and on the final they gave me ten questions, and I couldn't answer a single one of 'em. . . . I left 'em all blank. [Beat] I got a hundred."

There are several seemingly autobiographical elements in *Stardust Memories*. For instance, Sandy's sister tells Isobel that her and Sandy's parents were always fighting, and screaming at each other. Woody has often talked about his own parents constantly arguing when he was growing up. When the studio honchos rewrite the ending of Sandy's film, they have the characters go to "Jazz Heaven," telling Sandy, "[We] thought you'd like it, Sandy. You love jazz." Woody loves jazz and plays clarinet at Michael's Pub in Manhattan every Monday evening. At one point, Sandy tells one of the UFOers that he used to do magic tricks when he was a kid, but no more. Woody did perform magic as a child, and in his 1982 play, *The Floating Light Bulb*, Paul Pollack, a young boy living with his parents, is an aspiring magician who bombs during his first (and only) audition. And during a conversation with a space alien named Og, Sandy asks, "If nothing lasts, why am I bothering to make films, or do anything for that matter?" And Og replies, "We enjoy your films. Particularly the early funny ones." The alien then rebukes Sandy and tells him, "You want to do mankind a real service? Tell funnier jokes." And as the film festival weekend continues with screenings of Sandy's films, we find that Sandy Bates, too, has done science fiction/comedy films similar to *Sleeper* and segments of *Everything You Always Wanted to Know About Sex.*

There are other notable and interesting bits of business in *Stardust Memories*. In an eerie foreshadowing of John Lennon's murder, a fan comes up to Sandy, tells him, "I'm your biggest fan," and later shoots him. (Even though the shooting was actually a hallucination, it was remarkably like what happened with Lennon.) At one point, Daisy has one of the most astonishing phone conversations viewers have ever been privy to. She says that she's crazy, that she had a migraine and took some Darvon (in *Play It Again, Sam,* Felix likes Darvon and apple juice), which made her nervous, and that she then took forty milligrams of Valium. And not least, Daisy has a message on her service from her lesbian lover Sarah, with whom she lived in Israel, and the call made her so nervous, she ate a pound of cookies. So now she thinks she's fat, and told Jack she has herpes.

At the film's conclusion, we see that everyone has been watching Sandy's new film, which apparently included many scenes and people from *Stardust Memories,* making Woody's real-life film actually a film about a film.

Look for . . .

• The opening Bergman and Fellini homage. *Stardust Memories* begins with what is really a dark nightmare sequence that owes its genesis to Fellini's *8½* (except that instead of being trapped in a railroad car, Fellini was trapped in an automobile), and Ingmar Bergman's *Wild Strawberries,* with its ticking clock soundtrack.

• *Total Recall* and *Basic Instinct's* Sharon Stone as the beautiful blonde on the train opposite Sandy in the opening montage.

• John Rothman. Rothman, who plays Jack Abel, the Columbia screenwriting teacher and Daisy's boyfriend in *Stardust Memories,* was Meryl Streep's roommate at Yale.

• Laraine Newman of "Saturday Night Live" in an uncredited role as a studio executive.

• The "flying saucer"/hot-air balloons. Even though I greatly admire Roger Ebert's work and place great store in his opinions, I must argue one point with him here. Roger has a rule he calls "The Balloon Rule." He believes that "no good movie has ever contained a hot-air balloon." (Except for *The Wizard of Oz.*) Well, I think *Stardust Memories* is a good movie, and yes, it contains not one, but three, hot-air balloons. Readers, what do you think? Write both Roger and me (hey, another movie reference!) c/o Andrews and McMeel.

• The real artwork by Venet, Segal, and Cole seen during the film. Paintings included *Position of Two Arcs of 171.5° and 188.5°* and *Position of Two Angles of 90° and 35°* by Bernar Venet, *Girl in Chair Dangling Left Arm* by George Segal, *Montana* and *Anza* by Max Cole.

• The real photographs seen during the film. We see photographs by Lee Friedlander, a photo titled "Photo Mural/Ward 81" by Mary Ellen Mark, and selections from "Hot Spot" and "Colters Hell" by Robin Lehman. (Mary Ellen Mark was the photographer who took the "umbrella" photo of Woody that appeared on the cover of the *New York Times Magazine* on April 22, 1979.)

• The pigeon scene. During a scene with Dorrie in Sandy's apartment, a pigeon flies in through the window and Sandy freaks. He considers pigeons "rats with wings" and says that the one that flew into the apartment had a swastika under its wings. In real life, Woody Allen is so disgusted by pigeons that he once painted the terrace of his Manhattan apartment with a solution that was supposed to act as a "pigeon repellent." The next morning pigeons were stuck all over the terrace. "I didn't know what to do," he said. "I was all alone. They were struggling. In the end, I had to *prize* them off, one by one, with a spatula."

• Yet another masturbation reference. The critic John Lahr even saw a masturbation allusion in Sandy's name: "Sandy ('Master') Bates." Sandy says, "Jazz heaven. That is the stupidest thing I've ever heard. You can't control life. It doesn't wind up perfectly. Only art you can control. Art and masturbation. Two areas in which I am an absolute expert."

• The crossover of material. At a screening of one of Sandy's films, the audience views a film in which Sydney Fynklestein's hostility (an enormous furry monster) escapes. The Hostility Monster kills Sydney's schoolteacher, ex-wife (and her alimony lawyer), and his brother Alvin. (The Hostility Monster appears later at the UFO convention and attacks one of the UFO freaks.) On December 16, 1985, Woody read an unpublished short story at a benefit to raise money for the forty-eighth International PEN Congress to be held in January 1986. In the story, Phil Feldman's hostility escapes out of Phil (as a hairy black blob with red eyes) and goes on a rampage, attacking Feldman's psychiatrist and his parents as well as feeding a radio to a teenage boy who was playing it too loudly. And in Woody's early standup comedy routine "Pets" (on his first album, *Woody Allen*), we learn that Woody was once bullied by a *Sheldon* Fynklestein.

• The "Dorrie in the sanitarium" sequence. In a bravura editing job, we see quick cuts of Dorrie's face, and in each cut she says only a couple of words. This visual realization of her instability and irrationality is mesmerizing.

• The comedy albums reference. When Sandy finds a girl in his bed who wants to make it with him, she tells him that her husband has all his albums. Woody, of course, recorded three albums of his own standup comedy material early in his career.

A Few Words from Woody . . .

In an interview with Tom Shales that appeared in the April 1987 issue of *Esquire,* Woody Allen said, "The best film I ever did, really, was *Stardust Memories.* . . . It was the closest I came to achieving what I set out to achieve."

16.
A Midsummer Night's Sex Comedy
(Orion Pictures, 1982); Running Time: 88 minutes; Rating: PG; Color.

Why, this is very midsummer madness.
William Shakespeare, from *Twelfth Night*

A Midsummer Night's Sex Comedy—a visually stunning, whimsical, turn-of-the-century romantic comedy—is about six people who share a summer weekend in the country where they learn about love, metaphysics, and each other.

Critics have noted the nods to Shakespeare (*A Midsummer Night's Dream*) and Ingmar Bergman's *Smiles of a Summer Night* in Woody's *Midsummer*. The film has the tone and ambience of Woody's 1991 fantasy *Alice*, and even though it is not one of Woody's landmark efforts, much here is to be savored and appreciated. And like *Alice*, *A Midsummer Night's Sex Comedy* posits the existence of magic and operates on two levels: as a romantic comedy, and as a romantic fantasy. (And any film that gives us Woody Allen on a flying bicycle trying to seduce Mia Farrow through an open window is at least worth a couple of viewings, eh?)

Two couples, Maxwell and Dulcy, and Leopold and Ariel, arrive at Andrew and Adrian's house in the country to celebrate the marriage of Leopold and Ariel. (Leopold is Adrian's cousin.) Leopold is an older professor with an ego as big as all outdoors. He recites poetry whenever he feels like it (regardless of whether the others are in the mood for an ode) and sings Schubert lieder. His latest book is called *Conceptual Pragmatism*. Leopold is a realist. The film opens with the learned professor telling his class, "Ghosts? Little spirits or pixies? I don't believe in them." He firmly believes that "nothing is real but experience" and that "apart from this world there are no realities." This rigid rejection of the "unseen world" gives the perfect ironic touch to the end of the film when Leopold dies and his spirit joins the "spirits and pixies" that inhabit the enchanted woods outside Andrew's house.

There are in *Midsummer* interesting nods to previous Woody Allen films, most notably *Manhattan*. At one point one of Leopold's fellow professors says to Leopold, "I agree with you about Balzac, Leopold, he's vastly overrated." This refers us to "the Academy of the Overrated" scene in *Manhattan*. And Woody Allen adds a nice musical touch. As he had the fireworks exploding in time to Gershwin's music in the opening of *Manhattan*, here he has animals gamboling in time to the music of Mendelssohn. In another thematic nod to *Manhattan*, Andrew tells his wife, "I was never in love with Ariel Weynmouth and I don't love her now. Hey, trust me." This resonates off the final scene in *Manhattan* in which Mariel Hemingway's character Tracy insists to Ike (Woody) that he "[has] to have a little faith in people." Andrew also tells his wife that he had "a couple of lobsters" when he dated Ariel, referring to the *Annie Hall* scene wherein Alvy and Annie cook lobsters. Finally, when Andrew comes in after his "flight" with Ariel, he tells his wife he was chopping ice for dinner, acknowledging the scene in *Love and Death* in which Sonia (Diane Keaton) serves Boris sleet for supper.

Flights of fancy galore are in this film. Andrew, a self-acknowledged "crackpot inventor" who works on Wall Street (that ultimate bastion of realism), has successfully invented a flying bicycle, a device that bones fish (and "although there's no point to it, it puts bones *in* fish"), and, most notably, a "spirit ball" that operates on psychic energy and "penetrates the unseen world." Andrew pours all his energy into his inventions because he hasn't had sex with Adrian in six months. (She became frigid from guilt after an illicit affair with Andrew's best friend Maxwell.) As Andrew puts it, because of his sex problems with Adrian, he can now fly.

The story revolves around the group's dissatisfaction with their love lives. As mentioned, Adrian can't make love with Andrew because of her affair with Maxwell. Andrew loves his wife, but regrets not seizing the chance to make love with Ariel when they once dated. Maxwell (who Andrew says is "like one of those characters in Greek mythology who's half goat") has more sex partners than he can handle, but falls madly in love with Ariel the first time he sees (and smells) her. Dulcy, Maxwell's nurse and weekend date, is a free spirit who considers sex wonderful recreation, and who teaches Adrian how to do a "Mexican cartwheel." Ariel is marrying Leopold but over the weekend realizes she doesn't love him. And Leopold is marrying Ariel for the prestige he'll acquire with his colleagues for having such a young and luscious bride.

Complicating the turmoil and intricacies of all these "lust affairs" is Andrew's spirit ball. As Dr. Yang in *Alice* uses magic herbs to help Alice see her real self (*and* make her invisible to help the process along), so does Andrew's spirit ball "enlighten" the group by showing them ambiguous scenes that each is free to interpret in his own way. In fact, after Andrew finds out that Leopold is marrying Ariel, he's in bed with Adrian, and downstairs the spirit ball turns and lights up by itself. The frustrated psychic romantic energies in the house are already becoming restless.

The first time Andrew uses the spirit ball, it lights up and projects a man waiting for someone, and a woman in a summer dress. Our first reading of this is that it is either Maxwell or Andrew waiting for Ariel for a rendezvous, or a manifestation of everyone's unrequited love. Later we find out that the couple was actually Andrew's wife Adrian meeting Maxwell for an illicit meeting. After the group sees the vision, the ball explodes. It is presented as a given that such a fantastic manifestation was not only possible, but necessary, even though Leopold dismisses the whole thing as an optical illusion.

As the film builds to its conclusion (Leopold's death), Ariel reluctantly agrees to meet both Maxwell and Andrew in the woods at midnight. She rejects Maxwell, chooses Andrew, and in a line that contributes to the mystical tone of the scene (and film), they realize that the constellations are in the same place as they were when they first met there so long ago and Andrew blew his chance to make love to Ariel.

Meanwhile, back at the house, Leopold has just had a precognitive dream in which he came downstairs and found Dulcy reading "The Katzenjammer Kids." When he looks for Ariel, the spirit ball lights up and shows the silhouettes of Andrew and Ariel on the wall. Leopold goes after Andrew and shoots Maxwell with an arrow by mistake. As he lies wounded, thinking he's dying, Maxwell reveals to Andrew that he had an affair with Andrew's wife, Adrian. Andrew marches off to confront Adrian, while Leopold returns to the house and makes love to Dulcy.

Because the truth is now revealed, Adrian loses her frigidity, and she and Andrew make love and resolve their sexual problems.

In the meantime, Leopold dies making love to Dulcy.

When they all get back to the house (including a bandaged Maxwell—he was only wounded), the spirit ball explodes with Leopold's spirit, and he speaks to the others from the unseen world. He reveals that Andrew's woods *are* enchanted. They're filled with the spirits of people who died at the height of lovemaking. The film ends with Leopold the rationalist telling the others, "Promise me, all of you, to look for my glowing presence on starlit evenings, in these woods, under the summer moon, forever."

Then his soul flies out the house and joins the dance of the spirits in the woods.

Look for . . .

• Woody's "voice" coming out of Leopold, Adrian, and Maxwell's mouths. Acting as a spokesperson for Woody's own "teleologic existential atheistic" beliefs), Leopold lectures his students about "metaphysical gibberish."

> Nothing is real but experience, that which can be touched, tasted, felt or, in some scientific fashion, proved. . . . As I stated quite clearly in my latest paper, metaphysical philosophers are simply men who are too weak to accept the world as it is. Their theories of the so-called mysteries of life are nothing more than projections of their own inner uneasiness. Apart from this world, there are no other realities.

And Andrew's wife, Adrian, says something that would be more appropriate to Woody's own archetypal anhedonic characters: "Why does a beautiful day like today give me such a sad feeling?"

And then Woody gives Dr. Maxwell Jordan a speech that seems to be Woody speaking:

I see what goes on down at the hospital. I had a hell of a week. People with tumors, and brain damage, a guy with sudden heart failure. They're young men and women, Andrew. They've never lived, we tell them they're gonna die. And they never seized the moment. They never had a life. So gather ye rosebuds, Andrew.

• The first appearance of Woody's character, Andrew Hobbes. He's wearing a leather helmet, goggles, and giant wings, and trying to fly—with little success.

• The paradox of the agnostic/atheistic Woody playing a character (Andrew) who has such a fervent belief in an afterlife.

• The sequence of thirty pastoral scenes. For someone who has publicly affirmed that he is "a two with nature," Woody Allen certainly knows how to recognize bucolic glory when he sees it.

• The occasional Woody one-liner. Andrew is riding his flying bicycle as Maxwell and Dulcy arrive at the house. Early on, after Andrew "lands" his flying bicycle, he says, "I think I fractured my last remaining nose."

• Dulcy's scenes. Woody wrote some very funny lines and moments for scenes involving this sexual free spirit: When Dulcy sees a hammock, she tells Adrian hammocks were nostalgic for her. She lost it in a hammock. When Adrian is surprised, Dulcy tells her you have to have good balance. Another time, Dulcy tells Maxwell that she brought some contraceptives in case he forgot. Maxwell replies, "Oh, good. 'Cause I only brought three hundred." And when Dulcy asks Leopold about the "plot" of his book, he sardonically asks her what she does. She tells him she's a nurse and that she reads to patients. "And they die and I get to keep the copies." And when a lustful Leopold asks her if the older man she once made love to was a genius, she replies, "He was a dentist."

• Woody/Andrew's feelings about Mia/Ariel. "[S]he's so beautiful. I mean, that's a simple fact. A blind man could see that." (Because this is Woody's character speaking about Mia's character, we're aware of a sincerity and significance born of Woody and Mia's real-life relationship imbuing the line.)

• The eight-people/four-way conversation in the woods. Tony Roberts (quoted in *Woody Allen: A Biography*) remembers, "Even after the film had been wrapped and edited, we went back into the woods to do that damn scene." According to Eric Lax, "Woody wanted the dialogue to overlap and to have a natural feel to it, but at the same time there couldn't be any air in it, nor could there be any sense of deliberateness."

• Woody's "spirit box" gaffe(?). During the outdoor dinner scene, Andrew refers to his spirit "ball" as a spirit "box," the only time he called it anything other than a ball.

• Andrew and Adrian's hilarious kitchen love scene. Adrian tries to take Dulcy's advice and be spontaneous. She wants to make love on the kitchen table. Andrew is shocked: "We cannot have intercourse where we eat oatmeal!" They grapple on the stove and the table. Andrew breaks some eggs and says, "This is like a Flemish painting." She wants his pants off. Andrew protests: "There's a man in the next room singing 'The Lord's Prayer.' We'll go blind!" Andrew ends up past the point of no return, but Adrian is suddenly overwhelmed by feelings of disgust. "How can it be disgusting?" Andrew asks. "I don't have my clothes off yet."

• The recycling of a *What's Up, Tiger Lily?* joke. After Adrian and Andrew finally make love, she asks him if he can forgive her earlier adulterous behavior. Andrew replies, "Forgive you? I can ordain you this evening. You've cleared my sinuses for the summer." This joke originally appeared in *Tiger Lily.*

A Few Words from Woody . . .

In one scene, a randy Dulcy tells Leopold (José Ferrer), "Bite me." He explains that he can't: "These are not my teeth." In his biography of Woody, Eric Lax relates that Woody had José Ferrer repeat the "teeth" line so many times that Ferrer got quite angry. Woody recalled to Lax, "I thought he was a total delight in every way. Just that once I asked him to do a line over many times. Finally he said to me . . . 'Now I can't, you've turned me into a mass of terrors.' And I thought to myself, 'My God, you're José Ferrer. How can I turn you into a mass of terrors? You're this wonderful actor and all I'm doing is saying no, that's not really the way I wanted it, do it again.' So I guess I'm insensitive, because I take it for granted that they should take it for granted."

Footnote: The Paint Problem

From *Woody Allen on Location* by Thierry de Navacelle:

> By the end of the shooting [of *A Midsummer Night's Sex Comedy*] the trees were turning brown and yellow, so the leaves were painted green. But when the movie company left, the Rockefeller estate, which owns the property, complained because it didn't want its trees green in winter. So the company came back to paint the trees brown. The green paint was dye and difficult to get out. Then, when the rains came, the brown came off and the trees were green again, in the middle of January. [P. 130]

In addition, the set of the summer house built for the filming was scheduled to be destroyed after production ended. Instead, it was purchased for five thousand dollars by a man who moved it to another location, reinforced it, and installed water and electricity.

17.
Zelig

(Orion Pictures, 1983); Running Time: 79 minutes; Rating: PG;
Black and White.

Wanting only to be liked, he distorted himself beyond measure. One
wonders what would have happened if, right at the outset, he had
had the courage to speak his mind and not pretend. In the end,
it was, after all, not the approbation of many but the love
of one woman that changed his life.
F. Scott Fitzgerald

We are all serving a life-sentence in the dungeon of self.
Cyril Connolly, from *Unquiet Grave*

I once read that in order to make *Zelig*'s old film footage look as grainy
and scratchy as genuine film from the 1920s, Woody Allen had crew members take his newly exposed film into the shower and step on it while water
ran all over it.

It worked.

Zelig is a masterpiece of originality and the film that should convince
any remaining doubters that Woody Allen is, unquestionably, a genius. It
is also an almost unclassifiable film, although "fake fantasy documentary"
does as good a job as any other description.

Zelig is the story of a man in the 1920s who was so insecure he literally
"fit in" by changing himself physically into the person he was with—he
was a bona fide human chameleon. A woman psychiatrist takes his case as
her main professional interest and succeeds in curing him temporarily,
and also falling in love with him. His relapse is temporary, though, and
they end up together.

The first time one sees *Zelig*, it's easy almost not to get the joke. The
film is so technically sophisticated and so brilliantly compiled and edited
that it is easy to believe that Woody Allen has done a legitimate documentary about a 1920s figure named Leonard Zelig whom culture and society
no longer remembered. After all, Susan Sontag and Irving Howe open the
film, and we readily sense we're witnessing the story of a bizarre Jazz Age
celebrity impersonator. His first "transformations" were, after all, merely
into a Republican aristocrat, a Democratic kitchen worker, a baseball
player, and a gangster. Anybody could pretend to be any one of these characters. But we begin to grow suspicious when we hear a retired black waiter
named Calvin Turner tell of Zelig transforming himself into a black trum-
peter—complete with total skin color change.

That's when we get the joke.

Zelig is Woody Allen as ersatz historian.

The film transports us to the American 1920s, the Jazz Age, with impeccable attention to detail, and introduces us to the aforementioned Leonard Zelig.

I think that with *Zelig,* Woody Allen proves to all that he is one of the few directors who undoubtedly make excellent use of their oft-touted "total creative control." Regardless of its few flaws, *Zelig* is a clear and abiding testimony of a truly creative artist, and one more proof that Woody is America's premier cinematic auteur.

Zelig begins in the year 1928.

We learn that the first time Zelig began behaving like others around him was when he lied about reading *Moby Dick* in order to fit in with others who had read it. The theoretical causes for Zelig's amazing transformational abilities include being "glandular in nature," a "problem in the secretions," "something he picked up from eating Mexican food," being "neurological in nature," a brain tumor, and "poor alignment of the vertebrae." (The doctor who concluded that Zelig's condition traced to a brain tumor died two weeks later from a brain tumor.)

Zelig's abilities are limited to men. He cannot transform into women. After this is discovered, doctors experiment with a midget and a chicken. (The results of those tests are not revealed.)

Zelig is not only Woody Allen's statement on the popular culture celebrity in this country, but also an absurdist look at what the desire to conform could conceivably lead to—if our physiology allowed it.

Zelig operates as a fantasy on two levels. The first is Woody Allen's "fantastic" re-creation and impeccable duplication of old newsreel footage, old films, radio broadcasts, and newspapers and magazines from the 1920s. The technical virtuosity exhibited in *Zelig* is nothing short of astounding. Woody Allen, through intricate cutting techniques and film lab pyrotechnical wizardry, appears in photographs and newsreels with dozens of notables. The photos and films are seamless. *Zelig* makes it more than obvious that Woody Allen has spent a great many years watching just such old documentaries and getting lost in yesteryear's magazines and newspapers. He has captured the essence of that long-dead time flawlessly.

The second fantasy level of *Zelig* is the premise itself, here taken very seriously and treated not only as possible but as the logical result of the type of personality disorder from which Leonard Zelig suffers. The film posits that Zelig can change into other people.

And rather than try and explain (to the viewer) not only how a human can physically change his appearance depending on the person in whose company he is, but how his clothes can change too, we are given "just the facts," and then shown how such a disorder affected both Zelig and society. It is presented as a given that such chameleonlike behavior exists, and that *Zelig* is a documentary of one so afflicted.

Zelig's story is told entirely in documentary form. We see Dr. Eudora Fletcher work diligently to reconstruct Zelig's personality, until finally she succeeds, and Zelig is his own man. It seems as though he will now find true happiness for, in addition to realizing his true personality, he recognizes that he is in love with Dr. Fletcher—and the feeling is mutual. They plan to marry, but then things fall apart. Women from Zelig's past begin coming forward claiming that Zelig married them when he was in another personality. And he did.

"He is sued for bigamy, adultery, automobile accidents, plagiarism, household damages, negligence, property damages, and performing unnecessary dental extractions."

Zelig becomes a global scandal, and on the eve of his sentencing for his crimes, he disappears from sight. Dr. Fletcher, heartbroken and distraught, searches for him in vain, until one day she sees a newsreel of Hitler and glimpses someone who could be Zelig in the crowd. She travels to Germany, and in a hilarious scene (also shown to us in a scene from Zelig's film biography *The Changing Man*), Eudora and Zelig make contact while Hitler raves. Zelig had become a Nazi. They steal a plane, escape, and while in the air, Dr. Fletcher becomes so terrified that she loses control of the plane. Zelig transforms into a pilot, takes over flying the plane, and brings them both back to the United States safely. In fact, he set a record for flying nonstop across the Atlantic upside down.

Zelig's heroic rescue of Dr. Fletcher endears him to the American public, and he receives a full presidential pardon for his crimes. The film ends with Zelig lamenting on his deathbed that "the only annoying thing about dying was he had just begun reading *Moby Dick* and wanted to see how it came out."

Look for . . .

• The onscreen "color commentators" à la *Reds*. Parts of Leonard Zelig's story are told during interviews with Susan Sontag, Irving Howe, and Saul Bellow, among others.

• The presence of real-life notables. Seen or mentioned are Calvin Coolidge, Charles Lindbergh, Al Capone, F. Scott Fitzgerald, Babe Ruth, Eugene O'Neill, members of the Ku Klux Klan, Eddie Cantor, Clara Bow, Jack Dempsey, Herbert Hoover, Josephine Baker, Cole Porter, Fanny Brice, Billy Rose, Pope Pius XI, Mussolini, Jimmy Walker, Nils Andersen, William Randolph Hearst, Marie Dressler, Marion Davies, Charlie Chaplin, Tom Mix, Adolphe Menjou, Claire Windsor, Dolores Del Rio, James Cagney, Carole Lombard, Bobby Jones, Duke Ellington, Adolf Hitler, and, of course, Moby Dick.

• Woody's autobiographical references. We are told that Zelig's parents were always arguing, "so much so that although the family lives over a bowling alley, it is the bowling alley that complains of noise." (In Eric Lax's book, Woody describes his parents marriage as "a totally contentious relationship. They did everything except exchange gunfire.") And it is well documented that Woody hates the country, and loves baseball. Zelig feels the same way: "It's the worst . . . I hate the country . . . I hate the grass and mosquitos . . ."; and, "I love baseball. You know, it doesn't have to mean anything. It's just very beautiful to watch."

• Woody's KKK reference. We are told by the narrator, "To the Ku Klux Klan, Zelig, a Jew who was able to transform himself into a Negro or Indian, was a triple threat." One of Woody's early standup routines called "Down South" was about the Ku Klux Klan.

• Leonard Zelig's documented transformations. There are over thirty, including Pagliacci and Duke Ellington's brother.

• Woody's recycling of an *Annie Hall* joke. At one point Zelig says that he used to work with Sigmund Freud, and that they broke company over penis envy. Zelig didn't agree that it should be limited to women. This is the same joke that Woody used in *Annie Hall.*

• Zelig memorabilia and songs. Memorabilia included a Zelig doll, several Zelig clocks, a box with Zelig's face on the cover, "the Chameleon Game," a Zelig ashtray, a Zelig wristwatch, Zelig pens, Zelig lucky charms, Zelig books, Zelig aprons, chameleon-shaped earmuffs, a chameleon-bodied meat thermometer with a Zelig head, Leonard Zelig–approved live chameleons, Leonard Zelig–endorsed Camel cigarettes, and Leonard Zelig–endorsed Pendleton underwear. Original songs written by Dick Hyman for *Zelig* included "Leonard the Lizard"; "Doin' the Chameleon"; "Chameleon Days"; "The Chameleon Days Fox Trot"; "You May Be Six People, But I Love You"; "Reptile Eyes"; and "The Changing Man Concerto."

• The Hassidic rabbi. One of Zelig's transformations is into a rabbi. Other notable appearances of a rabbi (or rabbis) in Woody's films include *Take the Money and Run, Bananas, Everything You Always Wanted to Know About Sex* (*But Were Afraid to Ask)* (the "What's My Perversion?" segment), and *Radio Days.*

• Leonard Zelig's lines. Many of the wittiest lines in the film are spoken by Leonard Zelig himself. At one point during an interview, he tells Dr. Fletcher, "Perhaps you've read my latest paper on delusional paranoia? Turns out the entire thing is mental." He also tells her, "I have an interesting case treating two sets of Siamese twins with split personalities. I'm getting paid by eight people." During a hypnotic trance, Zelig tells Fletcher, "My brother beat me . . . my sister beat me . . . my father beat my sister and my brother and me . . . my mother beat my father and my sister and me and my brother . . . the neighbors beat our family . . . people down the block beat the neighbors and our family . . ." He also tells her about a rabbi who once told him the meaning of life . . . in Hebrew . . . and then wanted to charge him six hundred dollars for Hebrew lessons.

• One more use of the masturbation motif. Zelig tells Dr. Fletcher that he teaches a course in masturbation, and that if he's not there, "they start without me."

• The courage/*Manhattan* reference. At one point, Zelig says, "You have to be your own person, and make your own moral choices even when they do require real courage. . . ." This refers back to the opening scene of *Manhattan* where Isaac Davis tells Yale, Emily, and Tracy that the important thing in life is courage.

• The bloodhounds/*Stardust Memories* reference. The scene where bloodhounds sniff the clothing of Zelig the fugitive is reminiscent of the "escaped hostility" scene in one of Sandy Bates's films shown in *Stardust Memories.*

A Few Words from Woody . . .

According to Eric Lax, Woody's reservations about *Zelig* are that "the technical achievement . . . [is] so flamboyant that it obscure[s] the points [I] was trying to make about a man afraid to be himself."

18.
Broadway Danny Rose

(Orion Pictures, January 27, 1984); Running Time: 85 minutes; Rating: PG; Black and White.

Don't forget to do "My Funny Valentine" with the special lyrics about the moon landing.
Danny Rose

Broadway Danny Rose is about Danny Rose, a hapless schlemiel in "theatrical management" who gets a shot at the big time when the career of one of his clients, Lou Canova, starts to take off. Danny plays "the beard" by taking Lou's girlfriend to Lou's big night (a performance for Milton Berle), not knowing that behind the scenes the girlfriend has been orchestrating Lou's move to a bigger, more high-powered manager. Danny ends up betrayed. The whole story is told by a group of (real-life) comics sitting around a table at the Carnegie Delicatessen.

Broadway Danny Rose is marvelously entertaining, and Woody's character, Danny Rose, is a quintessential Woody manifestation (even though he is drawn with a rather "broad" stroke at times). It is clear from this film that Woody has been around in show business. He's got all the little

An early publicity photo of Woody in his mid– to late twenties, probably taken in the early sixties.

An early sixties publicity shot of Woody.

This is a photo taken during Woody's 1967 *Kraft Music Hall*
special, "The Year 1967 in Review."

Robert MacNeil, Woody Allen, Pauline Kael. It isn't often one finds
Woody detractor Pauline Kael and Woody in the same room, let alone
the same picture. Kael has been fairly negative in her criticism of Woody
over the years. They appeared together to discuss film with Robert MacNeil.
The year isn't known, but it's probably the late seventies.

Woody Allen and Barbara Brownell in a scene from Woody's 1969 play, *Play It Again, Sam*. Brownell played "Dream Sharon" and Woody was thirty-four years old at the time.

Woody Allen and Jerry Lacy in a scene from Woody's 1969 play,
Play It Again, Sam. Lacy played the spirit of Humphrey Bogart.

Woody Allen and Candice Bergen in a skit from Woody's 1969
CBS special, "The Woody Allen Special."

Francis Ford Coppola, Woody Allen, Martin Scorsese. The three directors during the production of their three-film collaborative effort, *New York Stories.*

Woody Allen discussing a shot with legendary cinematographer
Sven Nykvist on the set of *Crimes and Misdemeanors*.

Jack Warden, Elaine Stritch, Woody Allen, Mia Farrow. Woody discusses a scene on the set of his 1987 drama, *September*.

Woody Allen pauses between takes on the set of *The Front.*

Woody directs Diane Keaton in a scene from his 1978 drama, *Interiors*.

Woody Allen in a scene from *What's New, Pussycat?* This photo was taken on December 1, 1964, Woody's twenty-ninth birthday.

Mia Farrow, Halston, Woody Allen, Martha Graham, Yoko Ono
at the New York State Theater on March 13, 1984.

Louise Lasser and husband Woody Allen arriving at The Top of The Sixes for a party after the opening of *Henry, Sweet Henry* on December 28, 1967. Lasser was one of the stars.

Woody Allen playing clarinet during one of his regular Monday night gigs at Michael's Pub in Manhattan.

"quirks and mannerisms" down to a science, and is never better than when asking if he can "interject a concept at this juncture," or when he tries to get out of trouble at the Mafia party by talking about "*Mister* Danny Kaye," and "*Mister* Milton Berle." This is genuinely funny material. (One of the most hilarious moments is when the Water Glass Virtuouso is auditioning for Philly, and Danny is bopping in time to her music, which is so blatantly nonrhythmic.)

Mia Farrow is also very effective in this film. Her performance is perfect. She plays the brassy Italian blonde, Tina Vitale, and watching Mia bring this woman to life is as impressive as watching her transform herself into an irresistible temptress (thanks to Dr. Yang's herbs) in *Alice.* Her range is formidable, to say the least.

Broadway Danny Rose is one of Woody Allen's most accessible and entertaining films.

Look for . . .

• "Sincerest form of flattery?" The storyline of *Broadway Danny Rose* was "borrowed" for a 1991 episode of the short-lived TV series "The Fanelli Boys," even down to two people being tied together face-to-face and having to wriggle free from their bonds.

• Leo Steiner's Carnegie Delicatessen (854 Seventh Avenue, near Fifty-fifth Street), where Danny's story is told by a bunch of real-life comics.

• The real-life comics in the film. Corbett Monica, Howard Storm, Morty Gunty, Will Jordan, Jackie Gayle, and Sandy Baron all appear as themselves. Also at the table was Woody's real-life agent, Jack Rollins. (Howard Storm also appeared in *Take the Money and Run.*)

• The role of Lou Canova. Also up for the role of Canova were Robert De Niro and Danny Aiello.

• The Chomsky reference. The first time we see Danny, he's trying to sell Phil *Chomsky* his water glass act. Isaac Davis's analyst in *Manhattan* was named Dr. Chomsky.

• The Weinstein's reference. Danny is trying to get Philly to book one of his acts at Weinstein's Majestic Bungalow Colony. Weinstein's also appears in Woody's play *The Floating Light Bulb.*

• The real-life acts. Danny represents, for the most part, real acts. The Water Glass Virtuoso was Gloria Parker; the Balloon Act was husband and wife team Bob and Etta Rollins; Bob Weil was Herbie Jayson, the bird man; Mark Hardwick was the blind xylophonist; and Alba Ballard was the bird lady who dressed parrots up in costumes. (David Letterman has had Alba on his show several times.)

• Danny Rose's standup routine. At one point, we see Danny doing a standup routine in the Catskills. He is in a tuxedo, working the room, and tells a joke about a terrible accident. "Two taxicabs collided. Thirty Scotchmen were killed."

• The pre-*Oedipus Wrecks* backstage scene. Howard Storm tells a story about the time one of Danny's clients hypnotized a woman and she wouldn't come out of the trance. We then see the backstage scene, and it reminds us of a similar scene in Woody's 1989 short film *Oedipus Wrecks.* In the early *Danny Rose* version, the husband is enraged because Danny can't bring Tessie out of her trance.

• Danny Rose's one-liners. Woody gives Danny Rose some wonderful one-liners in this film. For instance, he tells Lou that his Aunt Rose was "not a beautiful woman. She looked like something you'd buy in a live bait store." Later, he tells the hoods that his cousin Ceil was "not pretty like Tina at all. She looks like something in the reptile house in a zoo." (This was another foreshadowing of *Oedipus Wrecks.* In *Wrecks,* Sheldon's aunt was named Ceil. "Aunt Ceil" also appears in *Radio Days.*) Danny also talks about his Uncle Morris, "the famous diabetic from Brooklyn."

• The real Joe Franklin appearing as himself on the real "Joe Franklin Show."

• Milton Berle, "Mr. Television," appearing as himself.

• The third Woody Allen "poet." Tina's spurned lover Johnny writes Tina a poem. This is the third Woody Allen character to be a poet (two of which were played by Diane Keaton). The first was Luna, in *Sleeper;* the second, Renata, in *Interiors;* and the third, Johnny.

• Woody's "guilt and the existence of God" theme. At a diner, Danny and Tina discuss the existence of God. Danny tells her, "My rabbi, Rabbi Perlstein, used to say, we're all guilty in the eyes of God." Tina then asks him, "You believe in God?" Danny replies, "No, no. But I'm guilty over it." (Guilt and the existence of God, as well as the metaphor "eyes of God," are explored in much greater depth in Woody's 1989 masterpiece, *Crimes and Misdemeanors.*)

• The Frank Sinatra reference. When Danny shows Tina the photographs in his apartment, Tina points to a picture and asks, "Who is this here?" Danny replies, "What do you mean, who's that? That's Frank. That's Frank. That's Frank, Tony Bennett, and me." (Mia Farrow, who, of course, plays Tina, was once married to Frank Sinatra.)

• Howard Cosell's third appearance in a Woody Allen film.

• More California-bashing. When Lou wants to move to California, Tina, speaking as proxy for Woody Allen, says, "I don't want to go to California, okay? It gives me the creeps out there."

• A pre-*Hannah and Her Sisters* Thanksgiving dinner scene. Woody would again have narrative events revolve around a Thanksgiving dinner two films later, in fact three of them in 1986's *Hannah.*

A Few Words from Woody . . .

According to Eric Lax, "Woody feels that [*Broadway Danny Rose*] was nicely executed in general and is largely entertaining."

19.
The Purple Rose of Cairo

(Orion Pictures, 1985); Running Time: 81 minutes; Rating: PG; Color and Black and White.

Yet mark'd I where the bolt of Cupid fell:
It fell upon a little western flower,
Before milk-white, now purple with love's wound . . .
William Shakespeare, from *A Midsummer Night's Dream*

And I seem to find the happiness I seek . . .
from "Cheek to Cheek" by Irving Berlin

The Purple Rose of Cairo tells the story of an abused and lonely Depression-era housewife who loses herself in the movies and who has her dream come true when a movie heart-throb steps off the movie screen, into her life, and falls in love with her. The fantasy is not to remain a reality, however; when the character returns to movie land, his real-life actor betrays her, and the woman remains lost and alone.

In this touching fantasy, Woody Allen tells the poignant story of a young woman named Cecilia who is a prisoner of two forces: a loveless marriage and a cruel economy, neither of which seems to be escapable. Cecilia does what many of us do when confronted with a reality too harsh to handle every minute of every day: she escapes into fantasy. And her fantasy of choice is the movies.

Cecilia (played with a real sincerity by Mia Farrow) is married to Monk, a bum who gambles, drinks, fools around with women (in his and Cecilia's apartment), and hasn't worked in two years. Monk, a real prince, has been known to slap Cecilia around a bit.

Cecilia works in a diner as a waitress and goes to the movies whenever she can. Flicks about romance, high society, and dashing heroes are her favorites, and for the brief time she's in the theater, it seems as though her troubles disappear. She feels free in the dark sanctuary of the moviehouse.

One day, though, as Cecilia is sitting through *The Purple Rose of Cairo* for the fifth time, reality and fantasy change places.

Tom Baxter, *Purple Rose*'s charming archaeologist "on the verge of a madcap Manhattan weekend," suddenly looks out at Cecilia and says, "My God, you must really love this picture." In Woody's world, movie characters watch the audience as we watch them and Tom has been watching Cecilia for the past five performances. Tom has become so enamored of Cecilia that he breaks down the wall separating us from them (the movie screen) and steps out into our reality.

Tom and Cecilia share a common sensibility: both felt trapped by their circumstances, and each one wanted to escape into the other's world in order to be "free." Woody is showing us that our reality is equated with freedom for denizens of the fantastic realm of cinema, just as, ironically, the movies "free" us from our worries and troubles, if but for a short time.

Woody gives no concrete explanation for Tom's sudden ability to move from one state of being to another. As he did with Leonard Zelig's chameleonic abilites, he simply presents it as a given and we, the real-world audience, along with the audience in the film (the characters watching *The Purple Rose of Cairo*), don't try to explain it—we just try to deal with it. (Although a good case can be made for Woody's implication that Cecilia's extreme emotional state acted as the catalyst for the intrusion of the fantastic into her life. One of fantasy's sacred credos is that if you believe it, you can make it happen, and in *Purple Rose,* it seems that Cecilia may have drawn Tom to her by her "belief" in the power of the movies to change her life. Interestingly, a line of dialogue after Tom's "escape" seems to substantiate this theory. Tom was the one who made the journey from film to our world, and it's Tom whom Cecilia was obviously smitten with in the movie. After Tom escapes and the theater manager demands to know what happened, Henry [a character in the film] says, "I don't know how he did it. *I* can't get out." [Emphasis added.] Apparently, though, some real-world people assumed that if Tom Baxter could do it, then any screen character could descend into our world. Later in the [real] film, Mr. Hirsch, the producer of *Purple Rose,* comes to the Jewel and tells the movie people, "I just want the whole cast to know how much I appreciate your staying up there on the screen.")

After Tom's escape, the fragile façade that keeps movie characters acting and movie watchers viewing disintegrates. Suddenly, the characters of the film are arguing among themselves with unscripted dialogue, and the moviegoers sit there for hours watching the "cast" wander around aimlessly.

Once Tom is in our world, he decides he wants to learn about reality from Cecilia—a woman who wanted nothing more than to escape reality. During their time together, Tom falls in love with Cecilia—because it is written into his character to fall in love with women, and to kiss, hold hands, and speak sweetly.

In the meantime, Tom's defection to the real world has caused all kinds of trouble. Reporters descend upon the theater, calling what happened "a miracle." The theater manager calls the producer to complain that the characters in his film are just sitting around up on the screen. People keep coming to the theater because they enjoy sitting there and "observing" the characters. And Gil Shepherd, the "real-world" actor who played Tom Baxter, is panicky that his "creation" will go off and rape somebody and that his career will be over.

Tom has some interesting experiences in our world. First, he tries to pay a large restaurant tab with stage money. Then he tries to drive a car without starting it because in *Purple Rose,* he drove a car but never had to start one, so consequently he doesn't know how to turn an ignition. He even visits a brothel where his gentle manner and sweet talk so seduce the ladies of the house, they offer him a party—for free. Tom turns their offer down because his character could never be unfaithful to the woman he loves—Cecilia.

His behavior in the brothel makes for a very funny scene because of his obvious naïveté and innocence. After waxing ecstatically about "the absolutely astonishing miracle of childbirth . . . with all its attendant feelings of humanity and pathos . . . ," the prostitute Martha asks him, "Do you want me to tie you up?"

At one point, Tom tells Cecilia that he plans on staying in her world and that if his stage money doesn't work, he supposes he'll have to get a job:

Tom   Oh, I guess I have to get a job.
Cecilia   But that's not going to be so easy . . . Right now, the whole country's out of work.
Tom   Well, then we'll live on love. We'll have to make some concessions, but so what? We'll have each other.
Cecilia   That's movie talk.

Later, the lawyers, agents, and producers gather for a conclave to discuss their next step, and during their meeting, the Press Agent says, "The real ones want their lives fiction, and the fictional ones want their lives real"—which is the premise of (Woody's) *The Purple Rose of Cairo.*

While Tom Baxter is running around reality falling in love and not fooling around with prostitutes, his real-life "creator" Gil Shepherd is falling apart emotionally. He envisions his career going down the tubes because of Tom's actions and decides to do something about it. This involves betraying Cecilia by tricking her into falling in love with him so that Tom will go back into the movie. (Although to be fair, it does seem that there are times when Gil is sincere and really is falling for Cecilia, but in the end, his career triumphs over his nascent love for Cecilia.)

Cecilia is in love with Tom and makes that clear to Gil: "I just met a wonderful new man. He's fictional, but you can't have everything."

Tom later brings Cecilia into *The Purple Rose of Cairo* and, in a very humorous scene, Tom tells the characters, "It's every man for himself!" Arturo the maître d' drops his menus, exclaims, "Then I don't have to seat people anymore!" and starts tap dancing across the stage of the Copacabana.

Finally, Cecilia has to make a choice: either stay in the movies with Tom or return to Hollywood with Gil. (The Countess, one of the characters in Tom's *Purple Rose* film, tells Cecilia, "Go with the real guy. . . .") Cecilia chooses to go with Gil, and goes home and tells Monk she's leaving him.

Monk screams at her, "Go! Go! See if I care. Go, see what it is out there. It ain't the movies! It's real life! It's real life, and you'll be back. You mark my words! You'll be back!"

In a poignant closing sequence, Cecilia arrives at the theater with her suitcase, ready to embark on a whirlwind Hollywood life of movies and parties with Gil. She finds the theater deserted and discovers that everyone went back to Hollywood after Tom Baxter went back up on the screen. Completely betrayed and rejected by Gil, she finally realizes that Monk was right: it ain't the movies.

So what does she do?

What she's always done to escape: she goes to the movies. She carries her ukelele and suitcase into the Jewel, and sits crying while Fred Astaire and Ginger Rogers dance across the screen. And after a while, the magic of the movies once again takes hold. She stops crying and becomes engrossed in the film. She may be lost in a fantasy but, once again, she's free . . . for a moment.

The Purple Rose of Cairo, like *Zelig,* is a meditation on reality and fantasy and the wall that separates the two. It is a look at our universal search for identity . . . and love, and the price we pay for finding both . . . or neither.

But lest such serious interpretive concerns blind us to the other pleasures of the film, let us remember: *The Purple Rose of Cairo* is a Woody Allen film—specifically, a Woody Allen comedy, and thus very funny.

And perhaps that is the most important thing to remember after all.

Look for . . .

• The real Kent Theater. Some of *Purple Rose*'s interior scenes were shot at the Kent Theater (called the Jewel in the film) before it was knocked down. Woody told Eric Lax that the Kent was "one of the great, meaningful places of my boyhood." (In Woody's 1975 *New Yorker* essay "Fine Times: An Oral Memoir," Big Flo Guinness used to dance at the Jewel Club in Chicago.)

• The Tom Baxter character. Tom was originally to be played by Michael Keaton, but after ten days of shooting, Woody decided that Keaton had a contemporary sensibility that was too much for the period of the film, and he replaced him with Jeff Daniels.

• Mia Farrow's sister Stephanie. She plays Cecilia's sister, Jane.

• The reference to Mia Farrow's mother, Maureen O'Sullivan. In one scene, Cecilia and Tom walk pass a shoe repair shop called O'Sullivan's.

• Mia Farrow's ability to cry on command. In *Mia Farrow: Flowerchild, Madonna, Muse,* Jeff Daniels remembered that Mia Farrow could cry on command—without the use of glycerin—for the scene in the church where Monk beats up Tom.

A Few Words from Woody . . .

In an interview with Tom Shales in the April 1987 issue of *Esquire*, Woody was asked if he shot an alternate "happy" ending to *The Purple Rose of Cairo*. He replied, "This *is* the happy ending."

20.
Hannah and Her Sisters

(Orion Pictures, 1986); Running Time: 103 minutes; Rating: PG-13; Color.

> The young ladies entered the drawing-room in the
> full fervour of sisterly animosity.
> **R. S. Surtees, from *Mr. Sponge's Sporting Tour***

Hannah and Her Sisters depicts the lives and relationships of Hannah, her two sisters, her philandering husband, her hypochondriac ex-husband, her contentious parents, and the assorted men, women, and children who attend these various and sundry lives. It is set in Manhattan.

Hannah and Her Sisters is a delightful experience, from its first moments in Hannah's apartment at Thanksgiving, to its last moments in Hannah's apartment at Thanksgiving. Everything works.

This film can genuinely be called novelistic—even down to the "chapter headings" between sections of the film's narrative. (And even though I mean "like a novel" when I use the word novelistic, a case can also be made for the adjectival definition of *novel,* as when it's used to mean "innovative and original.")

The writing is brilliant (Woody won an Academy Award for Best Screenplay—he wasn't there, he was busy; the direction, inspired (Woody was nominated for an Academy Award for Best Director); and the film comprises superb performances, wonderful New York locations, and a marvelous story. (*Hannah* was also nominated for an Academy Award for Best Picture, and Michael Caine and Dianne Wiest won Oscars for Best Supporting Actor and Actress.)

Hannah and Her Sisters is a brilliant look at a family told in Woody Allen's inimitable style.

The film is broken into sixteen separate sections, each with its own heading:

- "God, she's beautiful. . . ."
- "We all had a terrific time."
- "The hypochondriac."

- "The Stanislavski Catering Company in action."
- " '. . . nobody, not even the rain, has such small hands.' "
- "The anxiety of the man in the booth."
- "Dusty bought this huge house in Southampton."
- "The abyss."
- " 'The only absolute knowledge attainable by man is that life is meaningless.'—Tolstoy"
- "Afternoons."
- "The audition."
- "The big leap."
- "Summer in New York."
- "Autumn chill."
- "Lucky I ran into you."
- "One year later."

Hannah and Her Sisters must be counted as one of the five best films of Woody Allen's career, and perhaps one of the five best films of the past ten years as well.

Look for . . .

- Michael Caine's eyeglasses. In a 1986 *Boston Herald* interview with Nancy Collins, Michael Caine, speaking of his role in the film, said, "It was an unusual part for me. When I first decided to do it, I was talking to Woody and I said to him, 'Can I wear glasses?' And he said, 'Yeah, but what do you want to wear glasses for?' 'Because, I figure I'm playing you in it.' To me the character is an alter ego of Woody." When asked why working with Woody was something to which most actors aspired, Caine said, "You work with Woody because of the writing, the uniqueness of the situation and because he has complete power over his films. He's like a dictator. He's someone who's written, who's acted, and who's directed. So you know it's not going to be screwed up in the editing or the advertising."
- The Missing Scenes. According to Thierry de Navacelle, in *Woody Allen on Location,* "Only about 20 percent of [*Hannah's* original] script and the original shooting made it in. The rest was from the reshoot. And the result is entirely different from the original concept and script. Originally, [Tony Roberts] had more scenes, including one in an art gallery, and there were more scenes with Woody and Hannah together, Michael Caine and Barbara Hershey made love in a boat, and that was cut. At another point, Barbara Hershey was coming with her fiancé for dinner in Hannah's apartment; Michael Caine tried to kiss her and she accidentally stabbed him in the hand with scissors. The very beautiful scene where Hannah, in bed with Michael Caine, tells him she, too, is fragile was not in the original script." (P. 342)
- Mia Farrow's apartment. All scenes in Hannah's apartment were filmed in Mia Farrow's own New York apartment.

• Another hostile artist named Frederick. See *Interiors.*

• Mickey Sachs's TV skits. Mickey wants to air the "Pope/child molestation" sketch, or the "Cardinal Spellman/Ronald Reagan homosexual dance number," but Standards and Practices gives him a hard time.

• The e. e. cummings reference. In the segment "'. . . nobody, not even the rain, has such small hands'" Elliot "accidentally" bumps into Lee, and they go to the Pageant Book & Print Shop, where he buys her a volume of e. e. cummings's poetry. He tells her to read the poem on page 112. He tells her it reminded him of her. (The cummings poem which contains the line titling this section is "Somewhere I Have Never Travelled, Gladly Beyond." We hear Lee reading the second and fifth stanzas of the poem.)

• Mickey's terror. After tests find a gray area in his brain that the doctors want a closer look at, Mickey wakes up hysterical in the middle of the night, gasping, "There's a tumor in my head the size of a basketball!" Mickey the atheist is now willing to make a deal with God. He tries to assure himself that everything will be fine, that he always overreacts, but then he remembers back to the time he found out that he was infertile and that he and Hannah couldn't have children.

• The real Benno Schmidt. The doctor who gave Mickey the news that he was infertile was played by Benno C. Schmidt, the former president of Yale University.

• Classic anhedonic thinking. When Mickey is told he's fine, he leaps for joy, but then immediately sobers. He realizes that even though he's not dying *now,* he—like all of us—is still dying. He tells Gail that he planned on committing suicide if the news was bad. When Gail reminds Mickey that we're all going to die, Mickey responds with exquisitely anhedonic thinking: "Yes, but doesn't that ruin everything for you? . . . [I]t just takes the pleasure out of everything."

• Frederick's diatribe against American television. When Lee returns home to Frederick after her first tryst with Elliot, Frederick lectures her on the stupidity of American television: "Can you imagine the level of a mind that watches wrestling?"

• Mickey's angst-ridden existential one-liners. Mickey ponders the meaning of life, and knocks off a couple of superb one-liners while musing. We hear him thinking about Nietzsche's theory of eternal recurrence, the belief that the life we live we will live over and over again for eternity. Mickey thinks, "Great. That means I'll have to sit through the Ice Capades again." Then he thinks about being in analysis for years: "My poor analyst got frustrated. The guy finally put in a salad bar."

• Mickey's attempt to convert to Catholicism. He buys Wonder Bread, mayonnaise, a crucifix, and a 3-D portrait of Jesus.

• Symbolic book placement. In 1987, *New York Times* critic Janet Maslin noted that in *Hannah* Mia Farrow is seen reading Richard Yates' novel *Easter Parade,* which is about two adversarial sisters. Maslin called attention to the fact that Woody simply put the book there and did *not* call attention to it.

A Few Words from Woody . . .

• After casting Barbara Hershey as Lee, Woody Allen said, "She gives off enormous erotic overtones, and I don't know why it is, but you see it all the time with her."

• In an interview with Tom Shales in the April 1987 issue of *Esquire,* Woody Allen said of *Hannah and Her Sisters:* "I don't think *Hannah* is as good as *Blue Velvet*. The best picture of the year was *Blue Velvet,* in my opinion. I just liked everything about it."

21.
Radio Days

(Orion Pictures, January 30, 1987); Running Time: 85 minutes;
Rating: PG; Color.

[Woody] denies a lot of truths in his life. *Radio Days* was easy
to admit because he was six in it.
Charles Joffe, quoted in *Woody Allen: A Biography*

There was so much to write. He had seen the world change; not just the
events; although he had seen many of them and had watched the people,
but he had seen the subtler change and he could remember how
the people were at different times. He had been in it and he had
watched it and it was his duty to write of it. . . .
Ernest Hemingway, from *The Snows of Kilimanjaro*

Asked if she really had nothing on in the [*Playboy* calendar] photograph,
Marilyn, her blue eyes wide, purred, "I had the radio on."
From a feature on Marilyn Monroe, in *Time,* August 12, 1952

Radio Days is Woody Allen's glorious and nostalgic paean to his childhood, and a warm, funny, and heartbreakingly accurate look at life in the United States of the early 1940s.

Woody does not appear in *Radio Days* as an adult character, except as the narrator, and even though he is supposed to be fictional, the persona of Woody Allen permeates every scene, line, and moment of the film.

Radio Days is the story of a man reminiscing about his family, his neighborhood, World War II, and the importance of the radio in everyone's lives.

Radio Days is one of the most important films in Woody Allen's body of work. Overtly autobiographical, it is Woody's acknowledgment of his deep-seated nostalgia for his childhood and the 1940s in America.

Two stories run through *Radio Days.* First is the story of Little Joe and his large, extended family. The second consists of behind-the-scenes stories of radio personalities and their programs.

Radio Days is a charming and heartwarming exploration of a time that, as Little Joe laments at the end of the film, grows "dimmer and dimmer" as each year goes by. The film was shot in vivid hues, and is a wonderful re-creation of what many people recall as one of the most romantic times in America's history.

Woody Allen is a historian of the heart, and with *Radio Days* he peers deep within himself and remembers what it was like when families lived under one roof. This was a time when the radio was always playing, and Woody remembers blackouts and dance palaces, skating rinks and night-clubs, and he lets us experience what it was like growing up in a time many still consider magical. To communicate the magic is effective storytelling. To allow you to *feel* the magic is genius.

Watching *Radio Days,* one feels the magic.

Radio Days has an intrinsic sense of wonder, a sensibility that, when properly communicated (as it is here), elevates retold memories to a state approaching fantasy. We enter this other world so lovingly re-created by Woody and his excellent cast.

Reinforcing the fantasy feel to this film is Woody's script, one of his best. It begins with "Once upon a time . . ." and from that moment on, you know that you're going to be told a wondrous story, replete with romance, villains, and heroes (even if the heroes are radio characters like the Masked Avenger).

Woody Allen's Doppelgänger is Joe, a young Jewish kid growing up in Rockaway in the early forties: "The scene is Rockaway, the time is my child-hood. It's my old neighborhood, and forgive me if I tend to romanticize the past."

The story of *Radio Days* is like a wheel with many spokes. The spokes are Joe and his extended family, their neighbors, and the celebrities they hear and read about. The center of the wheel is the ubiquitous radio. It is on all the time, in every house. It is the focal point of these people's lives.

The movie opens with the story (probably apocryphal?) of the two burglars who answer the phone in a house they are robbing and correctly answer the jackpot questions on "Guess That Tune." In *Radio Days* the house belongs to a Mr. and Mrs. Needleman, and the next day a truckload of prizes is delivered to their house.

The characters in *Radio Days* use radio as a fantasy escape, and

Woody's script oft restates this theme throughout the film. Woody's parents listen to "Breakfast with Irene and Roger" and we're told that Irene and Roger and Joe's family lived in "two completely different worlds" and that Irene and Roger knew "people and places we only dreamt of." And when Joe's Aunt Bea and her current boyfriend take Joe to Radio City Music Hall, there's a strong sense of fantasy. We see Radio City through Joe's eyes. He has obviously never seen anything so beautiful in his life—it's almost as though he were entering another world.

At one point, Woody's mother (flawlessly played by Julie Kavner) acknowledges her fantasies to her sister with a very funny line. They're talking about romance, and Bea, played by Dianne Wiest, reminds her sister that she's always listening to romantic soap operas on the radio. Kavner replies, "I like to daydream, but I have my two feet firmly planted on my husband."

And then there's Uncle Abe, a guy who is always bringing home fish from Oscar's Dock. (He knows guys down there.) His wife, Ceil, always gets stuck cleaning them, and the adult Joe tells us that Ceil always "dreamed of a more exciting life than always having to filet his flounder." Abe's response? "If you don't like it, take the gas pipe."

Joe's parents argue about everything, but they truly love each other. An early scene shows them fighting over which is a greater ocean, the Atlantic or Pacific. Joe's father (who won't tell Joe he drives a cab for a living) is wont to tell his wife, "You're lucky I love you, you old douche bag." Once, Joe fantasizes his parents appearing on the radio show "The Court of Human Emotions" and complaining about each other. The radio psychiatrist tells the two of them that they deserve each other.

Joe also tells us about his neighborhood. The Waldbaums lived next door. Mrs. Waldbaum had a steel plate in her head and "it was said she couldn't walk near magnets." Ceil's daughter, cousin Ruthie, always used to listen in on their party line and that's how she found out that Mrs. Waldbaum had to have her ovaries removed. (Joe's mother wanted to know, one or two?) Then there was the old guy who had a nervous breakdown and ran through the business district of Rockaway in his underwear, waving a cleaver.

The film moves back and forth from Joe and his family to the radio people, focusing on floozy Sally White (played by Mia Farrow), a cigarette girl and would-be actress/singer who one day sees a murder committed by Rocco (Danny Aiello). Rocco brings Sally home, his mother takes a shine to her, and instead of killing her and dumping her body in Jersey, he decides to call in a favor and get her a job on the radio. She is about to make her debut when Pearl Harbor is bombed and her chance for stardom is shot down. But things work out after she takes diction lessons and becomes a society reporter.

There are some highly amusing vignettes in *Radio Days*. In one, a class-mate of Joe's brings one of his father's condoms to Show and Tell. In another, Joe and his friends, on a rooftop looking for German subs, watch through binoculars a woman dance naked in front of a mirror. The woman later becomes a substitute teacher of their class, and Joe thinks that it is a good thing to have seen his teacher dance naked in front of a mirror. And in another, Mrs. Silverman has a stroke on the spot upon seeing the girl across the street kiss a black guy.

In a radio vignette that scathingly parodies "sports legends," Bill Kern (obviously Bill Stern, who did just such a show), in "Bill Kern's Favorite Sports Legends" tells the story of a pitcher who lost a leg, an arm, and his sight—but kept on pitching. (In a hilarious scene, the blind pitcher with one leg and one arm holds out his glove as the ball goes elsewhere.) After the guy gets killed in an accident, we learn that the next season he won eighteen games in "the big league in the sky."

Joe also talks about "memory flashes" triggered by certain songs. The song "Lay That Pistol Down" brings back memories of the day he and a friend built a snowman in front of the school and used a carrot as the snowman's erection. A woman teacher came out, chased the boys away, pulled out the carrot, and proceeded to eat it.

Joe also remembers blackouts. During one, his mother remarks, "What a world. It could be so wonderful if it wasn't for certain people."

Aunt Bea, who wanted only to get married, is also lovingly remembered as she's seen dancing around the house, and bringing home one new boyfriend after another. In a very funny scene, Bea dates a guy still griev-ing for his dead fiancé—who it turns out was named Leonard.

Some of the dialogue in *Radio Days* is brilliantly reminiscent of the sardonic way people talked back then. When Joe's mother has a baby girl, her husband suggests calling his new daughter Ellen, in memory of his wife's cousin Eddie. But Eddie's not dead yet, his wife reminds him. "He should be," he replies.

One segment in the film is very dramatic and very touching. In another re-creation of a radio legend, Joe tells us about a little girl who fell in a well and was trapped. The country, glued to the radio, followed every turn of event regarding the rescue. But unlike the more recent (and very similar) Jessica McClure story, this one did not have a happy ending: the little girl died, and everyone found out about the failed rescue via the radio. The scene ends with Joe's father holding Joe on his lap, hugging him, and crying.

Radio Days ends on New Year's Eve 1943. We behold the roof of the King Cole Room where much of the story took place, the roof where Sally White used to go for her illicit rendezvous; the roof that overlooked New York, and from where we could view the giant smoking billboard and the moving top-hat sign. We had previously seen the New Year's Eve celebration at Joe's house, and couldn't help but feel a sense of loss . . . and change . . . and hope:

> I never forgot that New Year's Eve . . . when Aunt Bea awakened me to watch 1944 come in. And I've never forgotten any of those people. Or any of the voices we used to hear on the radio. Although the truth is, with the passing of each New Year's Eve, those voices do seem to grow dimmer and dimmer.

Look for . . .

• Ken Roberts. One of *Radio Day*'s "Radio Voices" belonged to Ken Roberts, Tony Roberts's father.

• The Bernsteins. Nick Bernstein, a member of the *Radio Days* Location Department, is the son of Walter Bernstein, the writer of *The Front.* Nick started working with Woody at age fourteen as a production assistant on *Manhattan.*

• The Paradise Garage. The "Breakfast with Irene and Roger" set was actually the Paradise Garage on King Street, the oldest gay bar in New York City.

• The Morosco reference. At one point, Roger (of "Breakfast with Irene and Roger") tells "Richard" (Rodgers) that the "show at the Morosco" was terrific. Woody's first play, *Don't Drink the Water,* opened on November 17, 1966, at the Morosco Theater.

• The Waldbaums. The Waldbaums were based on real people Woody lived next door to while growing up: "The family in the house on the other side [of the Konigsbergs] were both Russian Jews and Communists. They shocked the neighborhood by flagrantly not observing the Jewish high holy days; a mild version of them appears in *Radio Days.*" (Eric Lax, *Woody Allen: A Biography,* p. 32)

• The mail-order businesses. At one point, Little Joe's father wants to sell cultured pearls by mail order. He also considers learning jewelry engraving, and at one time, he sold "get well" greeting cards by mail. (In Woody's 1981 play, *The Floating Light Bulb,* Paul's mother Enid wants her sister Lena to help her start a business selling personalized matchbooks and guppies by mail order. Earlier, Enid had tried to start her own greeting card business, but "it was a nightmare. Who knew you had to keep books and records?" Enid also wanted to sell costume jewelry by mail at one point.)

• The "slapping Little Joe" scene. See the section below on Thierry de Navacelle's behind-the-scenes look at the making of this scene.

• The Whites. Mia Farrow's character is named Sally White, and in Woody's 1981 play, *The Floating Light Bulb,* Paul's father, Max, knew a guy named Danny White.

• Rebecca Schaeffer. The Communist's daughter who gave Mrs. Silverman a stroke by kissing a black guy was played by Rebecca Schaeffer.

Schaeffer starred in the sitcom "My Sister Sam," and in real life was later slain by a crazed fan.

• Jimmy Sabat. Bea's "Radio City" date, Chester, was played by Jimmy Sabat, a sound mixer who is Woody Allen's longest collaborator. Jimmy worked with Woody on *Bananas.* (Jimmy Sabat was also the location sound mixer on Martin Scorsese's *GoodFellas.*)

• The weekend whiz. The sequence in which Sally witnesses a killing at the nightclub was conceived and written by Woody over the May 2 weekend because he didn't have enough scenes to film while Dianne Wiest was away at her father's funeral.

• The Nazi sub. The Nazi submarine in *Radio D*ays had been previously used as a Japanese sub in Steven Spielberg's *1941.*

• Dylan Farrow. Little Joe's new sister, Ellen, was played by Dylan Farrow, Mia Farrow and Woody Allen's adopted daughter.

• The fur-dying incident. The scene in which Little Joe dyes his mother's fur coat is based on a real-life incident in Woody's childhood.

• The Two Voices of Mia Farrow. Sally White goes to the King Cole Room with the Masked Avenger for New Year's Eve 1943. Thanks to her diction lessons, her voice is now rich and sensuous. She accidentally lapses into her high, squeaky voice, though, when she asks if anyone has ever seen the King Cole roof. (Mia Farrow had to do two distinct voices for this role.)

Thierry de Navacelle's *Woody Allen on Location*
A Day-to-Day Account of the Making of *Radio Days*

Woody Allen on Location is a rather peculiar volume in the "Books About Woody Allen" library.

Essentially, the book is a diary of the making of *Radio Days.* Thierry de Navacelle had total access to Woody's set, script, and screening room, and thus, as would be expected, the book is *loaded* with minutiae about the making of the film.

But that's the problem with the book. While de Navacelle had access to all of the above, the one thing he did not have access to was the most important element in the film's production: the director. Based on the author's thorough chronicling of his experience watching *Radio Days* be made over the four-month period from November 1985 through February 1986, one can conclude that not a hundred words passed between Woody and de Navacelle. De Navacelle was allowed on the set, yes, but that was the end of Woody's involvement with the book.

The result is a book that, while very informative and accurate, is rather sterile and distant.

De Navacelle recorded the specifics of every take of every scene, throughout the entire four months of filming.

An example, from page 360:

> Shot 95: Ruthie, all dressed up, sings and dances in front of her mirror à la Carmen Miranda, to "South American Way," which plays on the radio. Pop and Abe come to watch, and join in at the end. *(1 minute, 30 seconds.)*
>
> His job finished, Carlo comes out to the balcony. After two hours of lighting, Carlo needs to relax, staying near the set, though. He cracks a few "Italian" jokes that the ladies appreciate. Ray joins us, too. The balcony is the place today.
>
> Take 1: Very good. "Hold your positions, kids!" Dickie screams. Woody checks the last framing: "That's perfect." Then to Ruthie: "Maybe, at the end . . ." But Ruthie already knows; she can do better.
>
> Take 2: Dickie cuts. There was a problem with the camera movement.
>
> Take 3: Cut. Ruthie lost one of her earrings.
>
> Take 4: Good. Woody asks Ruthie if she could dance as well with the music much lower. "Yes," she answers.
>
> Take 5: "Perfect," but Dickie thinks he saw somebody pass by in the background. But who? Nobody was back there. Woody: "Let's do one more."
>
> Take 6: Good.
>
> *(Takes 1, 4, and 6 are printed.)* It's 6:30 P.M.

The whole book is like that. Even though de Navacelle found all this detail fascinating and felt a pressing need to record it for posterity, after a hundred pages of this, you tend to find yourself skimming over the text. *Power*-skimming.

There are two other perplexing aspects to this book. First is de Navacelle's insistence on continually putting in "real-world" news headlines before his entries. He says he included items of news in his diary to stay grounded in reality during the shooting. Fine, but why include them in the book?

And second is his insistence on referring to the cast members *only* by their characters' names. It is ridiculous and insulting to read that "Bea's father has died. She's in her room, crying" when he's referring to the passing of Dianne Wiest's *real* father; and yet he refuses to refer to her as "Dianne." He also never refers to Mia Farrow—MIA FARROW! for heaven's sake—otherwise than by "Sally," the name of her character in the film, even when Mia is on the set in "civilian" clothes, obviously not participating in the film that day.

The book is definitely worth a look, however, because it does offer a glimpse into Woody's working habits, and it allows fans to see what it's like on a Woody Allen set. You will find many parts of it enthralling, and you will find yourself thinking about it for days after finishing it. De Navacelle does a very good job of capturing the ambience of a working film set, and for Woody fans—or any film buffs, for that matter—this will be an interesting read.

De Navacelle was thoughtful enough to include several fascinating and irresistible tidbits of "insider" information in the book. Here is a sampling:

• Several times during filming Woody was asked for an autograph. In most cases, he consented, and signed the proffered card, paper, whatever.

• At one point, de Navacelle thanked Woody for allowing him on the set and told him how interesting it was for him. Woody's response? "For us, it's a little sloppy."

• One Friday in early November, a sixteen-year-old girl successfully sneaked onto the set and stood next to Woody, staring at him. Woody reacted with embarrassment and tried to hide beneath his cap.

• During the scene when Abe brings home fish, a "real-world" woman from a neighboring house screamed out Woody's name. Woody simply looked at her and held a finger to his lips.

• Kay Chapin, Woody's script supervisor, told de Navacelle that Woody very often cuts a lot of scenes "for pace" but uses the gags themselves in later films. "It is said they are kept on what is called 'the black reels.' "

• Sydney Blake, who played the "nude dancing" teacher Miss Gordon, refused to allow two male members of the crew in the room with her while filming her nude scene. Fern Buchner, the woman who did makeup, speciously told her the guys were gay, and Sydney then allowed them to stay.

• De Navacelle tells of Woody blocking a scene by going through all the actions himself: "He hangs the drapes, he puts the babies to bed, he picks a baby up . . . You get the feeling that Woody is both precise in that he knows exactly the sort of effect he is looking for, and imprecise because he lets the atmosphere of the room lead him to that effect."

• At one point, Woody's assistant, Jane Read Martin, took de Navacelle aside and asked him again what he wanted: "She wants to be sure she is conveying it correctly to Woody." De Navacelle is distraught. He thinks that Woody has had second thoughts about giving his approval for the book, and that he will want him gone. At lunch, the crew tries to reassure him that everything is fine by telling him of their own experiences with Woody: One crew member tells him, "I'm seeing more of him than I do my own wife, and we never say a word." Bobby Ward (who has been with Woody since *The Front*) "hasn't talked to him in the ten years they worked together." They tell him that Jeff Daniels, during the filming of *The Purple Rose of Cairo,* only heard from Woody for direction. "And then there is the Marshall McLuhan story. When McLuhan came to the set to reshoot his scene in *Annie Hall,* Woody didn't want to talk to him anymore. It was very embarrassing." Everything worked out fine, however, and that afternoon, Jane handed de Navacelle a copy of the *Radio Days* script. When he waved the script at Woody and thanked him, Woody replied, "Guard it with your life!"

• Two teenagers asked de Navacelle about some of the rumors about

Woody Allen: "Is is true that he has two bodyguards? They say he comes by helicopter. Where is his limousine? Is it true that everybody has to stand up when he arrives?"

• One Friday, de Navacelle had to leave the set early. The following Monday, Jane Martin told him, "Woody noticed."

• The scene in which Rabbi Baumel and Little Joe's parents slap Joe for spending his Palestine Fund money on a Masked Avenger Secret Compartment Ring took ten takes, and ended with Little Joe (Seth Green) in tears from being slapped so much.

• There is a scene that was cut from the film in which a marine kisses his girl while Ruthie watches and swoons over the kiss. The actors playing the marine and the girl began kissing as soon as Tom Reilly, the first assistant director yelled out, "Rolling!" Woody remarked (to no one in particular), "I didn't say, 'Action.'"

• At one point, de Navacelle observed Woody typing out his script changes: "He types with all his fingers, though not very quickly."

• During one take, an extra waiting to be made up came on the set to watch Woody work. When Woody found out who he was, he said, "Out!" and the terrified extra fled the room.

• Woody was reading the *Daily News* prior to the filming of one scene with Mia Farrow. He waited until the absolute last second after "Action!" was called to lift his head from the paper and watch.

• A cake was brought onto the set for Nick Bernstein's birthday. De Navacelle reports that everyone sang "Happy Birthday," except Woody, but that Woody did whistle a few times during the applause before splitting.

• De Navacelle tells the story of a screening at the Zukor theater of some footage of the King Cole roof set. Woody was tense because he wasn't sure how the set looked on film. When people continued to open the door and come in after the screening had begun, Woody asked that the screening be stopped: "And immediately, [first assistant director] Tom [Reilly] act[ed]. Everybody [had] to leave, even [Mia] and Jane [Martin, Woody's assistant]! Only Woody, Carlo [Di Palma] and Tom remain[ed]."

• De Navacelle learned from John Doumanian and Judy Swerdlow that Woody does impersonations of Fred Astaire and excerpts from *West Side Story.*

A Few Words from Woody . . .

In Eric Lax's book *Woody Allen: A Biography,* Woody says, "When there's a role for me, I do it. But there was nothing for me in *Radio Days.* . . ."

22.
September

(Orion Pictures, December 18, 1987); Running Time: 82 minutes;
Rating: PG; Color.

Tell me not here, it needs not saying,
What tune the enchantress plays
In aftermaths of soft September
Or under blanching mays,
For she and I were long acquainted
And I knew all her ways.
**A. E. Houseman, from
"Epitaph on an Army of Mercenaries"**

August is a wicked month.
Edna O'Brien

September is the story of six people who share a summer in a Vermont beach house and try to cope with their pasts, their unrequited loves, and their crippling secrets.

September is one of Woody's three unadulterated dramas. (The two others are, of course, *Interiors* and *Another Woman.*) The entire film takes place in the beach house and never strays outdoors. Woody wanted to do a play on film, and that he has done. Does it work?

Yes and no.

As usual, the writing is, for the most part, razor-sharp. But there are moments when the dialogue is a bit affected. One instance comes to mind: Dianne Wiest's character, Stephanie, says that her husband is a radiologist, but that she never let him take X-rays of her because if he looked inside her he'd see things he wouldn't understand and be terribly hurt. Do real people *ever* speak so metaphorically? Sometimes, the preciseness of the dialogue comes off as stagy.

But then there are brilliant moments. When Diane (Elaine Stritch) looks in the mirror during her "it's hell gettin' older" speech, we *feel* the tragedy of aging, the sadness of regrets. And Lloyd's speech about the universe being "haphazard" and "morally neutral" is likewise quite gripping.

September is a qualified success. It's a success because Woody did something not many directors can do: satisfactorily stage a play on film. It's a qualified success because there are certain moments that don't work. But overall, it is well worth your time.

Look for . . .

• *September,* Take 1. The original version of *September* had an almost entirely different cast. Mia Farrow played Lane; Maureen O'Sullivan (her real mother) played her mother, Diane; Dianne Wiest played Stephanie; Denholm Elliott played Diane's husband, Lloyd; Charles Durning played next-door-neighbor Howard; and Christopher Walken played Peter the writer. Walken was replaced by Sam Shepard several weeks into shooting. (Woody told Eric Lax, "We couldn't get copacetic on what to do and decided that instead of his making concessions and my making concessions, we'd work on something else down the line.")

• The Lana Turner connection. Early on, we learn that Lane (supposedly) killed her mother's lover. Lane's story is based on the real-life story of Lana Turner's daughter, who stabbed her mother's abusive lover to death.

• The buying of music. Peter, who is in love with Stephanie, bought her an Art Tatum recording. In *Hannah and Her Sisters,* Elliot bought Lee a Bach recording.

• The blacklisting reference. A possible title of Peter's book is *The History Professor.* The history professor was Peter's father. He was fired during the McCarthy era. He was blacklisted. (See the section on *The Front* in this chapter for details on Woody's film on that period.) Peter's father supported his family by playing poker and betting the horses.

• Woody's "voice" coming out of Lloyd and Diane. Lloyd and Diane seem to speak for Woody in this film. (See Chapter 11, "Wooden Poses: The Reel Woody Allen," for a discussion of Woody's Doppelgängers.) At one point, Peter asks Lloyd, "Is there anything more terrifying than the destruction of the world?" They then have the following existential conversation:

> **Lloyd**   Yeah, the knowledge that it doesn't matter one way or the other. It's all random, resonating aimlessly out of nothing, eventually vanishing forever. I'm not talking about the world now. I'm talking about the universe. All space, all time, just a temporary convulsion. And I get paid to prove it.
> **Peter**   You feel so sure of that when you look out on a clear night like tonight and see all those millions of stars . . . and none of it matters?
> **Lloyd**   I think it's just as beautiful as you do. And vaguely evocative of some deep truth that always just keeps slipping away. But then my professional perspective overcomes me. A less wishful, more penetrating view of it all. And I understand it for what it truly is. Haphazard. Morally neutral. And unimaginably violent.

• The pond remark. Diane says she never liked the pond because there are "live things" in it. (Woody has made this remark himself.)

• Another boozy-blowzy mother character. Diane is another boozy-blowzy mother character à la Norma in *Hannah and Her Sisters.*

• The closed blinds. Throughout the picture, the blinds in the house are never shown open because the film was shot on one set.

A Few Words from Woody . . .

• Woody Allen told Eric Lax, "*September* is less cerebral and much, much warmer than *Interiors* but not as warm and familial as *Hannah,* which is a more amusing movie because I'm in it and I play a comic character in a comic predicament, and Michael Caine's predicament as a man infatuated with his wife's sister is in its way comic, too." He also said, "I knew very few people would like it because when you see something like this done on its most successful level, it's not widely seen because plays and movies are very different."

• In a 1987 *Rolling Stone* interview with William Geist (reprinted in Chapter 2) Woody said of *September,* "[I]t's a small film, a small idea; a small, intimate kind of film, principally dramatic but hopefully with some laughs in it.

23.
Another Woman

(Orion Pictures, 1988); Running time: 81 minutes; Rating: PG; Color.

Few love to hear the sins they love to act.
William Shakespeare, from *Pericles, Prince of Tyre*

Another Woman is about a detached and distant philosophy professor at midlife who comes to terms with her mistakes, her feelings, her family, and her life.

Another Woman—with *Interiors* and *September*—holds the distinction of being one of only three solely dramatic films by Woody Allen. The three form a somber trinity, as it were, and yet their pleasures are many.

Philosophy professor Marion Post is one of the three characters Woody has created with whom he identifies the most. (See "Wooden Poses: The Reel Woody Allen" [Chapter 11] for a discussion of Woody's Doppelgängers as well as a look at the creation of the "Woody Allen" myth.) Marion is lost. She is now in her fifties and her life is filled with regrets. She seems to have it all but in reality has nothing. And interestingly, it is the women in her world—Laura, Hope, even Claire—who recognize the truth.

Woody's films always make us think, but the dramatic works *really* make us ponder issues that are important to Woody. Sometimes in the comedies, when a character begins spouting existential angst reflecting Woody Allen's personal beliefs, we don't take their concerns that seriously because their worries will occasionally come off as somewhat excessive and extreme.

But in *Another Woman,* when Hope tells her psychiatrist that life itself enrages her—the inhumanity, the cruelty, even death—we respect her feelings, and we somehow sense that the truth is being spoken here.

With *Another Woman,* Woody Allen had released two dramas in a row (the first was *September.*) His next film would be the short *Oedipus Wrecks,* and with it some of his fans would commence wondering where was the Woody of *Hannah and Her Sisters,* his last box-office smash.

The answer was just around the corner with *Crimes and Misdemeanors.*

In the meantime, we were treated to the golden glories of *Another Woman,* a film that holds much for the filmgoer willing to give it a chance. To be sure, there is an *isolated* affected moment (such as the Heidegger reference—see below) in the film, but overall, *Another Woman* is consummately profound filmmaking, from a comic filmmaker whom we are beginning to get used to as being occasionally humorless and surprisingly serious.

The film takes us through the growing restlessness and unhappiness of Marion, and shows how she begins to project her fears and insecurities onto a young pregnant woman (deliberately named Hope) who, ironically, is considering suicide.

The film ends with what can justifiably be called the ultimate fantasy: Marion reading a novel in which she has become a character.

Look for . . .

• Mia Farrow's pregnancy. Mia's character Hope in *Another Woman* is pregnant. Mia Farrow was really pregnant with her and Woody's son Satchel when the film was made.

• The lost opening. *Another Woman* starts with the sound of a ticking clock, and Marion's voice-over (*before* the credits) in which she talks about turning fifty. (See Chapter 11, "Wooden Poses," for her opening speech.) In *Woody Allen: A Biography,* Eric Lax tells of the original opening shot for *Another Woman:*

> While making *Another Woman,* the crew set up what was supposed to be the first shot of Marion, in which she would come out of a neighborhood delicatessen with instant coffee and such supplies for her new office, and then walk along the street. It was to be accompanied by her voice-over, introducing herself and explaining her work. A dolly track had been laid out on the sidewalk so the camera could be moved to capture everything in one long master shot. . . . After all was ready, Woody sat on the camera seat and was dollied through the shot. Then he said, simply, "No," and stepped aside with [Sven] Nykvist and assistant director Tom Reilly. . . . "Nine of hearts on this," Reilly called out to the crew. Without surprise or saying a word, they started to dismantle the equipment that had taken two hours to set up. [P. 326]

• Marion's flawless assessment of the writing process. "A new book is always a very demanding project, and it requires that I really shut myself off from everything—but the work."

• "The big five-oh." At a birthday party, the guest of honor says, "It is with a mixture of some joy, but mostly paralyzing anxiety, I hereby plunge into the big five-oh." Woody Allen was fifty-three when *Another Woman* was released.

• Gena Rowlands's body language. Her physicality is indicative of Marion's mental state: When Ken asks her at the party if the song the pianist is playing takes her back, she says, oh, yeah, and casually turns her back on Ken. *Then* she asks him if he'd ever think of making love to *her* on the living room floor.

• Discipline and the borrowing of money. When Lynn tries to take a little time to talk to Marion about borrowing some money, Marion says, "I've just got to be disciplined when I'm writing, or else I'm not going to get it done in time." (In *Manhattan,* Yale whined about not being able to find the time to finish his O'Neill book, and in *Hannah and Her Sisters,* Holly was constantly borrowing money from Hannah.)

• The Heidegger reference. At the party where Larry kissed Marion, the guests toast Marion's new book: "German philosophy will never be the same." A guest says to Marion, *"You'll* go on forever, Heidegger definitely got what he deserved." Everyone laughs because it's clear these are people who get the references—and the joke.

• Ken and condemnation. The first time Ken says "I accept your condemnation" is to his ex-wife when she barges in on his and Marion's engagement party. The second time he uses the line is when Marion has an argument with him about his not sleeping with her (not knowing that he's having an affair with Claire). Ken says he's sorry, and if he's done anything wrong, would she forgive him? He then tells her, "I accept your condemnation," and it's clear he uses this line as a pat and insincere escape from difficult situations.

• Falling off the wagon. In a bar scene where Claire confronts Marion about her former lover David, Jack tells Claire, "This is outrageous. You should never drink." (This is the same line Yale says to Ike in *Manhattan* after he starts in about his ex-wife.)

• The Rilke symbolism. "Archaic Torso of Apollo" was Marion's mother's favorite Rilke poem. Her mother's tears stained the book page over the last line of the poem: "For here there is no place that does not see you. You must change your life."

• Marion's writing critique. Marion visits her brother Paul and he asks her if she remembers what she said when he showed her a piece he had written. He remembers her saying, "This is overblown. It's too emotional, it's maudlin. Your dreams may be meaningful but to the objective observer, it's so embarrassing." She doesn't remember saying it.

• The Marion Post/Mary Wilke connection. Marion goes back to her office and hears Hope talking about her to the doctor. She tells him Marion was a very sad woman. "She can't allow herself to feel. The result is she's led this cold, cerebral life, and it's alienated everyone around her." Marion has much in common with Mary Wilke in *Manhattan,* who also lived a cold and detached "life of the mind."

• Woody's fiction writing. An excerpt from Larry's novel (written, of course, by Woody) is included in the film:

> Helinka and I accidentally ran into one another one day while we were both buying tickets to a concert. I knew her because she was the lover of a man I knew quite well. Recently, they had decided to marry. This was a catastrophe for me personally because from the first moment he had introduced her to me, I was in love with her. I convinced her to have a drink with me. It was the only time I had ever been alone with her since we met. She was lovely, and I spoke too much and too rapidly because I was embarrassed over my feelings towards her, which I felt were painfully obvious. We walked around in Central Park and talked about lots of things. I told her about a book I was planning to write, and my wanting to live out west. She spoke enthusiastically about her upcoming marriage, but I thought it was too enthusiastic, as if she was trying to convince herself, rather than me. Soon it began to rain. We ducked into an underpass to avoid a cloudburst. I remember thinking how wonderful she was, and how beautiful she looked at that moment. And I wanted to tell her so many things, because my feelings were swirling so. And I think she knew everything, and that frightened her. And yet some instinct told me that if I kissed her she would respond. Her kiss was full of desire, and I knew I couldn't share that feeling with anyone else. And then a wall went up and just as quickly I was screened out. But it was too late, because I now knew she was capable of intense passion if she would one day just allow herself to feel.

A Few Words from Woody . . .

Eric Lax quotes Woody Allen as saying *Another Woman* is only "an improved picture. Like *September* and *Interiors,* its aims are high in terms of wanting to say something in a dramatic way. . . . I wasn't good enough to have it rise to the level I wanted."

24.
Oedipus Wrecks
(in *New York Stories*)

(Touchstone Pictures, 1989); Running Time: 41 minutes; (*New York Stories,* 119 minutes); Rating: PG; Color.

I'm fifty years old, I'm a partner in a big law firm . . . and I still
haven't resolved my relationship with my mother.
Sheldon Mills, *Oedipus Wrecks*

Mother knows best.
Edna Ferber

Oedipus Wrecks is the story of what happens when a fifty-year-old law-yer's domineering, bossy mother really disappears during a magician's trick, only to appear later in the skies over New York City. She comes back to earth only after her son's relationship with a blonde shiksa falls apart and he ends up with a nice Jewish girl who is very similar to mom.

Oedipus Wrecks was Woody Allen's contribution to the three-part "New York" anthology film, *New York Stories.* Woody's was the third film in the trilogy. The first short film (and definitely the best of the bunch) was Martin Scorsese's *Life Lessons,* starring Nick Nolte as an obsessed painter, and Rosanna Arquette as his assistant and the object of his desire. The second was Francis Ford Coppola's *Life Without Zoe,* starring Heather McComb as a young girl living a variety of implausible old-fashioned adventures in today's New York City.

Oedipus Wrecks came on the heels of two dramas, *September* and *Another Woman.* It is only forty-one minutes long and has a cartoonlike feel to it, at times similar to the mood of *Radio Days.*

Oedipus Wrecks had more potential than was realized. Some quintes-sential Woody comedic moments in the film are so short that you almost get no chance for the humor to register. (Any of the scenes in which Sheldon participates in Treva's occult rituals, for instance, should have been longer. Seeing Woody in a headdress, or a monk's robe dancing around chanting should have been high comedy. But the scenes were too short to have much impact.)

Mia Farrow walks through her role as Lisa but has little to do here. She is, as always, almost ethereally lovely, and the scenes wherein she and Woody embrace, or kiss, or drink champagne on the balcony have a con-crete sense of genuineness about them.

Overall, *New York Stories* is worth watching, but selectively. *Life Lessons* can be watched repeatedly. It is magnificent. In the case of *Life Without Zoe,* once is more than enough. And *Oedipus Wrecks* demands at least two or three viewings, if only to catch all the jokes, and to appreciate Woody's filmmaking.

As the epigraph to this section reveals, Sheldon Mills has an Oedipal problem. Specifically, his mother still treats him like a child, and he still responds to her as one. It is serious enough for him to seek therapy. One day during a session he tells his doctor about a dream he had. He dreamed his mother died, and he was driving the hearse to the cemetery. As he's driving, his mother begins instructing him from the coffin ("back-hearse driving"), giving him directions and telling him how to drive.

Sheldon tells his doctor, "What can I say? I love her, but I wish she would disappear."

Sheldon's wishes are understandable. Sadie Millstein (Mae Questel, the voice of Betty Boop) is an unbelievably domineering mother. She embarrasses him constantly, criticizes his appearance, and detests his girlfriend. Ever the good son, though, Sheldon agrees with his fiancée Lisa's (Mia Farrow) suggestion to take his mother out for a Sunday dinner and then to a magic show so she can meet Lisa's kids. (Sheldon has them seated at an outdoor table because his mother yells everything she says and he's humiliated when she makes a scene.)

At the magic show the trouble begins. Sheldon gets his wish. Shandu the magician picks Sadie out of the audience to use in his disappearance trick. He puts her in the box, performs the required trickery, and Sadie disappears. For good. Even after the trick is over, she can't be found, and Shandu doesn't know what happened. At first, when Sadie doesn't come back when she's supposed to, Sheldon smiles. But then he's distraught and hires a private detective to search for her.

As in *The Purple Rose of Cairo,* the magic that caused Sadie to disappear simply happens. No one can explain it. And yet at the end of the film, Sadie decides to come down after Lisa has left Sheldon and he's decided to marry Treva. Did she learn some arcane power while up in the air? We don't know. It's never explained.

When Sadie is gone for a few days and it looks as if she'll not be back, Sheldon becomes a new man. He becomes more relaxed, he smiles more easily, and he's generally in a much better frame of mind. His wish has come true. In fact, he makes a point of telling his psychiatrist how good he feels, and how glad he is that she wasn't murdered. But then his face darkens and he asks the doctor, "You don't think she's gonna come back, do you?"

Sadie first appears in the sky above New York City as Sheldon buys yogurt in a health-food store. She appears as a giant Sadie in the sky and Sheldon is aghast. He asks her, "Where are you?" She doesn't know—and doesn't care. All she wants to do is persuade him not to marry Lisa. She's had much time to think about "his problem" and has even discussed it with strangers on the ground. While Sheldon is trying to process this, Sadie starts showing his pictures around, and all the people whip out their own photos. Sheldon says this can't be happening, "I need oxygen . . . I need cyanide."

Sheldon is enraged. He says he's going to find the magician and dismember him. And then he's going to sue him.

The people of New York accept Sadie and begin to torment Sheldon. Ed Koch defends her right to stay in the sky, and construction workers make fun of Sheldon.

Sheldon can't take it. He tries to kill himself by sticking his finger in a light socket. It doesn't work.

His psychiatrist recommends a psychic named Treva. Sheldon reluctantly goes, but after three weeks calls her a fraud and decides to quit. Treva cries, Sheldon feels bad, she feeds him (boiled chicken), and he falls in love with her.

He comes home to find Lisa gone, and so he is free to propose to Treva. She accepts and he introduces her to his mother in the sky. Sadie likes Treva, decides to come down, and the movie ends with Sadie showing Treva baby pictures of Sheldon while Sheldon stands and watches, wondering what he's got himself into. As the film fades to black, "I Wanna Girl (Just Like the Girl That Married Dear Old Dad)" plays on the soundtrack.

Look for . . .

• The "Danny Rose" reference. During the Chinese Box Trick at the magic show, Shandu the magician asks Sadie how old she is, exactly as Danny Rose used to do when he did his standup act.

• The backstage "Where's my mother?" scene after Sadie disappears. This scene is reminiscent of the backstage "My wife won't come out of hypnosis" scene in *Broadway Danny Rose.* Another similarity occurs when Shandu tells Sheldon that if anything has happened to his mother he'd give him two free tickets to any show. In *Broadway Danny Rose,* Danny offered the husband of the hypnotized woman dinner at the restaurant of his choice.

• More California-bashing: As part of Treva's rituals, Sheldon wears a headpiece, gets his fortune told with tarot cards, and dances in a bizarre costume (while Treva orders pizza). Sheldon also dances in a monk's robe and chants. At one point, Sheldon tells Treva she should move out to California: "By now you'd have a swimming pool and your own church."

• The Teasing of Woody. While his mother is still floating around, hardhats tease Sheldon. In *Bananas,* hoods tormented Fielding on the subway.

• The chicken jokes. Sheldon tells Treva that boiled chicken was his mother's specialty: she was able "to render the bird completely devoid of any flavor. It's a culinary miracle." Woody once did a joke about his mother being home running a chicken through the deflavorizing machine.

• Julie Kavner's spontaneous laughter. As Sheldon leaves Treva's apartment after dinner, he says it was a nice idea to floss between every course; he'd never done that before. This sounds like an ad-libbed line by Woody because Julie Kavner breaks up over it, and one gets the sense she wasn't expecting it.

A Few Words from Woody . . .

About the scene where Sheldon realizes he's in love with Treva by staring wistfully at the dripping chicken leg, Woody explained to Eric Lax (*Woody Allen: a Biography*):

> I made the shot knowing there's going to be a sweet piece of music there. I'm just acting at the time, the way any actor would. I'm picking the leg up and I know I've got to smell it and make it romantic-looking. I'm pretending. I'm not thinking at the time that I'm the character and I'm not thinking, 'Oh, God I love her.' I'm thinking, 'Okay, I've waited enough time. I've dropped the letter and now I'm standing there and this is going to get boring if I don't move now; it seems enough time to notice the chicken. Keep it like this, don't be too feminine about it.' I'm not thinking motivation, I'm thinking mechanics.

25.
Crimes and Misdemeanors

(Orion Pictures, 1989); Running Time: 104 minutes; Rating: PG-13; Color.

Crimes, like virtues, are their own reward.
George Farquhar, from *The Inconstant*

Human happiness does not seem to have been included in the design of
creation. It is only we, with our capacity to love, that give
meaning to the indifferent universe. And yet, most
human beings seem to have the ability to keep
trying, even to find joy from simple things,
their family, their work, and from the hope
that future generations might
understand more.
Professor Louis Levy, from *Crimes and Misdemeanors*

Il n'y a pas de morts. ["There are no dead."]
Maurice Maeterlinck, from *L'Oiseau bleu* (*The Blue Bird*)

In *Crimes and Misdemeanors,* an adulterous ophthalmologist has his
lover killed and wonders about a universe (and a God) that lets him get

away with it, while a frustrated filmmaker abandons his ideals and does a film about a producer he loathes.

The sleeve copy of the video version of Woody Allen's *Crimes and Misdemeanors* says, "Hailed by critics everywhere, *Crimes and Misdemeanors* offers astonishing performances from an all-star cast and could be Allen's best film to date."

That pretty much sums up the overall impact of this film.

Crimes and Misdemeanors probably is Woody's best film, and, unfortunately for Woody, it was almost unanimously praised as such. I say "unfortunately" because Woody does not wish his films to be appreciated by a mass audience. When he is hailed for one of his movies, he gets suspicious: if too many people like it, he's certain he's done something wrong, and somehow feels as though he's sold out.

This is an extremely harsh personal artistic position to take, and yet, it is the way he feels.

But that doesn't change the fact that this film exists, and that it is a masterwork of contemporary filmmaking.

Crimes and Misdemeanors was written on hotel stationery as Woody, Mia, and a passel of children toured Europe in summer 1988. (Eric Lax reproduces some of Woody's original handwritten pages as the front and back endsheets of his book, *Woody Allen: a Biography,* and also gives copious details on the various "versions" the film went through before Woody and company came to this final one, and I heartily recommend Eric's book for a comprehensive look at the life and career of Woody.)

Crimes and Misdemeanors is an intricate, literate, philosophical study that tackles such questions as "Is there a God?," "Is evil ultimately punished?," and "Is murder ever justified—is it ever the 'right' thing to do?" The film also poses questions about the ethics of art. Should an artist ever sell out by working on a commercially viable project that he or she finds aesthetically offensive in order to make enough money to work on his or her true artistic endeavors? (Woody posed similar questions about the existence of God in *Love and Death,* but there it was in a much lighter, more humorous manner. In *Crimes,* these questions are serious business.)

Crimes and Misdemeanors is also about seeing. Sight, eyes, vision, and blindness (literal and figurative) all play important roles as symbols that represent the conflicts the characters are confronted with in the film.

Judah Rosenthal is a respected, wealthy ophthalmologist who has been having an affair with Dolores Paley, a stewardess he met on a flight to Boston. At some point, the relationship soured, and Judah began paying less attention to Dolores, a move she saw as being cast aside after being used. Dolores decides that Judah's wife, Miriam, must be made aware of her philandering husband's cheating, and she begins to harass him with letters, phone calls, and threats. Judah is devastated. He has never been threatened with such intensity; his life of "wealth and privilege" was the one constant he could always count on. Now it is possible that he, and his family, will be destroyed by his neurotic former lover.

Judah turns to his brother, Jack, for help. Jack knows people, and can get things done. And he does. With Judah's consent, he has Dolores killed. This almost destroys Judah. He ends up on the verge of a complete mental collapse, and at one point even considers turning himself in to the police to clear his conscience. But he doesn't, and by the film's end, he has resolved himself into carrying around this "sin" and facing the consequences in the next life—although it is quite clear that Judah doesn't believe there is a next life, and thus he essentially has got off scot-free.

At one point, Judah confides in Ben, a rabbi, and one of his patients. Ben is going blind. Ben tries to convince Judah of a "moral structure" to the universe.

In the film, Ben symbolizes God. And at the end of the film, Ben has gone completely blind (God *doesn't* see), and Judah has not been punished. An unseeing, uncaring universe does not punish the wicked. Our only consolation, for those with faith, is the belief that evil will be punished in the next life. For those nonbelievers living in this world, though, that threat really doesn't carry much weight.

A fantasy sequence amplifies the conundrum Judah faces. In this scene, though, his conscience is manifested as an hallucination of his family. In an emotional quandary, he returns to the house he grew up in. The woman living there allows him to roam through the rooms, and when he comes to the dining room, he peers into the past and watches his family at Seder. His father and his father's sister are arguing about the existence of God. The sister is a cynic and a nihilist. One of the guests says of Sol (Judah's father), "He believes, and you can use logic on him all day long and he still believes." Sol replies, "Must everything be logical?" Judah then asks his father, "If a man commits a crime, if he kills . . . ?" They all turn to him, and his father responds, "Then one way or another he will be punished." Sol asserts that whether it's the Bible or Shakespeare, murder will out. Judah asks, "Who said anything about murder?" and Sol answers, "You did." Judah asks, "Did I?" They then argue faith, and Sol asserts that if it came to a choice between God and truth, he would always choose God.

Against this main storyline is a second story, one involving the question of the ethics of art.

Woody Allen plays Cliff Stern, a filmmaker who specializes in documentaries on leukemia and toxic waste. His wife's brother is Lester, a hugely successful TV producer. Lester (as a favor to his sister) offers Cliff the chance to make a documentary on him for television. Cliff takes the job for the money, all the while despising both Lester and his work. While working on the film about Lester, Cliff is also trying to put together a documentary on a philosopher professor named Louis Levy who Cliff feels has remarkable insights on God, love, and the human condition.

With the help of Halley (Mia Farrow), Cliff works on Lester's film (cutting it so as to make Lester look like an idiot and getting fired because of it), and tries to put together a significant film on Professor Levy, who Cliff feels truly understands what it means to be alive. To Cliff, Professor Levy *sees,* and thus should be given exposure. (Cliff is also after Halley, but in the end she winds up with Lester.)

Eventually, the professor who saw so much couldn't deal with it all, and commits suicide. Did he see *too* much? We are left with the question and no answers.

⋅

The coda takes place at the wedding of Ben's daughter. Halley has returned from four months in Europe, and she announces to everyone that she's engaged to Lester. As she talks to Cliff about her betrothal, we learn how two people can "see" things differently: she finds Lester endearing, Cliff finds him self-important, boorish, and egotistical.

We're left with the realization that it's all in the interpretation. Everything, including the universe, the existence of God, and the vagaries of romantic love, is defined by the beholder, from whose eyes comes the only real truth.

Crimes and Misdemeanors may very well be *the* masterpiece of Woody Allen to date. It is brilliantly written, flawlessly directed, and superbly acted. It is consummately excellent. The film poses tough questions, addresses difficult issues, and still entertains—no easy task. The dialogue in *Crimes and Misdemeanors* is so penetrating, truthful, and important, it transcends mere conversation and the conventions of ordinary film dialogue and becomes something more, something approaching genius.

Look for . . .

• By any other name. . . . Woody considered the following titles for the film before deciding on *Crimes and Misdemeanors: Brothers, Dr. Shenanigans, Decisions, Decisive Moments, Make a Killing, Two Lives, Anything Else, Crimes and Vanity, High Crimes and Misdemeanors, The Lord's Prayer, Acts of Good and Evil, Moments of Good and Evil, Scenes of Good and Evil, The Eyes of God, Windows of the Soul, Visions of the Soul, Dark Vision, The Sight of God, Glimmer of Hope, Hope and Darkness, Faint Hope, A Matter of Choice, Choices in the Dark, Decisive Points, Empty Choices,* and *Split Decisions* (from *Woody Allen: A Biography*).

• Judah the skeptic's use of religious imagery. Throughout the film, Judah—the self-described religious skeptic—uses religious imagery in his language. During a speech at the opening of a new ophthalmology wing, he states that its realization was due, in part, to "answered prayers." He also discloses to the group that his father used to tell him that "the eyes of God" were always upon him, and thus, is it a coincidence that he made his specialty ophthalmology? Later, after Judah first convinces Dolores not to do anything rash, he says, "Oh, God." He later tells Dolores that by "a miracle" his wife didn't open the letter before he got home. And while examining Ben, Judah again says, "Oh, God," and then confides in Ben about his affair with Dolores. At the conclusion of Judah's phone conversation with Jack during which he learned that Dolores was dead, Judah says, "God have mercy on us, Jack."

• Cliff/Woody's "life lesson." "So while we wait for a cab I'll give you your lesson for today. Your lesson is this: Don't listen to what your school-teachers tell you, you know? Don't pay any attention to that. Just see what they look like and that's how you'll know what life is really gonna be like. Okay? You heard it here first. I think I see a cab. If we run quickly, we can kick the crutch from that old lady and get it."

• Daryl Hannah. Look for her uncredited role as actress Lisa Crosby.

• Wanda Horowitz. At the reception where Lester asks Cliff if he'd like to do his biographical documentary, a woman comes up to Lester and thanks him for inviting her. The part of the woman was played by Wanda Horowitz, Vladimir Horowitz's widow.

• Even more California-bashing. Lester says he's going to be working in New York because "out there" (the West Coast) it is "such a Mickey Mouse environment."

• The teachers. Dolores has a memory flashback to the time she and Judah were on the beach discussing music. She remembers telling him that she's ignorant, and that he'll have to teach her all about music and the arts. This is reminiscent of Lee and Frederick's relationship in *Hannah and Her Sisters.*

• The Steve Allen reference. At one point, Lester says, "Comedy is tragedy plus time." This was originally written by Steve Allen. (See the Steve Allen section in Chapter 3.)

• The Barbados reference. At one point, Lester invites Halley to Barbados. In *Manhattan* Jill and Connie wanted to go to Barbados for a weekend.

• The David Greenglass reference. Cliff says he loves Lester like a brother: David Greenglass. In *Woody Allen: A Biography,* Eric Lax explains that this was "a phrase that was a favorite of New York liberals in the 1950s. Greenglass was the brother of Ethel Rosenberg, who with her husband, Julius, was executed in 1953 for passing U. S. atomic secrets to the Russians. Greenglass, who supplied them with the information, turned prosecution witness and got off with fifteen years in prison."

• Woody's attentiveness. During Cliff and Hally's conversation about Dr. Levy, Woody casually reaches over and plucks a hair or a piece of lint off the front of Mia's sweater. She looks down at her chest, brushes her sweater, and sort-of smirks at Woody, because Woody's move was obviously ad-libbed.

• The fluids joke. While Cliff and Halley are eating Indian food and watching *Singing in the Rain,* Cliff tells Halley, "When you see Lester later be careful. Because if this guy tells you he wants to exchange ideas, what he wants is to exchange fluids."

• The acupuncture reference. At a dinner party, Miriam and her daughter discuss Mary, a friend who had had acupuncture. Their guest then tells the story of a woman friend who visited a Chinese doctor. The doctor inserted a cat's whisker into her tear ducts. The inspiration for *Alice* came when Woody visited a Chinese doctor who put cat's whiskers into *his* tear ducts to get rid of his sties. In that film, Alice considers acupuncture for her bad back. (See Roger Ebert's *Alice* interview with Woody in Chapter 2.)

• The eyes symbolism. When Judah first sees Dolores's dead body, her eyes are wide and staring. He then recalls his father's words to him, "The eyes of God see all." And as Judah examines Ben's eyes, he remembers back to Dolores telling him that her mother once said to her that the eyes are the windows to the soul, and that her soul would live on after she was gone.

• Judah's return to his childhood home. In Eric Lax's *Woody Allen: A Biography,* Woody spoke of that scene, and his own desire to go back to the house in which he grew up: "I'd love to go back in that house sometime. But I have a little trepidation about going up to the door and saying, 'I lived here once,' because that's such a pushy thing to do. The woman could either recognize me and say, 'Oh, really?' and let me come in. Or she could say, 'Are you kidding?' "

• The dog-eat-dog joke. When Cliff's niece Jenny tells him that she's thinking of becoming an actress, he tells her he doesn't want her to; she should be on the Supreme Court, or be a doctor. He tells her that "show business is dog-eat-dog. It's worse than dog-eat-dog. It's dog-doesn't-return-other-dog's-phone-calls."

• The London reference. While walking through Central Park, Halley tells Cliff that she's going to London to produce a couple of shows. In *Manhattan,* Tracy left New York—and Isaac—to study in London.

• The best one-liner in the film. At Ben's daughter's wedding, Cliff and his sister talk about the breakup of his marriage to Wendy. Barbara tells him, "Once the sex goes, it all goes." Cliff replies, "It's true. The last time I was inside a woman was when I visited the Statue of Liberty." (This, by the way, was the single most oft-quoted line from the film in the reviews. Everyone picked up on this fantastic line.)

• More white roses. Lester tells how he won Halley's heart: he sent her white roses around the clock for days. In *Broadway Danny Rose,* Lou Canova sent Tina a single white rose every day.

A Few Words from Woody . . .

In an interview with Eric Lax, Woody, upon hearing that *Crimes and Misdemeanors* was being exceptionally well received in Hollywood, said, "I know I must be doing something wrong if my film is being viewed in some Hollywood character's screening room and a group of people there are saying, 'It's his best film,' when many of the things I attack are what they stand for. If it really was a wonderful film, I feel it wouldn't get that interest."

26.
Alice
(Orion Pictures, 1990); Running Time: 106 minutes; Rating: PG-13; Color.

Steve   I want to buy this book on *How to Hypnotize.* It says here you can make girls do anything you want.
Paul   A p-person won't d-do anything under hypnosis th-that they won't d-do in real life.
Steve   So . . . we'll try it on Catholic girls.
From Woody Allen's 1981 play, *The Floating Light Bulb*

"I can't explain *myself,* I'm afraid, sir," said Alice, "because I'm not myself, you see." "I don't see," said the Caterpillar.
Lewis Carroll, from *Alice's Adventures in Wonderland*

"Curiouser and curiouser!" cried Alice.
Ibid.

Alice is the story of a Roman Catholic woman who is married to a wealthy businessman and who suddenly realizes that she's been living with a set of twisted and specious values. Thanks to some magical herbs prescribed by a Chinese acupuncturist, she is given the opportunity to change her life.

In some ways, *Alice* is *Another Woman, Part 2: The Funny Years.* In both films a woman undergoes a reevaluation process; she looks at her life through different eyes and attempts to make a judgment as to the worth of her existence and the integrity and value of her decisions.

Of course, *Another Woman* was much more somber, but the themes do intersect. (And interestingly, in *Crimes and Misdemeanors* Judah Rosenthal also reevaluated *his* life, but it was not his decision to do so. If his lover Dolores had not decided that the secrecy of their affair was intolerable, then Judah would have gone on, screwing around with the stewardess, screwing around with the charity's funds, and generally having a good old time.)

Alice Tait's period of reappraisal begins with, of all things, a backache. During one bright, wealthy, New York morning, fate has Alice hearing the name of Dr. Yang, a Chinese acupuncturist who also treats with special herbs, herbs that turn out to be magical, to say the least.

As in *The Purple Rose of Cairo*, in *Alice* Woody Allen takes an ordinary young woman and thrusts her into an extraordinary situation.

The film is a pure fantasy and has the whimsical/mystical ("whistical"?) feel of *Oedipus Wrecks*. Magic abounds in *Alice* (which was originally titled *The Magical Herbs of Dr. Yang*, but which Woody abandoned because he felt it divulged too much of the story).

When we first meet Alice Tait, she is complacent and bored, and yet she possesses a spark of defiance that empowers her to try such fringe health practices as shiatsu massage and Swedes walking on her back.

One day, like an incantation, she hears Yang's name three times. Apparently, he has worked wonders for her friends, and since Western medicine has not been able to offer her any relief for her backache, she decides to visit this mysterious Dr. Yang.

The first thing Yang does is hypnotize the "un-hypnotizable" Alice with a spinning "vortex wheel," which sends her into a trance in which she speaks to her absent husband, and which sends her back in time to the location of their first date. Dr. Yang not only can observe what's happening in her trance; he can also participate if he so chooses, by speaking to her and directing the questioning.

Throughout his treatment of her, Dr. Yang gives Alice four different types of herbs. The first changes her from a mousy, shy housewife into a Coltrane-loving sexpot. The second batch summons the ghost of her dead boyfriend Ed, who takes Alice flying over New York, and traveling into the past. The third batch renders her invisible and allows her to "observe without being observed." And the final batch, "a love herb," accidentally makes every man at her sister's Christmas party fall in love with her.

The mysticism of Catholicism plays a large role in *Alice*, and acts as a counterpoint to Alice's embrace of other ways to achieve inner peace. It is appropriate that Alice is a lapsed Catholic, yet still retains a lion's share of Catholic guilt. And an especially clever touch is the appearance of Mother Teresa in the film. It is often said that Mother Teresa is a "living saint"; that she has somehow transcended human weaknesses and petty concerns and elevated her interests and pursuits to those of the divine. In *Alice* she is a symbol of Alice Tait's quest for a higher power. And because Alice gives up her earthly possessions and decadent materialistic lifestyle to go work with Mother Teresa and emulate her ideals, it is clear that even though she has lost her worldly wealth, she has gained something more. And *that* is why Alice is happy at the end of the film.

What is Woody Allen, the agnostic, telling us here? That the only real wealth comes from within; from good works; from sacrifice? He better be careful, because that sounds awfully close to religious thought. But that might be the point Woody is trying to make. That even if there is no God, we can achieve higher states and advanced levels of being ourselves, by simply following a strict set of moral standards. If that's the case, though, then why did Judah Rosenthal end up so happy at the end of *Crimes and Misdemeanors*? In one sense, *Alice* is the inverse of *Crimes*: it shows that morality can be an end unto itself. And that is totally consistent with agnosticism, or even atheism, for that matter.

Once again, Woody has used "genre" elements to tell a wondrous story that ironically, in the end, is a more "human" story than anything else.

Look for . . .

• The penguins reference. Yang hypnotizes Alice with a spinning "vortex wheel," even though she assures him that she can't be hypnotized. Dr. Yang asks her what she sees and she tells him "penguins." He says, "What about penguins?" She says, "They mate for life." Here Woody Allen again addresses the issue of monogamy. In *Manhattan,* as Tracy and Ike are discussing Yale's philandering with Mary, Tracy suggests that perhaps monogamy has gone out of date, and that perhaps people "weren't meant to have one deep relationship." Ike says, "I'm old-fashioned. I don't believe in extramarital relationships. I think people should mate for life, like pigeons or Catholics." Alice is a lapsed Catholic who once wanted to be a nun. And following Alice's "penguin" line, Dr. Yang asks her if she thinks penguins are Catholic?

• The seduction of Joe Ruffalo. After taking Dr. Yang's first batch of herbs, Alice comes on like a siren to Joe. She is sexy, seductive, and alluring. Mia Farrow's performance in this scene is a revelation. We don't usually get to see her playing the vixen, and here she handles it masterfully.

• The women and their weight. After Alice agrees to a rendezvous with Joe, she confides her indiscretion to Nina, and swears her to secrecy. She then laments that she has nothing to wear, and that she's become so fat. Alice is another Woody Allen woman who worries about her weight. Daisy (Jessica Harper) in *Stardust Memories* devotes part of a phone conversation to a discussion of her weight. She too worries that she had put on a few pounds. The first time Alice and Joe make love, she tells him it's usually dark when she and Doug do it, and he says, "Then you can't see anything." As he begins to kiss her, she says, "I am going to be going on a diet."

• Cybill Shepherd as a fast-track TV producer. Alice's meeting with her old friend Nancy in her office is classic. Nancy has moved on, and Alice can't see the truth. She didn't even realize that she was proposing stories based on her own life. Nancy's brushoff at the end of the meeting is perfect: "Give me a jingle and one of these weeks we'll go to Le Cirque."

• The appearance of Eddie. Yang's third batch of herbs summons Eddie, Alice's dead boyfriend. Late one night, after burning the herbs in a teacup, she hears her name being called. It's the ghost of her dead lover, Eddie. This scene is very similar in tone and feel to the scene in *Crimes and Misdemeanors* in which Judah gets out of bed in the middle of the night and has a conversation with Ben, who really isn't there.

• Dylan and her mother. One evening Alice is putting her kids to bed and Woody's camera is looking down the hall to their bedroom. Alice exits the room, and then her daughter Kate (played by her and Woody's real-life adopted daughter Dylan) runs out and throws herself into her mother's arms. The scene feels unscripted. It appears as though Dylan just wanted a hug from her mother and Woody happened to catch it on film and decided to leave it in the picture. I may be wrong, but there's a natural, unplanned sense to the scene. If it *was* scripted, then it just is one more acknowledgment of Woody's masterful, intuitive direction.

• The Big Apple circus. See "Chips: Insiders Talk About Woody Allen" (Chapter 3) for star Joe Mantegna's behind-the-scenes look at the filming of this circus scene.

• Creative Writing 101. We attend Alice's writing class and learn the following: "Dialogue in fiction has two functions. In the novel to be read to oneself as voices in the mind, and in scripts and in plays to be read out loud. So that what we're really talking about here are the two aspects of the consciousness of words: internal and meditative in the novel, and external and expressive in the drama and in film."

• Bernadette Peters as the Muse. Dr. Yang gives Alice a special herbal tea which summons her muse, a brassy spirit who sets Alice straight about Nancy Brill and her writing teacher. "He's very deep," Alice says. Her muse replies, "Yeah, very deep is exactly where he wants to put it."

• Supermodel Elle Macpherson. Joe uses his time spent invisible to watch model Elle Macpherson undress in a store's dressing room.

A Few Words from Woody . . .

Of making *Alice,* Woody told Eric Lax, "It's so hard to get what I want. Theoretically I want to shoot everything over, and if I had twenty million dollars I could do just that. But the film doesn't deserve to be made for twenty million. It deserves to be done for the twelve it has." (From *Woody Allen: A Biography*)

The following article by Dan Scapperotti about the special effects in *Alice* originally appeared in the February 1991 issue of *Cinefantastique* magazine. In the piece, Dan does a terrific job at filling us in on just how Eddie was made to appear transparent, and exactly how he and Alice ended up flying over the New York City skyline.

Dan Scapperotti is the New York bureau chief of *Cinefantastique* and has been a contributor to the magazine for almost twenty years. Dan's work has also appeared in *Photon, Fangoria, Starlog,* and *Comics Scene* magazines, and he is the author of several books on Western movie stars. Special thanks to Dan and *Cinefantastique*'s editor Fred Clarke for their kindness, and their gracious assistance with the reproduction of this article.

Woody Allen's *Alice*
Filming Special Effects for the Director's Supernatural Comedy*
by Dan Scapperotti

One director rarely considered when discussing fantasy films is Woody Allen. But Allen has ventured several times into the genre, notably with *Sleeper* (1973), *Zelig* (1983), and *The Purple Rose of Cairo* (1985). Allen's latest feature, *Alice,* involves a transparent ghost, a strange invisibility potion and a scene where two of the characters fly around Manhattan.

Mia Farrow plays Alice, a woman married to a successful stockbroker (William Hurt). Alice becomes involved with another man (Joe Mantegna) and must resolve questions at a critical point in her life. Alec Baldwin plays the ghost of a former lover accidentally killed ten years before who appears for a single day and counsels Alice about what is happening in her life and the choices she must make.

Allen and director of photography Carlo Di Palma selected New York-based Randall Balsmeyer to supervise the film's complex special effects. Recently Balsmeyer has become more involved with spectres than Topper, having worked on the effects for films such as *Dead Ringers, Hello Again,* and last summer's *Ghost.*

Allen was emphatic in his desire that the effects of *Alice* not overpower the acting or his accustomed production regimen. While having people appear and disappear is hardly new to the screen, Balsmeyer's challenge was to find a technique that would least interfere with Allen's direction of the actors. The usual techniques of using mattes or mirror shots did not suit Allen's directorial style. Allen prefers to shoot a scene with one grand, sweeping camera shot when possible.

Balsmeyer said he ruled out motion-control techniques because of the bulky equipment and noise. "Woody refuses to loop dialogue," said Balsmeyer. "He's a real stickler for using only production sound." Balsmeyer settled on using a lock and pan technique, allowing camera movement in scenes until an effect was introduced.

When Alice visits Yang, a Chinese doctor, and expresses her curiosity about Mantegna's character, Yang tells her that the best way to get to know somebody is to observe without being observed. He gives her a potion of some strange herbs and Alice becomes invisible. In the time-honored tradition of invisibility movies, the effect tends to wear off at the most inopportune times. Balsmeyer said he used soft screen mattes as in *Dead Ringers* for the film's invisibility effects. "To make people appear and disappear, we used a soft-edged light so they would usually disappear from the feet up," said Balsmeyer. "The last visible part was their head, and then that would fade."

Allen decided that he would like to have Baldwin's ghost transparent all the time he was on the screen. But Allen wanted the effect only if it wouldn't interfere with directing the actors. Balsmeyer convinced Allen that the effect could be done easily using soft split screen techniques. "We could always photograph the ghost and whoever else was involved all together, get the matching background shots and put the ghost in as a percentage exposure," said Balsmeyer.

Baldwin's ghost is also capable of flying and taking Alice along for the ride. He suggests that they visit a beach resort where they once had a romantic weekend. Although Alice explains that the place burned to the ground ten years ago, the ghost tells her he will take care of it and they step out on the terrace of Alice's apartment and fly into the night sky, around Manhattan, along the coast to the ghost casino where they have a last dance. Balsmeyer used Preston Cinema Systems' Gyrosphere, a gyro-stabilized camera mount to shoot background plates for the flying effects using a helicopter.

Bob Harman, the flying rig specialist who managed the flying scenes for the *Superman* film series, was hired to put Farrow and Baldwin through their airborne paces. Harman suggested the use of blue screen to composite the actors. Balsmeyer erected a blue screen to film the Harman-rigged scenes at New York's Astoria Studios. "We were able to erect an 80-foot track for the camera to move on, which ultimately turned the sequence into a motion-control shoot," said Balsmeyer. "We built a platform 8 feet high, 8 feet wide and 80 feet long that we laid dolly track on. We set up our motion-control rig on that. We suspended the actors on flying rigs about twelve feet off the end of the track so that they could be made to rise and fall and swivel by an operator above them, like marionettes."

27.
Scenes from a Mall

(Touchstone Pictures, 1991); Running Time: 87 minutes; Rating: R; Color.

Marriage is a wonderful invention; but, then again,
so is a bicycle repair kit.
Billy Connolly

Scenes from a Mall is a Los Angeles story. A successful fortysomething couple spend the day at the mall picking up their sixteenth-anniversary gifts for each other (along with the sushi for their sixteenth-anniversary party that evening), and end up revealing their adulterous affairs to each other.

Scenes from a Mall marked Woody Allen's first work for a director other than himself in fifteen years. His last work solely as an actor was in Martin Ritt's 1976 film, *The Front.*

Scenes from a Mall cast Woody against type, giving us a Los Angeles products endorsement lawyer with two kids, a modern home, a cellular phone, a beeper, trendy clothes, and a ponytail. It almost worked. The reason it doesn't completely work is that the Woody Allen persona is so strong that ultimately what comes across is an "almost-Woody" rather than the intended "anti-Woody."

It is easy to understand why Woody decided to do this film. The script, while at times a little talky, is very, very good. The writing is sharp, the dialogue observant and honest, and the scenario a plausible and accurate rendering of the Los Angeles lifestyle. Paul Mazursky and Roger Simon know of where they write.

But the problem with the film is the casting. This may not have been the right role for Woody Allen. There are times during the film where a hint of the *real* Woody Allen persona comes through (and frankly, they sound like ad-libbed moments by Woody) and we end up catching a glimpse of what might have been. But overall, Woody seems like a fish out of water.

Bette Midler is scintillating, as usual. She is not as shrill here as she has been in the some of her recent films (*Big Business, Ruthless People,* and parts of *Beaches* come immediately to mind) and one can't help but wonder what she might do with any of the roles that usually go to Shirley MacLaine.

It is good to see Woody just *act.* Do you think he ultimately did it because the film owed such an obvious debt to his idol Ingmar Bergman's *Scenes from a Marriage?* Let's hope a script more suited to his talents comes along in the near future. And let's also hope he agrees to do it.

Look for . . .

• Woody's kids. The film opens with Woody seeing his son and daughter off for a ski vacation. This is only the fourth film in which

Woody has been a father. The three others are *Take the Money and Run* (a son), *Manhattan* (a son), and *Hannah and Her Sisters* (in *Hannah*, his wife gave birth to twin boys artificially inseminated by his best friend, and at the end of the film Holly is pregnant with Mickey's child).

• Woody Allen, fashion animal. Woody sports a stubby ponytail—known in L.A. as a "dork knob"—throughout the film.

• Woody-like lines. Woody's character, Nick, tells his wife Deborah, "We've done our duty to civilization: We've procreated and now we can die." And later, when Deborah tells Nick her anniversary gift (a surfboard) will head off his midlife crisis, he says, "It could only mean the full body vibrator." And when Deborah asks if Nick could handle two girls passing by, Nick says, "I could salivate on them."

• The JFK assassination conspiracy reference. While Deborah makes the seating plan for their anniversary party, she mentions Marty and says, "Oh, God, if he starts with that Kennedy assassination again." In *Annie Hall* Alvy Singer was at one time obsessed with Kennedy assassination conspiracy theories.

• New York bashing. In a line clearly planted as a blatant and conspicuous indicator of just how opposite New York apologist Woody and L.A. animal Nick are supposed to be, Nick says: "Let me tell you something. If Philip starts in with me one more time, I promise you, about New York is the cultural center of the world, and Los Angeles is a barren desert, I'm gonna stick my fingers in his eyes." The attempt at contrast and "against-type" casting is admirable; the execution of this thematic focus, however, doesn't really work.

• Woody's black horn-rimmed glasses. You won't find them. Instead of his traditional glasses, Woody wears round tortoiseshell eyeglasses in this film.

• The Mime connection. The first time Nick sees the mall Mime, he says to the guy, "I hate mimes." In Woody's *Getting Even* essay, "A Little Louder, Please," the narrator of the piece reveals that he doesn't understand—and doesn't like—mime. In *Scenes from a Mall* Nick also says that mimes are "worse than Hare Krishnas." In *Hannah and Her Sisters* Mickey considers joining the Hare Krishnas in his search for a religion.

• Director Paul Mazursky. The therapist that Deborah is having an affair with is played by *Scenes* director Paul Mazursky.

• Allen's expletives. When the Mime imitates Nick while he's on the phone and Nick sees him, he tells him, "Fuck off." Later in the theater, Nick tells Deborah, "I had love and reassurance with you and I blew it. I fucked it up." Still later, when Nick goes out to get his car, he discovers it's been towed because Deborah parked in a handicapped zone. He says, "Christ, where's my fucking Saab? Shit, I can't believe it." And finally, when Nick and Deborah fight in the caviar place, Nick throws some money down and says, "Fucking keep it." These profanities are the raunchiest

Woody has ever used in a film. The last time Woody used the word *fuck* in a film was in the only other film he did for another director, Martin Ritt's *The Front*.

• The clarinet reference. Nick tells Deborah his affair took place when he was supposed to be at a health club, and Deborah responds that that was when she was taking his daughter to her clarinet lessons. Woody Allen is a lifelong clarinetist.

• Joan Delaney. The woman interviewer in *Scenes from a Mall* was played by Joan Delaney, the actress who played Jackie Gleason's horny daughter, Susan Hollander, in the film version of Woody's *Don't Drink the Water*.

28.
Shadows and Fog

(Orion Pictures, March 20, 1992); Running Time: 87 minutes;
Rating: PG-13; Black and White.

What is your substance, whereof are you made,
That millions of strange shadows on you tend?
William Shakespeare, from the 53rd *Sonnet*

For in and out, above, about, below,
'Tis nothing but a Magic Shadow-show . . .
Edward Fitzgerald, from The Rubáiyát of Omar Khayyám

Fear death?—to feel the fog in my throat,
The mist in my face.
Robert Browning, from *Prospice*

Gina   You think there's life out there on any of those billions of stars out there?
Kleinman   I personally don't know. Although I hear there may be life on Mars, but the guy that told me that is only in the hosiery business.
From the play, *Death*

Shadows and Fog—Woody Allen's first genuine (albeit offbeat) murder mystery (he always said he wanted to do one, didn't he?)—may very well be the most beautiful film he has made.

As with *Manhattan,* any single frame of *Shadows and Fog* could be matted, framed, and hung on a wall. The cinematography and photography are breathtaking. They should win an award. The "shadows" and "fog" of the title live and breathe ominously in an unnamed European

town in the 1920s (although *Entertainment Weekly* film critic Owen Glei-
berman remarked that it looked like Prague and described the setting as
"Kafkaland"). The cobblestone streets are wet; the buildings loom; the
shadows distend; the fog creeps.

As *Zelig* paid tribute to Woody's much-loved newsreels and documentaries, so does *Shadows and Fog* pay homage—to German expressionist
films of the aforementioned 1920s, especially the work of Fritz Lang and
F. W. Murnau.

Shadows and Fog is a very funny expansion of Woody's 1975 play, *Death*.
(See the sections on the plays [Chapter 8] and *Without Feathers* [Chapter 6].)

Woody Allen plays Max Kleinman, a bumbling schlemiel of a hard-
ware clerk who is awakened in the middle of the night and told he must
join a vigilante group looking for a maniacal killer. When his marriage-
minded landlady gives him pepper to blow in the killer's eyes, Kleinman
says, "Very good. I'll ward him off with a seasoning."

Kleinman pays a visit to the local coroner, who is later killed by the
strangler. But before this murder, the two men discuss the existence of God
and debate whether or not we have an eternal soul. They also discuss the
killer and Kleinman admits his fears—and also acknowledges his less-
than-prodigious physical powers: "A deranged person is supposed to have
the strength of ten men. I have the strength of one small boy. With polio."

When the Doctor pulls the sheet off the corpse of one of the killer's
victims, Kleinman asks him to remind him not to order the sweetbreads
the next time he goes to a restaurant.

As Kleinman wanders around the dark streets, never knowing exactly
what his role is, we meet Irmy and Clown, two members of a small traveling circus. Clown seems to speak with Woody's voice: "We're artists. With
great talent comes responsibility." And: "I have a rare opportunity now: To
make people laugh. To make them forget their sad lives." Interestingly, this
sounds like Woody responding to the digs against his serious stuff and
admitting that the "earlier, funny" films have always been more warmly
received than his serious, more challenging material. Clown also pontifi-
cates, "A family means death to the artist, and I need peace and quiet."
Later, when he and Irmy find an abandoned baby, he changes his opinion
about having a family. This is an interesting development when looked at
vis-à-vis Woody's own experiences with Mia Farrow's children and the
start of his own family with the birth of their son, Satchel.

After Irmy catches Clown trysting with Marie, the trapeze artist, she
leaves him, and while walking into town, meets a prostitute played by Lily
Tomlin. When Lily brings her back to the whorehouse and tells Kathy
Bates's character that Irmy is a sword swallower, Bates replies, "That's my
specialty, too."

While visiting the girls, a customer named Student Jack persuades Irmy to "work" for him one time for seven hundred dollars. (He started at twenty dollars, and went to fifty, a hundred, two hundred, five hundred, and then six hundred, until she finally gave in at seven hundred—but only after making him prove he had the money.)

At the same time that this is going on, in the streets Kleinman witnesses the vigilante mob taking the Mintz family away. Kleinman says he knows Mr. Mintz: "He does quality circumcisions. I've seen his work."

Kleinman ends up meeting Irmy in the mist (after she is arrested for prostitution during a brothel raid and fined) and they walk through the fog-bound streets. They come upon one of the vigilante members who wants Kleinman to try and trap the killer. Kleinman is terrified, and the vigilante says, "What they say about you isn't true, is it? You're not really a coward, or a worm, or a yellow-belly?" Kleinman replies, "Keep going. You're in the right column."

Irmy offers to patrol with Kleinman. They see the killer, but it turns out to be Kleinman's boss, Mr. Paulson (whom Kleinman calls "Your Grace"), peeping in a window watching a woman undress. Because of the confrontation, Paulson fires Kleinman.

When Irmy asks Kleinman if taking money for sex one time made her a whore, he replies, "Only by the dictionary definition." Later, Irmy tells Kleinman her father used to say, "We're all happy. If we only knew it."

The vigilante groups split into factions and while Kleinman is being badgered to choose between the two, Spiro the clairvoyant sniffs him and declares him the killer after finding a wine glass that belonged to the slain coroner in his pocket.

In the funniest scene in the film, Kleinman flees to his ex-fiancée Alma's apartment. (He once left her at the altar and she later caught him naked in a closet with her sister.) He admits he once got her pregnant, but it was only a hysterical pregnancy—she wasn't really pregnant. When she throws him out, calling him a "filthy vermin," Max says, "It's good to see that you're not bitter."

Meanwhile, Clown confronts Irmy about her commercial use of the "furry little animal" between her legs (as Jodie Foster's character put it) and while they're screaming at each other, they find an abandoned baby. They decide to keep her.

Kleinman, meantime, ends up at the brothel where Student Jack is lecturing the whores on the Metaphors of Perversion.

Jack asks Kleinman if he believes in God and, in an exchange that resonates off Mickey Sach's search for meaning in *Hannah and Her Sisters,* Kleinman replies:

> I would love to. Believe me. I know I would be much happier . . . but I can't. . . . I can't make the leap of faith necessary to believe in my *own* existence.

Jack and the whores then discuss suicide and Jack admits he's thought of it, but his blood always said, "Live," and he always listened to his blood.

Kleinman then takes Jodie Foster to bed and can't perform. The vigilantes arrive and Kleinman flees. He meets his coworker, Simon Carr, who informs him that he got the promotion over Kleinman and that Kleinman is a vermin worthy of nothing but extermination.

Kleinman goes to the circus encampment looking for Irmy. While there, the killer appears. Kleinman and the circus Magician, Armstead, hide in a magic mirror which the killer smashes. Armstead manages to tie up the killer with magic chains and locks, but the strangler escapes and is not found.

The Magician offers Kleinman a job as his assistant, Kleinman accepts (literally "running away and joining the circus"), and the two magically disappear with a finger snap.

Shadows and Fog is a mood piece that is not moody. It is a period piece unlike any American film released in the past several years. It is a tour de force of brilliantly evocative filmmaking that also offers Woody Allen in a classic Woody Allen role.

It is humorous, interesting, and not to be missed.

Look for . . .

• Madonna, as a sensuous trapeze artist screwing around with John Malkovich's character, Clown. Brief as her on-screen role is, this might very well be her best performance ever. (See "A Few Words from Woody . . ." below.)

• Kate Nelligan in an almost impossible-to-identify cameo as Eve. (She hangs out a window and berates Kleinman for asking her if she'd take in Irmy for the night.)

• The "luck" line. Once again, we have a Woody Allen character (a whore, this time) attributing abstract concepts like love to luck and chance. (See *Manhattan*.)

• The "Max" reference. Kleinman's first name is Max, a first name Rob called Alvy in *Annie Hall*.

• The Oscar-winning whorehouse. The whorehouse is staffed by Academy Award winners Jodie Foster and Kathy Bates.

• Kleinman the magician. When Kleinman first meets Irmy and learns she's in the circus, he tells her he's an amateur magician. Woody has always had an interest in magic, and in his 1981 play, *The Floating Light Bulb,* the character Paul Pollack is also an amateur magician.

• John Cusack and John Malkovich's performances, particularly in the scene in the bar where Student Jack (Cusack) reveals to Clown (Malkovich) that he had made love to Irmy. Transcendently excellent.

• The music. Once again, Woody has chosen the perfect accompaniment to his story. The music of Kurt Weill is perfect for the tone and sensibility of the tale.

A Few Words from Woody . . .

• In a March 1992 interview with Sean Mitchell that appeared in the *Los Angeles Times,* Woody said of *Shadows and Fog*, "Even though it has a serious title and looks serious in the ad, it's a comic film. And like all my films, I made it for people who enjoy that sort of thing. It's an offbeat kind of film—I think more so than *Alice,* because *Alice* was the story of a contemporary woman with contemporary problems. People always have an easier time with that." Regarding his character in the film, he said, "If you see me on the screen like the character in *Shadows and Fog,* schlepping around, fumbling around, it isn't me. It just isn't. There may be some elements of me in it, but they're so exaggerated for comic purposes." And he observed about the 1920s time period of the film: "It's got to be set in a period, so I picked a period that I could believably play in. If I set it in a village in Europe in 1750, you couldn't believe me in that context—I'm just too contemporary. So I tried to go back as far as I could and still play the role believably."

• In a BBC interview broadcast in July 1991, when Woody was asked how he managed to acquire the stellar casts he uses in his films, he said, "You know, it's an odd thing because I just cast according to who would be right for the part, the obvious example being Madonna. All I knew was, I needed for [*Shadows and Fog*] a certain type of 1920s trapeze artist in a circus. . . . And Juliet Taylor, who is the lady I cast with, said, 'You mean someone like Madonna,' meaning only to show me the exact type we were looking for. And I said, 'Yeah, she would be perfect.' And so Juliet called her, and told her it's only a two- [or three-] minute part, and her response—typical of many performers—was, 'Sure, I'd love to.' You know, it's perfect. It's no demand on her. She'll come in quickly. She works for a week, or two days, she does it, she enjoys doing it."

• In the same BBC interview, Woody remarked about what these incredible casts mean to his ticket sales: "I wind up with casts that from a marquee point of view are very meaningful. On the other hand, it doesn't resonate in the box office, 'cause what happens, as will happen, say, in this case with Madonna—she's a huge, huge draw everywhere—but when the first flush of her fans who hear she's in this picture come, they'll go back and tell their friends, don't bother, 'cause she's not doing her thing. She's not singing or dancing or cutting up in the same way. She's acting a role that could have been done by another actress—probably not as well as Madonna, I think, 'cause she's right on the nose for it. So I really don't get a lot of commercial benefit from it."

CHAPTER 6

Woody Allen, Author
The Books and Essays

What I see for myself in my life's game plan, though I may be
struck down by an automobile before that happens, is, I see
stopping making films at a certain point because they're
strenuous, it's hard work, and I'd like to write
books. . . . It would be fun.
Woody Allen

Annotated Summaries of the Book Titles

By my count, through 1991, thirteen books have been published "by" Woody Allen. The majority of them have been either script versions of his films or book editions of his plays. The three books for which he is most well known are, of course, the three collections of essays, all of which are covered in detail in this section.

Many of the books listed below, while long out of print, are still available in libraries across the country. Many are also available in used bookstores, and through public and university libraries' interlibrary loan programs.

The script collections are still in print and should be available through most bookstores. [Same-year publications are listed alphabetically.]

B1.   *Don't Drink the Water* (Random House, 1967)
      A hardcover edition of Woody's play.

B2.   *Play It Again, Sam* (Random House, 1969)
      A hardcover edition of Woody's play.

B3.   *Getting Even* (Random House, 1971; Vintage Books, 1978)
      Woody's first collection of his *New Yorker* essays. (See the section "*Getting Even*" in this chapter.)

B4.   *Woody Allen's "Play It Again, Sam"* (Grosset & Dunlap, 1972)
      A frame-by-frame reproduction of the film, *Play It Again, Sam.*

B5.   *Death* (Samuel French, Inc., 1975)
      A performance edition of Woody's play *Death.* (*Death* had previously been published in the collection *Without Feathers.*)

B6.   *God* (Samuel French, Inc., 1975)
      A performance edition of Woody's play *God.* (*God* had previously been published in the collection *Without Feathers.*)

B7.   *Without Feathers* (Random House, 1975; Warner Books, 1976)
      Woody's second collection of his *New Yorker* essays. (See the section "*Without Feathers*" in this chapter.)

B8.   *Non-Being and Somethingness* (Random House, 1978)
      A selection of comic strips from the comic strip *Inside Woody Allen* by Stuart Hample.

B9.   *Side Effects* (Random House, 1980; Ballantine Books, 1981)
      Woody's third—and final—collection of his *New Yorker* essays. (See the section "*Side Effects*" in this chapter.)

B10. *The Floating Light Bulb* (Random House, 1982)
      A hardcover edition of Woody's play.

B11. *Four Films of Woody Allen* (Random House, 1982)
      A trade paperback that contained exact reconstructions of the scripts of the final screen versions of *Annie Hall, Interiors, Manhattan,* and *Stardust Memories.* Stage directions were added by the publisher to describe the action.

B12.   *Hannah and Her Sisters* (Random House, 1987)

A trade paperback that contained an exact reconstruction of the script of the final screen version of *Hannah and Her Sisters*. Stage directions were added by the publisher to describe the action.

B13.   *Three Films of Woody Allen* (Random House, 1987)

A trade paperback that contained exact reconstructions of the scripts of the final screen versions of *Zelig, Broadway Danny Rose,* and *The Purple Rose of Cairo*. Stage directions were added by the publisher to describe the action.

Update

In spring 1991 I spoke with someone in the publicity department at Random House and was told that the publication of further script collections was being discussed, but that nothing was definite. I was also told that *Four Films of Woody Allen, Hannah and Her Sisters,* and *Three Films of Woody Allen* were still in print.

Random House has a couple of options when it comes to choosing which films to publish in script form. If it wanted to catch up with Woody's output since the publication of the script version of *Hannah and Her Sisters,* then it would need to publish *Radio Days, September, Another Woman, Oedipus Wrecks, Crimes and Misdemeanors,* and *Alice*.

Here's a guess. If Random House does decide there is still a market for further Woody Allen script books, it will pass on *Oedipus Wrecks* because it's so short, and will do two volumes: one four-film volume consisting of *Radio Days, September, Another Woman,* and *Alice,* and, because of its importance, a separate *Crimes and Misdemeanors* volume. It took the same approach with *Hannah and Her Sisters,* and *Crimes* would seem to be worthy of the same attention.

Details on the Essays in Three Books

(1)
Getting Even
(1971)

Contents

1. "The Metterling Lists"
2. "A Look at Organized Crime"
3. "The Schmeed Memoirs"
4. "My Philosophy"

5. "Yes, But Can the Steam Engine Do This?"
6. *Death Knocks* (A Play)
7. "Spring Bulletin"
8. "Hassidic Tales"
9. "The Gossage-Vardebedian Papers"
10. "Notes from the Overfed"
11. "A Twenties Memory"
12. "Count Dracula"
13. "A Little Louder, Please"
14. "Conversations with Helmholtz"
15. "Viva Vargas!"
16. "The Discovery and Use of the Fake Ink Blot"
17. "Mr. Big"

Introduction

Getting Even was Woody Allen's first collection of comic essays. It was originally published by Random House in 1971. A Vintage Books edition was published in August 1978. *Getting Even* later appeared in a three-volume anthology published by the Quality Paperback Book Club in 1989.

The book consists of sixteen essays and one short play. Thirteen of the essays and the play were previously published.

Particularly strong pieces include "A Look at Organized Crime"; "My Philosophy"; "Spring Bulletin"; "The Gossage-Vardebedian Papers"; "Count Dracula"; "Conversations with Helmholtz"; and "Mr. Big."

The following section takes a look at the works in *Getting Even*. The essay's first appearance, the premise, and laugh-out-loud line are offered for each piece.

The Stories

1. "The Metterling Lists"

First Appearance: New Yorker; May 10, 1969; pp. 34–35.
Laugh-Out-Loud Line: "Freud writes of a key dream Metterling described to him: 'I am at a dinner party with some friends when suddenly a man walks in with a bowl of soup on a leash.'"
Premise: A writer reviews the publication of "*The Collected Laundry Lists of Hans Metterling,* Vol. 1, 437 pp., plus XXII-page introduction; indexed."

2. "A Look at Organized Crime"

First Appearance: New Yorker; August 15, 1970; pp. 24–25.
Laugh-Out-Loud Line: "Other illicit activities engaged in by Cosa Nostra members included gambling, narcotics, prostitution, hijacking, loansharking,

and the transportation of a large whitefish across the state line for immoral purposes."
Premise: A look at organized-crime operations in America.

3. "The Schmeed Memoirs"

First Appearance: New Yorker; April 17, 1971; pp. 36–37.
Laugh-Out-Loud Line: "Himmler was not accustomed to being invited to dinner at Berchtesgaden, because his eyesight was poor and Hitler could not bear to watch him bring the fork up to his face and then stick the food somewhere on his cheek."
Premise: A look at the memoirs of Hitler's barber.

4. "My Philosophy"

First Appearance: New Yorker; December 27, 1969; pp. 25–26.
Laugh-Out-Loud Line: "I remember my reaction to a typically luminous observation of Kierkegaard's: 'Such a relation which relates itself to its own self (that is to say, a self) must either have constituted itself or have been constituted by another.' The concept brought tears to my eyes."
Premise: A writer attempts to elucidate his own personal philosophy about such matters as "morality, art, ethics, life, and death."

5. "Yes, But Can the Steam Engine Do This?"

First Appearance: New Yorker; October 8, 1966; pp. 52–53.
Laugh-Out-Loud Line: "I was leafing through a magazine while waiting for Joseph K., my beagle, to emerge from his regular Tuesday fifty-minute hour with a Park Avenue therapist—a Jungian veterinarian who, for fifty dollars per session, labors valiantly to convince him that jowls are not a social drawback—when I came across a sentence at the bottom of the page that caught my eye like an overdraft notice."
Premise: A chronicling of the history of the invention of the sandwich.

6. "Death Knocks" (A Play)

First Appearance: New Yorker; July 27, 1968; pp. 31–33.
Laugh-Out-Loud Line:

> **Nat** (to Death)   You broke my drainpipe?
> **Death**   It didn't break. It's a little bent. Didn't you hear anything?
> I slammed into the ground.

Premise: In this parody of Ingmar Bergman's film *The Seventh Seal,* Death visits Nat Ackerman, and they play gin rummy for Nat's life.

7. "Spring Bulletin"

First Appearance: New Yorker; April 29, 1967; pp. 38–39.
Laugh-Out-Loud Line: "[Students] are also taught to identify various constellations such as the Big Dipper, Cygnus the Swan, Sagittarius the Archer, and the twelve stars that form Lumides the Pants Salesman."
Premise: An overview of Summer Session offerings from a rather strange school.

8. "Hassidic Tales, with a Guide to Their Interpretation
by the Noted Scholar"

First Appearance: New Yorker; June 20, 1970; pp. 31–32.
Laugh-Out-Loud Line: "A man journeyed to Chelm in order to seek the advice of Rabbi Ben Kaddish, the holiest of all ninth century rabbis and perhaps the greatest *noodge* of the medieval era."
Premise: A recounting of Hassidic tales not found in any great book of religious thought.

9. "The Gossage-Vardebedian Papers"

First Appearance: New Yorker; January 20, 1966; pp. 26–28.
Laugh-Out-Loud Line: "My Dear Vardebedian: I was more than a bit chagrined today, on going through the morning's mail, to find that my letter of September 16, containing my twenty-second move (knight to the king's fourth square), was returned unopened due to a small error in addressing—precisely, the omission of your name and residence (how Freudian can one get?), coupled with a failure to append postage."
Premise: Two extremely civil, refined, and deranged gentlemen play a game of chess by mail.

10. "Notes from the Overfed (After reading Dostoevski and
the new 'Weight Watchers' magazine on the same plane trip)"

First Appearance: New Yorker; March 16, 1968; pp. 38–39.
Laugh-Out-Loud Line: "Now, the reader may ask, are there advantages or disadvantages to being built like a planet?"
Premise: A meditation on obesity in the manner of Dostoevski.

11. "A Twenties Memory"

First Appearance: (as "How I Became a Comedian," in *Panorama,* the *Chicago Daily News*); as "A Twenties Memory" in *Getting Even* in 1971; reprinted in *The Saturday Evening Post;* July 1978; pp. 56–57. (Note: This essay utilizes material from a standup routine called "The Lost Generation," which Woody performed in the midsixties, and which was originally recorded at the Shadows in Washington, D.C., in April 1965. The original routine later appeared on the album *Woody Allen, Volume 2,* as well as on the 1978 compilation album *Woody Allen Standup Comic.* It begins: "I mentioned before that I was in Europe. It's not the first time that I was in Europe. I was in Europe many years ago with Ernest Hemingway. Hemingway had just written his first novel and Gertrude Stein and I read it, and we said that it was a good novel, but not a great one, and that it needed some work but it could be a fine book. And we laughed over it. And Hemingway punched me in the mouth."

"And that winter, Picasso lived on the Rue de Bac. He had just painted a picture of a naked dental hygienist in the middle of the Gobi Desert. And Gertrude Stein said it was a good picture, but not a great one. And I said it could be a fine picture. And we laughed over it. And Hemingway punched me in the mouth.")

Laugh-Out-Loud Line: "Juan Gris, the Spanish cubist, had convinced Alice Toklas to pose for a still life and, with his typical abstract conception of objects, began to break her face and body down to its basic geometrical forms until the police came and pulled him off."

Premise: A writer recounts his days with Ernest Hemingway, Alice B. Toklas, Gertude Stein, F. Scott Fitzgerald, and other artists of the twenties.

12. "Count Dracula"

First Appearance: Getting Even.

Laugh-Out-Loud Line: "Really, I'd like to stay but there's a meeting of old Roumanian Counts across town and I'm responsible for the cold cuts."

Premise: Dracula mistakes an eclipse for sundown, and ends up trapped in a closet.

13. "A Little Louder, Please"

First Appearance: New Yorker; May 28, 1966; pp. 39–41.

Laugh-Out-Loud Line: "Seizing the telephone with one wet hand while attempting to turn off the radio with the other, I ricocheted off the ceiling, while lights dimmed for miles around, as they did when Lepke got the chair."

Premise: A man who prides himself on being culturally sophisticated is forced to acknowledge a dreadful shortcoming: he doesn't understand pantomime.

14. "Conversations with Helmholtz"

First Appearance: Getting Even.

Laugh-Out-Loud Line: "I cured him with hypnosis, and he was able to achieve a normal healthy life, although in later years he constantly fantasized meeting a horse who advises him to take up architecture."

Premise: Excerpts from *Conversations with Helmholtz,* a forthcoming book by Fears Hoffnung about Helmholtz, a pioneer in psychoanalysis and a contemporary of Freud's.

15. "Viva Vargas! Excerpts from the Diary of a Revolutionary"

First Appearance: Evergreen Review; August, 1969; pp. 25–27.

Laugh-Out-Loud Line: "As it turned out, Arroyo's busy schedule did not include taking time away from being fanned to meet with our beloved rebel emissary, and instead he referred the entire matter to his minister, who said he would give our petitions his full consideration, but first he just wanted to see how long Julio could smile with his head under molten lava."

Premise: A would-be revolutionary keeps a diary of rebels' attempts to overthrow a corrupt regime. (Note: What came first, "Viva Vargas!" or *Bananas?* "Viva Vargas!" seems to be a first-draft *Bananas* [even down to using the same name for the rebel leader, General Emilio Molina Vargas], although it's not clear just what came into existence first, the story or the film script. According to Eric Lax, *Bananas* was written sometime in 1966 [with the original title *El Weirdo*], and then, because producer Robert Morse wasn't too crazy about it, was put away. *Bananas* was eventually produced, and was released in 1971. Since "Viva Vargas!" was published in the *Evergreen Review* prior to 1971 [the year of the first appearance of *Getting Even,* containing the story], and the script was in existence since 1966, it could be that both were conceived simultaneously, although from the level of writing, and the fact that *Bananas* is much funnier and more successful than "Viva Vargas!" it's likely that the story came first.)

16. "The Discovery and Use of the Fake Ink Blot"

First Appearance: Playboy; August 1966.

Laugh-Out-Loud Line: "However, with the discovery of the concept of smaller sizes by a Swiss physicist, who proved that an object of a particular size could be reduced in size simply by 'making it smaller,' the fake ink blot came into its own."

Premise: A look at the practical joke habits of some great men of history.

17. "Mr. Big"

First Appearance: Getting Even.

Laugh-Out-Loud Line: "My first lead was Rabbi Itzhak Wiseman, a local cleric who owed me a favor for finding out who was rubbing pork on his hat."

Premise: A beautiful blonde hires a hard-boiled detective to find a missing person: God. Woody Allen, "teleological existential atheist," lets loose with both barrels in this incredibly clever satire of detective stories. Accurately colored with the precise language of philosophy, "Mr. Big" is brilliant. And the following scene foreshadows a similar scene/conversation in 1975's *Love and Death* when Sonia spouts off a metaphysical speech about the concept of "being":

> She was fading fast, but I managed to get it in, in time.
>
> "The manifestation of the universe as a complex idea unto itself as opposed to being in or outside the true Being of itself is inherently a conceptual nothingness or Nothingness in relation to any abstract form of existing or to exist or having existed in perpetuity and not subject to laws of physicality or motion or ideas relating to non-matter or the lack of objective Being or subjective otherness."
>
> It was a subtle concept but I think she understood before she died.

(2)
Without Feathers
(1975)

Contents

1. "Selections from the Allen Notebooks"
2. "Examining Psychic Phenomena"
3. "A Guide to Some of the Lesser Ballets"
4. "The Scrolls"
5. "Lovborg's Women Considered"
6. "The Whore of Mensa"
7. *Death* (A Play)
8. "The Early Essays"
9. "A Brief, Yet Helpful, Guide to Civil Disobedience"
10. "Match Wits with Inspector Ford"
11. "The Irish Genius"
12. *God* (A Play)
13. "Fabulous Tales and Mythical Beasts"
14. "But Soft . . . Real Soft"
15. "If the Impressionists Had Been Dentists"
16. "No Kaddish for Weinstein"
17. "Fine Times: An Oral Memoir"
18. "Slang Origins"

Introduction

Without Feathers contains some of the finest comic writing of the twentieth century.

That's quite a rave, don't you think?

But it's true.

The collection is brilliant, and substantiates Steve Allen's comment that Woody's stuff was "just as funny as Perelman's or Benchley's."

And the senior Signore Allen is right. The essays in *Without Feathers* are blisteringly funny, although it must be acknowledged that the jokes are much funnier if you get the references. Unless you've read the pompous, anecdotal interpretation of some minor poet, "The Irish Genius" might amuse you, but its deepest humor will be lost.

And unless you're familiar with the seemingly endless debate about who actually wrote Shakespeare's works, "But Soft . . . Real Soft" might seem pointless.

But many essays in the volume are immediately accessible even to people who may not share Woody's artistic background. These include "Selections from the Allen Notebooks," "Examining Psychic Phenomena," "The Scrolls," "The Whore of Mensa," "The Early Essays," "Fabulous Tales and Mythical Beasts," and, most notably, "Slang Origins."

The Stories

1. "Selections from the Allen Notebooks"

First Appearance: New Yorker; November 5, 1973; pp. 48–49.
Laugh-Out-Loud Line: "Short story: A man awakens in the morning and finds himself transformed into his own arch supports."
Premise: "Following are excerpts from the hitherto secret private journal of Woody Allen, which will be published posthumously or after his death, whichever comes first." (In this essay, Woody takes another shot at a favorite target: insurance salesmen. In *Take the Money and Run,* when Virgil Starkwell complains about not being allowed to faint without permission while working on the prison rock pile, "For several days he is locked in a sweat box with an insurance salesman." There is also an insurance salesman joke in *Love and Death.*)

2. "Examining Psychic Phenomena"

First Appearance: New Yorker; October 7, 1972; pp. 32–33.
Laugh-Out-Loud Line: "Mr. Albert Sykes reports the following experience: 'I was sitting having biscuits with some friends when I felt my spirit leave my body and go make a telephone call.'" Tie: "I found this séance to pass the most stringent tests of credulity, with the minor exception of a phonograph, which was found under Madame Reynaud's dress."
Premise: Excerpts from a book on paranormal experiences by Dr. Osgood Mulford Twelge, "professor of ectoplasm at Columbia University."

3. "A Guide to Some of the Lesser Ballets"

First Appearance: New Yorker; October 28, 1972; pp. 34–35.
Laugh-Out-Loud Line: "Many people in gaily colored costumes dance and

laugh, to the accompaniment of flutes and woodwinds, while the trombones play in a minor key to suggest that soon the refreshments will run out and everybody will be dead." [From *Dmitri.*]

Premise: A look at some of the *truly* lesser-known ballets, with summaries and erudite commentary.

4. "The Scrolls"

First Appearance: New Republic; August 31, 1974; pp. 18–19.

Laugh-Out-Loud Line: "And the Lord made an bet with Satan to test Job's loyalty and the Lord, for no apparent reason to Job, smote him on the head and again on the ear and pushed him into an thick sauce so as to make Job sticky and vile and then he slew a tenth part of Job's kine and Job calleth out: 'Why dost thou slay my kine? Kine are hard to come by. Now I am short kine and I'm not even sure what kine are.'"

Premise: A look at recently uncovered parchment scrolls originally thought to date from 4000 B.C., but whose authenticity is now in question because of the appearance of the word "Oldsmobile" in the text.

5. "Lovborg's Women Considered"

First Appearance: New Yorker; October 28, 1974; pp. 44–45.

Laugh-Out-Loud Line: "Perhaps no writer has created more fascinating and complex females than the great Scandinavian playwright Jorgen Lovborg, known to his contemporaries as Jorgen Lovborg."

Premise: A comprehensive, analytical look at the women in the work of the Scandinavian author of such stage classics as *A Mother's Gums, Those Who Squirm, I Prefer to Yodel, While We Three Hemorrhage,* and *Mellow Pears.*

6. "The Whore of Mensa"

First Appearance: New Yorker; December 16, 1974; pp. 37–8.

Laugh-Out-Loud Line: "For three bills, you got the works: A thin Jewish brunette would pretend to pick you up at the Museum of Modern Art, let you read her master's, get you involved in a screaming quarrel at Elaine's over Freud's conception of women, and then fake a suicide of your choosing—the perfect evening, for some guys."

Premise: Gumshoe Kaiser Lupowitz busts an intellectual call girl ring. (Woody later used a line from this piece in *Annie Hall:* When one of the intellectual call girls comes clean to Kaiser, he thinks, "It all poured out—the whole story. Central Park West upbringing, Socialist summer camps, Brandeis." In *Annie Hall* Alvy asks Allison Portchnik: "You, like, New York Jewish Left Wing Liberal Intellectual Central Park West Brandeis University, the Socialist summer camps and the father with the Ben Shahn drawings?")

7. Death (A Play)

First Appearance: Without Feathers.
Laugh-Out-Loud Line: "All right, keep the door locked and don't open it for anyone—not even me, unless I happen to be screaming, 'Open the door!' Then open it quickly."
Premise: Kleinman is roused from his sleep to join a group of vigilantes on the prowl for a maniacal killer. Kleinman is never told what the plan is, and ends up murdered by a killer who looked like him. The other victims had all said that the killer looked like themselves, and the play ends with the survivors running off to catch the elusive murderer (who is actually death incarnate). [See the *Shadows and Fog* feature in Chapter 5.]

8. "The Early Essays" (consisting of "On Seeing a Tree in Summer," "On Youth and Age," "On Frugality," "On Love," and "On Tripping Through a Copse and Picking Violets")

First Appearance: New Yorker; January 20, 1973; pp. 32–33.
Laugh-Out-Loud Line (from "On Seeing a Tree in Summer"): "Of all the wonders of nature, a tree in summer is perhaps the most remarkable, with the possible exception of a moose singing 'Embraceable You' in spats."
Premise (from the headnote): "Following are a few of the early essays of Woody Allen. There are no late essays, because he ran out of observations. Perhaps as Allen grows older he will understand more of life and will set it down, and then retire to his bedroom and remain there indefinitely. Like the essays of Bacon, Allen's are brief and full of practical wisdom, although space does not permit the inclusion of his most profound statement, 'Looking at the Bright Side.'"

9. "A Brief, Yet Helpful, Guide to Civil Disobedience"

First Appearance: New York Times; July 15, 1972.
Laugh-Out-Loud Line: "The problem with the hunger strike is that after several days one can get quite hungry, particularly since sound trucks are paid to go through the street saying, "Um . . . what nice chicken—umm . . . some peas . . . umm . . . .""
Premise: An overview of selected revolutions, and a look at some particularly effective means of civil disobedience. (Such as "Phoning members of 'the establishment' and singing 'Bess, You Is My Woman Now' into the phone.")

10. "Match Wits with Inspector Ford" (consisting of "The Case of the Murdered Socialite," "A Curious Riddle," "The Stolen Gem," "The Macabre Accident," and "The Bizarre Kidnapping")

First Appearance: Playboy; December 1972.
Laugh-Out-Loud Line: (from "The Case of the Murdered Socialite"): "The

position of the body indicated that the victim had been surprised in the act of singing 'Sorrento' to his goldfish."
Premise: Five mini-mysteries, all solved by the brilliant Inspector Ford.

11. "The Irish Genius"

First Appearance: New Republic; February 22, 1975; pp. 14–16.
Laugh-Out-Loud Line: "O'Shawn was influenced by Celtic mythology, and his poem that begins, 'Clooth na bare, na bare, na bare' tells how the gods of ancient Ireland transformed two lovers into a set of the Encyclopaedia Britannica."
Premise: Analysis, with anecdotal background, of the poem "Beyond Ichor" by the great Irish poet, Sean O'Shawn.

12. *God* (A Play)

First Appearance: Without Feathers.
Laugh-Out-Loud Line: "Did you hear about Cyclops? He got a middle eye infection."
Premise: An existential play concerning ancient Greeks named Diabetes, Hepatitis, and Trichinosis, Blanche DuBois, the Civil War, the Academy Awards, *A Streetcar Named Desire,* Groucho Marx, orgasms, and Woody Allen as a character in his own play.

13. "Fabulous Tales and Mythical Beasts" (consisting of "The Nurk," "The Flying Snoll," "The Frean," "The Great Roe," and "The Weal")

First Appearance: New Republic; November 30, 1974; pp. 19–21.
Laugh-Out-Loud Line (from "The Flying Snoll"): "Chastened, Ho Sin looked into a mirror and instead of seeing his own reflection, he saw a man named Mendel Goldblatt who worked for the Wasserman Plumbing Company and who accused him of taking his overcoat."
Premise: (from the headnote): "The following is a sample of some of world literature's more imaginative creations that I am anthologizing in a four-volume set that Remainder and Sons plans to publish pending the outcome of the Norwegian shepherds' strike." (In "The Frean," Woody offers a variation on a joke from *Sleeper.* The first line of "The Frean" is, "The frean is a sea monster with the body of a crab and the head of a certified public accountant." In *Sleeper,* after seeing a giant chicken, Miles asks Luna if the year 2173 has any weird futuristic animals—"like something with the body of a crab and the head of a social worker.")

14. "But Soft . . . Real Soft"

First Appearance: Without Feathers.
Laugh-Out-Loud Line: "We all realize Shakespeare (Marlowe) borrowed his

plots from the ancients (moderns); however, when the time came to return the plots to the ancients he had used them up and was forced to leave the country under the assumed name of William Bard (hence the term 'immortal bard') in an effort to avoid debtor's prison (hence the term 'debtor's prison')."

Premise: An in-depth analysis of the various theories concerning who actually wrote the work we know today as William Shakespeare's.

15. "If the Impressionists Had Been Dentists"

First Appearance: Without Feathers.
Laugh-Out-Loud Line: "Today I pulled a tooth and had to anesthetize the patient by reading him some Dreiser." Tie: "He held my head under the X-ray machine for ten straight minutes and for several hours after I could not blink my eyes in unison."
Premise: A series of letters from Vincent van Gogh—the dentist—to his brother Theo.

16. "No Kaddish for Weinstein"

First Appearance: New Yorker; March 3, 1975; pp. 34–35.
Laugh-Out-Loud Line: "At twelve, he had translated the poems of T. S. Eliot into English after some vandals had broken into the library and translated them into French." Tie: "He was positive that collectivization could work if everyone would learn the lyrics to 'Rag Mop.'"
Premise: The Jewish, political, social, religious, and sexual paranoia and anxiety of one Isaac Weinstein, a divorced man with no children who pays his wife four hundred dollars a week for child support.

17. "Fine Times: An Oral Memoir"

First Appearance: New Yorker; March 17, 1975; pp. 34–35.
Laugh-Out-Loud Line: "Liked the rural life, too, although Dad got struck by lightning in the north forty and for six years afterward when asked his name could only say the word 'Kleenex.'"
Premise: "The following are excerpts from the soon-to-be-published memoirs of Flo Guinness [—c]ertainly the most colorful of all speakeasy owners during Prohibition . . ."

18. "Slang Origins"

First Appearance: Without Feathers.
Laugh-Out-Loud Line: "A typical dinner (according to DeRochet) consisted of a thin crêpe appetizer, some parsley, an ox, and custard." Tie: "So obese was the French monarch that he had to be lowered onto the throne with a winch and packed into the seat itself with a large spatula." Tie: "Whenever

a man in the banking profession announced his marriage to a circus pinhead, it was the custom for friends to present him with a bellows and a three-year supply of wax fruit."

Premise: Perceptive (but questionable) explanations of the origins of certain slang expressions, including, "to eat humble pie," "take it on the lam," "got into a beef," "to look down one's nose," "spiffy," "to beat the band," "fiddlesticks," and "the cat's pajamas."

(3)
Side Effects
(1980)

Contents

1. "Remembering Needleman"
2. "The Condemned"
3. "By Destiny Denied"
4. "The UFO Menace"
5. "My Apology" (A Play)
6. "The Kugelmass Episode"
7. "My Speech to the Graduates"
8. "The Diet"
9. "The Lunatic's Tale"
10. "Reminiscences: Places and People"
11. "Nefarious Times We Live In"
12. "A Giant Step for Mankind"
13. "The Shallowest Man"
14. "The Query" (A Play)
15. "Fabrizio's: Criticism and Response"
16. "Retribution"
17. "Confessions of a Burglar"

Introduction

Side Effects was Woody Allen's final collection of short essays. By 1980, his film work had become so demanding that he stopped writing things for *New Yorker,* instead channeling his creative energies into his films.

There are some very funny pieces in this collection, but perhaps what is most noteworthy about it is the presence of some less absurd, more traditional narrative essays. "The Shallowest Man" and "Retribution", for instance, are entirely possible stories, unlike some of the more bizarre concoctions. "The Shallowest Man" tells the story of a man who repeatedly visited a dying friend just so he could see a nurse he lusted after; "Retribution" is the tale of a man who ends up married to his girlfriend's mother.

It is interesting to see Woody working with these longer, more straightforward pieces. It bodes well for the novel he keeps talking about writing someday.

For newcomers to this collection, the best pieces in *Side Effects,* in my opinion, are probably "The Kugelmass Episode" and "Fabrizio's: Criticism and Response."

The Stories

1. "Remembering Needleman"

First Appearance: New Republic (as "At the Cremation: Remembering Needleman"); July 24, 1976; pp. 4–6.
Laugh-Out-Loud Line: "I was present at the cremation and at his son's request, brought the marshmallows, but few of us could think of anything but our pain."
Premise: A remembrance of the famous philosopher Sandor Needleman, the man who often would leave the coat hanger in his jacket while he wore it, the man who was fond of saying, " 'God is silent, now if we can only get Man to shut up.' "; and the man who authored such classics as *Time, Essence, and Reality: A Systematic Reevaluation of Nothingness; The Best Places to Eat While in Hiding; Non-Existence: What to Do If It Suddenly Strikes You; Semantic Modes of Non-Essential Functioning* ("which was made into the hit movie *They Flew by Night*"); and *Styles of Modes.*

2. "The Condemned"

First Appearance: New Yorker; November 21, 1977; pp. 57–59.
Laugh-Out-Loud Line: "She was one of the few women he knew who could hold two disparate concepts in her mind at once, such as Hegel's dialectic and why if you stick your tongue in a man's ear while he is making a speech he will start to sound like Jerry Lewis."
Premise: The story of Cloquet, a man falsely arrested for a murder he didn't commit. Condemned to die, he ponders the meaning of life, the existence of God, and his desire to show up at the Louvre in bikini underwear, with a fake nose and glasses. (This essay seems to have sprung from the same idea kernel as *Love and Death,* as there are several similarities to the stories.)

3. "By Destiny Denied"

First Appearance: New Yorker; February 23, 1976; pp. 33–35.
Laugh-Out-Loud Line: "His small trading post will go on to become a giant modern department store, and when he dies at eighty-five, from a combination of smallpox and a tomahawk in the skull, he is happy." Tie: "John

Higby, the owner, is a stubby man with bushy hair who fell off a ladder at the age of nine and requires two days' advance notice to stop grinning."
Premise (from the headnote): "Notes for an eight-hundred-page novel—the big book they're all waiting for." First chapter notes for a novel called *By Destiny Denied*. The notes are broken into sections as follows: "Background—Scotland, 1823"; "Locale and observations, 1976"; "Blanche (Base her on Cousin Tina)"; "Carmen (A study in psychopathology based on traits observed in Fred Simdong, his brother Lee, and their cat Sparky)"; and "The Meeting (rough)." The last sentence of the notes is "Late in January, Entwhistle's closed its doors for the last time, and Julie Entwhistle, the owner, took his family, whom he loved very dearly, and moved them into the Bronx Zoo." The author then makes a parenthetical notation reading, "This last sentence should remain intact. It seems very great." (Woody has often said that if he couldn't make films anymore, he would love nothing better than to stay home and write novels.)

4. "The UFO Menace"

First Appearance: New Yorker; June 13, 1977; pp. 31–33.
Laugh-Out-Loud Line: "All UFOs may not prove to be of extraterrestrial origin, but experts do agree that any glowing cigar-shaped aircraft capable of rising straight up at twelve thousand miles per second would require the kind of maintenance and sparkplugs available only on Pluto." Tie: "And, again, were those 'orange objects' similar to what is described in a recently discovered twelfth-century Saxon church manuscript: 'A lauch lauched he, wer right laith to weet a cork-heild schonne; whilst a red balle lang owre swam aboone. I thank you ladies and gentlemen'?"
Premise: An overview of the UFO experience throughout history, as well as a look at recent UFO sightings.

5. *My Apology* (A Play)

First Appearance: Side Effects.
Laugh-Out-Loud Line: "Agathon: Oh, I ran into Isosceles. He has a great idea for a new triangle."
Premise: Woody Allen has a dream in which he is a Greek philosopher sentenced to death who is reprieved at the last minute. The dream is told in stageplay form.

6. "The Kugelmass Episode"

First Appearance: New Yorker; May 2, 1977; pp. 34–39.
Laugh-Out-Loud Line: "What he didn't realize was at this very moment students in various classrooms across the country were saying to their

teachers, 'Who is this character on page 100? A bald Jew is kissing Madame Bovary?'"

Premise: Sidney Kugelmass enters *Madame Bovary* with the help of the magician, the Great Persky, and begins an affair with Emma Bovary. He then brings her to New York for a visit and she almost gets stuck there. After she's back in her own book, he decides he'd like to visit *Portnoy's Complaint,* but after Persky has a heart attack, he ends up instead in *Remedial Spanish* being chased by the word *tener* ("to have")—"large and hairy irregular verb." (This is reminiscent of a routine on *The Third Woody Allen Album* in which Woody tells of a dream he had in which he was chased by two big hairy letters, "N," and "O." See the feature on Woody's records in Chapter 7.)

7. "My Speech to the Graduates"

First Appearance: New York Times; August 10, 1979; pg. 25.

Laugh-Out-Loud Line: "(Modern man is here defined as any person born after Nietzsche's edict that 'God is dead,' but before the hit recording 'I Wanna Hold Your Hand.')"

Premise: An alienated, frustrated, angst-ridden, agnostic technophobic commencement speaker addresses a graduating class.

8. "The Diet"

First Appearance: New Yorker; February 25, 1980; pp. 36–37.

Laugh-Out-Loud Line: "Three weeks earlier, F. had been discovered in the Xerox room behaving like a woodpecker."

Premise: A paranoid and portly drone of a worker in a "Big Brother" type of office environment finds his lot improving after he loses weight.

9. "The Lunatic's Tale"

First Appearance: New Rebublic; April 23, 1977; pp. 17–19.

Laugh-Out-Loud Line: "The bullet passed through my ceiling, causing Mrs. Fitelson in the apartment overhead to leap straight upward onto her bookshelf and remain perched there throughout the high holidays."

Premise: A doctor who successfully switched the brains of his wife and his mistress—and then lost interest in *both* women—relates his descent into madness. (Note: This essay has elements from Woody's life and work. After his divorce, Woody repeatedly did a joke about his first wife being "violated" in Central Park (in the routine "Second Marriage" on *The Third Woody Allen Album*), but that knowing his ex-wife, he was pretty sure it wasn't a "moving violation." [See the interview with Steve Allen and his essay on Woody in Chapter 3 for details on the lawsuit against Woody that resulted from Woody's use of that joke on Steve's show.] In "The Lunatic's

Tale," while the "lunatic" is talking about his second wife, he says, "I recall once, while we were making love, a curious optical illusion occurred and for a split second it almost looked as though she was moving." The mad doctor in the story successfully switches the brains of his sexpot mistress and his intellectual wife. This is a scenario director Sandy Bates (in *Stardust Memories*) used for a science fiction film he made, with the results being the same: he wasn't satisfied with the "redesigned" women.)

10. "Reminiscences: Places and People"

First Appearance: New Yorker; December 29, 1975; pp. 20–21.
Laugh-Out-Loud Line: "A small boy helps a bearded old man across the street and says, 'Good Sabbath.' The old man smiles and empties his pipe on the boy's head."
Premise: A writer remembers (rather peculiar) encounters with André Malraux, William Maugham, Paris, Brooklyn, Mexico, and New Orleans.

11. "Nefarious Times We Live In"

First Appearance: New Republic; November 22, 1975.
Laugh-Out-Loud Line: "More precisely, a group of us had been fed roast chicken stuffed with lysergic acid, in a research program designed to determine the quantity of LSD a man can ingest before he attempts to fly over the World Trade Center." Tie: "I also recall being made to take peyote and cocaine and eat a white substance that came from boiled cactus, which caused my head to revolve completely around like a radar dish."
Premise: A failed presidential assassin recounts his life story, from being an experimental subject in the army, to his brainwashing by being tickled by experts and having country and western music sung to him until he agreed to do whatever he was told.

12. "A Giant Step for Mankind"

First Appearance: New Yorker; June 9, 1980; pp. 36–38.
Laugh-Out-Loud Line: "Placing his fist just under Goldworm's sternum, he hugged sharply, causing a side order of bean curd to rocket out of the victim's trachea and carom off the hat rack."
Premise: Excerpts from the diary of the scientific team that tried to develop the Heimlich maneuver before Dr. Heimlich. (Note: A variation of a joke in this essay appears four years later in *Broadway Danny Rose*. In the essay, he writes, "Wolfsheim, unable to part with the old theories, tried administering a glass of water, but unfortunately seized it from the table of a gentleman well placed in the cement and contracting community, and all three of us were escorted out of the service entrance and up against a

lamppost, over and over." In *Danny Rose,* the following exchange takes place:

> **Danny** Well, what do you do, Rocco?
> **Rocco** Ah, cement.
> **Danny** Cement?
> **Rocco** I own a fleet of cement mixers.
> **Danny** Oh, no kidding? Well, isn't that a very big organized cr—
> Cement. That's fantastic, cement.

13. "The Shallowest Man"

First Appearance: Kenyon Review; Winter, 1980; pp. 1–8.
Laugh-Out-Loud Line: "Mendel did stop short of bringing Iskowitz a pair of antique earrings although he saw some he knew Miss Hill would adore."
Premise: The story of Lenny Mendel, who regularly visited a dying friend because he had the hots for his nurse.

14. *The Query* (A Play)

First Appearance: New Republic; September 18, 1976; pp. 11–13.
Laugh-Out-Loud Line: "I plant turnips and corn comes up? You think that doesn't hurt a man?"
Premise: A play recounting the story of a farmer who wanted Abraham Lincoln to commute his son's death sentence, but instead of asking for a pardon, became tongue-tied and asked Lincoln, "How long do you think a man's legs should be?" The non sequitur causes Abe to reevaluate his life, and the son is pardoned.

15. "Fabrizio's: Criticism and Response"

First Appearance: New Yorker; February 5, 1979; pp. 31–32.
Laugh-Out-Loud Line: "Who can forget his scampi: four garlic-drenched shrimp arranged in a way that says more about our involvement in Vietnam than countless books on the subject?"
Premise: Renowned food critic Fabian Plotnick reviews Fabrizio's Villa Nova Restaurant ("His fettuccine, though wry and puckish in an almost mischievous way, owes a lot to Barzino, whose use of fettuccine as an instrument of social change is known to us all") in "one of the more thought-provoking journals." A selection of responses to Plotnick's review is included, as well as the critic's reply to the letter writers.

16. "Retribution"

First Appearance: Kenyon Review; Summer, 1980; pp. 23–34.
Laugh-Out-Loud Line: "Actually, I had a rather dim view of my family's

physical appearance, likening the relatives on my mother's side to something usually cultured in a Petri dish."

Premise: A young Jewish man named Harold Cohen enters into a relationship with a beautiful Connecticut WASP named Connie Chasen, and falls for her mother, Emily. He abandons the idea of an affair with Emily because of his love for Connie, but then Connie turns off to him. The two split up, and he ends up marrying Emily. This re-ignites the daughter's libido toward Harold ("Marrying Mom has made you my father") and the story ends with Harold sitting on the bed, muttering, "Oy vey." (In Woody's 1981 play, *The Floating Light Bulb,* Paul's mother Enid had a friend named *Carol* Chasen.)

17. "Confessions of a Burglar"

First Appearance: New Yorker; October 18, 1976; pp. 35–37.

Laugh-Out-Loud Line: "My brother Vic got in with a gang of plagiarists. He was in the middle of signing his name to "The Waste Land" when the feds surrounded the house."

Premise: The memoirs of a burglar who apparently came from the same genetic pool as Virgil Starkwell.

CHAPTER 7

Woody Allen, Recording Star
The Records

Alvy Singer. I'm a comedian.
Alvy Singer to Allison Portchnik, in *Annie Hall*

If people come away relating to me as a person, rather than just enjoying my jokes; if they come away wanting to hear me again, no matter what I might talk about, then I'm succeeding.
Woody Allen

You're gonna like nightclubs. They're a lotta fun.
Alvy Singer to Annie Hall, in *Annie Hall*

THIS CHAPTER examines the three original albums and the two compilation albums of standup comedy material Woody Allen released between 1964 and 1978.

The last two albums *Woody Allen: The Night-Club Years* and *Woody Allen Standup Comic* are identical and consist of material from the three albums of new, original material Woody released in 1964, 1965, and 1968.

Woody's first album, titled *Woody Allen,* was released in 1964 on Colpix and contained 37 minutes and 8 seconds of material.

Woody's second album, titled *Woody Allen Volume 2* was released in 1965 on Colpix and contained 30 minutes and 35 seconds of material.

Woody's third—and final—album of original material was released in 1968 on Capitol Records. It was called *The Third Woody Allen Album* and contained 34 minutes and 59 seconds of material.

In 1976 a two-record compilation album called *Woody Allen: The Night-Club Years,* which consisted of material from the first three albums was released by United Artists. This two-record set contained 74 minutes and 59 seconds of material.

253

In 1978 *Woody Allen Standup Comic* was released by Casablanca Records and Film Works. This was identical to *Woody Allen: The Night-Club Years.*

This chapter probes the thirty or so routines Woody wrote and performed in the early sixties. Each piece has a "Premise," a section called " 'The Big, Big Laughs' " (the title of which is a quotation by Woody from his interview with Stephen Banker reprinted in Chapter 2), and a section titled "Ch-Ch-Ch-Changes," which looks at the changes made to the routine when it was rereleased on the compilation albums. (And of course, the title "Ch-Ch-Ch-Changes" comes from the chorus of David Bowie's classic song "Changes" off his *Hunky Dory* album.)

To compile this section, I transcribed verbatim every routine on the three original Woody albums, and then compared it line by line with the routine as it was released on the compilation albums.

As of this writing, *Woody Allen Standup Comic* was still available on album and cassette from select mail-order dealers. This is not a plug, but I did see it in the "Postings" catalogue in the fall of 1991. I would suggest you try them first if you are interested in obtaining a copy. The "Postings" address is P. O. Box 8001, Hilliard, Ohio 43026-8001. The toll-free order number is 1-800-262-6604.

For Woody fans, the opportunity to hear this brilliant, early work should not be passed up.

R1.
Woody Allen
(Colpix, 1964; Recorded Live at Mr. Kelly's; Chicago, March 1964)
[Approx. 37:08]

Introduction: "Ladies and gentlemen, Woody Allen."

SIDE 1: [19:29]
R1a. "Private Life" [6:00]
R1b. "Brooklyn" [3:45]
R1c. "The Army" [1:20]
R1d. "Pets" [1:00]
R1e. "My Grandfather" [:53]
R1f. "My Marriage" [5:55]
R1g. "Bullet in My Breast Pocket" [:36]

SIDE 2: [17:39]
R1h. "N.Y.U." [4:28]
R1i. "A Love Story" [4:54]
R1j. "The Police" [7:40]
R1k. "Summing Up" [:37]

SIDE 1

R1a. "Private Life" [6:00]

Premise: Woody informs the audience about certain "significant things that have occurred" in his private life. This piece is one of the most quoted routines of Woody Allen's career. It seems that everyone writing about Woody's standup comedy act at one time or another referred to his bit about taking all the "abstract philosophy courses" at NYU, like "Truth and Beauty," "Advanced Truth and Beauty," "Intermediate Truth," "Introduction to God," and "Death 101."
"The Big, Big Laughs": "Private Life" contains some classic lines, such as, "I cheated on my metaphysics final. I looked within the soul of the boy sitting next to me." (Woody later used this bit in *Annie Hall*, as well as the follow-up line about his mother taking an overdose of mah-jongg tiles.) Other riotous bits include Woody's discussion of being in analysis. He was "captain of the Latent Paranoid Softball Team. Nailbiters against the Bedwetters." Another funny line is the one about his wife's cousin. She had orgasmic insurance: "If her husband fails to satisfy her sexually, Mutual of Omaha has to pay her every month." While trying to get into the role of God for the play *Gideon*, Woody told a guy who hit his fender, "Be fruitful and multiply . . . but not in those words."

Ch-Ch-Ch-Changes: "Private Life" was included on both compilation albums, only seven lines were edited out, and they were mostly about his first wife. The omitted lines included the barbs "I ran into my ex-wife . . . who I did not recognize with her wrists closed" and "The Museum of Natural History found her shoe and based on the measurements, they reconstructed a dinosaur." The first compilation album, *Woody Allen, The Night-Club Years* came out in 1976, a full fourteen years after Harlene and Woody were divorced, so it's safe to assume that the bitterness had diminished some, and Woody and the producers felt that it was unnecessary to include blatant insults about his ex-wife, whom he hadn't even seen in over a decade.

R1b. "Brooklyn" [3:45]

Premise: Woody talks about his childhood and growing up in Brooklyn. Interestingly, there's a line in the first segment of "Brooklyn" (about Coney Island) that foreshadows a similar scene in *Radio Days.* Woody mentions that "there were rumors during the war that enemy submarines, German subs came into the bathing area at Coney Island and they were destroyed by the pollution." In the fourth segment of this routine (about Floyd the tough kid), Woody foreshadows *Take the Money and Run* when he says that he used to take violin lessons when he was a kid, and that after he stood up to Floyd for calling him "Red, . . . doctors labored to remove a violin." He then remarks that he was "lucky it wasn't a cello." (In *Take the Money and Run,* Virgil Starkwell was a [very bad] cellist.)
"The Big, Big Laughs": "Brooklyn" contains several funny one-liners, among them those mentioned above, as well as, "When I go to the beach, I don't tan. I stroke." "Brooklyn" also contains very bizarre, suggestive, and highly humorous word sketches, including one of Woody water-skiing . . . and his wife "in the boat ahead . . . rowing frantically."
Ch-Ch-Ch-Changes: "Brooklyn" was included complete and uncut on both compilation albums.

R1c. "The Army" [1:20]

Premise: Woody ends up as a member of the canine corps instead of the regular army.
"The Big, Big Laughs": In "The Army" we learn that Woody's father "was caddy at a miniature golf course in Brooklyn." The routine contains Woody's hysterical bit, "I was classified 4-P by the draft board. In the event of war I'm a hostage," which he later did on "The Dick Cavett Show." (The "Cavett" segment was excerpted and used later in *Annie Hall.*) "The Army" also informs us of a shop that sold "damaged pets," such as bent pussycats, straight camels, and a dog that stuttered.

Ch-Ch-Ch-Changes: "The Army" was included complete and uncut on both compilation albums.

R1d. "Pets" [1:00]

Premise: As a child, Woody got an ant instead of a dog as a pet. This is a very short routine that hinges on the absurd notion that one could have an ant as a pet, train it, and sic it on a bully. The August 21, 1964, issue of *Life* magazine ran an article about Woody called "Man with an Ant on a Leash," which featured a photo of Woody holding a leash with the neck piece on the floor.

"The Big, Big Laughs": "Pets" is so short that the majority of Woody's lines are setups for the final punchline. After Woody is bullyed by Sheldon Finklestein, he tells his ant, Spot, to "Kill!" The payoff line was "And Sheldon stepped on my dog."

Ch-Ch-Ch-Changes: "Pets" was included complete and uncut on both compilation albums.

R1e. "My Grandfather" [:53]

Premise: Woody tells the audience about his grandfather, shows them his grandfather's watch, and describes the old man's funeral. It seems as though Woody wrote this bit specifically to give him an excuse to check his timing. He knew he had to be at a certain time mark when he got to "My Grandfather" and if he wasn't, then he could stretch. But instead of simply wearing a watch and casually glancing at it, Woody used a pocket-watch and built a routine around checking the time.

"The Big, Big Laughs": "It is a gorgeous gold pocketwatch . . . and I am proud of it. My grandfather, on his deathbed, sold me this watch." We also learn how insignificant his grandfather was: "At his funeral, his hearse followed the other cars." And in a line that foreshadows the character of Walter Hollander the caterer (the "Potato Salad Picasso") in the 1969 film, *Don't Drink the Water* (which was based on Woody's stageplay), we are told that at his grandfather's funeral, "On the buffet table there was a replica of the deceased in potato salad."

Ch-Ch-Ch-Changes: Other than the elimination of the first line of this bit (which was "Strange life."), "My Grandfather" was included complete and uncut on both compilation albums.

R1f. "My Marriage" [5:55]

Premise: Woody reveals details of his first marriage and subsequent divorce to the audience. "My Marriage" was a routine that Woody did quite often in the midsixties. Steve Allen sent me a videotape of Woody's appearance on Steve's show on November 15, 1963, during which Woody did "My

Marriage" and "My Grandfather." The routine is hilarious but does have a measure of cruelty to it. Many of the laughs come from jokes about Woody's persona ("I would be home in the bathroom taking a bath and my wife would walk right in whenever she felt like it and sink my boats." In the aforementioned "Man with an Ant on a Leash" article, Woody was photographed sitting in a bathtub as a woman sunk his boats with a broom). But there were also a few digs (calling his ex-wife "Quasimodo," and saying she spent her time listening to Conelrad on the radio) that seemed gratuitous when leveled against someone who couldn't fire back—except with a lawsuit. And speaking of the lawsuit: Harlene Rosen sued Woody in 1967 for one specific remark that Woody made in the routine known as "Second Marriage." The bit was "She [Harlene] was violated. . . . And I said, knowing my ex-wife, it probably was not a moving violation." Woody and Harlene were divorced in 1962. "Second Marriage" was included on Woody's third album, which was released in 1968. But according to Steve Allen, Woody did the "moving violation" joke on Steve's 1963 show, but it was cut out and didn't air.

"The Big, Big Laughs": The jokes in this routine play on Woody's "schlemiel" character. He saw himself single again, living in a bachelor apartment with "some of those great Picassos by van Gogh." He sold the memoirs of his love life to Parker Brothers and they were going to make them into a game. And what is probably the funniest line in the bit: Because New York State required adultery as grounds for divorce, Woody decided to ask for the help of his wife's friend Nancy: "So I called up Nancy on the phone and I asked her if she would have adultery with me. And she said, 'Not even if it would help the space program.' "

Ch-Ch-Ch-Changes: "My Marriage" was drastically edited for the compilation album. Over three minutes of material were cut out of the bit, and for the most part, the cuts were judicious and correct: they strengthened the piece. After Woody explains that adultery was required for a divorce, he says the lines, "And that is weird because the Ten Commandments say, 'Thou shalt not commit adultery.' But New York State says you have to." The piece then skips thirty-five lines of material and moves to Woody explaining that his wife finally committed adultery for him. "She's always been more mechanically inclined than I have." In between those two segments was a long, rambling bit about Woody trying to find someone with whom he could commit adultery. The only funny lines in this cut material are the aforementioned "Parker Brothers" and "space program" lines. Also cut was a reference to a bordello masquerading as a bar called the Agnostic Bagel Shop. Woody did a similar joke on his second album in the routine called "What's New, Pussycat?" (which appeared on the compilation album as "European Trip"). In that bit, Woody said he appeared at a Greenwich Village coffeehouse called the Integration Bagel Shop and Freak Parlor. This is a stronger joke, and since the producers obviously couldn't include both "Bagel Shop" jokes on the compilation album, they wisely went with the better one.

R1g. "Bullet in My Breast Pocket" [:36]

Premise: Woody's life is saved when a Gideon Bible hurled out a window by a berserk evangelist is stopped from penetrating his chest by a bullet in his breast pocket. Woody takes a cliché here and, for sharp comic effect, turns it upside down.

"The Big, Big Laughs": This short piece has the one big laugh at the punch line: "The Bible would have gone through my heart if it wasn't for the bullet."

Ch-Ch-Ch-Changes: "Bullet in My Breast Pocket" was included complete and uncut on both compilation albums.

SIDE 2

R1h. "N.Y.U." [4:28]

Premise: Woody tells the audience about his college experiences. "N.Y.U." is a series of jokes all linked by the umbrella heading of Woody's (very brief) college days. He starts off the routine with what seems like a reprise of his "thrown out of school for cheating" bit from "Private Life," only this time it's a much weaker joke: "I was thrown out of N.Y.U. in my freshman year for cheating. It was a very delicate situation at the time because it was with the dean's wife." He then tells a joke about a woman he knew who was practicing "rhythmic birth control" which has as its only laugh the line "she has not been able to keep a beat, because she's densely populated." And he also tells a joke about junkies that he now considers distasteful: he decided to get his junkie and junkette friends a complete set of silverware as a wedding present: all spoons. "N.Y.U." was very well-received by audiences because it sounded autobiographical, and Woody was always appreciated when he did material that seemed to spring from his real life. It reaffirmed his public persona and made audiences feel as if they really knew him. Little did they know.

"The Big, Big Laughs": "N.Y.U." contains some very strong material. Woody tells about a religious conflict with the first girl he fell in love with: "She was an atheist and I was an agnostic. We didn't know what religion not to bring the children up in." He tells about the "reformed" rabbi that married him. He was *very* reformed: he was a Nazi. We learn that his father was watching the Indiana Home for the Criminally Insane Glee Club on Ed Sullivan when Woody told his parents about his divorce, and that his mother put down the chicken she was knitting, "went over to the furnace . . . and got in."

Ch-Ch-Ch-Changes: The "dean's wife," "birth control," "and "junkies" bits were all edited out of "N.Y.U." for the compilation albums.

R1i. "A Love Story" [4:54]

Premise: Woody informs the audience of an affair he had with a Bennington girl. She was a beatnik who was "studying at Bennington to be a woman male nurse." (She was also working on a term paper "on the increasing incidence of heterosexuality amongst homosexuals.") He picked her up at the ballet, they went to her apartment, and she ended up dumping him because he was not intellectually her equal. Throughout the narrative, Woody inserts a series of very funny gags. He says his weak spot is women: "I always think someday they're going to make me a birthday party and wheel out a tremendous birthday cake, and a giant naked woman is going to leap out of the cake, and hurt me, and leap back in." The piece ends with Woody being hired as a "show Jew" by an advertising agency and getting fired for taking off too many Jewish holidays.

"The Big, Big Laughs": The big laughs in "A Love Story" come from humorous asides Woody offers while telling the story of his affair with the Bennington beatnik. He says that while he was dating her, "she lived with . . . a sort of post-Impressionist, mock, pseudo-psychotic, neo-quasi-cretin painter . . . who tried to cut off his ear with an electric razor." Initially, Woody told the audience that the girl had a "Bird Lives" tattoo. This "Charlie Parker" reference didn't work for many audiences and so, on Charles Joffe's suggestion, Woody expanded the joke so that it was "tattooed on her inner thigh," and "had it been printed in Braille, I would have had a great thing going with her." We also learn that the girl's friends used to try and "make opium out of the poppies given out by veterans on street corners" while they listened to "the record albums of Marcel Marceau."

Ch-Ch-Ch-Changes: This piece was fairly heavily edited for the compilation albums. They cut a pointless passage about Woody wearing an Italian suit, and, surprisingly, the aforementioned "electric razor" gag. A couple of lines about the girl's brother's rubber sheets being returned to his parents after he was shot at military school were cut, as was a final unnecessary passage about the girl winning a scholarship to secretarial school in Switzerland.

R1j. "The Police" [7:40]

Premise: Woody gets mugged. "The Police" is a lengthy piece that is only moderately funny. Probably the funniest part of the routine is the opening passage in which the New York Public Library surrounds Woody's house and a librarian lobs in tear gas grenades because Woody had an overdue book. The storyline basically concerns Woody's attempts to protect himself by buying a tear gas fountain pen which doesn't work when he is confronted by a "Neanderthal Man" in the lobby of his apartment building. The concluding thematic punch line (which was cut from the piece for the compilation albums) is that after the cops come, "they took his side."

"The Big, Big Laughs": Aside from the "library policeman" bit, the funny stuff in this piece concerns Woody's neighbor, Mr. Russo, who tried to sign for the money he was robbed of, and Woody's confrontation with the "tree-swinger, mouth-breather" mugger. When the tear gas pen doesn't work, Woody tries writing on the guy with it, and the guy tap dances on his windpipe. A line that got a big laugh from the audience was the next line, "Very quickly I lapsed into the old Navajo Indian trick of screaming and begging." Interestingly, the next line, which I consider hilarious, was cut: "He started to remove my wisdom teeth." Another funny line that was omitted was "I have on my chest the words, 'Do Not Fold, Spindle, or Mutilate.'" A short bit that was part of "The Police" was a routine I've subtitled "Rio," which displays Woody's brilliance with language. The routine begins with a fairly straightforward gag: "I was flying down to Rio to check on reports that a silver mine left to me by my uncle was tarnishing." But the next two lines are sheer brilliance: "With me on the plane was the daughter of a Maharaja, six escaped Litvaks, and a defrocked Mother Superior who ran a floating nunnery. Opposite me was a man named Leo who was part Mexican, part nonfat dry milk." The bit ends with the Maharaja's daughter giving Woody a "mammoth" hickey for saving the plane.

Ch-Ch-Ch-Changes: Besides the final four lines already discussed, the only lines cut (surprisingly) were the entire "Rio" routine, and four lines from early in the routine about the Japanese losing the war.

R1k. "Summing Up" [:37]

Premise: Woody ends his act with a kidnapping joke.

"The Big, Big Laughs": "Summing up" contains two laughs. Woody begins, "In summing up, I wish I had some kind of affirmative message to leave you with. I don't. Would you take two negative messages?" The second foreshadows his classic routine "The Kidnapping" on *Woody Allen, Volume 2*: "My mother used to say to me when I was younger, if a strange man comes up to you and offers you candy, and wants you to get in the back of his car with him . . . Go." (A kidnapping motif also appears in Woody's vignette "The Bizarre Kidnapping," which is part of the short story "Match Wits with Inspector Ford" in *Without Feathers*.)

Ch-Ch-Ch-Changes: "Summing Up" was included complete and uncut on both compilation albums.

R2.
Woody Allen, Volume 2
(Colpix, 1965; Recorded Live at the Shadows; Washington, D.C.,
April 1965) [Approx. 30:35]

[No Introduction]

[The album has quotations on the back from *New York, Newsweek,* and *Life* magazines; the album sleeve also has a collage of photos titled "The Real Actual Life of Woody Allen, Man and Boy."]

SIDE 1: [14:50]

R2a. "The Moose" [2:38]
R2b. "The Kidnapping" [2:54]
R2c. "Superman" [5:27]
R2d. "Science Fiction Movie" [1:48]
R2e. "Eggs Benedict" [1:36]
R2f. "Footnote [:27]

SIDE 2: [15:45]

R2g. "What's New, Pussycat?" [7:12]
R2h. "Reminiscences" [3:20]
R2i. "Swedish Movie" [2:21]
R2j. "Taking a Shower" [:54]
R2k. "The Lost Generation" [1:58]

SIDE 1

R2a. "The Moose" [2:38]

Premise: Woody shoots a moose, doesn't kill it, and it wakes up on the fender of his car on the way home. This routine can rightfully be considered a classic. It is brilliantly constructed, very funny, and performed flawlessly. "The Moose" is reprinted in its entirety in Steve Allen's article "Woody Allen," which appears in Chapter 3, and Steve deftly analyzes the piece line by line and explains why it's funny, and why it works.
"The Big, Big Laughs": Almost every line of "The Moose" is a "big, big laugh." See the transcript in Steve Allen's article in Chapter 3.
Ch-Ch-Ch-Changes: "The Moose" appears complete and uncut on both compilation albums.

R2b. "The Kidnapping" [2:54]

Premise: Woody is kidnapped and ransomed. "The Kidnapping," like "The Moose," is another classic Woody standup routine. It is almost funnier than "The Moose" because of its brilliant absurdity. "The Kidnapping" also foreshadows *Take the Money and Run.* The last line of this routine is "They're sentenced to fifteen years on a chain gang and they escape, twelve of them chained together at the ankle, getting by the guards posing as an immense charm bracelet."

"The Big, Big Laughs": Nearly every line of "The Kidnapping" is high humor, but to me the best lines are: "The FBI decides to lob in tear gas. But they don't have tear gas. So several of the agents put on the death scene from *Camille.*" See the transcript in Steve Allen's article, Chapter 3.

Ch-Ch-Ch-Changes: "The Kidnapping" appears complete and uncut on both compilation albums.

R2c. "Superman" [5:27]

Premise: Woody tells the audience about his unhappy childhood and his Superman fixation. This piece is a perfect example of how less can be more. "Superman" (which is the original unedited version of this material), in its entirety, is not nearly as strong as the edited version, "Unhappy Childhood," which appears on both compilation albums. "Superman" starts with a standard gag: "My parents did not want me as a child. They put a live teddy bear in my crib." Woody next mentions his father's milk bottle concession at Coney Island ("[A] tidal wave ripped up the boardwalk and did about a million dollars worth of damage . . . [and] the only thing left standing were those little milk bottles"); and his prom night (he had to be home by 9:30). He then goes into an extended bit about wearing a Superman cape (his parents' Hotel Dixie tablecloth) to Seymour Gutkin's birthday party and having to defend Hermina Jaffe against the annoying Guy de Maupassant Rabinowitz. After a funny gag about his father's attempts to play "Flight of the Bumblebee" on the tuba ("He blew his liver out through the horn"), he moves into an episode based on his actual adolescent experiences of being harassed on the New York subways. (He later used this routine in *Bananas,* featuring a young Sylvester Stallone as one of the offending hoods.) He was on his way to an amateur musical contest when he was assaulted by a gang of hoods. One of them kneed him in the groin and he "did one of the greatest imitations of Lily Pons you ever heard. I hit an M over high C on the BMT." (Eric Lax also mentions this routine in his book, *Woody Allen: A Biography,* and notes that in the performance of "Superman" that he saw, Woody said he hit "an L over high C." Personally, I think "L" is funnier. What do you think?) The routine ends with Woody coming in second at the contest and winning two weeks at Interfaith Camp, "where I was sadistically beaten by boys of all races and creeds."

"The Big, Big Laughs": "Superman" is pretty funny; "Unhappy Childhood" is hilarious. One of the big laughs retained in both versions is Woody's

account of his prom night: "I made a reservation at the Copacabana for five o'clock. I took my date and we watched them set up." Another funny line not included in the edited version was the one about Hermina Jaffe's overbite: "She used to eat a piece of toast and finish the outer edge first all the time." But probably the single funniest line in the bit is Woody's observation about the "hairy knuckle" types who confronted him on the subway: "Apparently they had just come from a settlement house because they were dribbling a social worker as they went through the car."

Ch-Ch-Ch-Changes: The entire "Seymour Gutkin/Superman" segment of the routine was edited out for the compilation album, shortening the bit by almost three minutes, but also greatly improving it.

R2d. "Science Fiction Movie" [1:48]

Premise: This is basically a laundry joke. But as is usually the case with Woody Allen, the premise is run through a blender and revolved on a Rotissemat before being offered for consumption to the public. The premise of the routine is that Woody once wrote a science fiction film. Everyone in the world falls asleep for exactly an hour, and upon awakening, "everybody in the world finds themselves in the pants business." Aliens land, they want their pants, and everyone tells the visitors the pants aren't ready, and "could you come back Thursday?" The aliens insist the pants be ready because they're going to a wedding. They return Thursday, and this time bring their laundry to do, but "they're foiled because . . . they forget their ticket."

"The Big, Big Laughs": What's funny here (in addition to the hilarious notion of everyone in the world waking up in the pants business) is hearing of aliens spouting the classic laundry cliché about needing pants for a wedding, and of everyone on earth becoming a tailor and not having the work ready when promised. (Woody also used a tailor joke in *Sleeper:* Miles Monroe visits the computerized tailors, Ginsberg & Cohen Computerized Fittings.) "Science Fiction Movie" was very well received by Woody's live audiences.

Ch-Ch-Ch-Changes: "Science Fiction Movie" was included complete and uncut on both compilation albums, but it was retitled "The Science Fiction Film."

R2e. "Eggs Benedict" [1:36]

"Eggs Benedict"* by Woody Allen

1. I had once a pain in the chestal area.
2. Now I was sure it was heartburn, you know, because that time I was married, and my wife, cooking with her Nazi recipes.
3. Chicken Himmler.

* © 1965 by Woody Allen. From the 1965 Colpix record album, *Woody Allen Volume 2.*

4. And I didn't want to pay twenty-five bucks to have it reaffirmed by some medic that I had heartburn.
5. But I was worried because it *was* in the chestal area.
6. And then it turns out my friend, Eggs Benedict, has a pain in his chestal area in the same exact spot.
7. And I figured if I could get Eggs to go to the doctor, I could figure out what's wrong with me.
8. At no charge.
9. So I con Eggs.
10. And he goes.
11. Turns out he's got heartburn.
12. Cost him twenty-five dollars and I feel great.
13. 'Cause I figure I beat the medic out of twenty-five big ones, you know?
14. Call up Eggs two days later.
    [beat]
15. He died.
16. I check into a hospital immediately.
17. Have a battery of tests run.
18. X-rays.
19. Turns out I got heartburn.
20. Cost me a hundred and ten dollars.
21. Now I'm furious.
22. I run to Eggs's mother and I say, "Did he suffer much?"
23. And she says, "No, it was quick. Car hit him and that was it."

Premise: Woody gets a pain in his "chestal" area and cons a friend with the same pain to go to the doctor so he won't have to spend the money himself. "Eggs Benedict" is the kind of joke you'd tell your friends, but you'd start it off, "This guy had a pain in his chest, right?" Instead, Woody's comedic genius gives us, "I had once a pain in the chestal area." He thereby immediately snares us by personalizing the story, and then adding a fillip of humor by the construct of the nonexistent adjective "chestal." "Eggs Benedict" is quick: a minute and a half and it's over. But it has no less than seven payoffs in a routine of only twenty-three lines. (Interestingly, Woody also uses "Eggs Benedict" as an opportunity to get in another blast at his ex-wife by accusing her of giving him the pain in his chest with her "Nazi recipes.") Another important point to remember is that "Eggs Benedict," unlike some of Woody's more surrealistic verbal cartoons, could actually happen. This adds a level of immediacy and believability that contributes to the humor.

"The Big, Big Laughs": If you read through the transcript (which I have numbered by line to show you how Woody puts together a routine), you'll see that the laughs come at lines 1, 2, 3, 6, 15 (big laugh), 16, and 23 (big laugh).

Ch-Ch-Ch-Changes: Originally, "Eggs Benedict" was twenty-six lines. On *Woody Allen Volume 2,* it began, "I had once a pain in my chest over here.

You didn't know it was a musical act. I did. I had a pain in the chestal area."
For the compilation album, this was edited out (except for the first five
words of line 1) since it is obvious that Woody made a physical gesture,
and that its accompanying words ("musical act") were not appropriate for
an album.

R2f. "Footnote [:27]

Premise: Side 1 of *Woody Allen Volume 2* ends with a brilliant twenty-seven-
second, three-sentence bit:

> I must pause for one fast second and say a fast word about oral contracep-
> tion. I was involved in an extremely good example of oral contraception
> two weeks ago. I asked a girl to go to bed with me and she said no.

There was a brief pause while the joke sank in, and then riotous laughter
and applause.
"The Big, Big Laughs": The laugh comes when the proper interpretation of
"oral contraception" hits the audience.
Ch-Ch-Ch-Changes: "Footnote" appeared on both compilation albums retitled as "Oral Contraception."

SIDE 2

R2g. "What's New, Pussycat?" [7:12]

Premise: Woody bares his romantic experiences filming *What's New, Pussycat?* in Europe. Woody starts off the routine by talking about his early
childhood acting experiences ("I played the part of Stanley Kowalski in . . .
Streetcar Named Desire and I was one of the great five-year-old Stanleys")
and then informs the audience that *Pussycat* is "an autobiographical
movie: It's based on the experiences of a great ladies' man." This sets the
audience up for his discussion of a girl he met at his European analyst's.
The piece ends with Woody being "aced out" by Peter O'Toole's advances
toward a girl Woody was after. The ever-optimistic Woodman, however,
asks the girl, "Could you bring a sister for me? And she did. Sister Maria
Teresa."
"The Big, Big Laughs": There are some quick, very funny gags in "What's
New, Pussycat?" We learn of a discotheque he worked at called B'Nai a Go-
Go. It was a synagogue that was not doing well so it was converted into a
disco. A funny "honeymoon" one-liner has been often quoted: "On my
honeymoon night, my wife stopped in the middle of everything to give me
a standing ovation." One great joke was surprisingly cut from the compilation albums: about an Italian girl who "ran away to Venice and became a
streetwalker and drowned." Probably the funniest part of the routine,
though, is Woody's account of preparing his hotel room for a rendezvous

with a girl he met at his analyst's. The radiator in the room breaks, it's freezing, and Woody resorts to "an old Brooklyn trick to heat the apartment." He turns on the hot water in the shower, and leaves the bathroom door open. "And hot water comes down, and billows of steam come into the living room. And ice cold air is seeping in under the window sill, and the two fronts meet in the living room, and it starts to rain in my hotel room."

Ch-Ch-Ch-Changes: The seven minutes and twelve seconds of "What's New, Pussycat?" became the five minutes and forty-three seconds of "European Trip" on the compilation albums. The B'Nai a Go-Go introduction was eliminated, as was an entire segment of Woody's ex-wife bashing. (See the feature on Louise Lasser, Diane Keaton, and Mia Farrow in Chapter 11 for a discussion of Woody's public blasts against his first wife, Harlene Rosen.) Other than these cuts, and a few minor word eliminations for pace, the rest of the routine was included on the compilation albums as originally performed.

R2h. "Reminiscences" [3:20]

Premise: Once again, Woody tells the audience about his divorce. The premise of this piece, however, is that his wife divorced him because she thought he was weird. And, "She disapproved of my friends." He then informs the audience of three particularly weird friends. First, there was Nathan, who raised sheep. "Used to feed them silkworms and try and get jackets with linings." He was also friends with a Japanese boy who "had flown nine successful kamikaze missions for the Japs in World War II." And finally, there was the boy in his analysis group who was "a southern bigot and a bedwetter. . . . He used to go to his Klan meetings in rubber sheets." He next discloses that he got caught cheating on his algebra test. He took the answers off Alvin Beckman's paper by using a mirror in his palm. "I got them all backwards. He got a 94; I got a 49." One segment that is indicative of Woody's interest in language and words concerns his attempts to learn Spanish from record albums. He played the records at the wrong speed for a year and a half. He then says, "Spoke a fairly torpid Castilian," and it gets a big laugh. That's quite an accomplishment when you consider that the punch line came in a five-word sentence, of which two words ("torpid" and "Castilian"), it might be assumed, would be unfamiliar to many people. After this series of gags about his friends and himself, Woody returns to his ex-wife for a couple of jokes. First, he says he bought her a "novelty gift": an electric chair. "Told her it was a hairdryer." He then reveals that his wife divorced him because she caught him with his head inside the Rotissemat, trying to hear the police calls that were coming in on the appliance from the electrical trouble caused by her use of the electric chair. "Charged me with conversing with a revolving chicken."

According to Woody, his wife got "the house, car, bank account, Rotisse-mat." He ends the piece with a funny one-liner: "In the event that I re-marry and have children, she gets them."

"The Big, Big Laughs": The big laughs in this piece came during Woody's description of his three friends (particularly the bigot joke), the "torpid Castilian" line, Woody's pronunciation of the three rows of keys on a type-writer keyboard ("The first line is Qwertyuiop"), and at the final line about the children.

Ch-Ch-Ch-Changes: "Reminiscences" was not included on either compila-tion album.

R2i. "Swedish Movie" [2:21]

Premise: While waiting to see a film by Ingmar Bergman, Woody views a short subject about the Faroe Islands, a group of islands which are in the Norwegian Sea west of Norway, but which Woody says are off the coast of Denmark and Sweden as a setup for this routine. "Swedish Movie" begins with Woody describing a visit to an art movie theater where "they serve pre-Columbian coffee," and where the "ushers are all there on Fulbrights." He recalls that as a kid he watched the bouncing ball and sang along at the movies, but at this art theater the audience consists of "a group of hardcore fanatic intellectuals" who watch the bouncing ball, but sing Gregorian chants. Woody tells us that Denmark and Sweden are sexually progressive: "They have mixed nude bathing, and they teach sex education in school. It's like a wild, swinging country. Everybody scores. You don't have to be tall." And then he gets in a dig about America's sexually repressed attitudes: "I always get the impression American cops are gonna knock on the country and say, 'All right Sweden, we know what you're doing in there.'" Up to this point the routine has been a fairly straightforward com-mentary on intellectualism and sexual repression. But then Woody takes off in what turns out to be one of his quintessential commentaries on the food/sex paradigm. According to Woody, the big bugaboo/taboo on the Faroe Islands is food. "Food is a dirty subject. Little strange guys are always running up to you and saying, 'Hey, buddy. How'd you like to get a rye bread? Or else I can get you a picture of a grilled cheese sandwich." Certain women, he says, won't put cream cheese on a bagel, and when you ask them about it, they say, "Well, I don't do that." One guy checked into a hotel for a convention "and the elevator operator fixed him up with a mixed green salad. He ate the salad in the middle of the night, and he put on his pants and went home. He said it was a very empty experience." "Swedish Movie" is an early exploration of a subject Woody would tackle visually in *Everything You Always Wanted to Know About Sex,* and thema-tically in *Love and Death* and elsewhere. Woody has said that he's always considered food a funny subject. In "Swedish Movie" he shows just how funny it can be.

"The Big, Big Laughs": The big laughs in this routine came at the "Gregorian chant" line, and throughout the food jokes.

Ch-Ch-Ch-Changes: "Swedish Movie" was not included on either compilation album.

R2j. "Taking a Shower" [:54]

Premise: I assume this is a routine about taking a shower, although I haven't a clue. I say not a clue because there was nothing on my copy of *Woody Allen Volume 2* for this cut except what sounded like backward audience sounds. I do not know if my copy was defective, or if all copies of this album had a bad cut. If you have a copy of the album that has audible material for this cut, I'd appreciate a cassette of it sent to me in care of Andrews and McMeel. I will then be able to include details on the routine for the second edition of this volume. Thanks.

"The Big, Big Laughs": There were a few explosions of what sounded like big laughter, but I can't be sure.

Ch-Ch-Ch-Changes: There is no cut on either compilation album called "Taking a Shower," although Woody does talk about taking a shower in the routine "Mechanical Objects" on *The Third Woody Allen Album.*

R2k. "The Lost Generation" [1:58]

Premise: Woody's early years in Europe with Ernest Hemingway, Gertrude Stein, Pablo Picasso, and Scott and Zelda Fitzgerald. This piece was later transformed into the essay "A Twenties Memory" (which originally appeared in *Panorama* magazine, and was later reprinted in both the *Saturday Evening Post* and *Getting Even*). This is a rare instance of Woody using material from one form (a standup routine) and expanding it into another (an essay). (Another instance of this type of transmutation of material is Woody's use of his image of a "hostility monster" in *Stardust Memories,* and in a short story, which is still unpublished. See Chapter 1, "The Woody Allen Time Line," December 16, 1985, for details on Woody's public reading of this unpublished short story.)

"The Big, Big Laughs": The laughs in this routine come from Woody's mantralike repetition of the phrase "And Hemingway punched me in the mouth." See "A Twenties Memory" in *Getting Even* (Chapter 6) for what amounts to a text version of this routine.

Ch-Ch-Ch-Changes: The closing line from this routine was eliminated for both compilation albums: "And then the war came, and Hemingway went to Africa to do a book, and Gertrude Stein moved in with Alice Toklas, and I went to New York to see my orthodontist." The piece was strengthened by excising this somewhat weak ending.

R3.
The Third Woody Allen Album
(Capitol, n.d.; [Actually 1968]; Recorded Live at Eugene's; San Francisco, August 1968) [Approx. 34:59]

[No Title Listings]

INTRODUCTION: "Eugene's is moderately proud to present actor, author, comedian, and spoiler of women, Mr. Woody Allen."

SIDE 1: [17:35]
R3a. "The Vodka Ad" [5:26]
R3b. "Las Vegas" [1:53]
R3c. "Second Marriage" [10:16]

SIDE 2: [17:24]
R3d. "The Great Renaldo" [2:07]
R3e. "Mechanical Objects" [6:04]
R3f. "Down South" [3:24]
R3g. [Question & Answer Session] [5:43]
R3h. ["Encore"] [:06]

SIDE 1

R3a. "The Vodka Ad" [5:26]

Premise: Woody refuses to do a vodka ad on moral grounds (and the advice of his rabbi), and the ad (which paid fifty thousand dollars) goes to the rabbi instead. This is a blatantly autobiographical routine except for one catch: Woody *did* do a vodka ad in the early sixties. He appeared as a celebrity endorser of Smirnoff vodka, Foster Grant sunglasses, and Van Heusen shirts, but for the purposes of this routine, he ostensibly passed it up. What's ironic is that the routine begins with an admission by Woody that he did do the ad ("Let me start at the very beginning. I did a vodka ad"), but later in the routine he says he passed the ad up. This gaffe was due to the construction of the piece. He couldn't tell the joke if he admitted accepting the ad. But somehow the first few lines in which he says he did the ad were not edited out. He tells the audience that he was not the company's first choice. It originally wanted Noël Coward, but "he had acquired the rights to *My Fair Lady* and he was removing the music and lyrics." The company finally got Woody's name from "a list in Eichmann's pocket." After a gag about Kate Smith doing *Peter Pan* ("They're having trouble flying her. The chains keep breaking all the time"), Woody informs the audience about the phone call from the vodka company. When asked to do the ad, Woody replied, "I'm an artist. I don't do commercials. I don't pander. I don't drink vodka, and if I did, I wouldn't drink your product." And the guy on the other end said, "Too bad. It pays fifty thousand dollars." And Woody said, "Hold on. I'll put Mr. Allen on the phone." After explaining that he has been in analysis for years because of a traumatic childhood, Woody says, "I was breast-fed through falsies," a line he later used in the "Are the Findings of Doctors and Clinics Who Do Sexual Research and Experiments Accurate?" segment of *Everything You Always Wanted to Know About Sex.* The piece concludes with Woody spotting a vodka ad featuring Monique Van Vooren and his rabbi on a beach in Jamaica.

"The Big, Big Laughs": This hilarious piece has been always well received by audiences. The laughs come at the *Pygmalion* joke, the Eichmann joke, the Kate Smith joke, after the phone call bit, and at the "falsies" line. Woody also got a big laugh from this line: "I was in a strict Freudian analysis for a long time. My analyst died two years ago and I never knew it." Another *very* topical line that got a huge response was Woody's remark about how he needed the money for the ad because he was writing: "I was working on a nonfiction version of The Warren Report."

Ch-Ch-Ch-Changes: "The Vodka Ad" ran five minutes and twenty-six seconds on *The Third Woody Allen Album.* It was edited down to four minutes and fifty-four seconds for the compilation albums by eliminating some expendable introductory remarks that totaled ten lines, as well as a single unnecessary line ("I was really adorable") from the end of the piece.

R3b. "Las Vegas" [1:53]

Premise: Woody picks up a girl at the crap table in Las Vegas and brings her back to his room where they both undress. After Woody has winked at the girl and taken off his pants, he realizes he's looking into a mirror.

"The Big, Big Laughs": There are two big laughs in this piece. The first comes from an unrelated (to the story) line about a racehorse Woody bet on named Battlegun: "And all the horses come out, and mine is the only horse in the race with training wheels." The final laugh comes from the punch line when Woody reveals that all his romantic moves were for naught, that he's been looking into a mirror the whole time.

Ch-Ch-Ch-Changes: "Las Vegas" became simply "Vegas" for the compilation albums, and nineteen seconds of the routine were trimmed by eliminating Woody's final lines (after the "looking into a mirror" punch line): "I don't want to go into details, but I was pulling glass out of my legs for two weeks. I was the best I ever had, I must say." By cutting those final lines, the piece ends up stronger.

R3c. "Second Marriage" [10:16]

Premise: Woody tells the audience how he met his second wife, Louise Lasser, and about the first time they made love. This long piece contains much witty material, including the remark Woody made about his first wife, Harlene, that got him sued. Woody starts by mentioning that he has married for a second time. Then he hurls a few barbs at Harlene (see Chapter 4 for details on Woody's public verbal blitz on Rosen) which culminates with the lawsuit remark: "She was violated. . . . And they asked me to comment on it. And I said, knowing my ex-wife, it probably was not a moving violation." He then talks about meeting his second wife on a blind date at New York University, going to a party, and then returning to her apartment to make love. Woody then does his famous "I think of baseball players" bit, and the piece ends with their wedding.

"The Big, Big Laughs": There are many very funny jokes in "Second Marriage," some of which have to do with Harlene, some of which are drug jokes, and some of which have nothing to do with the premise at all. One hilarious bit is Woody's account of the time he went to work at his father's grocery store as a delivery boy. He unionized the workers, struck, and drove his father out of business. Then there is the oft-quoted gag about sex: "I believe that sex is a beautiful thing between two people. [Beat] Between five, it's fantastic." Another very funny gag is Woody's reminiscence of the time he smoked a joint: "I took a puff of the wrong cigarette at a fraternity dance once. The cops had to get me. I broke two teeth trying to give a hickey to the Statue of Liberty."

Ch-Ch-Ch-Changes: The ten-minute, sixteen-second "Second Marriage" was pared to seven minutes and forty-eight seconds for the compilation albums by the elimination of the following material: a couple of lines about Woody tipping the process server who brought him his lawsuit summons; a segment about one of his dates being arrested by Israeli agents at the Stork Club; a line about Woody's parents wanting to bronze his baby shoes with his feet still in them; a bit about the party host who had six sex change operations but couldn't come up with anything he liked; and a bit about Woody's confrontation with a cop on the George Washington Bridge.

SIDE 2

R3d. "The Great Renaldo" [2:07]

Premise: Woody (and several other guys) gets hypnotized by a hypnotist on "The Ed Sullivan Show" and believes he is a red fire engine. Woody falls asleep during the Great Renaldo's act, and when he wakes up, he's seized "with an uncontrollable impulse to dress up in [his] red flannel underwear." When the phone rings, he bursts out his apartment door, and dashes down Fifth Avenue making a siren noise. This fairly straightforward comic routine is bizarre, surrealistic, and classically Woody. Interestingly, Woody insists on a wholehearted, all-out suspension of disbelief by the audience by adding the following lines after the "fire engine" piece: "I should just add parenthetically these stories are true. These things actually happen to me. I don't make them up. My life is a series of these crises." The piece ends with another appropriately fantastic story. Woody came home one night and found that a moth had eaten his yellow-and-green-striped jacket and was lying on the floor, nauseated. Woody gave him two plain brown socks: "I said, 'Eat one now, and eat one in a half hour.'"

"The Big, Big Laughs": The laughs in this routine come when Woody describes his meeting another hypnotized fire engine and their decision "to work as one truck." He draws a big laugh at the line about the cops trying to haul him and his fellow "trucks" off to police headquarters: "And I start giggling hysterically, 'cause this jerk's trying to get a fire engine into a lousy little Chevy." The moth routine got a big laugh as well.

Ch-Ch-Ch-Changes: "The Great Renaldo" was included complete on both compilation albums. One "Listen to this" line was eliminated from the beginning of the routine.

R3e. "Mechanical Objects" [6:04]

Premise: Woody details his difficulties with mechanical objects. He ends up in Hollywood to talk to a producer about making "an elaborate, Cinemascope musical comedy out of the Dewey Decimal System." He gets in an elevator which operates by voice control, and on his way up, he begins to feel self-conscious: "I talk, I think, with a slight New York accent. And the elevator spoke quite well." He continues, "This is the strange part of the story. That was the normal part." He then talks about gathering all his possessions into the living room and telling them to "cut it out." His clock ran counterclockwise, his tape recorder answered him back, his sun lamp rained on him. After he puts everything back, his TV threw a tantrum and started jumping up and down. So he beat it. Two days later he goes to see his dentist in New York. His dentist is in a building that has the talking elevators, and when he gets in, the elevator says, "Are you the guy that hit the television set?" and throws him off in the basement. The elevator also makes an anti-Semitic remark. The piece ends with Woody telling the audience that his father was replaced at his job by a tiny gadget that did everything his father did but much better. "The depressing thing is my mother ran out and bought one."

"The Big, Big Laughs": The laughs in this piece come at the "Dewey Decimal" line, and throughout Woody's recounting of his altercations with his "mechanical objects." A line that got a big laugh, but that was cut from the compilation album version, was "I'm watching Dr. Joyce Brothers, and she's explaining to a Bronx housewife how it's possible for her daughter to have gotten pregnant from joining the Peace Corps." The joke about his father also got a big laugh.

Ch-Ch-Ch-Changes: "Mechanical Objects" was cut from six minutes and four seconds to five minutes and thirty-eight seconds for the compilation albums by eliminating the "Peace Corps" joke, by cutting a few irrelevant one-liners, and by excising a few lines at the conclusion of the piece in which Woody asks his listeners if they have any questions before he moves to "Down South."

R3f. "Down South" [3:24]

Premise: "Down South," the last original Woody Allen piece released, is another Woody classic. The premise is simple: Woody Allen, the quintessential New York Jew, ends up "down South" in a car filled with Ku Klux Klansmen. Woody is invited to a costume party and decides to throw a sheet over his head and go as a ghost. The aforementioned car of Klansmen picks him up as he walks to the party. The KKK guys think he's on his way to a Klan rally. He tries to pass by saying "grits" and "you all" but they realize who he is and decide to lynch him. "And suddenly my whole life passed before my eyes. I saw myself as a kid again in Kansas going to school, and swimmin' at the swimmin' hole, and fishin' and fryin' up a mess o' catfish, goin' down to the general store, gettin' a piece of gingham for Emmy Lou." [Beat] "And I realized it's not my life. They're gonna hang me in two minutes, the wrong life is passing before my eyes." Woody wiggles out of it by giving the Klansmen a speech about brotherhood: "And they were so moved by my words that not only did they cut me down and let me go, but that night I sold them two thousand dollars' worth of Israel bonds."

"The Big, Big Laughs": The laughs in this piece come primarily at the "grits" line and the "not my life" sequence. The "Israel bonds" line at the end also got a huge laugh. A line that also drew a big laugh was the one in which Woody explained how he knew he was in the presence of the leader of the Klan: "He [was] the one wearing contour sheets."

Ch-Ch-Ch-Changes: "Down South" was included complete and uncut on both compilation albums.

R3g. [Question & Answer Session] [5:43]

Premise: Woody takes audience questions. This was a good idea, but it doesn't work on the album because the audience wasn't miked and Woody didn't repeat their questions.

"The Big, Big Laughs": Woody gets in a few excellent and quick one-line responses to some of the questions. A *woman* asks Woody if he's ever been picked up—or excited—by a homosexual, and Woody replies, "No, sir." A man asks if anything new has happened with his family corporation and Woody replies, "Nothing new has happened. My family remains the same: The only sharecroppers in Brooklyn. I have to go easy on my family because my mother is also suing me." A man asks Woody if he's an only

child, and he responds, "I am, yes. I have a sister." And then, in a remarkable exchange, a man in the audience asks Woody, "What are your chances of survival?" Woody bounces a joke off the question by saying, "That you ask a man who has had carnal knowledge of a vegetable?" But then he reveals some of his existential angst and replies (somewhat) seriously: "Actually, very little, when I analyze it. Not so good. I'm thirty-two, I'll be thirty-three, December first, so what are my chances of survival? I'm coming to a turning point in my life." Then Woody decides to go for the laugh: "I've passed my sexual peak. Twenty-two years ago, I think. On my honeymoon night, I was making love to my wife, and I dropped my notes." A woman then asks him what his birth sign is, and Woody replies, "I'm a Sagittarius, which is part man, part horse. Meet me later, I'll explain that in detail." A man then asks Woody when they would see another of his plays on Broadway and he replies, "I'm working on a play now. A pro-Catholic, pornographic musical." A man asks Woody if Richard Nixon is an unfrocked priest and Woody doesn't do anything with the question. He simply says, "A religious question in this section of the room." The final audience question was, "Would you accept the vice presidential nomination?" and Woody replies, "I'm apolitical. I have no political convictions whatsoever. I'm a registered pervert."

Woody then informs the audience of a strange dream he had in which he was being chased by a giant "NO," two big black hairy letters, "N" and "O." As he flees from the word, he keeps putting commas in front of it so it has to pause. He escapes by hiding inside a parenthesis. He continues the "dream" motif by telling the audience that he has a strange dream life and that he had a bad dream last night: "I dreamt I was changed by a fairy godmother into a sixty-pound suppository." And then he says "Good night."

Ch-Ch-Ch-Changes: None of this question and answer session was included on the compilation albums.

R3h. ["Encore"] [:06]

Premise: Woody merely returns to say thank-you to the audience.
"The Big, Big Laughs": There are three lines, and one laugh in this "Encore": "Thank you very much. I really appreciate that. I accept that with a tremendous sense of megalomania."
Ch-Ch-Ch-Changes: This "bow" was not included on the compilation albums.

The Compilation Albums

The following listing details the cuts on the two identical compilation albums of Woody's standup material. For complete details on the actual routines and how they were edited for the compilation albums, see the preceding features on Woody's three albums of comedy material in this chapter.

R4.
Woody Allen: The Night-Club Years, 1964–1968
(1976; United Artists) [74:59]

and

R5.
Woody Allen Standup Comic, 1964–1968
(1978; Casablanca Records and Film Works)

SIDE 1: (Recorded Live at Eugene's; San Francisco, August 1968) [22:05]

R4/R5a. "The Vodka Ad" [4:54]
R4/R5b. "Vegas" [1:34]
R4/R5c. "Second Marriage" [7:48]
R4/R5d. "The Great Renaldo" [2:11]
R4/R5e. "Mechanical Objects" [5:38]

SIDE 2: (Recorded Live at the Shadows; Washington, D.C., April 1965) [20:10]

R4/R5f. "The Moose" [2:38]
R4/R5g. "Kidnapped" [2:54]
R4/R5h. "Unhappy Childhood" [2:43]
R4/R5i. "The Science Fiction Film" [1:48]
R4/R5j. "Eggs Benedict" [1:36]
R4/R5k. "Oral Contraception" [:27]
R4/R5l. "European Trip" [5:43]
R4/R5m. "The Lost Generation" [2:21]

SIDE 3: (Recorded Live at Mr. Kelly's; Chicago, March 1964) [16:23]

R4/R5n. "Private Life" [5:43]
R4/R5o. "Brooklyn" [3:47]
R4/R5p. "The Army" [1:20]
R4/R5q. "Pets" [1:06]

R4/R5r. "My Grandfather" [:53]
R4/R5s. "My Marriage" [2:47]
R4/R5t. "Bullet in My Breast Pocket" [:47]

SIDE 4: (Recorded Live at Mr. Kelly's; Chicago, March 1964) [16:21]

R4/R5u. "N.Y.U." [2:27]
R4/R5v. "A Love Story" [3:32]
R4/R5w. "The Police" [5:08]
R4/R5x. "Down South" [3:49]
R4/R5y. "Summing Up" [1:25]

CHAPTER 8

Woody Allen, Playwright
The Plays

I think *Play It Again, Sam* made a better movie instead of a play. I have a
tendency to not really have mastered playwriting too much. I have a
tendency to create a lot of problems for the director, and my stuff,
I think, is more suited to more movement, and a bigger
production and more mobility.
Woody Allen

WOODY began his stage career in 1966 with *Don't Drink the Water,* and the
last time he wrote something specifically for the stage was in 1981, *The Floating Light Bulb.*

Even though Woody has written eight plays, only three have been
professionally produced so far, *Don't Drink the Water* (1966); *Play It Again,
Sam* (1969); and *The Floating Light Bulb* (1981). There is also an "unknown"
play of Woody.

Woody's plays run the gamut from frivolous comedy (*Water* and *The
Query*)to absurdist farce (*Death* and *God*).

The following is a list of Woody Allen's work as a playwright/dramatist:

P1. *Don't Drink the Water* (1966)
P2. *Death Knocks* (1968)
P3. *Play It Again, Sam* (1969)
P4. *Death* (1975)
P5. *God* (1975)
P6. *Sex* (unwritten/unpublished?)
P7. *The Query* (1976)
P8. *My Apology* (1980)
P9. *The Floating Light Bulb* (1981)

We will now take a brief look at each of these works.

P1.
Don't Drink the Water
(1966)

There's always got to be something beyond the laughs or people will get
bored. That was the trouble to some extent in *Don't Drink the Water*.
It was one laugh on top of the next. Every line was a joke.
The problem was, every time a laugh didn't work,
the thing went down the toilet.
Woody Allen,in *Los Angeles Times* interview, 1969

Don't Drink the Water was Woody Allen's first produced play. He completed writing the play in spring 1966 at the age of thirty-one, and it
opened on Broadway at the Morosco Theater on Thursday, November 17,
1966. (Woody obviously holds the Morosco dear. Twenty-two years later
he had a character in *Radio Days* mention the theater by name. See the
Radio Days and "Seen Scenes" features in Chapters 5 and 12, respectively.)

The play opened with the following cast:

(In order of appearance)
Dick Libertini (Father Drobney); House Jameson (Ambassador Magee);
Gerry Mathews (Kilroy); Anthony Roberts (Axel Magee); Kay Medford
(Marion Hollander); Lou Jacobi (Walter Hollander); Anita Gillette (Susan
Hollander); James Kukas (Krojack); Curtis Wheeler (Burns); Gene Varrone
(Chef); Oliver Clark (Sultan of Bashir); Donna Mills (Sultan's First Wife);
John Hallow (Kasnar); Sharon Talbot (Countess Bordoni); Luke Andreas
(Novotny); Jonathan Bolt (Walter)

(Vivian Vance had originally been cast as Marion Hollander, but she
was replaced by Kay Medford before the play opened.)

The play ran for 598 performances.

Production Credits

Director: Stanley Prager; Producer: David Merrick, in association with Jack
Rollins and Charles Joffe.

The 1980 Samuel French *Basic Catalogue of Plays* described the play as
follows:

(All Groups.) Farce. 12 males, 4 females. Produced on Broadway by David
Merrick. A cascade of comedy from one of our funniest comedians, and a
solid year's hit on Broadway, this affair takes place inside an American
embassy behind the Iron Curtain. An American tourist, caterer by trade,
and his family of wife and daughter rush into the embassy two steps

ahead of the police who suspect them of spying and picture-taking. But it's not much of a refuge, for the ambassador is absent and his son, now in charge, has been expelled from a dozen countries and the whole continent of Africa. Nevertheless, they carefully and frantically plot their escape, and the ambassador's son and the caterer's daughter even have time to fall in love.

The October 6, 1966, issue of *Variety* said of the play's Philadelphia tryout:

> The author reveals both an ear and imagination attuned to the times. . . . But while the laugh lines are fresh and frequently inventive, story and staging format suggest pre-World War II farce.

Don't Drink the Water was reviewed in the February 1967 *Playboy*:

> Woody Allen, *Playboy* contributor, pint-sized Perelman and puny Pepys, has put quill to parchment and penned his first play, *Don't Drink the Water*, about a pushy caterer from Newark who gets entangled in the Iron Curtain. *Don't Drink the Water* is a grab bag of gags, many great, a few terrible, all of them dyed-in-the-wool Woody, and the sharp-witted cast happily downplays them all. The play is farce-fetched and unshapely but, like its author, it is compulsively funny.

The *New York Times* said:

> Because Mr. Allen is a working comedian himself, a number of the lines are perfectly agreeable and there's quite a bit of delectable business laid out by the author and maniacally elaborated by the actor . . . the gag is pleasantly outrageous and impeccably performed.

The *New York Daily News* observed:

> Moved the audience to great laughter . . . Allen's imagination is daffy, his sense of the ridiculous is keen and gags snap, crackle and pop.

The *New York Post* noted:

> [Woody Allen is] a master of bright and hilarious dialogue and has provided so much material for laughter in his farcical comedy that it is upsetting to find that the final result falls disturbingly short of satisfaction. . . . The fun grows too mechanical for its own good.

In 1969 *Don't Drink the Water* was made into a film directed by Howard Morris, with a screenplay by R. S. Allen and Harvey Bullock, based on Woody's play.

P2.
Death Knocks
(1968)

Death Knocks is a short play by Woody that first appeared in the July 27, 1968, issue of *New Yorker* magazine. The play was later collected in *Getting Even*. *Death Knocks* is a parody of Ingmar Bergman's film *The Seventh Seal*. (See the section on *Getting Even* in Chapter 6.)

P3.
Play It Again, Sam
(1969)

I was scared because—first of all, I had never acted in my life. I was strictly
a nightclub comic. And then, when we called [Diane Keaton] back we
were worried that she'd be too tall, you know, and we didn't want
the joke of the play to be that I was in love with a, you know,
super-looking woman. And we got on stage together, and
both of us were nervous. I felt, "Oh, this is a real
actress, she was in *Hair*, and I'm just going
to waste her time" . . . and we measured
back to back, and it was like
being in the third grade.
Woody Allen, in *Rolling Stone*, June 30, 1977

Play It Again, Sam was first presented on February 12, 1969, by David Merrick in association with Jack Rollins and Charles Joffe at the Broadhurst Theater in New York City, and it ran until March 14, 1970, for a total of 453 performances.

The cast consisted of the following:

(In order of appearance)

Woody Allen (Allan Felix); Sheila Sullivan (Nancy); Jerry Lacy (Bogart); Anthony Roberts (Dick Christie); Diane Keaton (Linda Christie); Barbara Brownell (Dream Sharon); Diana Walker (Sharon Lake); Jean Fowler (Gina); Cynthia Dalbey (Vanessa); Lee Anne Fahey (Go-Go-Girl); Barbara Press (Intellectual Girl); Barbara Brownell (Barbara)

Production Credits

Director: Joseph Hardy; Setting: William Ritman; Lighting: Martin Aronstein; Costumes: Ann Roth; Associate Producer: Samuel Liff.

The published edition of the play gave the following synopsis of scenes:

> The entire action of the play takes place in the apartment of Allan Felix on West 10th Street in New York.
>
> ACT ONE, SCENE ONE: A late summer afternoon. SCENE TWO: Later that night.
>
> ACT TWO: Two weeks later.
>
> ACT THREE: The following morning.

(See the section in Chapter 5 on the film version of *Play It Again, Sam,* for details on the story and the differences between stage and screen.)

P4.
Death
(1975)

Death is a short play by Woody that first appeared in *Without Feathers.* In the play, the character Kleinman is roused from his sleep to join a group of vigilantes on the prowl for a maniacal killer. Kleinman is never told what the plan is, and ends up murdered by a killer who looked like him. The other victims had all said that the killer looked like themselves, and the play ends with the survivors running off to catch the elusive murderer (who is actually death incarnate).

Woody reworked *Death* into his 1992 film, *Shadows and Fog.*

The 1980 Samuel French *Basic Catalogue of Plays* described the play as follows:

> Comedy. 18 males, 2 females (many double). Bare stage, simple props. A maniacal killer is at large and Kleinman, "the protagonist," is caught up between conflicting factions and plans on how to catch the killer. Kleinman is a logical man in a mad world. But he is also indecisive and insecure. He doesn't want to get involved and everyone is after him to make a choice. He is even accused of being the killer himself. Finally, the real killer confronts Kleinman who finds the maniac looks no different from anyone else. He stabs Kleinman who dies and everyone rushes off to pursue the still elusive killer.

P5.
God
(1975)

God is a short play that first appeared in *Without Feathers*. *God* is an existential work about ancient Greeks named Diabetes, Hepatitis, and Trichinosis, Blanche DuBois, the Civil War, the Academy Awards, *A Streetcar Named Desire,* Groucho Marx, orgasms, and Woody Allen as a character in his own play.

The 1980 Samuel French *Basic Catalogue of Plays* described the play thus:

> Comedy. 20 males, 8 females (much doubling). Chorus. Set suggests empty Greek amphitheater. A mad play within a play that switches back and forth between Athens, 500 B.C., and today in a Broadway theater. An ancient Greek actor and writer are discussing how to end a play. People in the play pop up from the audience including one Doris Levine from Great Neck, Blanche DuBois, Groucho Marx among others. Peppered with metaphysical and philosophical questions, the play skids along farcically and actor and writer conclude that the play not only doesn't have an ending but also no beginning.

P6.
Sex
(unpublished and/or unwritten?)

Eric Lax, in his first book about Woody, *On Being Funny,* wrote that *Sex, Death,* and *God* were to be the three components of a stage trilogy by Woody Allen. There has been no confirmation that *Sex* was, in fact, ever written, although *Death* and *God* obviously were. The play is worth a mention, though, because it makes sense that Woody would consider writing a stage trilogy composed of *Death, God,* and *Sex,* three subjects for which he has more than a passing concern.

P7.
The Query
(1976)

The Query is a short play by Woody that first appeared in the September 18, 1976, issue of *New Republic.* The play recounts the story of a farmer who wanted Abraham Lincoln to commute his son's death sentence, but instead of asking for a pardon, became tongue-tied and asked Lincoln, "How long do you think a man's legs should be?" The non sequitur causes Abe to reevaluate his life, and the son is pardoned. *The Query* was collected in *Side Effects.* (See Chapter 6, the section on *Side Effects.*)

P8.
My Apology
(1980)

My Apology is a short play by Woody that first appeared in *Side Effects.* In the play, Woody has a dream in which he is a Greek philosopher sentenced to death who is reprieved at the last minute. The dream is told in stageplay form. (See the section *on Side Effects* in Chapter 6.)

P9.
The Floating Light Bulb
(1981)

Woody Allen's dramatic play *The Floating Light Bulb* was first presented on Monday, April 27, 1981, at the Vivian Beaumont Theater in New York City by the Lincoln Center Theater Company.

The cast consisted of:

(In order of appearance)
Brian Backer (Paul Pollack); Eric Gurry (Steve Pollack); Beatrice Arthur (Enid Pollack); Danny Aiello (Max Pollack); Ellen March (Betty); Jack Weston (Jerry Wexler)

Production Credits

Director: Ulu Grosbard; Producer: Richard Crinkley; Settings and Costumes: Santo Loquasto; Lighting: Pat Collins; Sound: Richard Fitzgerald; Production Stage Manager: Franklin Keysar; Stage Manager: Wendy Chapin; Standby: Beatrice Arthur–Tresa Hughes.

The published edition of the play gave the following synopsis of scenes:

THE SCENE
The entire action of the play takes place in and around a dingy apartment in the Canarsie section of Brooklyn, 1945.

ACT ONE
Scene One: Four-thirty in the afternoon.
Scene Two: Later that day.
Scene Three: Around seven-thirty, the following morning.
Scene Four: Late afternoon, the same day.
Scene Five: Three in the morning, the next day.
Scene Six: Midmorning, the same day.

ACT TWO
Scene One: Early evening, a few days later.
Scene Two: That same evening.

The Floating Light Bulb was one of the "Best Plays" of the 1981–82 Broadway season and was included in Otis Guernsey's *Best Plays* series.

The story of a disintegrating family, it is a sad and touching meditation on failed hopes and lost dreams.

Enid is married to Max, and they have two sons, Paul and Steve.

Steve is on the verge of going bad. He has already been caught setting fires, and he is too interested in gambling, cheating, and his father's gun.

Paul is a stuttering, solitary loner with a genius IQ who spends days in his room practicing magic tricks that he's too nervous to perform for anyone.

Enid wanted to be a Broadway dancer, but now she spends all her time working behind a hosiery counter, planning worthless mail-order schemes, and asking her sister for money.

Her husband, Max, is a small-time hood who cheats on his wife, lies to his lover, tries to stiff his loansharks, and doesn't even attempt to support his family.

The Pollacks live in "an apartment reeking of hopelessness and neglect" that "looks out on the bleak brick courtyard in the back and rear of the surrounding buildings, giving one the feeling of being at the bottom of a well."

Into these lost and desperate lives comes a ray of hope. A neighbor's brother, a theatrical manager, one Jerry Wexler, is in town and agrees to see

Paul's "routine." The only problem is, Paul doesn't have a routine. This doesn't deter Enid, however, from literally forcing Paul to audition for Mr. Wexler. This, after all, could be their ticket out of Canarsie.

Paul finally surrenders to his mother's will and attempts to put on a show for Wexler. He fails miserably and flees in an emotional state near nervous breakdown.

Enid attempts to make a bad situation better by apologizing for Paul and being very friendly to Wexler. When she begins to fall for him, the rug is once again pulled out from under her: She finds out that he doesn't represent any big names, that there wasn't much chance of Paul hitting the big time even if he was any good, and that he is soon to move to Arizona to care for his mother.

Wexler leaves and Max—after receiving his "secret code" phone call that signals him to leave to meet his lover, Betty—pushes Enid too far. She explodes, telling him, "Get out of here! Get out! I'll kill you!"

The stage directions describe the action:

> *Unable to bear her frustration any longer, Enid flies off the handle and runs at him, beating him in rage with her towel. . . . Enid looks around for something to hit him with. She sees a cane on the magic table, picks it up and goes to hit Max with it.*

The cane, however, is Paul's magic cane, and as she whacks Max with it, it turns into a bouquet of flowers. But this is not funny. It is heart-breakingly sad, and as she chases him with the bouquet, Max leaves, telling her, "I'm getting out of here for good, Enid! Soon!"

That brings us to the play's last moments:

Enid   Get out! I'll kill you!

> *(There is a pause. In his room PAUL puts "In a Persian Market" on the phonograph and begins to practice the floating light bulb. ENID, spent, slowly walks to the sofa. She sits and looks at the flower bouquet for a time, reflecting on her life. she smiles and turns, calling to PAUL.)*

Enid   Paul, are you hungry? Let me fix you something to eat. You haven't had anything all day. *(No answer)* Paul! Paul?
Paul   *(Still with the light bulb)* I'm p-practicing . . . p-practicing.

> *The lights fade as he practices and she looks at the flowers*

The Floating Light Bulb, with its debts to Tennessee Williams's *The Glass Menagerie* and Edward Albee's *Who's Afraid of Virginia Woolf?* is Woody in his serious mode. Although not as intense or thematically rich as *Interiors* or *Another Woman*, the play is nonetheless a successful exploration of issues and dilemmas Woody has always found perplexing, interesting, and perhaps unsolvable, but still worthy of consideration and dramatic exposition.

The Floating Light Bulb was published in book form in 1982 by Random House. It is now out of print. The book should be available, though, in many libraries throughout the country, and I recommend tracking it down and reading it. It exists in no other form now.

CHAPTER 9

(Tele)Visions of Woody
The TV Work

There's no reason for me to be really nationally known because I do very little television. I've only appeared on a few shows in the last three years or the last four years. I've been on a half-dozen times, really, and generally it's been late at night.
Woody Allen

WOODY ALLEN did much television work in the fifties and sixties and though it is virtually impossible to track and document *every* appearance, this chapter attempts to note some of his more memorable appearances and writing credits.

The list below begins with what is generally considered to be Woody's first involvement with television: his job as a writer—at the age of nineteen, no less—on "The Colgate Comedy Hour," and concludes with one of his last appearances on television, that as a guest on his friend Dick Cavett's talk show.

T1. "The Colgate Variety Hour" (NBC; September 10, 1950–December 25, 1955) (*Writer, 1955*)

At age twenty Woody flew to California to work on "The Colgate Variety Hour" with Danny Simon. He roomed with Milt Rosen and worked on sketches for the show. "The Colgate Variety Hour" folded in May 1956 and Woody and his new wife Harlene returned to New York City. One line of Woody's that Milt Rosen remembered, and that is quoted in Eric Lax's *Woody Allen: A Biography,* was in a skit being written for Fred MacMurray. "A girl is on her first date, and her parents are waiting for her to return. They are worried. 'There's too much laxity in this house,' Rosen wrote as the father's line. . . . Woody added, 'From now on, there's going to be a lot more strictity.'" (P. 96)

T2. "Stanley" (NBC; September 24, 1956–March 11, 1957) (*Writer, 1956*)

This half-hour sitcom starred Buddy Hackett as the manager of a newsstand, and Carol Burnett as Celia, his girlfriend. Woody was hired by Max Liebman to write for the show, but Hackett did not appeal to the audience. Even with Danny Simon trying to save the show (as well as the terrific Carol Burnett in the cast), the show bombed.

T3. "Sid Caesar's Chevy Show" (NBC; November 2, 1958) (*Writer*)

For this show Woody and Larry Gelbart won a Sylvania Award and were nominated for an Emmy Award. (For complete details on the skits Woody and Gelbart wrote for this show [which starred Art Carney and Shirley MacLaine], see Eric Lax's *Woody Allen: A Biography,* pp. 111–14.)

T4. "The Pat Boone–Chevy Show" (ABC; October 3, 1957–June 23, 1960) (*Writer, 1958*)

Woody worked on this musical/variety show for a brief time in 1958.

T5. "The Gary Moore Show" (CBS; September 30, 1958–June 14, 1964) (*Writer, 1960*)

Woody worked on this variety show somewhat reluctantly (even though he was now making $1,700 a week). According to Eric Lax, Woody was "itching to get out of television" and was spending much of his time working on other projects, including a play.

T6. "P.M. East—P.M. West" (Syndicated; 1961–62) (*Guest, 1961*)

On this ninety-minute nightly talk show Woody guested a half-dozen times in 1961. The first hour of the show was broadcast from New York and was hosted by Mike Wallace and Joyce Davidson. The last half hour was from San Francisco and was hosted by Terrence O'Flaherty.

T7. "The Ed Sullivan Show" (CBS; June 20, 1948–June 6, 1971) (*Guest, the sixties*)

Woody appeared several times on the Sullivan show in the sixties. Lax tells the story of the time Woody did his "orgasmic insurance" joke (from "Private Life," off his first album) during a dress rehearsal and Sullivan exploded. He thought the term was too lewd for his show. (Woody hadn't even planned on using this routine on the air. He only did it so he wouldn't have to repeat a routine twice in one day.) Woody apologized and Sullivan was placated. Woody went on to appear on the show "all the time."

T8. "The Tonight Show" (NBC; Jack Paar; July 29, 1957–March 30, 1962) (*Guest, 1962*)

In 1962 Woody appeared as a guest on Paar's show and performed material that later appeared on his first album, *Woody Allen.*

T9. "The Laughmaker" (ABC; Undeveloped half-hour pilot; 1962) (*Writer*)

This was a half-hour pilot show written by Woody and starring Louise Lasser, Alan Alda, and Paul Hampton. ABC declined to put the show into production. (Woody would later work with Alan Alda in *Crimes and Misdemeanors.*)

T10. "Candid Camera" (CBS; October 12, 1960–September 3, 1967) (*Guest, 1963*)

Woody appeared several times on Allen Funt's show in 1963, each time in a skit in which he played pranks on unsuspecting people. Eric Lax gives details on several of Woody's "Candid Camera" stunts in *Woody Allen: A Biography.* (Not surprisingly, Woody does not hold these appearances dearly. Of his participation, he told Lax, "The degrading things I had to do when I started. But they're funny. Funny in the context of the show. I did the show for pure career advancement. Now I'm trying to do Dostoevski, trying to live down this shit.")

T11. "The Tonight Show" (NBC; Johnny Carson; October 1, 1962–May 20, 1992) (*Guest, 1963*)

Woody made several appearances on "The Tonight Show" early in his career.

T12. "The Steve Allen Show" (Syndicated; 1962–64) (*Guest, November 15, 1963*)

This appearance was Woody's first performance on one of Steve Allen's shows. Steve Allen kindly made a videotape of Woody's appearance available to me, and thus I was able to include details on his routine in this feature. Steve introduced Woody with the following remarks:

> **Steve Allen**   And we also have a young comedian who's a great favorite of the young people today, Woody Allen. . . . This man was born and schooled in New York. At seventeen, he was writing gags for newspaper columnists [like] Earl Wilson. Woody was soon writing TV jokes for Herb Shriner, Peter Lind Hayes, Sid Caesar, Art Carney, Gary Moore . . . and in

one two-year period, he wrote twenty-five thousand gags. So it is asserted. I doubt that. Twenty-five *thousand* gags? That's questionable. He's one of our most gifted gag writers, but I question that. About three years ago, he started doing his own stuff in nightclubs and people liked him right off the bat. You've seen him since then on a great many television shows, so I'm sure he's no newcomer to you. But I'm sure he will bring you new material—seven or eight of those twenty-five thousand gags—and they'll all be great. Let's make him feel at home. Woody Allen!

Woody then did a routine lasting exactly six minutes and twenty-one seconds (including bows). It consisted of a combination of parts of "Private Life," "My Marriage," and "My Grandfather," all from his first album, *Woody Allen.*

Woody Allen was twenty-eight years old when he made this appearance and watching him today—almost thirty years later—is a revelation. Seeing this gangly, awkward, stammering, lip-smacker talking about adultery, his ex-wife, and Parker Brothers making his love life into a game gives one a perspective that helps us understand why these early performances are unbearable for Woody to watch. Yes, the routines were very funny, but they bespoke a leering preoccupation with sex that Woody now finds deplorable. Commenting on some of his early standup routines, Woody told Eric Lax:

> I'm no better than any bad comic, any pushy comic. I'm pushy. I think I'm cuter than I am. I hate what I stand for. All those stupid girl-chasing jokes and sex jokes and, you know, self-deprecating stuff. It's repugnant to me now.

Basically, what that reaction indicates is an artistic growth that has changed an artist's perception of his early work. This paradigm can be seen today in Woody's refusal to see any of his own films after they're released. It's too painful: he knows he'd find things he'd change. As for his stand-up routines, Woody himself has changed so much from that twenty-eight-year-old sex fiend that essentially he no longer knows who that person is.

Nonetheless, reviewing his early appearances is a valuable tool to understanding where Woody came from, and how he became who he is today. (Special thanks to Steve Allen and his staff for the video of Woody's appearance.)

T13. "The Joe Franklin Show" (Syndicated; 1954–Present) (*Guest, midsixties*)

Woody Allen, quintessential New Yorker, appeared during his "nightclub years" on "The Joe Franklin Show," the quintessential "New York" talk show.

T14. "Hootenany" (ABC; April 6, 1963–September 12, 1964) (*Guest*)

"Hootenany" was television's first folk music series, and it was hosted by Art Linkletter (known for his devotion to folk music, right?). It was broadcast from a different college campus each week.

T15. "The Tonight Show" (Carson) (*Guest Host, 1964*)

As guest host on this television institution, Woody forged a trail for Joan Rivers and Jay Leno.

T16. "The Tonight Show" (Carson) (*Guest, New Year's Eve, 1965*)

On Johnny's New Year's Eve program, Woody talked about living in Paris during the making of *What's New, Pussycat?* and also did standup material. Eric Lax reproduces the transcript of Woody's appearance on this show in his book *Woody Allen: A Biography.*

T17. "Hippodrome" (CBS; July 5, 1966–September 6, 1966) (*Guest Host, 1966*)

"Hippodrome" was an hour-long series that featured European circus acts. Woody appeared as a guest host on the program in 1966, and other hosts included Eddie Albert, Trini Lopez, and Tony Randall. (Woody has used circus scenes in *Alice* and *Shadows and Fog.*)

T18. "The Kraft Music Hall: The Year 1967 in Review" aka "Woody Allen Looks at 1967" (NBC; September 13, 1967–May 12, 1971) (*Writer/Star, December 27, 1967*)

Woody casts his particular and singular glance on 1967, a year which included increasingly negative popular sentiment against the war in Vietnam; the debut of *Rolling Stone* magazine; the opening of the musical *Hair;* and the release of the Beatles album *Sergeant Pepper's Lonely Hearts Club Band.*

T19. "The Merv Griffin Show" (CBS; August 18, 1969–February 11, 1972) (*Guest, 1969*)

Woody appeared as a guest on this show in 1969, the year in which his first film, *Take the Money and Run,* was released. "The Merv Griffin Show" was intended to compete with Johnny Carson's extremely successful late-night program, "The Tonight Show."

T20. "The Kraft Music Hall: The Woody Allen Special" (NBC; September 13, 1967–May 12, 1971) (Guests: Billy Graham, Candice Bergen, Fifth Dimension) (*Writer/Star, September 21, 1969*)

This was one of a number of comedy specials produced under the banner title of "The Kraft Music Hall." (Another was Groucho Marx's special, "A Taste of Funny.") Three of the most notable features of the special were a short film called *Cupid's Shaft,* which starred Candice Bergen and parodied Charlie Chaplin's classic film, *City Lights;* a somewhat spontaneous conversation between evangelist Billy Graham and atheist Woody Allen; and a Pygmalion spoof in which Rabbi Woody promised to pass off "Liza" (played by Candice Bergen) as "one of the country's leading pseudo-intellectuals" at the "annual Norman Mailer cocktail party." [See the photo section.]

T21. "Hot Dog" (NBC; September 12, 1970–September 4, 1971; 26 episodes.) (*Guest Host*)

This was a Saturday morning educational program for children which explained, by using short films, how everyday things are made, including footballs, felt tip pens, baseballs, cuckoo clocks, blue jeans, rope, bricks, pencils, hot dogs, and paper. The show, which featured music by The Youngbloods, was hosted by Jonathan Winters, Woody Allen, and Jo Anne Worley. "Hot Dog" was created by Frank Buxton, its executive producer was Lee Mendelson, and it won a Peabody Award in 1971.

T22. "The Steve Allen Show" (Syndicated; 1967–72) (*Guest, April 30, 1971*)

This was Steve Allen's third daily syndicated talk/comedy show. Woody appeared on the show with his ex-wife Louise Lasser. He was plugging *Bananas.* The other guests that day included Frederick Mellinger (of Frederick's of Hollywood), and Anthony Greenbank (who did a "Strength and Survival" demonstration).

T23. "The Politics of Woody Allen" aka "The Politics—and Comedy—of Woody Allen" (PBS; Scheduled: February 21, 1972; Never aired) (*Writer/ Star*)

This scathingly satirical slap at the Nixon administration (including the president's aide "Harvey Wallinger," whose father performs openheart surgery by mail) was never aired because PBS felt that if it was, it would be obligated to offer equal time to other candidates. (See Eric Lax's 1975 book, *On Being Funny: The Comedy of Woody Allen,* for complete details on both the script and final filmed version of this special.)

T24. "The Dick Cavett Show" (ABC; May 26, 1969–December 29, 1972) (*Guest, 1969*)

Woody appeared on his friend Dick Cavett's talk show in late 1969, and an excerpt from one of his appearances was later used in *Annie Hall.*

PART III

Out of the Woodwork

Reflections on the Work of Woody Allen

CHAPTER 10

Woody Allen, Culture Animal
Woody's Cultural Influences

You take some of those Bergman films that are enormously complex. . . .
They're the best films in the world, I think.

Maybe I'll get lucky and come up with a *Bicycle Thief* or something one
day, and then they'll have that, too. And if not—so they'll pay their six
dollars and it'll stink and they'll go home. It's not the end of the world.
Woody Allen

Canst thou bind the sweet influences of Pleiades,
or loose the bands of Orion?
Job 38:31, Bible

Culture may even be described simply as that which
makes life worth living.
T. S. Eliot, *Notes Towards a Definition of Culture*

RECIPE DIRECTIONS: Mix the cultural legends below with a liberal quantity of Jewish angst, red hair, and Brooklyn; add an immeasurable helping
of genius, and you *might* get something approaching the legendary Woody
Allen.

In this chapter you will meet, by way of an overview, many of the
writers, directors, musicians, philosophers, and comics that, over the
years, have been mentioned by Woody himself as having influenced him
and his work, been cited by critics during the discussions of Woody's influences, or been mentioned by any of the characters in Woody's films or
essays. These artists have in some way contributed to the development of
Woody Allen's sensibility, as well as to the creation of the Woody Allen
persona.

For instance, Gustav Mahler is included because he is mentioned in

297

Manhattan, and because Woody used Mahler's Symphony no. 4 in *Another Woman.*

Norman Mailer is listed because he is mentioned in *Sleeper,* his book *Advertisements for Myself* is mentioned in "The Whore of Mensa," and a quote from *The Prisoner of Sex* is used in *Annie Hall.*

Buster Keaton is logged because of the obvious influence of his film *Sherlock, Jr.* on *The Purple Rose of Cairo.*

Although the following list is but a sampling of the hundreds of artists whose influence has touched Woody, it will suffice as a starting point for further study and enjoyment.

A

Edward Albee   (American playwright)
See: *The Floating Light Bulb.*
Michelangelo Antonioni   (Italian director)
See: The "Why Do Some Women Have Trouble Reaching an Orgasm?" segment of *Everything You Always Wanted to Know About Sex* (*But Were Afraid to Ask).*
Aristotle   (Greek philosopher)
See: *God* (in *Without Feathers*); *My Apology* (in *Side Effects*).
Louis Armstrong   (American jazz musician)
See: *Manhattan; Stardust Memories.*
Fred Astaire   (American dancer and actor)
See: *Stardust Memories; The Purple Rose of Cairo; Crimes and Misdemeanors.*

B

Johann Sebastian Bach   (German baroque composer)
See: *Hannah and Her Sisters; Another Woman; Crimes and Misdemeanors; Alice.*
Honoré de Balzac   (French novelist)
See: *Annie Hall; A Midsummer Night's Sex Comedy.*
James Barrie   (British writer)
See: *What's Up, Tiger Lily?*
L. Frank Baum   (American writer)
See: *Annie Hall.*
Ernest Becker   (American writer)
See: *Annie Hall.*
Saul Bellow   (American writer)
See: *Zelig;* "No Kaddish for Weinstein" (in *Without Feathers*).
Robert Benchley   (American humorist writer)
See: *Getting Even; Without Feathers; Side Effects.*

Jack Benny   (American comedian)
See: *The Floating Light Bulb.*
Beowulf   (Old English poem)
See: *Annie Hall.*
Nikolai Aleksandrovich Berdyaev   (Russian Christian existentialist)
See: *Love and Death;* "The Condemned" (in *Side Effects*).
Ingmar Bergman   (Swedish director)
See: *Love and Death; Annie Hall; Interiors; Stardust Memories; Manhattan; A Midsummer Night's Sex Comedy; Hannah and Her Sisters; September; Another Woman; Crimes and Misdemeanors; Scenes from a Mall; Shadows and Fog;* "Death Knocks" (in *Getting Even*).
Milton Berle   (American comedian)
See: *Broadway Danny Rose.*
Irving Berlin   (American composer and songwriter)
See: *The Purple Rose of Cairo; September; Crimes and Misdemeanors.*
Bernardo Bertolucci   (Italian director)
See: The "Why Do Some Woman Have Trouble Reaching an Orgasm" segment of *Everything You Always Wanted to Know About Sex* (*But Were Afraid to Ask).*
Humphrey Bogart   (American actor)
See: *Don't Drink the Water; Play It Again, Sam;* "The Whore of Mensa" (in *Without Feathers*).
Heinrich Böll   (German writer)
See: *Manhattan.*
James Boswell   (British writer)
See: *A Midsummer Night's Sex Comedy.*
Marlon Brando   (American actor)
See: *Sleeper;* "Mr. Big" (in *Getting Even*).
Bertolt Brecht   (German playwright and poet)
See: *Manhattan; Another Woman; Shadows and Fog.*
Dave Brubeck   (American jazz composer and pianist)
See: *Hannah and Her Sisters; Another Woman.*
Lenny Bruce   (American comedian)
See: *Manhattan.*
Martin Buber   (German-Israeli existential philosopher)
See: "Mr. Big."
William F. Buckley, Jr.   (American writer)
See: *Annie Hall.*

C

Sammy Cahn   (American songwriter)
See: *Hannah and Her Sisters; Radio Days.*

Thomas Carlyle   (Scottish critic and essayist)
See: *A Midsummer Night's Sex Comedy.*
Hoagy Carmichael   (American songwriter and composer)
See: *Stardust Memories.*
Lewis Carroll   (English writer)
See: *Alice.*
Paul Cézanne   (French impressionist painter)
See: *Manhattan; A Midsummer Night's Sex Comedy.*
Charlie Chaplin   (American actor and director)
See: *Sleeper; Love and Death; Annie Hall.*
Anton Chekhov   (Russian dramatist and short-story writer)
See: *Interiors; Manhattan; Hannah and Her Sisters; Radio Days; September.*
Maurice Chevalier   (French singing entertainer and actor)
See: *Annie Hall.*
Noam Chomsky   (American linguistic philosopher)
See: *Manhattan;* "The Whore of Mensa" (in *Without Feathers*).
John Coltrane   (American jazz saxophonist)
See: *Alice.*
Alice Cooper   (American rock musician)
See: *Annie Hall.*
Howard Cosell   (American sportscaster)
See: *Bananas; Sleeper; Broadway Danny Rose.*
Bing Crosby   (American singer)
See: *The Floating Light Bulb.*
Xavier Cugat   (American composer)
See: *Radio Days; Crimes and Misdemeanors.*

D

Vittorio de Sica   (Italian director)
See: The "Why Do Some Woman Have Trouble Reaching an Orgasm" segment of *Everything You Always Wanted to Know About Sex* (*But Were Afraid to Ask).*
Charles Dickens   (English novelist)
See: "Mr. Big" (in *Getting Even*).
Emily Dickinson   (American poet)
See: *Crimes and Misdemeanors.*
Isak Dinesen   (Danish writer)
See: *Manhattan.*
Walt Disney   (American animator and filmmaker)
See: *Annie Hall.*
Tommy Dorsey   (American bandleader)
See: *Annie Hall; Interiors; Radio Days.*

Fyodor Dostoevski   (Russian writer)
See: *Love and Death; Crimes and Misdemeanors;* "Notes from the Over-fed" (in *Getting Even*).
Alexander Dovzhenko   (Russian writer-director)
See: *Love and Death; Annie Hall.*
Theodore Dreiser   (American novelist)
See: "If the Impressionists Had Been Dentists" (in *Without Feathers*).
Jimmy Durante   (American comedian)
See: *The Floating Light Bulb.*
Bob Dylan   (American singer-songwriter)
See: *Annie Hall.*

E

Nelson Eddy   (American actor-singer)
See: *Annie Hall.*
Sergei Eisenstein   (Russian director)
See: *Bananas; Love and Death.*
T. S. Eliot   (American dramatist and poet)
See: *Love and Death;* "No Kaddish for Weinstein" (in *Without Feathers*); "Confessions of a Burglar" (in *Side Effects*).
Duke Ellington   (American musician)
See: *Alice.*

F

Federico Fellini   (Italian director)
See: *What's New, Pussycat?;* the "Why Do Some Women Have Trouble Reaching an Orgasm?" segment of *Everything You Always Wanted to Know About Sex* (*But Were Afraid to Ask); Annie Hall; Stardust Memories; The Purple Rose of Cairo; Radio Days; Crimes and Misdemeanors; Alice; Scenes from a Mall; Shadows and Fog.*
Henry Fielding   (English writer)
See: *Bananas.*
Dorothy Fields   (American popular composer)
See: *Hannah and Her Sisters; Another Woman; Alice.*
W. C. Fields   (American actor)
See: *Manhattan; Radio Days.*
F. Scott Fitzgerald   (American novelist and short-story writer)
See: *Manhattan;* "A Twenties Memory" (in *Getting Even*).
Gustave Flaubert   (French writer)
See: The "What Happens During Ejaculation?" segment of *Everything*

You Always Wanted to Know About Sex* (*But Were Afraid to Ask); Manhattan; "The Kugelmass Episode" (in *Side Effects*).

Richard Fleischer   (American director)
See: The "What Happens During Ejaculation?" segment of *Everything You Always Wanted to Know About Sex* (*But Were Afraid to Ask)*.

Sigmund Freud   (Austrian psychologist and writer)
See: *Annie Hall; Manhattan; Another Woman;* "The Metterling Lists"; "Yes, But Can the Steam Engine Do This?"; "The Gossage-Vardebedian Papers"; "Conversations with Helmholtz" (all in *Getting Even*); "The Whore of Mensa" (in *Without Feathers*).

G

George Gershwin   (American composer)
See: *Manhattan.*

Jackie Gleason   (American comedian)
See: *Don't Drink the Water.*

Jean-Luc Godard   (French director)
See: *King Lear.*

Benny Goodman   (American popular jazz musician)
See: *Stardust Memories; Radio Days; Oedipus Wrecks.*

H

Marvin Hamlisch   (American popular composer and songwriter)
See: *Take the Money and Run; Bananas.*

Oscar Hammerstein II   (American popular composer and songwriter)
See: *September; Another Woman; Oedipus Wrecks.*

Lorenz Hart   (American popular composer and songwriter)
See: *Hannah and Her Sisters; Crimes and Misdemeanors.*

Moss Hart   (American playwright)
See: *Don't Drink the Water.*

Hugh Hefner   (American publisher)
See: *What's Up, Tiger Lily?; Don't Drink the Water; Sleeper; Annie Hall.*

Georg Wilhelm Friedrich Hegel   (German dialectic Absolutist philosopher)
See: "The Condemned" (in *Side Effects*).

Martin Heidegger   (German existential philosopher)
See: *Another Woman;* "Mr. Big" (in *Getting Even*); "Remembering Needleman" (in *Side Effects*).

Ernest Hemingway   (American writer)
See: "A Twenties Memory" (in *Getting Even*).

Alfred Hitchcock   (American director)
See: *Crimes and Misdemeanors.*

Bob Hope   (American comedian and actor)
See: *Bananas; Sleeper; Love and Death.*
Irving Howe   (American writer)
See: *Zelig.*
Victor Hugo   (French poet, dramatist, and novelist)
See: The "Are the Findings of Doctors and Clinics Who Do Sexual Research and Experiments Accurate?" segment of *Everything You Always Wanted to Know About Sex* (*But Were Afraid to Ask).*
David Hume   (British empiricist philosopher)
See: *Love and Death;* "Mr. Big" (in *Getting Even*).
Anjelica Huston   (American actress)
See: *Annie Hall.*
Aldous Huxley   (English writer)
See: *Sleeper.*

I

Henrik Ibsen   (Norwegian poet and dramatist)
See: *Annie Hall; Hannah and Her Sisters.*
Hiroshi Inagaki   (Japanese director)
See: *Annie Hall.*

J

Harry James   (American bandleader)
See: *Hannah and Her Sisters; Radio Days.*
Henry James   (American writer)
See: *Annie Hall.*
Samuel Johnson   (English writer)
See: *A Midsummer Night's Sex Comedy.*
James Joyce   (Irish writer)
See: *Crimes and Misdemeanors;* "The Irish Genius" (in *Without Feathers*).
Carl Jung   (Swiss psychiatrist)
See: "Yes, But Can the Steam Engine Do This?" (in *Getting Even*).

K

Franz Kafka   (Austrian writer)
See: *Annie Hall; Manhattan; Shadows and Fog;* "Yes, But Can the Steam Engine Do This?" and "The Metterling Lists" (both in *Getting Even*).

Immanuel Kant   (German transcendental philosopher)
  See: *Love and Death.*
George S. Kaufman   (American playwright)
  See: *Don't Drink the Water.*
Buster Keaton   (American comic film actor)
  See: *Sleeper; The Purple Rose of Cairo.*
Jerome Kern   (American popular composer)
  See: *Hannah and Her Sisters; Another Woman; Alice.*
Aram Khachaturian   (Armenian composer)
  See: *The Floating Light Bulb.*
Sören Kierkegaard   (Danish existential philosopher and writer)
  See: *Love and Death.*
Gustav Klimt   (Austrian artist)
  See: *Another Woman.*
Akira Kurosawa   (Japanese director)
  See: *Annie Hall.*

L

Fritz Lang   (German director)
  See: *Shadows and Fog.*
Veronica Lake   (American actress)
  See: *Manhattan; Crimes and Misdemeanors.*
Laurel & Hardy   (American comedic actors)
  See: *Sleeper.*
Gottfried Wilhelm Leibniz   (German logical rationalistic philosopher
  and mathematician)
  See: "Mr. Big" (in *Getting Even*).
Mervyn Leroy   (American director)
  See: *Take the Money and Run.*
Jerry Lewis   (American comedian)
  See: "The Condemned" (in *Side Effects*).
Peter Lorre   (American actor)
  See: *What's Up, Tiger Lily?*

M

Ross MacDonald   (American writer)
  See: "Mr. Big" (in *Getting Even*); "The Whore of Mensa (in *Without
  Feathers*).
Gustav Mahler   (Austrian composer)
  See: *Another Woman.*
Norman Mailer   (American writer)
  See: The "What Happens During Ejaculation?" segment of *Everything*

F. W. Murnau   (German director)
See: *Shadows and Fog.*

N

Paul Newman   (American actor)
See: *Take the Money and Run.*
Jack Nicholson   (American actor)
See: *Annie Hall.*
Friedrich Nietzsche   (German existentialist philosopher)
See: "My Speech to the Graduates" (in *Side Effects*).

O

Clifford Odets   (American playwright)
See: *The Floating Light Bulb.*
Laurence Olivier   (British actor)
See: The "Do Aphrodisiacs Work?" segment of *Everything You Always Wanted to Know About Sex* (*But Were Afraid to Ask).*
Eugene O'Neill   (American playwright)
See: *The Floating Light Bulb.*
Marcel Ophuls   (French director)
See: *Annie Hall; Manhattan.*

P

G. W. Pabst   (German director)
See: *Shadows and Fog.*
Blaise Pascal   (French pragmatist philosopher and mathematician)
See: "Mr. Big."
John Patrick   (American playwright)
See: *Don't Drink the Water.*
S. J. Perelman   (American essayist and humorist)
See: *Getting Even; Without Feathers; Side Effects.*
Pablo Picasso   (Spanish painter and sculptor)
See: The "What Is Sodomy?" segment of *Everything You Always Wanted to Know About Sex* (*But Were Afraid to Ask).*
Sylvia Plath   (American poet)
See: *Annie Hall.*
Plato   (Greek rationalistic philosopher)
See: *God* (in *Without Feathers*); *My Apology* (in *Side Effects*).
Cole Porter   (American songwriter and composer)
See: *Stardust Memories; Hannah and Her Sisters; Radio Days; September; Another Woman; Crimes and Misdemeanors.*

Sergei Prokofiev (Russian composer)
See: *Love and Death.*
Marcel Proust (French writer)
See: The "What Happens During Ejaculation?" segment of *Everything You Always Wanted to Know About Sex* (*But Were Afraid to Ask); Stardust Memories.*
Giacomo Puccini (Italian operatic composer)
See: *The Floating Light Bulb.*

R

Jean-Pierre Rampal (French classical flutist)
See: *Manhattan.*
Raphael (Italian painter)
See: *A Midsummer Night's Sex Comedy.*
Jean Renoir (French writer-director)
See: *Manhattan.*
Rainer Maria Rilke (German poet)
See: *Another Woman.*
Martin Ritt (American director)
See: *The Front.*
Richard Rodgers (American composer)
See: *Hannah and Her Sisters; Crimes and Misdemeanors.*
Rolling Stones (British rock group)
See: *Annie Hall.*
Cesar Romero (Latin-American actor)
See: *The Floating Light Bulb.*
Rosicrucianism (American-German religious-fraternal organization)
See: *Annie Hall.*
Robert Rossen (American director)
See: *Take the Money and Run.*
Philip Roth (American novelist)
See: "No Kaddish for Weinstein" (in *Without Feathers*); "The Kugelmass Episode" (in *Side Effects*).

S

Mort Sahl (American comedian and social commentator)
See: *Woody Allen; Woody Allen, Volume 2; The Third Woody Allen Album.*
J. D. Salinger (American writer)
See: *Annie Hall.*
Jean-Paul Sartre (French existentialist philosopher, novelist, and dramatist)
See: *Love and Death.*

Erik Satie   (French composer)
See: *Another Woman.*
Franz Schubert   (Austrian composer)
See: *A Midsummer Night's Sex Comedy; Crimes and Misdemeanors.*
Mack Sennett   (American director)
See: *Take the Money and Run; Bananas.*
Ben Shahn   (American artist)
See: "The Whore of Mensa" (in *Without Feathers*).
William Shakespeare   (English dramatist and poet)
See: *What's New, Pussycat?;* The "Do Aphrodisiacs Work" segment of *Everything You Always Wanted to Know About Sex* (*But Were Afraid to Ask); A Midsummer Night's Sex Comedy; Annie Hall; Zelig.*
Percy Bysshe Shelley   (British poet)
See: *What's New, Pussycat?*
Frank Sinatra   (American popular singer)
See: *Annie Hall; Radio Days.*
Socrates   (Greek realist philosopher)
See: *Love and Death.*
Susan Sontag   (American writer)
See: *Zelig.*
Benedict (Baruch) Spinoza   (Dutch monistic philosopher)
See: *Love and Death; Another Woman;* "My Philosophy" and "Spring Bulletin" (both in *Getting Even*).
August Strindberg   (Swedish dramatist and novelist)
See: *Manhattan;* "Lovborg's Women Considered" (in *Without Feathers*).
Preston Sturges   (American director)
See: *Bananas.*

T

Frank Tashlin   (American director)
See: *Sleeper; Love and Death.*
Art Tatum   (American jazz pianist)
See: *September.*
James Thurber   (American writer and cartoonist)
See: *Getting Even; Without Feathers; Side Effects.*
Leo Tolstoy   (Russian novelist)
See: *Love and Death; Hannah and Her Sisters.*
Henri de Toulouse-Lautrec   (French painter)
See: *What's New, Pussycat?*
Ivan Turgenev   (Russian novelist)
See: *Love and Death.*

V

Vincent van Gogh   (Dutch painter)
See: *What's New, Pussycat?; Play It Again, Sam; Manhattan.*
Edgard Varèse   (American composer)
See: *Another Woman.*
Voltaire   (French writer)
See: *What's New, Pussycat?*

W

Richard Wagner   (German operatic composer)
See: *What's New, Pussycat?; Annie Hall.*
John Wayne   (American actor)
See: *What's Up, Tiger Lily?*
Kurt Weill   (German composer)
See: *Shadows and Fog.*
Orson Welles   (American director)
See: The "What Is Sodomy?" and the "Do Aphrodisiacs Work?" segments of *Everything You Always Wanted to Know About Sex* (*But Were Afraid to Ask); Zelig.*
Walt Whitman   (American poet)
See: *Manhattan.*
Tennessee Williams   (American playwright)
See: *Sleeper; The Floating Light Bulb.*
Robert Wise   (American director)
See: *Take the Money and Run.*

CHAPTER 11

Wooden Poses:
The Reel Woody Allen

The Characters Woody Has Written for Himself & the Creation of the "Woody Allen" Myth

Most of the time,
I don't have much fun.
The rest of the time,
I don't have any fun at all.
Woody Allen

On the stage he was natural, simple, affecting;
'Twas only that when he was off he was acting.
Oliver Goldsmith

There's one clear autobiographical fact in [*Annie Hall*].
I've thought about sex since my first
intimation of consciousness.
Woody Allen, interview with *New York Times*, 1977

I'm a little more morbid than the average person.
Woody Allen

ON JULY 17, 1991, the British Broadcasting Corporation broadcast on the "Kaleidoscope" radio program a thirty-minute interview with Woody Allen conducted by Nigel Andrews. The interview originally took place in the spring of 1991 in New York City as *Alice* was just opening in England.

Andrews asked Woody a question that had to be one of the most unusual questions ever asked of a celebrity, but that, upon reflection, should also be deemed one of the most trenchant.

The question (and Woody's response) is reproduced below, but here's a head start: "How strange is it to be a myth?" The reason the question struck me as so odd is that it was so on the money.

There is no quarrel with the question: Woody Allen is a myth; an icon; an archetype. As Andrews acknowledges, his persona is known around the world. In a sense, Allan Konigsberg created Woody Allen (somewhat?) in his own image, and the rest is cinematic history.

But exactly what has Woody done to mythologize himself? And how would the "Woody Allen" myth be defined? Most fans would describe his character as a bumbling schlemiel who is (usually) a loser in love; an agnostic who is abundantly intelligent and stunningly verbal; a sourpuss who is occasionally hostile and paranoid; and a neurotic analysand who is undeniably anal-retentive, obsessive-compulsive, and a hypochondriac to boot. Is that the real Woody Allen?

If the "Woodman" persona and the "real" Woody don't jibe, *why* don't they jibe? And was the creation of this "Woody" character—with all its exaggerated "quirks and mannerisms"—a conscious decision of Mr. Konigsberg, or just an artistic manifestation of certain aspects of his personality that Woody realized could be used to comic advantage?

Probably there are no carved-in-stone answers. But it's interesting to observe popular culture's somewhat indiscriminate embrace of icons and our lust for personas rather than persons.

The acknowledgment of this hunger goes a long way toward understanding American society's appetite for tell-all unauthorized biographies, the proliferation of gossip rags, and the (recent) ubiquitousness of tabloid television shows.

It seems that the more we behold the mask, the more we want to peek beneath it.

Why has Woody Allen become something more than the sum of his parts, so to speak?

The real truth can probably never be known, since such artistic/cultural/personal psychoanalysis would require being inside Woody Allen's sensibility in order to understand fully which elements of the Woody recipe were home-cooked (intrinsic to Allan Konigsberg), and which were store-bought (used as an artistic device for effect).

Interestingly, Woody doesn't actually answer the interviewer's question about his status as a myth. His response is to a question more along the lines of, "How does it feel to be a celebrity?" So perhaps even he doesn't relish delving too deeply into the how and why of his role as a legend?

Nigel Andrews/BBC When you developed your standup comedy, and one of the things that distinguished it, was that it was *about* Woody

Allen. You were creating a persona, and not just a series of gags. And you've become almost a mythological character in American popular culture. You've been turned into a newspaper cartoon; everyone recognizes you on the movie screen or on television. How strange is it to be a myth?

Woody Allen   It's a surprise when you first get recognized. This happened to me years ago when I first made the transition from a writer's life, which is reclusive, to a popular performer. And that was strange for me. I've never really gotten used to it completely. But, it's fine. But it's not a natural feeling, and particularly since it came to me comparatively late in life . . . I mean, most performers begin when they're twenty years old, you know, and I didn't turn to performing until I was in my late twenties or something. Well, mid-twenties.

Are the characters Woody Allen writes for himself cinematic manifestations of his own real personality? Is Alvy Singer an autobiographical creation? Or are the Woody Allen characters really just highly stylized interpretations of specific facets of Woody's sensibility—characters acting out certain aspects of his life?

The answers to these questions are "Sometimes," "In some ways," and "In most cases, yes."

Every writer brings to the creation of his fictional characters elements from his own life, from people he knows, from things he has read and seen, and from his own particular and unique imaginary inventiveness.

Woody Allen is no different. *Broadway Danny Rose* has a character named Tina Vitale, played by Mia Farrow. The character was written after Mia saw a woman like her in a restaurant and mused aloud that she would someday love to play a character like her. So Woody wrote Tina for her.

But Woody's own characters almost mandate the questions posed earlier. Woody's early "bumbling schlemiel" standup persona set up an expectation for his audiences, and thus they weren't surprised when they first met Virgil Starkwell (*Take the Money and Run*), Fielding Mellish (*Bananas*), Miles Monroe (*Sleeper*), Boris Grushenko (*Love and Death*), and the other Woody Allen characters in his films. That the disenchanted, borderline misogynist Sandy Bates in *Stardust Memories* might be closer to the real Woody (or at least one side of his personality) may have contributed to the hostile reaction that film received when it was first released.

In Eric Lax's *Woody Allen: A Biography,* Woody reveals (through Lax) the three characters he has written that he feels are closest to his real personality, the characters with whom he identifies the most. Is one Alvy Singer, the comic, from *Annie Hall*? Isaac Davis, the writer, from *Manhattan*? Mickey Sachs, the television producer, from *Hannah and Her Sisters*? Cliff Stern, the filmmaker, from *Crimes and Misdemeanors*? Or even the aforementioned Sandy Bates? No to all.

Woody feels that the three characters closest to the real Woody are (are you ready for this?) Eve from *Interiors,* Cecilia from *The Purple Rose of Cairo,* and Marion from *Another Woman.*

Three women. And each of them disillusioned and morose, although Cecilia is apparently the token optimist of the bunch. (And it's very revealing that her character gets tricked and left alone by the one man she thought she could trust.)

At one point or another in the films, these three female manifestations of Mr. Allen all speak for Woody.

In *Interiors* Eve is a cold and suicidal woman, rigid, distant, and mentally unstable, who turned her home into an "ice palace," and who couldn't bear the living of her own life. Even though Woody may have told Lax that Eve was one of his alter egos, it seems that in *Interiors* Woody has given Diane Keaton's character, Renata, the lines that come closest to verbalizing his own concerns.

Here Renata talks to her psychiatrist about her fears of death, the permanence/impermanence of art, and the artist's ability (or inability) to live on through the work:

> **Renata** [I]t started happening last winter. Increasing thoughts about death just seemed to come over me . . . a preoccupation with my own mortality. These feelings of futility in relation to my work. I mean, just what was I striving to create anyway? I mean, to what end? For what purpose? What goal? I mean, do I really care if a handful of my poems are read after I'm gone forever? Is that supposed to be some sort of compensation? I used to think it was. But now, for some reason, I can't seem to shake . . . the real implication of dying. It's terrifying. The intimacy of it embarrasses me.

Perhaps there are facets of Eve's character that Woody believes most resemble parts of himself, but has he not elected to have Renata verbalize his true feelings? (One particularly powerful and revealing scene is set in a church. Arthur tells Eve he wants to finalize their divorce and she weeps, "Oh!! I just want to die! I just hate myself!" Then, after sweeping the red (Pearl's color) candles to the floor, she tells Arthur, "I'm fine, I'm fine. Oh, I hate myself, I hate myself!")

Later, Renata tells her husband Frederick of an especially distressing existential angst-filled moment:

> **Renata** I just experienced the strangest sensation. It was if I had a sudden, clear vision where everything seems sort of awful and predatory. It was like I was here, and the world was out there, and I couldn't bring us together.

As *Interiors* moves toward Eve's suicide, Joey speaks frankly to her mother on the night of Arthur's marriage to Pearl:

Joey I think you're really too perfect to live in this world. I mean, all the beautifully furnished rooms, carefully designed interiors . . . everything so controlled. There wasn't any room for any real feelings. None. Between any of us. . . . You're not just a sick woman. That would be too easy. The truth is, there's been perverseness—and willfulness of attitude—in many of the things you've done. At the center of a sick psyche, there is a sick spirit.

The film ends with Eve's death seeming finally to release *Joey's* creative paralysis as we hear her writing in a journal thoughts that "seemed very powerful to me."

In *The Purple Rose of Cairo* Cecilia is a starry-eyed optimist who gets dumped on by life in general, and men in particular, and who can find sanctuary only in the dark womb of the movie theater, a place where flights of fantasy transport her away from the real world. But even when fantasy becomes reality she finds little solace. In the following exchange of dialogue with Tom Baxter, the "come-to-life" movie hero who falls in love with the real-world Cecilia, Cecilia seems to express some of Woody Allen's personal feelings about life on earth:

Cecilia Oh, it's been hard for everyone. You know, living in the world with no jobs and wars. You probably never heard of the Great War.
Tom No, I'm sorry. I missed it.
Cecilia Yeah, well, people get old, and sick, and never find true love.
Tom Well, you know, where I come from, people, they don't disappoint. They're consistent. They're always reliable.
Cecilia You don't find that kind in real life.

A great similarity also exists, it seems, between Woody Allen and Mia Farrow. In their 1989 biography of Mia, *Mia Farrow: Flower Child, Madonna, Muse,* authors Sam Rubin and Richard Taylor tell us that "Mia herself was pleased with the role in *Purple Rose,* and she acknowledged that many aspects of the character undoubtedly were the result of Woody's knowing her so well." Mia said:

She's a nice character, very simple and ingenuous, and I liked her. I think she's a lot better than I am, but I can identify with some parts of her and *she is closer to me than some of the other characters I have played.* She is sweet and innocent and really a good person, who is trying very hard to cope with her lot in life. . . . *This character was the closest in a way to my own.* [Emphasis added]

Woody, reflecting their genuinely symbiotic personal and professional relationship, apparently combined elements of his own personality with elements of Mia's, to come up with Cecilia. And it seems the two of them also share a common obsession. Mia also said of Cecilia (and

Woody?), "She has an absolute commitment to the movies. I too can be completely absorbed in the reality of a movie."

In *Another Woman* Marion is a brilliant professor and philosopher who, in middle age, has so closed herself off that she is unable to accept (even though she may recognize the truth) that she has botched several relationships in her life, and that there is now no going back.

Woody Allen's voice is present in the very first lines spoken in the film. The film opens with Marion's voice-over:

> **Marion**   If someone had asked me when I reached my fifties to assess my life, I would have said that I had achieved a decent measure of fulfillment, both personally and professionally. Beyond that, I would say I don't choose to delve. Not that I was afraid of uncovering some dark side of my character. But I always feel if something seems to be working, leave it alone.

In 1988, when *Another Woman* was released, Woody Allen was fifty-three years old.

Compare that speech with this one by Elaine Stritch's character Diane (another female alter ego of Woody's?) to her daughter Lane (Mia Farrow) from Woody's 1987 film, *September*:

> **Diane**   It's hell gettin' older. Especially when you feel twenty-one inside. All the strengths that just sustain you all through your life just vanish one by one. And you study your face in the mirror, and you notice something's missing. And then you realize it's your future. So that's why I want you to find yourself while there's still time left to enjoy it.

This armchair analysis of the three (or four, if you count Diane) female Dopplegängers of Woody Allen is revealing, if only for the fact that one would think that Woody would reveal more of his personality in his male characters.

Woody *has* written male characters for himself to play; through 1992's *Shadows and Fog,* there have been seventeen. Are there autobiographical elements in these guys? Certainly. The following list comprises Woody's male creations that he has played himself. (Characters marked with a bullet (•) are those who are either writers or involved in entertainment or the film industry.)

- 1. Victor Shakapopolis, stripper dresser (*What's New, Pussycat?*, 1965)
- 2. Virgil Starkwell, small-time crook (*Take the Money and Run,* 1969)
- 3. Fielding Mellish, products tester and revolutionary (*Bananas,* 1971)

- 4. Allan Felix, film critic (*Play It Again, Sam,* 1972)
- 5. Victor Shakapopolis, sex researcher and writer (*Everything You Always Wanted to Know About Sex* (*But Were Afraid to Ask),* 1972)
  6. Miles Monroe, health-food store owner and revolutionary (*Sleeper,* 1973)
  7. Boris Grushenko, soldier and failed assassin (*Love and Death,* 1975)
- 8. Alvy Singer, comedian (*Annie Hall,* 1977)
- 9. Isaac Davis, television writer and novelist (*Manhattan,* 1979)
- 10. Sandy Bates, film director (*Stardust Memories,* 1980)
  11. Andrew Hobbes, Wall Street worker and crackpot inventor (*A Midsummer Night's Sex Comedy,* 1982)
  12. Leonard Zelig, human chameleon (*Zelig,* 1983)
- 13. Danny Rose, talent agent (*Broadway Danny Rose,* 1984)
- 14. Mickey Sachs, television writer and producer (*Hannah and Her Sisters,* 1986)
  15. Sheldon Mills, lawyer (*Oedipus Wrecks,* 1989)
- 16. Cliff Stern, documentary filmmaker (*Crimes and Misdemeanors,* 1989)
  17. Kleinman, persecuted ersatz detective (*Shadows and Fog,* 1992)

Of these seventeen, nine are writers, or filmmakers, or in show business. (Including Woody's "wish-fulfillment" job of dressing strippers.)

Perhaps from this list of Woody characters, we can gain some insight into Woody Allen's own personal interests and development.

Woody began his screenwriting career with *What's New, Pussycat?* in 1965 and wrote for himself a character who dressed strippers as his job. Woody was thirty when he did *Pussycat,* and thus it is understandable how his interests would lean toward the risqué and more broad (no pun intended) humor.

From there he went on to playing a crook in *Take the Money and Run* and a products tester and revolutionary in *Bananas,* both creations that were unabashed inventions. Pseudoautobiographical references were lightly sprinkled in both films, but there was no intense drawing upon his own personal life, something that would characterize later works.

In 1972 we meet the first genuine Woody Allen character, Allan Felix, the writer and film critic in *Play It Again, Sam.* The persona has come alive. His wife has left him, he can't score with girls, and he takes advice from the shade of Humphrey Bogart. Also in 1972, this time in *Everything You Always Wanted to Know About Sex* (*But Were Afraid to Ask),* we meet Woody's second writer character: Victor Shakapopolis. (His latest book was *Advanced Sexual Techniques—How to Achieve Them Without Laughing.*)

From there, we go back to Nebbish Unlimited for the next two films: *Sleeper* (starring Miles Monroe, who develops an attachment to certain future "inventions"), and *Love and Death* (featuring Boris Grushenko, the cowardly hero who's interested more in bedding his cousin than in defeating Napoleon.)

Fans were not surprised by either of these characters. Fielding Mellish and Virgil Starkwell were written all over them.

But in 1977 things changed.

Annie Hall introduced us to Alvy Singer. To be sure, Alvy was still neurotic, paranoid, and obsessive (as were most of Woody's earlier characters), but he was also less of the "fool," and definitely more real. Alvy Singer was the most complex, fully developed, and fully realized character Woody Allen had ever written.

His Isaac Davis in *Manhattan* continued this focus, as did Sandy Bates in *Stardust Memories.* These characters seemed to spring from a place deep inside Woody Allen himself. They were too honest not to have come from somewhere within. (And no, we're not venturing on a Shirley MacLaine "inner voyage" with this discussion. But when we deal with someone [as Bernadette Peters's Muse in *Alice* describes this type of sensibility] as "psychological" as Woody, a little examination of the subtext to his characters becomes necessary.)

Woody seemed to tap into something in himself to create these characters. To this day, regardless of Woody's protests, critics and fans consider *Annie Hall, Manhattan,* and *Stardust Memories* to be Woody's autobiographical trilogy.

The next role he played was closer to the bumbling Woody "persona" than to Woody the real-life writer/director. Andrew Hobbes, the Wall Street worker/weekend inventor in *A Midsummer Night's Sex Comedy,* even goes so far as to describe himself as a "crackpot." Significantly, the very first time we see Woody's character, he's wearing wings, and dashing across a field like a lunatic, trying to fly. Andrew is also sexually obsessed—as are even the more serious Woody characters—but his interest in carnal knowledge is far less serious in *Midsummer.* It's more lustful than erotic, if such a distinction can be made. For instance, in *Manhattan,* Woody's character, Ike, and his seventeen-year-old girlfriend, Tracy, make love constantly, and Ike himself describes their affair as very "erotic." We get the sense that their affair is mature and—Tracy's age notwithstanding—definitely adult. We believe that their lovemaking is, indeed, erotic and intense. In *Midsummer,* however, when Adrian tries to take Dulcy's advice and be spontaneous by making love to Andrew in the kitchen, the scene is played for laughs, with Woody getting off no fewer than four jokes in the short scene.

This shift in characterization begs the question. Did Woody feel he was approaching psychic exhibitionism by baring what seemed to be autobiographical and personal feelings and thus decided to retreat from this type of "confession"?

Interestingly, from Andrew Hobbes he moved on to Leonard Zelig (in 1983's *Zelig*), a character so insecure that he not only was unsure of his own identity, but also assumed the identity of *others* rather than come to terms with his own psyche.

His next character Danny Rose, in 1984's *Broadway Danny Rose,* was still outside the classic Woody Allen persona. Danny Rose was a caricature, a very funny one, certainly, but clearly drawn with a bold stroke. Woody seemed, however, to be nearing a reality-based character that he would be willing to play, and in 1986 we met that character, and indeed, as Jonathan Swift put it, we were "well met."

Mickey Sachs, in *Hannah and Her Sisters,* brought us back to the days of Alvy Singer, Isaac Davis, and Sandy Bates, and it is not coincidental that *Hannah* won Woody an Academy Award for Best Screenplay, as well as nominations for Best Picture and Best Director. Woody was on home turf; he was in his own neighborhood again, and his work was never stronger. *Hannah and Her Sisters*—and Woody's character, Mickey Sachs—was real, and it was honest. This is not to say that his less personally focused films were dishonest; they weren't. They were from another neighborhood, though. Here, we got the sense that Woody was writing from the heart— his heart—rather than just telling a story.

We sample of this ultimate Woody character again with Sheldon Mills in *Oedipus Wrecks,* but that film was essentially a cartoon come to life. It was great fun to watch, and I'm sure Woody had a ball writing it. (As Phil Donahue is fond of saying, you can't cry, "the sky is falling" all the time. Sometimes you need the male strippers.) But there were not too many of what Jack Handey on "Saturday Night Live" calls "deep thoughts" in the film.

One of Woody's most recent characters (aside from his character in *Scenes from a Mall,* a role which was written for him) was the documentary filmmaker Cliff Stern, in 1989's brilliant *Crimes and Misdemeanors.* Cliff was closer to Sandy Bates than to Alvy Singer. He was frustrated, anhedonic, and obsessively driven.

Sort of like Woody Allen?

He winds up losing the girl, as did Alvy and Isaac, and having more questions than answers.

Woody Allen has been in what Stephen King once described (I'm paraphrasing) as the enviable and luxurious position of being able to write what he wants. He is one of the few American directors who insist on total creative control of his films, and get it. In writing. But with Orion's financial troubles, and Woody's move to TriStar for one film, it isn't clear just how long he'll be able to insist upon that kind of autonomy—especially when films like *September* and *Another Woman* don't even recover their costs.

In the future, studios and theaters may lean more heavily on Woody to do *Annie Hall II,* or *Hannah and Her Other Sister,* instead of what he really wants to do, *September II: Another Summer of Pain.*

The level of excellence of Woody Allen's work over the past twenty-five years is evidence of one very important fact: the autonomy he has possessed has freed him creatively. It will be interesting to see if—as he is pushed toward more overtly commercial works—he'll do them simply because he wants to make films, or if he'll follow through on his long-spoken promise to retire from filmmaking and write books.

CHAPTER 12

Seen Scenes

Woody Allen's (Almost) Obligatory "Going to the Movies" Scenes and References in His Films

I'm being paid to do what I like.
Woody Allen

ONE OF the more noteworthy idiosyncrasies of Woody Allen's films is that, like Woody himself, his screen characters attend movies, watch them at home, write for and/or watch television, take in live concerts, listen to the radio, visit museums, go to nightclubs, attend theatrical events, and discuss films. These "movie moments" are many, and have so taken on an appeal of their own that not a few Woody fans eagerly await these scenes in each new release. And usually, Woody does not disappoint. Through 1990's *Alice*, "seen scenes" have seasoned almost every Woody Allen movie to hit the screen.

Herein is a rundown of Woody Allen's cineastic allusions. (For ease of reference, characters are referred to by their screen names. To find out who's who, check the cast credits for the films in Appendix 1. In addition, for fun, I have included details on films which Woody didn't make, but in which he did appear.)

What's New, Pussycat?

- Fritz Fassbender and Michael James lasciviously ogle a stripper at a club. Michael tells Fritz that he's seen the show a hundred times.
- Fritz Fassbender's wife is performing in a production of Richard Wagner's *Die Walküre.*

What's Up, Tiger Lily?

- The film begins with real footage from the original Japanese film, *Kagi No Kagi,* which Woody "adapted."
- Before *What's Up, Tiger Lily?* begins, Woody and an interviewer discuss the "new and improved" film. (During the discussion, Woody reveals that *Gone With the Wind* underwent the same dubbing process as *Tiger Lily,* but that it was quiet because of "the war.")
- *What's Up, Tiger Lily?* is shown on a movie projector in Woody's office, and we get to watch.
- The opening credits spoof the opening of every James Bond movie ever made.
- Phil Moskowitz stares at a stripper (whose bare breasts are covered by the words "Foreign Version").
- In another film reference, during a scene where Phil and Terry are looking out the window of an observation tower, Phil says, "This is the obligatory scene. The director always has to walk through with his wife."
- About halfway through the film, the projector stops and the interviewer asks Woody if he'd like to explain the story because it's kind of hard to follow. (Woody says, "No.")
- During a scene on the ship, Shepherd Wong says, "Men, we're on water. I don't want any of you walking too far to the left or to the right. Remember the training films we saw about how people sink."
- About two-thirds of the way through the film, the projector stops once again, and hands appear in the light and make shadow puppets. It's "Dolores" and "Max" (Woody and Louise Lasser) fooling around in the projection room.
- At the end of the film, stripper China Lee does a striptease while the credits roll, and at the conclusion of an "Eye Chart" scroll (for those who were actually watching the credits instead of the striptease), Woody says, "I promised I'd put her in the film. Somewhere."

Don't Drink the Water

- Father Drobney puts on a magic show for the Hollanders while they're trapped in the American embassy in Vulgaria.

Take the Money and Run

• The entire film is a phony documentary, foreshadowing and setting the stage for Woody's much more ambitious and technically sophisticated pseudodocumentary, 1983's *Zelig*.

• We see rare film footage of Virgil's "grandfather," who after being struck in the head by a foul ball at a Washington Senators' game, became convinced he was Kaiser Wilhelm. The footage seen is actual old newsreel coverage of the real Kaiser Wilhelm.

• We see black-and-white film footage of happy-go-lucky people enjoying 1956, including skiing and swimming scenes; bizarre scenes of a "wacky" family having a picnic underwater; a giant woman getting into a VW bug (and then her husband driving off with her sticking up through the sunroof); two kids and a man taking golf swings; and Richard Nixon (at Camp David?) fishing with President Eisenhower.

• A running gag throughout the film is that Virgil plays cello with the Philharmonic.

• During Virgil's job interview with an insurance company, he tells the interviewer he once worked with products, and they then play an abbreviated version of the television game show "What's My Line?" as the interviewer tries to guess what kind of product Virgil worked with.

• Before the big bank robbery, Virgil shows his fellow robbers films taken surreptitiously of the bank (the camera was hidden in a loaf of rye bread), but before they begin, there's a "boring short" called *Trout Fishing in Quebec*.

• The plan Virgil concocts to rob the bank involves their pulling up to the bank and pretending they're making a movie. An ex-con named Fritz (who said he worked with John Gilbert and Valentino) will "play" the director.

• We see Virgil's final capture on film. A freelance photographer named Stanley got the only pictures of Virgil being arrested by Eddie Haynes.

Bananas

• The film opens with Howard Cosell anchoring live "Wide World of Sports" coverage of a political assassination.

• When Fielding asks his coworker Norma out on a date, she tells him she can't; she's having some people over that evening to watch pornographic movies. Fielding then asks her, "Do you need an usher?"

• A rebel soldier is tortured by having the entire score of *The Naughty Marionette* played for him.

• During the dinner with the president of San Marcos, an orchestra plays in mime.

• During the battle scene in San Marcos, a baby carriage rolls unattended down the steps of a municipal building, re-creating the same scene seen in Sergei Eisenstein's 1925 silent classic *The Battleship Potemkin.*

• Roger Grimsby anchors the "News at Six" and gives details on Fielding's Mellish's "subversive imposter" trial.

• A commercial for "New Testament" cigarettes (with the "revolutionary incense filter") is inserted into Roger Grimsby's newscast.

• The film ends with Howard Cosell's live "Wide World of Sports" wedding night coverage of the sexual consummation of Fielding and Nancy's marriage. ("Well, Howard, it all went by so fast. I just had no idea that it would be so quick, really. I was expecting a longer bout.")

Play It Again, Sam

• The film opens with Allan Felix in a theater watching *Casablanca.* (In the play he was watching *The Maltese Falcon.*)

• There is a giant poster of Bogart's *Across the Pacific* in Allan's bedroom.

• Allan is a film reviewer for a magazine called *Film Weekly.* (In the play it was *Film Quarterly.*)

• Allan's date Sharon was the only female actress (with nine men) in a sixteen-millimeter underground "arty" film called *Gang Bang.*

• While on their date, Julie takes Allan to a biker bar, where he gets into a fight. Allan had wanted to go to the Erich von Stroheim film festival.

• Allan asks the biker who comes on to Julie if he has seen the new production of *The Trojan Women.* (In 1972 [the year the film version of *Play It Again, Sam* was released], the Greek-American film *The Trojan Women* was also released. The film was directed by Michael Cacoyannis and starred Katharine Hepburn, Vanessa Redgrave, Genevieve Bujold, and Irene Pappas.)

• Allan invites Linda to his apartment for dinner while Dick is in Cleveland, telling her that *The Big Sleep* is on the late show. (In the play no film is mentioned.)

• Allan invites Linda to see the new Truffaut film (*Two English Girls?*) playing at the Regency. (In the play it was a Godard film.)

• Linda tells Allan she'd like to see the Ida Lupino film (*They Drive by Night?*) playing on Channel 4.

• Allan remarks to Bogart that Fred Astaire looks great in tails, but he (Allan) just looks silly. (Woody eventually dons tails in one of the "Sandy Bates" films shown at the film festival weekend in *Stardust Memories.*)

• Allan has *Casablanca* and *Key Largo* posters in his apartment.

• As Allan and Linda kiss, scenes from *Casablanca* are intercut.

• Allan walks by a theater showing the Vittorio de Sica film *Le Coppie,* which triggers his "Italian bakery" confrontation fantasy with Dick.

• Allan recites Bogart's final speech from *Casablanca* to Linda.

• The film ends with "As Times Goes By" from *Casablanca* playing on the soundtrack.

Everything You Always Wanted to Know About Sex* (*But Were Afraid to Ask)

• In Segment 5, "What Are Sex Perverts?" we see a commercial for a men's hair product.

• Also in Segment 5, we view a complete episode of the TV show "What's My Perversion?"

• In Segment 7, "What Happens During Ejaculation?" various video displays detail the functioning of Sidney's various bodily organs and systems.

Sleeper

• Miles watches old videotape of Howard Cosell and Richard Nixon.

• We see television footage of the leader of the future society.

• The doctors watch a video presentation about the death of the Leader and the rescue of his nose.

Love and Death

• Boris and the other soldiers see a hygiene play. ("A puckish satire . . .")

• Boris attends a performance of Mozart's opera *The Magic Flute*.

The Front

• The film opens with newsreel footage of fifties scenes.

• An Old Gold commercial is on a TV monitor the first time Howard meets Florence Barrett.

• We see prebroadcast monitor scenes of "Grand Central," then the opening sequence in which Hecky the Hackie talks to the audience.

• Alfred watches "Grand Central" on his television at home.

• A family watches "Grand Central" while eating dinner.

• We see the "Grand Central" credits roll ("Teleplay by Howard Prince") in the diner where Howie works.

• In a bar Hecky watches Howard being interviewed on a television talk show.

• We see the end of the last song ("Anything for a Laugh") of Hecky's mountain resort show.

• Howard tells Florence he wanted to get tickets to a Paul Robeson concert, but it was the same night as a basketball game, so he didn't.

Annie Hall

• We watch Alvy Singer on Dick Cavett's talk show.
• Annie and Alvy plan to see Ingmar Bergman's *Face to Face* but Alvy won't go in because Annie arrives two minutes late:

Alvy I'm sorry, I can't. I've gotta see a picture exactly from the start to the finish 'cause I'm anal.
Annie Hah. That's a polite word for what you are.

• The obnoxious know-it-all film "critic" behind Alvy and Annie in the theater lobby discusses Fellini's new film (1974's *Amarcord*, perhaps?) as well as *La Strada, Juliet of the Spirits,* and *Satyricon.*
• Annie and Alvy see *The Sorrow and the Pity.*
• We watch Alvy performing standup comedy at an Adlai Stevenson political rally.
• During a flashback of Annie's old boyfriend Jerry, we see the marquee of the Plaza Theater behind him announcing Marilyn Monroe in the 1961 film *The Misfits.*
• Alvy watches the New York Knicks play the Cleveland Cavaliers on television at an intellectuals' party his wife Robin (*Take the Money and Run*'s Janet Margolin) dragged him to.
• Annie sings "It Had to Be You" in front of a nightclub audience that Alvy acknowledges was "a tad restless."
• Alvy performs standup comedy at the University of Wisconsin.
• We see an animated version of *Snow White and the Seven Dwarfs* in which Annie is the Wicked Queen.
• Annie sings "Seems Like Old Times" in front of a more responsive nightclub audience.
• Annie and Alvy see *The Sorrow and the Pity*—again.
• Alvy agrees to go to California to give an award on a TV show.
• When Alvy first arrives in California, he and Rob pass a movie theater announcing the films *House of Exorcism* and *Messiah of Evil.*
• We watch Rob's "laughtrack-enhanced" TV sitcom.
• Rob once acted in *Richard II* in Central Park.
• Annie and an escort see *The Sorrow and the Pity.*
• When Alvy tells us that he realizes he made a mistake by breaking up with Annie, he has just come out of a movie theater.
• While in Los Angeles, Alvy tells Annie he's trying to write a play.
• Annie tells Alvy that Tony is up for several Grammys.
• Alvy and an unnamed date (played by Sigourney Weaver) see *The Sorrow and the Pity.*

• We watch Alvy's "first" play, an obviously autobiographical account of his trip to California to win Annie back—only in the play he and Annie get back together. As he put it, "Whatta you want? It was my first play."

Interiors

• The first time we see Mike, he is dictating notes into a tape recorder for a film documentary about Chairman Mao.
   • Flyn is an actress who is preparing to shoot a made-for-TV movie.
   • On a plane flight, Arthur views a (bad) film Flyn made.
   • Eve watches a religious program in bed, during which an interviewer asks a boy, "What nationality were you at the time of your birth?" and the boy replies, "Hebrew." (This might be the only real joke in the film.)
   • Arthur, Pearl, Renata, Frederick, and Joey discuss a play about Algerians they had all seen.

Manhattan

• Ike's favorite film is *Grand Illusion.*
   • Ike writes a TV show called "Human Beings Wow!"
   • Ike and Tracy watch a movie on TV about a cab driver, which starred a guy with an unseemly toupee.
   • The late show the evening Ike and Tracy watch the "toupee" movie has a W. C. Fields film.
   • Ike, Mary, Yale, and Emily attend a classical concert.
   • Ike tells Tracy, "We'll always have Paris" (which is a line from *Casablanca*).
   • Mary and Ike see Inagaki's *Chushingura* and Dovzhenko's *Earth.*

Stardust Memories

• The studio executives screen Sandy's new film (for which they shoot a new "Jazz Heaven" ending).
   • Sandy is guest of honor at a "Film-Culture Weekend."
   • Sandy's film, in which he sings "Three Little Words" in top hat and tails, is shown during the weekend.
   • Sandy's film, in which Sydney Finklestein's hostility escapes, is shown during the weekend.
   • Sandy, Jack, and Daisy go to a cabaret.
   • Sandy directs Dorrie in his film, *Suppression.*
   • Sandy's science fiction film, in which he switches Doris's and Rita's brain, is shown during the weekend. (This is the film which had a scene in

a wax museum which Tony Roberts denied was "an homage to Vincent Price's horror movie *The House of Wax*" [actually just called *House of Wax*] because they "just stole the idea outright.")

• Sandy and Daisy see *The Bicycle Thief.*

• We see Sandy directing, and with Dorrie acting in, a film in which he wears a monk's costume.

• We attend a memorial service for the "dead" Sandy in which scenes from the film *The Creation of the Universe* are shown.

• One of Sandy's films wins an Academy Award, and Sandy is nominated for an Oscar for his portrayal of God. (This harks back to the scene in Woody's 1979 film *Manhattan* in which Ike and Yale have an argument about Ike's narcissistic self-righteousness:

> **Yale** You are so self-righteous, you know. I mean, we're just people, we're just human beings, you know. You think you're God!
> **Ike** I gotta model myself after someone!)

• We see the audience leaving a screening of the final version of what is assumed to be Sandy's "Jazz Heaven" film.

A Midsummer Night's Sex Comedy

• Andrew, Ariel, Dulcy, Leopold, Maxwell, and Adrian witness the image of a ghostly couple projected out of Andrew's "spirit ball."

Zelig

• Early in the film, during a montage of scenes of the 1920s, we spot the Paramount Theater.

• We see newsreel footage from the 1920s which includes a biplane, couples dancing, President Coolidge, Al Capone, and weird stunts.

• Footage is shown of a black band performing in a speakeasy.

• Zelig was the son of a Yiddish actor named Morris Zelig, who performed as Puck in an Orthodox version of *A Midsummer Night's Dream.*

• We watch footage of Zelig's father performing as Puck.

• We glimpse "quick cuts of a bygone America" (from *Three Films of Woody Allen*), which include eight scenes with a total of nineteen people and two dogs listening to the radio.

• We see clips of "Man in the Street" reactions to the phenomenon known as Leonard Zelig.

• A "Chameleon Dance Contest" is held at the Varsity Dance Hall.

• A large city parade passes before us in which there is an "anti-Zelig" faction.

- Martin Geist and Ruth Zelig tour with Zelig as a carnival oddity billed as the Human Chameleon.
- We see several excerpts from the 1935 Warner Bros. film about Leonard Zelig called *The Changing Man*.
- During the height of his popularity, Zelig appears at a theater, billed *above* Eddie Cantor.
- Zelig poses for photos in front of Graumann's Chinese Theater.
- Zelig is offered a Hollywood film contract.
- Clara Bow invites Zelig to her home for a private weekend and "tells him to bring all his personalities."
- Zelig appears in Parisian music halls.
- At the Folies Bergère, Josephine Baker does her version of the Chameleon Dance.
- Zelig visits the Parisian nightclub Bricktop's.
- We see Fanny Brice serenading Zelig.
- Footage of Jazz Age events includes men twirling themselves in giant hoops and unicycle riders.
- Footage shows Pope Pius XI in St. Peter's Square in Rome.
- We see the filmed footage of Paul Deghuee's recordings of Dr. Fletcher's White Room sessions with Zelig.
- Eudora Fletcher and her fiancé— go to Broadway and a nightclub.
- We see newsreel footage of coverage announcing Dr. Fletcher's "cure" of Zelig.
- Footage is shown of old film stars, including Marion Davies, Charlie Chaplin, Tom Mix, Adolphe Menjou, Claire Windsor, Dolores Del Rio, James Cagney, and Carole Lombard.
- We see footage of Zelig on the boardwalk in Atlantic City, sparring with a boxer; in Times Square; and at an outdoor art show.
- Showgirl Lita Fox states that she was married to Zelig, and that Zelig said he was an actor.
- We see the Vilification Woman in a radio station condemning Leonard Zelig as a "bad moral influence." (She says, "In keeping with a pure society, I say, lynch the little hebe.")
- While in hiding, Zelig plays guitar with a Mexican mariachi band.
- As we listen to an older Dr. Fletcher talk about how much she missed Zelig when he was a fugitive, we see a theater marquee in New York City.
- While the older Dr. Fletcher continues to speak, we see the Loew's State moviehouse in New York City advertising *Grand Hotel* on its marquee.
- Newsreel footage of Zelig and Hitler is shown.
- We see home movies of the marriage ceremony of Zelig and Eudora Fletcher.

Broadway Danny Rose

- We see several of Lou Canova's stage performances.
- Danny Rose performs his standup routine for a Catskills audience.
- We watch Canova on "The Joe Franklin Show."
- Milton Berle is putting together a television show about stars of the fifties.
- A scene from *The Bicycle Thief* is alluded to when Tina visits a fortune teller.
- Tina and Danny run into Ray Webb, the actor, while he's filming a commercial.
- Tina and Danny try to elude mobsters in the Macy's Thanksgiving Day Parade float warehouse.
- Tina and Ray attend the Macy's Thanksgiving Day Parade.
- Lou moves to Las Vegas and California to perform his act.

The Purple Rose of Cairo

- Cecilia spends much of her time in the Jewel Theater watching a film called *The Purple Rose of Cairo,* starring "Gil Shepherd, Beatrice Kelly, Sidney Oliver, and Kate Payson."
- Cecilia tells her sister about the film she saw last week at the Jewel starring Jane Froman and James Melton. In the film Melton was a hotel porter who became a radio singer, and then an opera singer.
- Jane tells Cecilia that she especially liked the film *Okay America* with Lew Ayres. Cecilia tells her she saw *Okay America* twice. (*Okay America* was a 1932 film starring Ayres, and Mia and Stephanie Farrow's mother, Maureen O'Sullivan.)
- Gil Shepherd's next role is supposed to be Charles Lindbergh.
- Gil Shepherd's other films included *Broadway Bachelors, Honeymoon in Haiti,* and *Dancing Doughboys.*
- After Gil and Cecilia sing "I'm Alabamy Bound" in the music store, they perform a short scene from *Dancing Doughboys.*
- At one point, Tom takes Cecilia inside *The Purple Rose of Cairo,* and she turns black and white.
- Tom Baxter and Gil Shepherd argue over the role of Tom Baxter. Tom asserts that he could have been played by Frederic March or Leslie Howard. The Countess tells Tom, "The part's too insignificant to attract a major star."
- At the end of the film, after being betrayed by Gil Shepherd, Cecilia goes into the Jewel and watches *Top Hat* with Fred Astaire and Ginger Rogers.

Hannah and Her Sisters

- At Thanksgiving dinner, we learn that Hannah has just completed a performance as Nora in Ibsen's *A Doll's House.*

• On her way home from Thanksgiving dinner, Lee's cab drives by the Winter Garden theater where *Cats* is playing.

• Mickey is a television producer and the first time we meet him he's arguing with a Standards and Practices guy over a "Pope/child molestation" sketch.

• Mickey's ex-partner Norman moves to California and becomes a very successful TV producer.

• Hannah tells Mickey she's trying to persuade Elliot to produce a play.

• Lee tells Elliot that she and Frederick went to the Caravaggio exhibition at the Met.

• Norman and Mickey once won an Emmy for a television show they had written together.

• Holly and David attend Puccini's opera *Manon Lescaut* at the Metropolitan Opera House. (The segment from the opera was actually filmed at the Regio Theater of Turin, Italy.)

• Frederick's potential customer, rocker Dusty Frye, had six gold records.

• The day Hannah's mother Norma fell off the wagon, she and Evan had been making a commercial at the mayor's office.

• While Elliot and Lee were together in the hotel for the first time, Frederick was home watching TV. He saw a documentary on Auschwitz, a deodorant commercial, wrestling, a beauty contest, and fundamentalist preachers.

• On their first date Mickey and Holly saw the 39 Steps at a rock club, and then Bobby Short at the Carlyle Club.

• April and Holly both audition for a singing role in a Broadway musical.

• Evan and Norma once took a trip to a show in Buffalo.

• Holly becomes a writer and turns out two (very good) scripts.

• After Mickey accidentally fires his rifle while contemplating suicide, he goes out, stops at a theater, and sees *Duck Soup* with the Marx Brothers. This experience somehow triggers in Mickey a newfound joy of living.

• Hannah agrees to play Desdemona in Shakespeare's *Othello* on public television.

Radio Days

• The Needlemans had gone to a movie when their house was broken into by the two burglars who won the jackpot on the radio program "Guess That Tune."

• We see one of Little Joe's favorite singers singing "Let's All Sing Like the Birdies Sing."

• Little Joe's mother listens to the radio program "Breakfast with Irene and Roger." Irene and Roger had attended an opening night: Rodgers and Hart were there, as was Cole Porter.

• Irene and Roger were planning to see the new Moss Hart play, and the next morning told their audience about it.

• Little Joe's favorite radio show is "The Masked Avenger."

• Little Joe's parents complain to the rabbi that Little Joe spends all his time listening to "The Lone Ranger," "The Shadow," and "The Masked Avenger."

• Bea's date with Mr. Manulis is interrupted by Orson Welles's "War of the Worlds" radio broadcast.

• Roger (of "Breakfast with Irene and Roger") tells "Richard" (Rodgers) that the "show at the Morosco" was magnificent. (Woody's first play, *Don't Drink the Water*, opened on November 17, 1966, at the Morosco Theater.)

• Irene informs Roger that she saw Ernest Hemingway at the bar at the King Cole Room.

• We see a Latin orchestra performing at the King Cole Room.

• We see a Latin singer perform "Tico, Tico."

• During Sally's romantic rendezvous with Roger on the roof of the King Cole Room building, the "Loew's" sign can be seen in the distance.

• Uncle Abe's favorite radio program was "Bill Kern's Favorite Sports Legends."

• Ceil's favorite program was a ventriloquist show. This drove Abe crazy: "How do you know he's not moving his lips!?"

• Ruthie loved a "romantic boy crooner" program.

• Little Joe's mother and father's favorite radio show was "The Court of Human Emotions."

• At the circus, Little Joe and his parents meet the fourteen-year-old mathematical genius star of the radio program "The Whiz Kids."

• Aunt Bea and a date take Little Joe to Radio City Music Hall where they see *It's a Wonderful Life*.

• Rocco and his mother get Sally a job on radio (they ask an "unrefusable favor") in a production of Chekhov's stories.

• We see Sally performing "I Don't Wanna Walk Without You" at a USO show.

• We watch Biff Baxter perform in a radio play about the German and Japanese "Axis rats."

• After seeing Miss Gordon naked, Little Joe and his friends discuss their favorite movie starlets: one picks Rita Hayworth, another Betty Grable, and another Dana Andrews. He is stunned to find out that Dana is a man.

• We see Kitty Carlisle Hart performing "They're Either Too Young or Too Old."

• Tess likes to listen to romantic soap operas on the radio.

• Bea and her gay date, Fred, go to a movie on their first date.

- We see Sally singing the "Re-Lax" laxative jingle.
- After taking diction lessons, Sally White ends up with her own radio show, "The Gay White Way." Her first exclusive was about Clark Gable. She also talked about Rita Hayworth at the Copacabana.
- Aunt Bea and her date Sy take Little Joe to his first radio show, "The Silver Dollar." Bea ends up a contestant on the show and wins fifty silver dollars. She buys Little Joe a chemistry set with part of her winnings.
- We see a band performing at a Broadway dance palace where Bea takes Little Joe and Sy with the rest of her silver-dollar winnings.
- The country gathers round the radio to learn the sad fate of Polly Phelps, the little girl who fell down a well.
- We watch Monica Charles performing "You'd Be So Nice to Come Home To" at the King Cole Room on New Year's Eve.

September

- Diane tells Peter that she didn't date Errol Flynn (as rumor would have it) because she was too old when she met him. She was sixteen: "For Errol, fifteen was over-the-hill."
- Before Diane invited the Richardsons to the house for drinks, Lane and Peter had plans to drive into town to see the new Kurosawa film.

Another Woman

- Claire is an actress who is starring in a play staged by her husband, Jack. When Marion runs into Jack and Claire outside a theater, the play is closing.
- When Marion, Claire, and Jack stop for drinks, Marion and Jack discuss opera, theater, and Brecht. Jack once staged a production of Brecht's *Mother Courage* that Marion had seen. (She didn't like the translation.)
- Marion has a dream in which Jack puts on a play of her life and Claire plays the lead.
- Marion once gave Sam a white mask from a French production of the opera *La Gioconda*.
- Ken, Marion, Lydia, and Mark attend a concert, during which Marion is very restless.
- On the evening of the day Marion sees Ken and Lydia in a restaurant, Ken and Marion were supposed to go to the opera. Marion refuses to go.
- Marion remembers running into Larry at a box office where they were both buying theater tickets. Larry later used the scene in his novel.

Oedipus Wrecks (in New York Stories)

- When Sheldon's mother and his Aunt Ceil visit Sheldon's office, they have just been to see *Cats*. Sheldon had bought them the tickets. (*Cats* is also referred to in a cab scene in *Hannah and Her Sisters*. See above.)

• Sheldon, Lisa, Sheldon's mother, and Lisa's kids attend a magic show, during which Sadie disappears.

• Sheldon and Lisa watch television coverage of his mother's appearance in the New York City skies.

• We see Ed Koch in a television interview about Sadie.

Crimes and Misdemeanors

• Cliff and his niece Jenny watch *Mr. and Mrs. Smith* in a theater.

• Lester tells Cliff and Wendy about a new TV series he produced. Lisa Crosby plays a lawyer for the ACLU, and she's married to a guy who writes for a conservative magazine.

• Lester dictates an idea for a series to be shot in New York about a high-profile builder who is always trying to realize grandiose ideas, à la Donald Trump.

• The documentary on Lester is part of Public Television's "Creative Minds" series.

• Cliff wants to make a documentary on Dr. Levy, the philosophy professor.

• Lester has "a closetful of Emmys."

• Lester dictates "Idea for farce: A poor loser agrees to do the story of a great man's life and in the process comes to learn great values."

• After Lester's first "If it bends, it's funny . . . " line, Cliff tells him he shot ten rolls of film on his first question. Lester then says he has to get to CBS.

• Cliff shows Halley his footage of Dr. Levy, in which the doctor discusses the paradox of the early Israelites' conception of a God that demanded moral behavior and yet commanded that Abraham sacrifice his son to Him.

• Cliff and Halley go to the movies in the afternoon and see *This Gun for Hire.*

• Cliff films Lester walking the streets of New York from the backseat of a station wagon. We see him peering through a camera as he films.

• Cliff runs backward with a camera filming Lester walking through a college campus.

• Cliff films Lester in the back seat of a limousine.

• Cliff films Lester during a staff meeting in his office.

• In Cliff's screening room, Cliff and Halley watch footage of Dr. Levy talking about the emotional process of falling in love.

• Also in the screening room, Cliff and Halley watch Cliff's print of *Singing in the Rain.*

• Lester tells Cliff and Wendy that he's putting together a special on jazz.

• Halley had an idea that Lester liked: she wanted to produce a different Chekhov story every month.

• Lester used to edit newsreel footage but quit because it was depressing.

• One afternoon Cliff and Jenny see *Happy Go Lucky* at a theater.

• After Dr. Levy commits suicide, Cliff watches some of his footage of the doctor speaking.

• Cliff had 600,000 feet of film on Dr. Levy at the time of the doctor's suicide. He says he'll cut it up and make it into guitar picks.

• Lester and Cliff watch Cliff's cut of his documentary on Lester, during which we see Lester telling one of his staff members that a story on the homeless is five pages too long, and that he wants a guy with cancer off a show. Also during the film, we see footage of Mussolini and Francis the Talking Mule.

• After Halley tells Cliff she's going to London for three or four months, Cliff says he feels as if he's been handed a prison sentence, and then we see him and his niece Jenny watching the film *The Last Gangster.*

Alice

• Nancy Brill buys scripts ("blood and guts stuff") for a big cable TV station.

• Joe and his ex-wife watch commercials in her office.

• Alice, Joe, and their kids attend the Big Apple circus.

• Perry's mom invites Alice's daughter to watch *The Little Mermaid* in Perry's daddy's screening room.

• Alice and Doug attend an evening in honor of Mother Teresa, during which they watch a documentary on her work.

Scenes from a Mall

• Nick and Deborah watch the Home Shopping Club on television while they make love.

• In a bookstore in the mall, Nick and Deborah see a videotape about Deborah's new book.

• Nick and Deborah chat in a line at a mall theater that is showing *Predator II, The Godfather, III, Rocky V,* and *Salaam Bombay!*

• Nick has an anxiety attack at the theater.

• Nick and Deborah go in to see *Salaam Bombay!* from which we see scenes.

• Nick performs oral sex on Deborah in the theater.

• After Deborah tells Nick about her affair, she goes to the bookstore and watches the video of the doctor she's having an affair with, but this time she hallucinates him telling everyone that he's having an affair with her, three times a week.

• Deborah says she and Nick never made love unless the television was on.

CHAPTER 13

"This Is Really a Great City"

Big Apple Landmarks in Annie Hall, Manhattan, and Hannah and Her Sisters

---

I'm definitely a child of the city streets. . . .
In Manhattan, I know the town.
Woody Allen

PROBABLY no other contemporary artist is more intimately associated with a specific location and its environs than Woody Allen is with New York, New York, the town so nice, they named it twice.

Woody Allen is a native New Yorker and proud of it.

In this chapter we'll visit New York (and vicinity) locations Woody used for the "New York trio"—his three most "NYC-specific" films, *Annie Hall, Manhattan,* and *Hannah and Her Sisters.* When I could, I supplied addresses for specific buildings or businesses.

Woody Allen, Native New Yorker

Some of Woody's personal bites of the Big Apple:

• Woody's first apartment after he married Harlene Rosen was at 110 East Sixty-first Street.

• Woody has an apartment on Fifth Avenue on Central Park East.

• Woody plays clarinet every Monday evening with the New Orleans Funeral and Ragtime Orchestra at Michael's Pub (211 East Fifty-fifth in Midtown Manhattan).

• Woody and Mia's relationship started after a lunch at Lutèce (249 East Fiftieth).

• Mia Farrow has an apartment across Central Park from Woody on Central Park West.

• Woody is a regular at Elaine's Restaurant (1702 Second Avenue).

• Woody has an office and editing room complex, complete with his own screening room, on Park Avenue. The screening room is small; it has a dark-green carpet, and dark-green velvet lines its walls. The room contains about ten swivel chairs, and a sofa. The cutting room Woody has used since *Manhattan* is to the left; there is a small kitchen to the right.

• Woody occasionally likes to drop into the Regency Theater.

• Allan Felix's apartment in *Play It Again, Sam* was on West Tenth Street.

Annie Hall

Annie Hall, Woody's breakthrough film, led us on a tour of the New York Woody loves. A great part of the film's fun was seeing the actual theaters, streets, and neighborhoods Woody lives and works in.

• Alvy's childhood home was in the Coney Island section of Brooklyn.

• During a flashback to Alvy's childhood, we see Steve's Famous Clam Bar at Coney Island.

• Alvy tells Rob about meeting with some guys at NBC (in Rockefeller Center).

• Annie and Alvy almost went in to see Ingmar Bergman's *Face to Face* at the Beekman Theater (East Sixty-fifth Street in Midtown Manhattan).

• Alvy's first wife, Allison Portchnik, was raised on Central Park West.

• Alvy and Annie (almost) make lobsters at a beach house in the Hamptons on Long Island.

• Annie and Alvy see *The Sorrow and the Pity* at the New Yorker Theater.

• Alvy, Annie, Rob, and Janet play tennis at the Wall Street Tennis Club.

• Alvy and Annie rank on passersby in Central Park.

• Alvy remembers auditioning as a writer for an obnoxious comic in an office on Broadway in Times Square.

• Alvy briefly attended New York University in Washington Square in Greenwich Village.

• Pam, Alvy's date, once saw Mick Jagger at Madison Square Garden.

• During a flashback, we see Alvy's father defending their cleaning woman, who had been stealing. The cleaning woman was from Harlem.

• Alvy walks the FDR Drive after breaking up with Annie.

• Alvy runs into Annie at the Thalia Theater (on the Upper West Side of Manhattan).

• After Annie moved back to New York, she lived in Soho.

Manhattan

Woody must have had a ball making *Manhattan*. The film is loaded with New York scenes and landmarks, and one can easily imagine the sheer pleasure he must have had filming all of his favorite earthly places.

• The film's stunning opening visual montage shows black-and-white scenes of Manhattan, including the New York City skyline, the Empire State Building, the Brooklyn Bridge, Broadway, Park Avenue, Central Park, Fifth Avenue, the Plaza Hotel (Fifth Avenue and Fifty-ninth Street), Gucci (Fifth Avenue), Sotheby Parke Bernet (1334 York Avenue), the Guggenheim Museum (Fifth Avenue and Eighty-ninth Street), the Fifty-ninth Street Bridge, Yankee Stadium (in the Bronx), the Delacorte Theater (Central Park at Eighty-first), and Radio City Music Hall.

• The film opens with Ike, Tracy, Yale, and Emily having drinks at Elaine's (1702 Second Avenue), a favorite haunt of Woody's.

• Ike confronts his ex-wife Jill outside the Time-Life Building (Rockefeller Center) about the book she's planning to write.

• Ike wants to take Tracy to the Bleecker Street Cinema (144 Bleecker Street) to see a Veronica Lake movie.

• Ike and Tracy meet Yale and Mary at the Guggenheim Museum (Fifth Avenue and Eighty-ninth Street).

• Tracy and Isaac shop at Dean and DeLuca's Food Shop.

• Ike tells Yale about quitting his job in the Rizzoli Bookstore.

• Ike tells Yale that because he quit his job he won't be able to take the Southampton house.

• Ike attends a reception in support of the Equal Rights Amendment at the Museum of Modern Art's Sculpture Gallery (Eleven West Fifty-third Street).

• After spending a night talking, Ike and Mary sit on a bench and look at the Fifty-ninth Street Bridge.

• Yale and Mary meet at Bloomingdale's (1000 Third Avenue at Fifty-ninth Street) for an afternoon rendezvous.

• Ike buys Willy a toy boat at FAO Schwarz (Fifth Avenue).

- Ike and Willy lunch at the Russian Tea Room (150 West Fifty-seventh Street).
- Ike and Mary get caught in an electrical storm in Central Park.
- Ike and Mary take shelter from the storm in the Hayden Planetarium (Central Park West and Eightieth Street) in Central Park.
- On their way home from Emily's parents' house, Yale and Emily get off the George Washington Bridge and drive down the Henry Hudson Parkway.
- Ike and Tracy have pizza at John's Pizza in Greenwich Village (302 East Twelfth Street).
- Ike and Tracy take a carriage ride through Central Park while "He Loves and She Loves" plays on the soundtrack.
- Mary and Yale break up at the Stanhope Café.
- Ike and Yale play squash at the Uptown Squash Club.
- Mary and Ike visit the Whitney Museum (Madison Avenue and Seventy-fifth Street).
- Ike and Mary eat at a restaurant in Brooklyn (they had Chianti from Warsaw) and return home via the West Side Highway.
- Tracy attends the Dalton School.
- Mary and Ike go boating on the lake in Central Park and Ike pulls up a handful of mud and dirt out of the water.
- Ike and Mary peruse the delicacies in Zabar's window.
- Yale buys his Porsche from a guy in Brooklyn Heights.
- Yale calls Mary from a phone booth on Park Avenue.
- Ike tells Yale and Emily that Viking Press (Hudson Street) loved his book.
- After Yale buys the Porsche, he, Ike, Mary, and Emily drive north, and then over the Tappan Zee Bridge to Nyack, New York, where they find copies of Jill's new book.
- Ike plays football with Willie ("The Divorced Fathers and Sons All Stars") in a Central Park field.
- Ike and Emily lunch at the Soho Charcuterie.
- While hurrying to stop Tracy from leaving for London, Ike races down Second Avenue in the Yorkville section of Manhattan and past Gramercy Park to Tracy's apartment building.

Hannah and Her Sisters

Viewing *Hannah and Her Sisters,* you almost don't realize that it's in color. It has the same magical black-and-white "Gershwin" New York feel to it that *Manhattan* has, and it was a major triumph for Woody. We're on home ground again, and Woody again does New York, New York, justice.

- Hannah's apartment is actually Mia Farrow's apartment in New York City on Central Park West.

- When Lee leaves Hannah's Thanksgiving dinner party, she takes a cab down Broadway, and passes the Winter Garden Theater (1634 Broadway).
- Mickey sees Dr. Abel, who has an office on the West Side of Manhattan.
- Holly tells David she saw *Ernani* at the Met (the Metropolitan Opera House at Lincoln Center).
- David has a private box at the Metropolitan Opera House (at Lincoln Center).
- When asked about his favorite New York buildings, David takes April and Holly on a tour and shows them the Dakota Apartments (One West Seventy-second); the Graybar Building on Lexington Avenue; an ornate building on Seventh Avenue and Fifty-eighth Street; an old building with bulging, embellished windows on West Forty-fourth Street; the Chrysler Building; Abigail Adams's Old Stone House; and the Pomander Walk (off Broadway on the Upper West Side).
- Holly lives in Chelsea (between Greenwich Village and the Lower West Side).
- Elliot runs past the Canal Lumber Company (and other Soho buildings) and through the Soho streets in order to bump "accidentally" into Lee.
- Lee takes Elliot to the Pageant Bookstore in Soho.
- Lee tells Elliot she and Frederick went to the Caravaggio exhibition at the Metropolitan Museum of Art (Fifth Avenue and Eighty-second Street).
- Mickey has his sophisticated audiometry tests at Mount Sinai Hospital (Fifth Avenue and One Hundredth Street).
- Mickey and Hannah walk Grove Street in Greenwich Village (between Seventh Avenue South and Hudson Street) and discuss Mickey's infertility.
- Frederick and Lee live in Soho (just south of Greenwich Village, west of Little Italy).
- Dusty Frye, the rock star, buys a house in Southampton on Long Island.
- Evan and Norma live in an apartment building on the West Side of Manhattan.
- Elliot and Lee have their illicit trysts at the St. Regis Hotel (Fifth Avenue and Fifty-fifth Street).
- Mickey and Holly see Bobby Short at the Carlyle Café (at 983 Madison Avenue on the Upper East Side) in the Carlyle Hotel (at Thirty-five East Seventy-sixth Street).
- Holly and Hannah shop in a Soho boutique for clothes for Holly's audition.
- Holly and Lee have a catering job for Mr. Morris Levine's eightieth birthday party on Riverside Drive (or Riverside Memorial Chapel, "depending on his health").
- After Lee breaks up with Frederick, she takes classes at Columbia University (Broadway and 116th).

• Mickey talks to a Hare Krishna in Central Park.

• Mickey runs into Holly at Tower Records (692 Broadway at Fourth Street).

• Mickey and Holly stroll a path in Central Park.

• Mickey shambles into the Metro Cinema (Broadway at West Ninety-ninth) after his failed suicide attempt.

CHAPTER 14

When Harry Met Sally . . .

The "Woody Allen Movie" Not Made by Woody Allen

Rob Reiner and Nora Ephron's Homage to Woody Allen

Alvy   I'm gonna have a corned beef.
Annie   Yeah . . . oh, and I'm gonna have a pastrami on white bread with, uh, mayonnaise and tomatoes and lettuce.
                      from *Annie Hall*

Waiter   Who ordered a plain pie?
Ike   Uh, me.
Waiter   So you must be anchovies, sausage, mushrooms, garlic, and green peppers.
Tracy   Mm-hm.
Ike   You forgot the coconut.
                      from *Manhattan*

Harry   I'll have a number three.
Sally   I'd like the chef's salad, please, with the oil and vinegar on the side, and the apple pie à la mode. But I'd like the pie heated, and I don't want the ice cream on top, I want it on the side, and I'd like strawberry instead of vanilla if you have it. If not, then no ice cream, just whipped cream, but only if it's real. If it's out of a can, then nothing.
Waitress   Not even the pie?
Sally   No, just the pie, but then not heated.
from *When Harry Met Sally . . .*, screenplay by Nora Ephron

THE OCTOBER 1989 issue of *Premiere* magazine, in "Short Takes," carried a feature called "When Harry Met Woody" (of which the headnote was "What, No Dr. Chomsky?").

The article noted, "Many, many critics have observed that Rob Reiner's latest film, *When Harry Met Sally . . .*, seems incredibly reminiscent of a Woody Allen movie. And why? Just because it features a neurotic relationship that takes place in New York to the tunes of Gershwin, kind of like the one in *Manhattan*? Just because Meg Ryan wears a bowler hat and mannish attire, kind of like Diane Keaton in *Annie Hall*? You could simply chalk it up to coincidence. But we decided that the matter warranted further investigation. Here's what we found."

The article then offered a chart, reproduced here, which detailed the similarities between *When Harry Met Sally . . .* and Woody Allen's films, most notably *Manhattan* and *Annie Hall*. But more connections exist than those delineated in the *Premiere* chart, and they are noted following the chart.

When comparing Woody's films with *When Harry Met Sally . . .*, one may easily conclude that Nora Ephron is the world's biggest Woody Allen fan. Her screenplays (most notably *Heartburn* and *When Harry Met Sally . . .*) are so obviously influenced by Woody's work, that it's clear that we're talking world-class homage. And this influence-admiration-acknowledgment must meet with Woody's approval: Nora Ephron appeared in Woody's 1989 masterpiece *Crimes and Misdemeanors*.

The *Premiere* Magazine *When Harry Met Sally . . .* / Woody Allen Comparison Chart*

Title Sequence

When Harry Met Sally . . .   White letters on a black background
Woody Allen   White letters on a black background (*Annie Hall*)

First, Inauspicious Meeting

When Harry Met Sally . . .   Harry and Sally, graduates of the same college, share a ride from Chicago to New York, during which they argue about such things as the ending of *Casablanca* and whether or not men and women can have a relationship that doesn't include sex; they part agreeing that they can't be friends.
Woody Allen   Isaac and Mary meet at the Guggenheim Museum, where they disagree about the exhibits, Mary's suggestion for the Academy of the

Overrated, and her pronunciation of van Gogh as "van Goch." After they part, Isaac calls her "overbearing" and "pedantic." (*Manhattan*)

Obsession with Death

When Harry Met Sally . . .   Harry to Sally: "Do you think about death? . . . Sure you do. A fleeting thought that drifts in and out of the transom of your mind. I spend hours, I spend days—"
Woody Allen   Alvy to Annie: "I'm obsessed with—with, uh, with death, I think. Big—big subject with me, yeah. I've a very pessimistic view of life." (*Annie Hall*)

Careers

When Harry Met Sally . . .   Sally is a journalist.
Woody Allen   Mary is a journalist. (*Manhattan*)

Fear of Commitment

When Harry Met Sally . . .   Harry on women: "How long do I have to lie here and hold her before I can get up and go home? Is thirty seconds long enough?"
Woody Allen   Isaac on women: "When it comes to relationships with women, I'm the winner of the August Strindberg Award." (*Manhattan*)

Establishing the Relationship on Central Park West

When Harry Met Sally . . .   Harry and Sally stroll past the American Museum of Natural History, discovering that they like each other more than they originally thought.
Woody Allen   Isaac and Mary stroll through the Museum of Natural History's planetarium, discovering that they like each other more than they originally thought. (*Manhattan*)

Chance Encounter with an Ex-Spouse

When Harry Met Sally . . .   Harry and Sally run into Harry's ex-wife, Helen, while shopping for a housewarming gift.
Woody Allen   Isaac and Mary run into Mary's ex-husband, Jeremiah, while shopping for men's clothing. (*Manhattan*). [Also, Allan runs into Nancy in an antique shop while buying a music box for Linda in *Play It Again, Sam*.—sjs]

Late-Night Call for Help

When Harry Met Sally . . .   Sally asks Harry to come over when she is depressed that an old boyfriend is getting married; they sleep together.
Woody Allen   Annie asks Alvy to come over to kill a spider; they sleep together. (*Annie Hall*)

Early-Morning Phone Call

When Harry Met Sally . . . Harry and Sally call their respective best friends shortly after 6 A.M. to talk about the night they spent together.
Woody Allen Isaac calls his best friend at 7:15 A.M. to talk about the night he spent with Mary. (*Manhattan*)

Activities That Aren't as Much Fun Without the Other Person

When Harry Met Sally . . . Harry and Sally buy a Christmas tree together; the next year, Sally awkwardly lugs one home by herself.
Woody Allen Alvy and Annie chase lobsters; it's hilarious. When Alvy does the same thing with another woman, she's impatient. (*Annie Hall*)

The Importance of Putting Your Name in Your Books

When Harry Met Sally . . . Harry: "Put your name in your books. Now, while you're unpacking them, before they get all mixed up together and you can't remember whose is whose."
Woody Allen Alvy: "Whose *Catcher in the Rye* is this? . . . You know, you wrote your name in all my books 'cause you knew this day was gonna come." (*Annie Hall*)

Flashback Sequence

When Harry Met Sally . . . Harry realizes he's in love with Sally during a montage flashback of all the fun times they had.
Woody Allen Alvy realizes why he loved Annie during a montage flashback of all the fun times they had. (*Annie Hall*)

Climactic Jog to Get the Girl

When Harry Met Sally . . . Harry runs to catch Sally at a New Year's Eve party before she leaves.
Woody Allen Isaac runs to catch Tracy at home before she leaves for London. (*Manhattan*)

Our Song

When Harry Met Sally . . . The soundtrack features four renditions of "It Had to Be You."
Woody Allen Annie sings "It Had to Be You." (*Annie Hall*)

In addition to the similarities noted in the *Premiere* chart, numerous other elements in *When Harry Met Sally . . .* confirm the debt to Woody Allen's work:

The Best Friends' Occupation

When Harry Met Sally . . .   Harry's best friend Jess is a writer.
Woody Allen   Isaac's best friend Yale is a writer. (*Manhattan*)

The Bogart Connection

When Harry Met Sally . . .   Harry and Sally first discuss the ending of *Casablanca,* and then watch the end of the film together, in their separate apartments, while talking on the phone.
Woody Allen   Allan Felix is a Humphrey Bogart fanatic, and is visited by the spirit of Bogart throughout *Play It Again, Sam.* The final scene of the film is a direct lift from *Casablanca.*

The Baseball Scenes

When Harry Met Sally . . .   Harry and Jess hit balls at a range while discussing Harry's love life.
Woody Allen   In *Manhattan,* Isaac plays softball with his son in Central Park. (They play on the "Divorced Fathers and Sons All-Stars" team.)

The Airplane Scenes

When Harry Met Sally . . .   Harry and Sally's relationship essentially begins when Harry sees Sally on a plane and they catch up with what they've each been doing for the past five years.
Woody Allen   In *Annie Hall,* Alvy and Annie's relationship essentially ends on an airplane as they fly back from Alvy's disastrous West Coast trip.

The Pivotal Eating Scene(s)

When Harry Met Sally . . .   Sally fakes an orgasm while she and Harry are eating in a deli to prove that Harry's macho and sexist attitude about women could derive from his lovers faking their way through their lovemaking. And Sally reveals during a dinner scene that she thought making love to Harry was a mistake.
Woody Allen   Alvy and Annie truly bond during the lobster scene in *Annie Hall,* and Isaac and Tracy discuss Tracy's future while eating pizza in *Manhattan.*

The Singing Scenes

When Harry Met Sally . . .   Sally sings on a singing machine in a Sharper Image store.
Woody Allen   Annie Hall sings in a nightclub. (*Annie Hall*)

The Documentary Couples

When Harry Met Sally . . .   Seven couples (including Harry and Sally) discuss their relationship between segments of the film.

Woody Allen In the pseudodocumentary film *Take the Money and Run,* Virgil Starkwell's parents (wearing fake nose disguises), as well as other characters, discuss Virgil's life of crime between narrative segments of the film. In Woody's pseudodocumentary film *Zelig,* people discuss Leonard Zelig between film clips of his history. (This seems to have been a parody of *Reds,* which used a similar device to reveal information.)

The Reading Scenes

When Harry Met Sally . . . Harry reads Robert Ludlum and Stephen King.
Woody Allen In *Manhattan,* Emily reads from Jill's book (*Marriage, Divorce, and Self-Hood*) about the breakup of her marriage to Isaac.

The "Days of the Week" Underwear Scenes

When Harry Met Sally . . . Sally tells Harry that Sheldon broke up with her because he didn't believe that there were no Sunday panties in her "Days of the Week" underwear set, instead thinking that she was cheating on him.
Woody Allen In the film version of *Play It Again, Sam,* after they have an affair, Linda tells Allan, "I even saw you in your underwear with the days of the week written on them."

The Park Scenes

When Harry Met Sally . . . Harry and Sally discuss the intricacies of male/female relationships (and, circuitously, their own) as they stroll through Central Park.
Woody Allen In *Bananas,* Fielding and Nancy discuss their own failed relationship while ambling through a park (which could also be Central Park.)

Another Eating Scene

When Harry Met Sally . . . After Harry and Sally sleep together, they go out for dinner, and a disconcerted Sally watches Harry eat his salad, as though she's seeing him for the first time.
Woody Allen In *Take the Money and Run,* when Virgil first takes Louise out to dinner, he tells her, "I could watch you eat all night." She replies, "Why?"

The Bookstore Scenes

When Harry Met Sally . . . Sally runs into Harry while they're both browsing in a bookstore.

Woody Allen In *Manhattan,* Isaac tells Yale he quit his job as they browse in Rizzoli's Bookstore.

The "Repeat After Me" Scenes

When Harry Met Sally . . . Harry speaks with a funny accent and makes Sally repeat what he says.
Woody Allen In *What's New, Pussycat?,* Michael bursts in on Carol while she's teaching an "English as a second language" class, and while the two of them argue, the class repeats their shouted accusations back at them.

CHAPTER 15

Driving Mr. Woody

Woody ("You Know I Don't Drive Well") Allen's Driving Scenes

I don't drive in real life.
Woody Allen

IT'S NOT HARD to understand why Woody Allen would want to forget the times he's driven in his films. He hates cars. Or better, he hates driving cars. And considering the fact that Woody never (that's *never*) sees his films after they're made, you easily apprehend how he can forget the regrettably necessary times he has manned the wheel of one of those infernal driving machines.

Over the past twenty-five years Woody *has* driven more often than just during his memorably disastrous excursion in *Annie Hall,* and herein we'll note the many scenes in his films showing him behind the wheel of a car.

What's New, Pussycat? (1965)

The first time Woody is shown driving on screen is in the first movie he ever made.

Woody's character, Victor Shakapopolis, is first seen behind the wheel of a car about two-thirds of the way through the film. He's tooling a red convertible through the streets of Paris. Sporting a leather helmet and goggles (as he would many years later in *A Midsummer Night's Sex Comedy*), he drives through an outdoor café, crashing into tables and sending Parisians scattering.

Later, Victor wheels into a gas station on his way to Chateau Chantel.

And then, at the very end of this eminently successful film, all the cast members jump into go-carts and chase one other around a track in what must be considered a quintessential wacky ending to a quintessential sixties madcap romp.

Take the Money and Run (1969)

No fewer than four times is Woody's character, Virgil Starkwell, seen driving in this film. The first time, in a deliciously funny scene, finds Virgil trying to murder his blackmailing coworker Miss Blair by running her over with his rented car. In her living room.

The next time Virgil drives he's fleeing from the police after Miss Blair's death. Accompanied by wife and son, he is ordered by an officer to pull over. He continues driving, and the cop ends up on the hood of his car.

The third time Virgil's behind the wheel he's headed toward the big "fake movie" bank robbery. (Alas, another group of robbers appeared at the same time to rob the same bank so Virgil polled the employees to see by whom they wished to be robbed.)

And finally, Virgil, again on the lam, is seen tooling down the highway. His wife is reading to their son, while a cop car pursues with lights flashing and siren screaming.

Bananas (1971)

Fielding Mellish drives but once in *Bananas*. Early on, Fielding, operating a beat-up old Volkswagen with a bad headlight, parks the car and steps out into an open manhole.

There is also a driving reference in the film. When rebel leader Esposito tells Fielding he'll not be able to return to New York for six months, Fielding snaps, "Six months! I got a rented car!"

Play It Again, Sam (1972)

Woody's character, Allan Felix, takes the wheel once in *Sam*. On a date with Julie, he drives to a sleazy bar (so Julie can "get stoned and watch the freaks"), and there brawls with two bikers.

Everything You Always Wanted to Know About Sex (*But Were Afraid to Ask)* (1972)

Woody's characters are seen driving in two of the segments of *Everything You Always Wanted to Know About Sex* (*But Were Afraid to Ask)*.

In the first, "Why Do Some Women Have Trouble Reaching an Orgasm?" Fabrizio pulls up in a hot red sports car to pick up his new wife, Gina, on their wedding night. (We don't actually see Woody behind the wheel, but it's clear that it's his character.)

In the second segment, "Are the Findings of Doctors and Clinics Who Do Sexual Research and Experiments Accurate?," Victor Shakapopolis drives twice.

The first time, he pulls up at a gas station, where he orders fifty cents' worth of gas, and then meets Helen Lacy.

The second time, Victor chauffeurs Helen to Dr. Bernardo's house, pulls up in front, and parks. (While fleeing from Dr. Bernardo's giant escaped breast, Victor gets back into the car, but it won't start because he's out of "gas, oil, and water.")

Sleeper (1973)

Woody's character, Miles Monroe, drives an antique Volkswagen he and Luna found in the cave after they escaped from the security police.

Later, Miles and Luna escape in a futuristic car (with Miles driving) after they destroy the Leader's nose.

The Front (1976)

Howard Prince is seen driving only once. One weekend Howard chauffeurs Hecky Brown to Hecky's club date up in the mountains.

Annie Hall (1977)

Alvy Singer drives twice in *Annie Hall*.

The first is when Alvy arrives in Los Angeles and he drives his rented car to the health-food restaurant to see Annie.

The second is after Annie, now living in California, rejects his attempts at reconciliation, and he drives his rented car back to the airport. On this return trip, he first smashes into some trash cans, and then deliberately crashes into two cars. He is subsequently arrested for tearing up his license rather than giving it to the police officer investigating his collisions.

In the Random House volume, *Four Films of Woody Allen,* the scene is described as follows:

> Alvy gets behind the wheel, starts the motor. Putting the car in gear, he inadvertently moves forward, hitting a bunch of trash cans with a loud crash. Putting the car in reverse, Alvy notices a beige car that has just turned into the parking lot. . . . Alvy . . . backs up his convertible, purposefully smashing the side of the beige car . . . [then] . . . moves his car over to another parked car and hits it full force. . . . He sits behind the wheel as people rush out of various cars and as sirens start blaring, coming closer and closer, stopping finally as a motorcycle cop gets off beside Alvy's car and walks over to him.

Throughout Alvy's crash scene, flashbacks show Alvy as a young boy driving a bumper car at his father's concession at Coney Island.

Another famous motoring scene in *Annie Hall* worth mentioning is Annie's drive through New York after she and Alvy play tennis. Alvy tells her she is "the worst driver I've ever seen in my life . . . including any place . . . Asia." When they finally arrive at Annie's apartment building and Annie parks the car, he tells her "we can walk to the curb from here." At one point in their conversation, Alvy yells at Annie, "I gotta problem with driving. I got a license but I have too much hostility."

Manhattan (1979)

We see Woody's character Ike actually drive once in *Manhattan,* and we're also given details on another notorious driving "incident." Ike and Mary drive out to the country and we see Woody behind the wheel. Also, one reason Ike and Jill split up was that Ike once tried to run her lover Connie over with a car. Instead, he sheared off a porch. He rationalized, "You know I don't drive well."

Stardust Memories (1980)

Woody's character Sandy Bates is mostly shown *being driven* in this film. But there is a scene wherein he asserts that he can drive if he must, as well as one wherein he drives.

In the first, his driver, George, has just been stopped and arrested for mail fraud. The arresting officer (who recognizes Sandy) asks him, "Listen, do you have a license? I mean, can you drive this car?" And Sandy replies, "I can drive it if I have to."

In the scene where Sandy actually drives, he and Daisy are returning to their hotel after an afternoon at the movies, Sandy is driving, and the car breaks down. Sandy curses George, and they end up walking.

Zelig (1983)

We don't see Leonard Zelig drive in *Zelig*, but apparently he not only had a license, but was a terrible driver as well.

A "Mr. Stoner" speaks of Zelig: "He was the guy who smashed my car up. It was brand new. Then he backed up over my mother's wrist. She's elderly, and she uses her wrist a lot." (It wasn't explained what Zelig was doing in Mr. Stoner's car.)

Broadway Danny Rose (1984)

Woody drives three times in this film, although twice he's not seen.

The first time, Danny Rose leaves his apartment building, unlocks his car (by reaching through the window and pulling up the lock), and gets into the car. We then see a long shot of the car on its way to pick up Tina.

Later, we see Danny's car driving into the circular driveway of Tina's Uncle Rocco's country estate.

The third time finds Danny and Tina returning from the Mafia party, and Danny is shown behind the wheel. (The camera is in the car.)

Oedipus Wrecks (in *New York Stories*) (1989)

In the dream sequence that takes place right after the opening analysis session, Sheldon, clad in a chauffeur's uniform, is driving a hearse containing the body of his dead mother—who gives him directions from the casket as he drives.

Scenes from a Mall (1991)

Nick tools a Saab Turbo to the mall to pick up the sushi for that evening's anniversary party. While driving, he talks on a cellular phone.

Postscript

A Midsummer Night's Sex Comedy (1982)

Woody doesn't drive in this film, but does "pilot" a flying bicycle invented by his character, Andrew Hobbes. It's quite a sight to behold Woody flying over a country pond on a bike with a pedal-powered propeller.

Crimes and Misdemeanors (1989)

Although he never drives, Cliff Stern is shown riding in the back seat of a station wagon as he films Lester strolling the streets of New York City.

Woody Allen (1964)

On Woody's first record album of his standup comedy material, in the routine "Private Life," he refers to owning a car.

CHAPTER 16

"Woody in Wonderland"
by John Taylor

"WOODY in Wonderland," which originally appeared in the September 30, 1991, issue of *New York* magazine, is a knee-slapping spin on what would happen if the big Hollywood studios got their weasel hands on Woody Allen.

John Taylor takes us on a tour through the labyrinthian minds of five studio heads (barely disguised heads, I might add) and lets us peruse the kind of letters they might write to "Woodsky" regarding his new script, *Autumn Interlude.*

The spark of inspiration for this piece came in fall 1991 when Orion wasn't able to come up with the funding for Woody to begin work on his film after *Shadows and Fog,* and so Woody signed with TriStar for at least one picture.

John Taylor took this scenario one step further by asking the obligatory writer's question, What if? The result is his scintillating "Woody in Wonderland."

(Special thanks to John Taylor and Gia Kourlas at *New York* magazine for their assistance with the reprinting of this piece.)

"Woody in Wonderland"*

by John Taylor

Now that Orion's in trouble, the other big Hollywood studios
would love to give an Allen movie their special spin

Woody Allen has always insisted on complete creative control over the
movies he makes. They're his babies. He writes them; he directs them. As
long as he kept them under a certain limited budget, Orion Pictures, which
has financed and distributed all his movies since 1982, let him do what he
wanted. Sure, they like to joke in Hollywood, no one outside New York ever
went to his movies, Orion wouldn't even bother to book them in the Corn
Belt, but Woody's core New York audience, together with a few cultish fans
in half a dozen other cities, kept his pictures in the black.

Most of the time.

Not that profit was ever the object, anyway.

But now, with Orion close to bankruptcy, Allen has been talking to
other studios. Every studio head would love to do a deal with the Woodster. He's America's one true auteur filmmaker. He's prestige. He's class. But
few studio heads seem to be as willing as Arthur Krim, Woody's old friend
and a founder of Orion, to grant him unlimited freedom.

Earlier this month, Allen signed a deal to make one movie with TriStar
Pictures. The details have remained secret, but everyone is intrigued. Does
the Woodchuck have final cut? If not, what might a Woody Allen TriStar
picture resemble? TriStar, after all, though now run by former Orion executive Mike Medavoy, is best known these days for *Terminator 2*. Would
TriStar want Woody to do an action-adventure movie? What would the
other studios want? Imagine the result as Hollywood executives try to
force one of Allen's angst-ridden, ruefully funny ensemble pieces into the
various commercial formulas now in vogue.

Paramount Pictures

Woody,

Loved the script for "Autumn Interlude." It's quintessential you.
The scene picking strawberries in Maine had me in stitches.

But we owe it to the shareholders to ask, How many people in Wisconsin are going to drive through the snow to the multiplex to see the
story of a depressed, middle-aged woman's affair with her psychiatrist?

Now, how many people might make that drive if Clair instead were young, beautiful—and deadly? We brainstormed a narrative line at the story meeting this morning. Clair becomes sexually obsessed with Robert, see. When Robert ends their affair after that one liaison in the strawberry patch, her psychopathic personality emerges. She begins to stalk and kill his other patients. To round out the triangle, a burned-out cop brought in to investigate falls for Clair at the same time that he begins to suspect she's the killer.

We could keep the strawberry scene, but my gut tells me that instead of playing the bit with the thorns for laughs, we should go full-throttle erotic: a blistering sex scene in act one—passionate coupling, the trickle of strawberry juice foreshadowing the blood to be spilled later—will put it over the top.

Which brings me to casting. You're right, Michael Caine makes a great Robert, and he's cheap, but Marketing says if we get Harrison Ford we could open on 1,700 screens. Also, I see Clair as a Greta Scacchi type—what's that line she uses, "a vagina with teeth." Mia could instead play Robert's wife. She's more long-suffering, anyway.

About the title, Marketing again—but you've got to hand it to them, they do their research—Marketing thought "Dark Interlude" or "Evil Interlude" would have more subliminal kick. I'm thinking "Fatal Interlude."

This could be your first movie to net serious money, Woodsky, so think hard, then call me. Anytime. If they don't patch you through to wherever I am, I'll have them fired.

Warner Bros. Inc.
4000 Warner Boulevard
Burbank, California 91522

Woody,

"Autumn Interlude" made me laugh and made me cry. It's so rare in this business to read a quality script. I hadn't even finished act one when I said to myself, "This is a movie."

You didn't promise Mia the lead, did you? Because I took the liberty of showing it to Goldie. Woody, she's available, and she's as excited as I am.

I know you're thinking right now you can't believe your luck. But it gets better.

I also took the liberty of showing it to Clint. He's available, too, and he liked it so much he wanted to direct it as well as star in it. But don't worry, you're my first choice.

Fly out Friday. Clint said he'll come down. He and Goldie will give you their input. Clint's already got a lot of ideas for his character. The rewrite shouldn't take more than a month. We can begin shooting in January and fill a window in our release schedule by opening on May 18.

I know you're now thinking two things. First, you're thinking, He wants me to shoot and finish postproduction in five months? What is he, nuts? But I know you're a professional, and even though you may not think you can do it, I know you can do it.

Second, I know you're thinking May 18 is a terrible release date. You're thinking, What movie has ever done any business that opened on May 18?

But let me tell you, if you've got the product, there is no such thing as a bad release date. And I'll let you in on a secret. Goldie's last picture, "Bird on a Wire," opened on May 18. No one thought it would do any business, but it's grossed $71 million. So it's a lucky date for Goldie, and it'll be a lucky date for you.

Friday, then. Be there or be square, you incredible genius.

Walt Disney Pictures

Woody,

Fabulous script. Funny, tender, with your special New York take on these crazy times we live in. Clair's encounter with the homeless woman at the automatic-teller machine is particularly hilarious.

But here we're wondering, Could "Autumn Interlude" be even funnier? And we're thinking, it could.

Start with casting. Mia's a wonderful actress, but her gift is the subtly nuanced moment. She would be the first to admit she's never had them rolling in the aisles. We're thinking: Bette Midler.

Bette's not in Mia's league at all craftwise, but she does have that fabulous manic energy. She can get them screaming. I've always liked to think, and "Premiere" quoted me once on this, she makes you laugh with her by letting you laugh at her.

Michael Caine's one of the industry's greatest assets, Woody, as you well know. But our thinking is that he's a little too European to play off Bette. We just don't see the chemistry. Our choice: Danny DeVito.

He's not as cheap as he was a few years ago, but he can match Bette's manic energy, and with the two of them you can play up the odd-couple motif that's at the heart of the script.

Now, a couple of nits to pick. Why does Clair seek out this psychiatrist? What's her motivation? Vague ennui? You've got to admit it's a little squishy.

Our suggestion: Have her dog die in the opening scene. He could be run over by a New York cab. Come to think of it, Danny could be the driver. An unemployed psychiatrist? I see a recession angle there.

Second nit. Why do they have to separate at the end? Why not marry them? Do we really want to disappoint the audience just to make a point about the futility of human relationships?

By starting with the dead dog and ending with marriage, you'll start with tears and end with cheers. You'll have a movie with heart that's also packed full of laughs.

In fact, we like this concept so much that if you don't want to proceed, we'll buy the idea, give you story credit, and sign Paul Mazursky to direct. But wait a minute—I'm dictating off the top of my head here—we don't need to buy it from you. We thought it up. Well, Legal can decide.

Hugs to Satchel.

Columbia Pictures Entertainment, Inc.
711 Fifth Avenue
New York, New York 10022

Woody,

Re "Autumn Interlude," one word. Unbelievable. In a single elegant script you've said more about this country's psychological crisis than all the professors at Yale and Harvard, and I know already that you are going to have your first overseas hit.

To do it, though, Woody, you've got to leave the planet. Fortunately, all that requires is minor tinkering. In fact, I can't think of a better way to dramatize your theme of existential anxiety than to have the subtly menacing psychiatrist turn out to be, in fact, an evil alien.

Clair discovers his true nature, as we see it here, and with the aid of a brilliant, gentle Japanese engineer she modifies a Sony Walkman to intercept his broadcasts up to the mother ship. Since no one believes Clair, she and the engineer must battle the aliens themselves. And those battle scenes, particularly the one where the engineer heroically dies to save Clair, will be shot as only Woody Allen can shoot them.

I've got to be frank, Woody—the younger V.P.s here think casting Mia as Clair would be a disaster. The kids are often right; they've got the pulse of the audience. But this time I disagree. I'm behind her—and you—all the way on this. If someone like Jake trains her intensively for six weeks—well, maybe twelve—and she gets a good tan, she could give Linda Hamilton a run for the money.

Now for my own small contribution: We make Jean-Claude Van Damme the psychiatrist. First off, since he's a psychiatrist, we don't have to worry about his foreign accent, always a problem with Jean-Claude. But the main thing, Woody, is that Jean-Claude is ready for his first big crossover role. "Double Impact" will gross over $30 million. That's 50 percent more than we expected it to make, and it'll do even better overseas, where they love him.

Jean-Claude's going to be the next Schwarzenegger, and we've got him under contract for at least two more pictures. If "Autumn Interlude"—we'll need a new title, start thinking—becomes the blockbuster I know it will, you'll be along for the whole sweet ride.

Sign up a trainer for Mia today, fella. We want her pumped and hard by the time she tests with Jean-Claude.

Universal Studios
Universal City, California 91608
Phone: (818) 777–1293

Woody:

Loved the script. I showed it to Mike, who should be representing you, by the way, and he's wild about it. Also sent it to Osaka. Haven't heard back yet, but that in itself is a good sign, according to Mike.

I know you've been in this business too long to be hurt if I tell you my one small problem with "Autumn Interlude" is that it lacks a certain punch. Mike agreed, and he had an idea. Several ideas, in fact.

First, and this shows Mike's genius at work, he thought you should play the psychiatrist. The role you've given yourself, the embittered little television writer, has some funny lines, but it's really just a walk-on part. Why not star?

Mike's second stroke of genius is to have John Goodman play the role of the patient. That means changing Clair from a woman to man and getting rid of the affair—we're not making a gay movie here, though AIDS is a terrible tragedy—but just think: John Goodman and Woody Allen. It's a classic buddy matchup, and Mike is confident that in return for pairing the two of you, you'll both become his clients.

Mike's plot concept is his third stroke of genius. John comes to you saying people are out to get him. You think he's paranoid, but then the villains try to break into your office and kill him during a session, and you both have to set off cross-country for John's childhood home, pursued all the time, to rekindle his suppressed memories—this is where the therapy comes in—about his long-gone sister who's trying to kill him so she can claim the inheritance he doesn't know he has.

The sister, of course, is Mia. You didn't think we'd write her out of the picture, did you? Mike, you know, feels she's got incredible potential; she's just been mishandled.

If you don't want to sweat the details on this—and why should you, you're a star—Mike said he'd be happy to put a couple of his writers on it. You'd still get sole screen credit, of course.

Instead of getting back to me, why don't you just phone Mike directly? Don't worry, he'll take the call—you *are* Woody Allen—and I'd really like to see the two of you come together.

Appendices
Annotated Bibliography

Appendix 1

The Film Credits
The Cast and Crew of Woody Allen's Films

1. **WHAT'S NEW, PUSSYCAT?** (1965) Peter Sellers (Dr. Fritz Fassbender); Peter O'Toole (Michael James); Romy Schneider (Carol Werner); Capucine (Renée Lefebvre); Paula Prentiss (Liz Bien); Woody Allen (Victor Shakapopolis); Ursula Andress (Rita); Edra Gale (Anna Fassbender); Katrin Schaake (Jacqueline); Eleanor Hirt (Mrs. Werner); Jean Paredes (Marcel); Jacques Balutin (Etienne); Jess Hahn (Perry Werner); Howard Vernon (Doctor); Michel Subor (Philippe); Sabine Sun (Nurse); Nicole Karen (Tempest O'Brien); Jacqueline Fogt (Charlotte); Daniel Emilfork (Gas Station Attendant); Tanya Lopert (Miss Lewis); Barbara Somers (Miss Marks); Robert Rollis (Car Renter); Annette Poivre (Emma); Colin Drake (Durell); Richard Saint-Bris (Le Maire); Marion Conrad (First Stripteaser); Maggie Wright (Second Stripteaser); Françoise Hardy (The Mayor's Secretary); Jean Yves Autrey, Pascal Wolf, Nadine Papin (Fassbender Children); Norbert Terry (Kelly); F. Medard (Nash); Gordon Felio (Fat Man); Douking (Renée's Concierge); Louise Lasser (The Nutcracker); Richard Burton (Man in Bar).
Production Credits Director: Clive Donner; Producer: Charles K. Feldman; Screenplay: Woody Allen; Photography: Jean Badal; Art Direction: Jacques Saulnier; Special Effects: Bob MacDonald; Music: Burt Bacharach; Editor: Fergus McDonnell; Sound: William-Robert Sivel; Title Song Sung by: Tom Jones.

2. **WHAT'S UP, TIGER LILY?** (1966) Tatsuya Mihashi (Phil Moskowitz); Mie Hana (Terry Yaki); Akiko Wakayabayashi (Suki Yaki); Tadao Nakamura (Shepherd Wong); Susumu Kurobe (Wing Fat); China Lee (Stripper).
Rerelease Screenplay and Dubbing Woody Allen; Frank Buxton; Len Maxwell; Louise Lasser; Mickey Rose; Julie Bennett; Bryna Wilson.
Production Credits Kagi No Kagi: Director: Senkichi Taniguchi; Producer: Tomoyuki Tanaka; Screenplay: Hideo Ando; Photography: Kazuo Yamado. *What's Up, Tiger Lily?*: Director: Woody Allen; Production Conception: Ben Shapiro; "Writings and Vocal Assists": Frank Buxton, Louise Lasser, Julie Bennett, Len Maxwell, Mickey Rose, and Bryna Wilson; Editor: Richard Krown; Executive Producer: Henry G. Saperstein; Music: Jack Lewis, with songs by the Lovin' Spoonful; Associate Producer: Woody Allen; Production Manager: Jerry Goldstein.

3. **CASINO ROYALE** (1967) Peter Sellers (Evelyn Tremble); Ursula Andress (Vesper Lynd); David Niven (Sir James Bond); Orson Welles (Le Chiffre); Joanna Pettet (Mata Bond); Deborah Kerr (Widow McTarry); Daliah Lavi (The Detainer); Woody Allen (Jimmy Bond); William Holden (Ransome); Charles Boyer (Le Grand); John Huston ("M"); Kurt Kaznar (Smernov); George Raft (Himself); Jean-Paul Belmondo (French Foreign Legion Soldier); Terence Cooper (Agent .007); Barbara Bouchet (Miss Moneypenny); Angela Scoular (Buttercup); Gabriella Licudi (Eliza); Tracey Crisp (Heather); Jacqueline Bisset (Miss Goodthighs); Anna Quayle (Frau Hoffner); Bernard Cribbens (Taxi Driver); Tracy Reed (Fang Leader); Fiona Lewis (Fang Girl); Percy Herbert (First Piper); Peter O'Toole (Man in Bar).
Production Credits Directors: John Huston, Kenneth Hughes, Val Guest, Robert Parrish, and Joseph McGrath; Producers: Charles K. Feldman, Jerry Bresler; Screenplay: Wolf Mankowitz, John Law, and Michael Sayers, from an Ian Fleming novel; Photography:

Jack Hildyard; Special Effects: Cliff Richardson, Roy Whybrow; Production Designer: Michael Ayringer; Music: Burt Bacharach; Editor: Bill Lenny.

4. DON'T DRINK THE WATER (1969) Jackie Gleason (Walter Hollander); Estelle Parsons (Marion Hollander); Ted Bessell (Axel Magee); Joan Delaney (Susan Hollander); Michael Constantine (Krojack); Howard St. John (Ambassador Magee); Danny Meehan (Kilroy); Richard Libertini (Father Drobney); Pierre Olaf (The Chef); Avery Schreiber (The Sultan); Mark Gordon (Merik); Phil Leeds (Sam); Howard Morris (Pilot of Escape Plane).
Production Credits Director: Howard Morris; Producer: Charles H. Joffe; Screenplay: R. S. Allen and Harvey Bullock, based on the play by Woody Allen; Photography: Harvey Genkins; Art Director: Robert Gundlach; Music: Pat Williams; Editor: Ralph Rosenblum; Assistant Director: Louis Stroller; Associate Producer: Jack Grossberg; Executive Producer: Joseph E. Levine; Operating Cameraman: Urs Furfer; Casting Director: Jay Wolf; Editorial Supervision: Ralph Rosenblum; Title Song: Lyrics by Kelly Gordon and Pat Williams; Title Song Sung by: Jake Holmes; Costume Design: Gene Coffin.

5. TAKE THE MONEY AND RUN (1969) Woody Allen (Virgil Starkwell); Janet Margolin (Louise); Marcel Hillaire (Fritz); Jacqueline Hyde (Miss Blair); Lonny Chapman (Jake); Jan Merlin (Al); James Anderson (Chain Gang Warden); Howard Storm (Fred); Mark Gordon (Vince); Micil Murphy (Frank); Minnow Moskowitz (Joe Agneta); Nate Jacobson (The Judge); Grace Bauer (Farm House Lady); Ethel Sokolow (Mother Starkwell); Henry Leff (Father Starkwell); Don Frazier (The Psychiatrist); Mike O'Dowd (Michael Sullivan); Louise Lasser (Kay Lewis); Stanley Ackerman (The Photographer); Jackson Beck (The Narrator).
Production Credits Director: Woody Allen; Producer: Charles H. Joffe; Screenplay: Woody Allen and Mickey Rose; Photography: Lester Shorr, ASC; Art Direction: Fred Harpman; Special Effects: A. D. Flowers; Music: Marvin Hamlisch; Supervising Film Editor: James T. Heckert; Assistant Director: Stanley Ackerman; Editors: Paul Jordan, Ron Kalish; Editorial Consultant: Ralph Rosenblum; Associate Producer: Jack Grossberg; Executive Producer: Sidney Glazier; Set Direction: Marvin March; Sound: Bud Alper.

6. BANANAS (1971) Woody Allen (Fielding Mellish); Louise Lasser (Nancy); Carlos Montalban (General Emilio Molina Vargas); Natividad Abascal (Yolanda); Jacobo Morales (Esposito); Miguel Suarez (Luis); David Ortiz (Sanchez); Renée Enriquez (Diaz); Jack Axelrod (Arroyo); Howard Cosell (Himself); Charlotte Rae (Mrs. Mellish); Dan Frazer (Priest); Martha Greenhouse (Dr. Feigen); Axel Anderson (Tortured Man); Dorthi Fox (J. Edgar Hoover); Dagne Crane (Sharon); Conrad Bain (Semple); Allen Garfield (Man on Cross); Princess Fatosh (Snakebite Lady); Hy Anzell (Patient); Sylvester Stallone (Street Hood).
Production Credits Director: Woody Allen; Producer: Jack Grossberg; Screenplay: Woody Allen and Mickey Rose; Photography: Andrew M. Costikyan; Production Design: Ed Wittstein; Set Decorator: Herbert Mulligan; Special Effects: Don B. Courtney; Music: Marvin Hamlisch; Editor: Ron Kalish; Assistant Director: Fred T. Gallo; Executive Producer: Charles H. Joffe; Associate Producer: Ralph Rosenblum.

7. PLAY IT AGAIN, SAM (1972) Woody Allen (Allan Felix); Diane Keaton (Linda Christie); Tony Roberts (Dick Christie); Jerry Lacy (Bogey); Susan Anspach (Nancy); Jennifer Salt (Sharon); Joy Bang (Julie); Viva (Jennifer the Nymphomaniac); Suzanne Zenor (Disco Girl); Diana Davila (Suicidal Museum Girl); Mari Fletcher (Fantasy Sharon); Michael Green (Motorcycle Hood 1); Ted Markland (Motorcycle Hood 2).
Production Credits Director: Herbert Ross; Producer: Arthur P. Jacobs; Production Supervisor: Roger M. Rothstein; Screenplay: Woody Allen, based on his play; Assistant Director: William Gerrity; Photography: Owen Roizman; Production Designer: Ed Wittstein;

Music: Billy Goldenberg; Editor: Marion Rothman; Associate Producer: Frank Capra, Jr.; Executive Producer: Charles Joffe; Costume Designer: Anna Hill Johnstone.

8. EVERYTHING YOU ALWAYS WANTED TO KNOW ABOUT SEX* (*BUT WERE AFRAID TO ASK) (1972) "Do Aphrodisiacs Work?" (Segment 1) Woody Allen (Fool); Lynn Redgrave (Queen); Anthony Quayle (King); Alan Caillou (Fool's Father); Geoffrey Holder (Sorcerer); "What Is Sodomy?" (Segment 2) Gene Wilder (Dr. Douglas Ross); Elaine Giftos (Mrs. Ann Ross); Titos Vandis (Stavros Milos); Daisy the Sheep (Herself); "Why Do Some Women Have Trouble Reaching an Orgasm?" (Segment 3) Woody Allen (Fabrizio); Louise Lasser (Gina); "Are Transvestites Homosexuals?" (Segment 4) Lou Jacobi (Sam Waterman); Sidney Miller (George); "What Are Sex Perverts?" (Segment 5) Jack Barry (Himself); Toni Holt (Herself); Robert Q. Lewis (Himself); Pamela Mason (Herself); Regis Philbin (Himself); Don Chuy (Football Player); Tom Mack (Football Player); H. E. West (Bernard Jaffe); Baruch Lumet (Rabbi Chaim Baumel); "Are the Findings of Doctors and Clinics Who Do Sexual Research and Experiments Accurate?" (Segment 6) Woody Allen (Victor Shakapopolis); Heather MacRae (Helen Lacy); John Carradine (Dr. Bernardo); Ref Sanchez (Igor the Hunchback); Dort Clark (The Sheriff); "What Happens During Ejaculation?" (Segment 7) Woody Allen (Sperm); Tony Randall (Brain Room Operator); Burt Reynolds (Switchboard Operator); Erin Fleming (Sidney's Date); Stanley Adams (Stomach Operator); Oscar Beregi (Brain Control Technician); Jay Robinson (The Priest); Robert Walden (Sperm); "What Makes a Man a Homosexual?" (the eliminated segment) Woody Allen (Male Spider); Louise Lasser (Female Spider).
Production Credits Director: Woody Allen; Producer: Charles H. Joffe; Screenplay: Woody Allen, from the book by Dr. David Reuben; Assistant Directors: Fred T. Gallo; Terry M. Carr; Editor: Eric Albertson; Supervising Film Editor: James T. Heckert; Photography: David M. Walsh; Production Design: Dale Hennesy; Music: Mundell Lowe; Associate Producer: Jack Grossberg.

9. SLEEPER (1973) Woody Allen (Miles Monroe); Diane Keaton (Luna Schlosser); John Beck (Erno Windt); Mary Gregory (Dr. Melik); Don Keefer (Dr. Tryon); John McLiam (Dr. Agon); Bartlett Robinson (Dr. Orva); Chris Forbes (Rainer Krebs); Marya Small (Dr. Nero); Peter Hobbs (Dr. Dean); Susan Miller (Ellen Pogrebin); Lou Picetti (Master of Ceremonies); Brian Avery (Herald Cohen); Jessica Rains (The Woman in the Mirror); Spencer Milligan (Jeb Hrmthmg); Stanley Ross (Sears Swiggles).
Production Credits Director: Woody Allen; Producer: Jack Grossberg; Screenplay: Woody Allen and Marshall Brickman; Assistant Directors: Fred T. Gallo, Henry J. Lange, Jr.; Editor: Ralph Rosenblum; Photography: David M. Walsh; Production Design: Dale Hennesy; Set Designer: Dianne Wager; Costume Designer: Joel Schumacher; Special Effects: A. D. Flowers; Stunt Coordinator: M. James Amett; Associate Producers: Marshall Brickman and Ralph Rosenblum; Executive Producer: Charles H. Joffe; Music: Woody Allen, with the Preservation Hall Jazz Band and the New Orleans Funeral Ragtime Orchestra.

10. LOVE AND DEATH (1975) Woody Allen (Boris Grushenko); Diane Keaton (Sonia); Olga Georges-Picot (Countess Alexandrovna); Jessica Harper (Natasha); Jack Lenoir (Krapotkin); James Tolkan (Napoleon); Alfred Lutter III (Young Boris); Lloyd Battista (Don Francisco); Frank Adu (Drill Sergeant); Harold Gould (Count Anton); C. A. R. Smith (Father Nikolai); Georges Adet (Old Nehamkin); Patricia Crown (Cheerleader); Harry Hankin (Uncle Sasha); Denise Peron (Spanish Countess); Zvee Scooler (Father); Beth Porter (Anna); Henry Czarniak (Ivan); Despo Diamantidou (Mother); Florian (Uncle Nicolai); Brian Coburn (Dmitri); Luce Fabiole (Grandmother); Edmond Ardisson (Priest); Feodor Atkine (Mikhail); Albert Augier (Waiter); Yves Barasco (Rimsky); Jack Berard (General Lecoq); Eva Bertrand (Woman in Hygiene Play); George Birt (Doctor); Yves Brainville (Andre); Gerard Buhr (Servant); Henri Coutet (Minskov); Sandor Eles (Soldier);

Jacqueline Fogt (Ludmilla); Sol L. Frieder (Leonid Voskovec); Tony Jan (Vladimir Maximovitch); Tutte Lemkow (Pierre); Leib Lensky (Father Andre); Ann Lonnberg (Olga); Roger Lumont (Baker); Ed Marcus (Raskov); Jacques Maury (Second); Narcissa McKinley (Cheerleader); Aubrey Morris (Soldier); Alan Rossett (Guard); Shimen Ruskin (Borslov); Persival Russel (Berdykov); Chris Sanders (Joseph); Fred Smith (Soldier); Bernard Taylor (Soldier); Clement-Thierry (Jacques); Alan Tilvern (Sergeant); Helene Vallier (Madame Wolfe); Howard Vernon (General Leveque); Glenn Williams (Soldier); Jacob Witkin (Sushkin).

Production Credits Director: Woody Allen; Producer: Charles H. Joffe; Screenplay: Woody Allen; Assistant Directors: Paul Feyder, Bernard Cohn; Photography: Ghislain Cloquet; Art Direction: Willy Holt; Special Effects: Kit West, Peter Dawson; Music: Sergei Prokofiev; Editors: Ralph Rosenblum, Ron Kalish; Costume Design: Gladys de Segonzac; Associate Producer: Fred T. Gallo; Executive Producer: Martin Poll.

11. THE FRONT (1976) Woody Allen (Howard Prince); Zero Mostel (Hecky Brown); Herschel Bernardi (Phil Sussman); Michael Murphy (Alfred Miller); Andrea Marcovicci (Florence Barrett); Remak Ramsay (Hennessey); Marvin Lichterman (Myer Prince); Lloyd Gough (Delaney); David Margulies (Phelps); Joshua Shelley (Sam); Norman Rose (Howard's Attorney); Charles Kimbrough (Committee Counselor); M. Joseph Sommer (Committee Chairman); Danny Aiello (Danny La Gattuta); Georgann Johnson (TV Interviewer); Scott McKay (Hampton); David Clarke (Hubert Jackson); L. W. Klein (Bank Teller); John Bentley (Bartender); Julie Garfield (Margo); Murray Moston (Boss); McIntyre Dixon (Harry Stone); Rudolph Wilrich (Tallman); Burt Britton (Bookseller); Albert M. Oppenheimer (School Principal); William Bogert (Parks); Joey Faye (Waiter); Marilyn Sokol (Sandy); John J. Slater (TV Director); Renee Paris (Girl in Hotel Lobby); Gino Gennaro (Stage Hand); Joan Porter (Myer's Wife); Andrew Bernstein, Jacob Bernstein (Alfred's Children); Matthew Tobin (Man at Party); Marilyn Persky (His Date); Sam McMurray (Young Man at Party); Joe Jamrog (FBI Man); Michael Miller (FBI Man); Lucy Lee Flippin (Nurse); Jack Davidson (Congressman); Donald Symington (Congressman); Patrick McNamara (Federal Marshal).

Production Credits Director: Martin Ritt; Producer: Martin Ritt; Assistant Directors: Peter Scoppa, Ralph Singleton; Screenplay: Walter Bernstein; Photography: Michael Chapman; Art Direction: Charles Bailey; Music: Dave Grusin; Editor: Sidney Levin; Executive Producer: Charles H. Joffe; Associate Producer: Robert Greenhut; Costume Designer: Ruth Morley.

12. ANNIE HALL (1977) Woody Allen (Alvy Singer); Diane Keaton (Annie Hall); Tony Roberts (Rob); Carol Kane (Allison); Paul Simon (Tony Lacey); Shelley Duvall (Pam); Janet Margolin (Robin); Colleen Dewhurst (Mom Hall); Christopher Walken (Duane Hall); Donald Symington (Dad Hall); Helen Ludlam (Grammy Hall); Mordecai Lawner (Alvy's Dad—Leo); Joan Newman (Alvy's Mom); Jonathan Munk (Alvy Aged 9); Ruth Volner (Alvy's Aunt); Martin Rosenblatt (Alvy's Uncle); Hy Anzell (Joey Nichols); Rashel Novikoff (Aunt Tessie); Russell Horton (Man in Theater Line); Marshall McLuhan (Himself); Christine Jones (Dorrie); Mary Boylan (Miss Reed); Wendy Girard (Janet); John Doumanian (Coke Fiend); Bob Maroff (Man 1 Outside Theater); Rick Petrucelli (Man 2 Outside Theater); Lee Callahan (Ticket Seller at Theater); Chris Gampel (Doctor); Dick Cavett (Himself); Mark Lenard (Navy Officer); Dan Ruskin (Comedian at Rally); John Glover (Actor Boyfriend-Jerry); Bernie Styles (Comic's Agent); Johnny Haymer (Comic); Ved Bandhu (Maharishi); John Dennis Johnson (L. A. Policeman); Lauri Bird (Tony Lacey's Girlfriend); Jim McKrell (Tony Lacey Party Guest); Jeff Goldblum (Tony Lacey Party Guest); William Callaway (Tony Lacey Party Guest); Roger Newman (Tony Lacey Party Guest); Alan Landers (Tony Lacey Party Guest); Jean Sarah Frost (Tony Lacey Party Guest); Vince O'Brien (Hotel Doctor); Humphrey Davis (Alvy's Psychiatrist); Veronica

Radburn (Annie's Psychiatrist); Robin Mary Paris (Actress in Rehearsal); Charles Levin (Actor in Rehearsal); Wayne Carson (Rehearsal Stage Manager); Michael Karm (Rehearsal Director); Petronia Johnson (Tony's Date at Nightclub); Shaun Casey (Tony's Date at Nightclub); Ricardo Bertoni (Waiter 1 at Nightclub); Michael Aronin (Waiter 2 at Nightclub); Lou Picetti (Street Stranger); Loretta Tupper (Street Stranger); James Burge (Street Stranger); Shelly Hack (Street Stranger); Albert Ottenheimer (Street Stranger); Paula Trueman (Street Stranger); Beverly D'Angelo (Actress in Rob's TV Show); Tracey Walter (Actor in Rob's TV Show); David Wier (Alvy's Classmate); Keith Dentice (Alvy's Classmate); Susan Mellinger (Alvy's Classmate); Hamit Perezic (Alvy's Classmate); James Balter (Alvy's Classmate); Eric Gould (Alvy's Classmate); Amy Levitan (Alvy's Classmate); Gary Allen (Schoolteacher); Frank Vohs (Schoolteacher); Margaretta Warwick (Schoolteacher); Lucy Lee Flippen (Waitress at Health-Food Restaurant); Gary Muledeer (Man at Health-Food Restaurant); Sigourney Weaver (Alvy's Date Outside Theater); Walter Bernstein (Annie's Date Outside Theater).
Production Credits Director: Woody Allen; Producer: Charles H. Joffe; Screenplay: Woody Allen and Marshall Brickman; Assistant Directors: Fred T. Gallo, Fred Blankfein; Photography: Gordon Willis; Art Direction: Mel Bourne; Animated Sequences: Chris Ishii; Editor: Ralph Rosenblum; Costume Design: Ruth Morley; Associate Producer: Fred T. Gallo; Executive Producer: Robert Greenhut.

13. INTERIORS (1978) Kristin Griffith (Flyn); Mary Beth Hurt (Joey); Richard Jordan (Frederick); Diane Keaton (Renata); E. G. Marshall (Arthur); Geraldine Page (Eve); Maureen Stapleton (Pearl); Sam Waterston (Mike); Missy Hope (Young Joey); Kerry Duffy (Young Renata); Nancy Collins (Young Flyn); Penny Gaston (Young Eve); Roger Morden (Young Arthur); Henderson Forsythe (Judge Bartel).
Production Credits Director: Woody Allen; Producer: Charles H. Joffe; Screenplay: Woody Allen; Assistant Director: Martin Berman; Photography: Gordon Willis; Production Design: Mel Bourne; Editor: Ralph Rosenblum; Costume Designer: Joel Schumacher.

14. MANHATTAN (1979) Woody Allen (Isaac Davis); Diane Keaton (Mary Wilke); Michael Murphy (Yale); Mariel Hemingway (Tracy); Meryl Streep (Jill); Anne Byrne (Emily); Karen Ludwig (Connie); Michael O'Donoghue (Dennis); Victor Truro (Party Guest); Tisa Farrow (Party Guest—Polly); Helen Hanft (Party Guest); Bella Abzug (Guest of Honor); Gary Weiss (Television Director); Kenny Vance (Television Producer); Charles Levin (Television Actor 1); Karen Allen (Television Actor 2—Caroline Payne-Whitney Smith); David Rasche (Television Actor 3); Damion Sheller (Ike's Son); Wallace Shawn (Jeremiah); Mark Linn Baker (Shakespearean Actor); Frances Conroy (Shakespearean Actor); Bill Anthony (Porsche Owner 1); John Doumanian (Porsche Owner 2); Ray Serra (Pizzeria Waiter).
Production Credits Director: Woody Allen; Producer: Charles H. Joffe; Screenplay: Woody Allen and Marshall Brickman; Assistant Directors: Frederic B. Blankfein, Joan Spiegel Feinstein; Director of Photography: Gordon Willis; Production Design: Mel Bourne; Music: George Gershwin, adapted and arranged by Tom Pierson, and performed by the New York Philharmonic, conducted by Zubin Mehta; additional Gershwin songs arranged by Don Rose, and performed by the Buffalo Philharmonic, conducted by Michael Tilson Thomas; Editor: Susan E. Morse; Costume Design: Albert Wolsky; Executive Producer: Robert Greenhut; Woody Allen's Wardrobe by: Ralph Lauren; Waffles trained by Dawn Animal Agency.

15. STARDUST MEMORIES (1980) Woody Allen (Sandy Bates); Charlotte Rampling (Dorrie); Jessica Harper (Daisy); Marie-Christine Barrault (Isobel); Tony Roberts (Tony); Daniel Stern (Actor); Amy Wright (Shelley); Helen Hanft (Vivian Orkin); John Rothman (Jack Abel); Anne de Salvo (Debbie—Sandy's Sister); Joan Neuman (Sandy's Mother); Ken

Chapin (Sandy's Father); Leonardo Cimino (Sandy's Analyst); Louise Lasser (Sandy's Secretary); Eli Mintz (Old Man); Bob Maroff (Jerry Abraham); Gabrielle Strasun (Charlotte Ames); David Lipman (George, Sandy's Chauffeur); Robert Munk (Young Sandy); Jaqui Safra (Sam); Sharon Stone (Pretty Girl on Train); Andy Albeck, Robert Friedman, Douglas Ireland, Jack Rollins, Laraine Newman (Studio Executives); Howard Kissel (Sandy's Manager); Max Leavitt (Sandy's Doctor); Renee Lippin (Sandy's Press Agent); Sol Lomita (Sandy's Accountant); Irving Metzman (Sandy's Lawyer); Dorothy Leon (Sandy's Cook); Roy Brocksmith (Dick Lobel); Simon Newey (Mr. Payson); Victoria Zussin (Mrs. Payson); Francis Pole (Libby); Bill Anthony, Filomena Spagnuolo, Ruth Rugoff, Martha Whitehead (Fans—Hotel Arrival); Judith Roberts ("Three Little Words" Singer); Barry Weiss ("Three Little Words" Dancer); Robin Ruinsky, Adrian Richards, Dominick Petrolino, Sharon Brous, Michael Zanella, Doris Dugan Slater, Michael Goldstein, Neil Napolitan (Question Askers—Screening); Stanley Ackerman (Reporter—Screening); Noel Behn (Doug Orkin); Candy Loving (Tony's Girlfriend); Denice Danon, Sally Demay, Tom Dennis, Edward Kotkin, Laura Delano, Lisa Friedman, Brent Spiner, Gardenia Cole, Maurice Shrog, Larry Robert Carr, Brian Zoldessy, Melissa Slade, Paula Raflo, Jordan Derwin, Tony Azito, Marc Murray, Helen Hale, Carl Don, Victoria Page, Bert Michaels, Deborah Johnson (Fans in Lobby); Benjamin Rayson (Dr. Paul Pearlstein); Mary Mims (Claire Schaeffer); Charles Lowe (Vaudeville Singer); Marie Lane (Cabaret Singer—"Brazil"); Gustave Tassell, Marina Schiano, Dimitri Vassilopoulos, Judith Crist, Carmin Masrin (Cabaret Patrons); Sylvia Davis (Hostility Victim); Joseph Summo (Hostility Monster); Victor Truro (Hostility Psychoanalyst); Irwin Keyes, Bonnie Hellman, Patrick Daly, Joe Pagano, Wayne Maxwell, Ann Freeman, Bob Miranti (Fans Outside Hotel); Cindy Gibb, Manuella Machado (Young Girl Fans); Judith Cohen, Madeline Moroff, Maureen P. Levins (Friends of Sandy's Sister); E. Brian Dean (Police Sergeant Arresting George); Marvin Peisner (Ed Rich); Robert Tennenhouse, Leslie Smith, Samuel Chodorov (Autograph Seekers on Boardwalk); Philip Lenkowsky (Autograph Seeker/Assassin); Vanina Holasek (Isobel's Daughter); Michel Touchard (Isobel's Son); Kenny Vance, Iryn Steinfink (New Studio Executives); Frank Modell (Rewrite Man); Anne Korzen (Woman in Ice Cream Parlor); Eric Van Valkenburg (Man in Ice Cream Parlor); Susan Ginsburg (Usherette); Ostaro (Astrologer); Wade Barnes, Gabriel Barre, Charles Riggs III, Geoffrey Riggs, Martha Sherill, Anne Risley, Jade Bari, Marc Geller, Daniel Friedman, James Otis, Judy Goldner, Rebecca Wright, Perry Gewertz, Larry Fishman, Liz Albrecht, Sloane Bosniak, James Harter, Henry House, Largo Woodruff, Jerry Tov Greenberg, Mohammid Nabi Kiani (UFO Followers); Alice Spivak (Nurse at Hospital); Armin Shimerman, Edith Grossman, Jacqueline French (Eulogy Audience); John Doumanian (Armenian Fan); Jack Hollander (Cop Arresting Sandy).
Production Credits Director: Woody Allen; Producer: Robert Greenhut; Screenplay: Woody Allen; Assistant Director: Frederic B. Blankfein; Photography: Gordon Willis; Production Design: Mel Bourne; Music: Dick Hyman; Editor: Susan E. Morse; Costume Design: Santo Loquasto; Executive Producers: Jack Rollins and Charles H. Joffe; Animals provided by Dawn Animal Agency.

16. A MIDSUMMER NIGHT'S SEX COMEDY (1982) Woody Allen (Andrew Hobbes); Mia Farrow (Ariel Weynmouth); José Ferrer (Leopold); Julie Hagerty (Dulcy Ford); Tony Roberts (Dr. Maxwell Jordan); Mary Steenburgen (Adrian Hobbes); Adam Redfield (Student Foxx); Moishe Rosenfeld (Mr. Hayes); Timothy Jenkins (Mr. Thomson); Michael Higgins (Reynolds); Sol Frieder (Carstairs); Boriss Zoubok (Purvis); Thomas Barbour (Blint); Kate McGregor-Stewart (Mrs. Baker).
Production Credits Director: Woody Allen; Producer: Robert Greenhut; Screenplay: Woody Allen; Photography: Gordon Willis; Production Design: Mel Bourne; Executive Producer: Charles H. Joffe; Associate Producer: Michael Peyser; Assistant Director: Frederic B. Blankfein; Music: Felix Mendelssohn; Editor: Susan E. Morse; Casting: Juliet Tay-

lor; Costume Design: Santo Loquasto; Art Director: Speed Hopkins; Set Decorator: Carol Joffe; Animation Effects: Kurtz and Friends; Flying Machines and Inventions: Eoin Sprott Studio, Ltd.

17. ZELIG (1983) Woody Allen (Leonard Zelig); Mia Farrow (Dr. Eudora Fletcher); John Buckwalter (Dr. Sindell); Martin Chatinover (Glandular Diagnosis Doctor); Stanley Swerdlow (Mexican Food Doctor); Paul Nevens (Dr. Birsky); Howard Erskine (Hypodermic Doctor); George Hamlin (Experimental Drugs Doctor); Ralph Bell, Richard Whiting, Will Hussong (Other Doctors); Robert Iglesia (Man in Barber Chair); Eli Resnick (Man in Park); Edward McPhillips (Scotsman); Gale Hansen (Freshman 1); Michael Jeeter (Freshman 2); Peter McRobbie (Workers Rally Speaker); Sol Lomita (Martin Geist); Mary Louis Wilson (Sister Ruth); Alice Beardsley (Telephone Operator); Paula Trueman (Woman on Telephone); Ed Lane (Man on Telephone); Marianne Tatum (Actress Fletcher); Charles Denney (Actor Doctor); Michael Kell (Actor Koslow); Garrett Brown (Actor Zelig); Sharon Ferroll (Miss Baker); Richard Litt (Charles Koslow); Dimitri Vassilopoulos (Martinez); John Rothman (Paul Deghuee); Stephanie Farrow (Sister Meryl); Francis Beggins (City Hall Speaker); Jean Trowbridge (Dr. Fletcher's Mother); Ken Chapin (On-Camera Interviewer); Gerald Klein, Vincent Gerosa (Hearst Guests); Deborah Rush (Lita Fox); Stanley Simmonds (Lita's Lawyer); Robert Berger (Zelig's Lawyer); Jeanine Jackson (Helen Gray); Erma Campbell (Zelig's Wife); Anton Marco (Wrist Victim); Louise Deitch (House-Painting Victim); Bernice Dowis (Vilification Woman); John Doumanian (Greek Waiter); Will Holt (Rally Chancellor); Cole Palen (Zelig's Stunt Double); Pam Barber (Fletcher's Stunt Double); Bernie Herold (Carter Dean); Marshall Coles, Sr. (Calvin Turner); Ellen Garrison (Older Dr. Fletcher); Jack Cannon (Mike Geibell); Theodore R. Smits (Ted Bierbauer); Sherman Loud (Older Paul Deghuee); Elizabeth Rothschild (Older Sister Meryl); Kuno Spunholz (Oswald Pohl); *Contemporary Interviews with:* Susan Sontag; Irving Howe; Saul Bellow; Bricktop; Dr. Bruno Bettelheim; Professor John Morton Blum; *Announcers:* Pathe News (Ed Herlihy); Hearst Metrotone (Dwight Weist); Radio (Gordon Gould); Universal Newsreel (Windy Craig); German U. F. A. Newsreel (Jurgen Kuehn).
Production Credits Director: Woody Allen; Producer: Robert Greenhut; Screenplay: Woody Allen; Photography: Gordon Willis; Production Design: Mel Bourne; Music: Dick Hyman; Editor: Susan E. Morse; Executive Producers: Charles H. Joffe and Jack Rollins; Associate Producer: Michael Peyser; Costume Design: Santo Loquasto; Optical Effects: Joel Hyneck and Stuart Robertson; Stills Animation: Steven Plastrik and Computer Opticals, Inc.

18. BROADWAY DANNY ROSE (1984) Woody Allen (Danny Rose); Mia Farrow (Tina Vitale); Nick Apollo Forte (Lou Canova); Sandy Baron (Himself); Corbett Monica (Himself); Jackie Gayle (Himself); Morty Gunty (Himself); Will Jordan (Himself); Howard Storm (Himself); Jack Rollins (Himself); Milton Berle (Himself); Craig Vandenburgh (Ray Webb); Herb Reynolds (Barney Dunn); Paul Greco (Vito Rispoli); Frank Renzulli (Joe Rispoli); Edwin Bordo (Johnny Rispoli); Gina DeAngelis (Johnny's Mother—Mrs. Rispoli); Peter Castellotti (Hood at Warehouse); Sandy Richman (Teresa); Gerald Schoenfeld (Sid Bacharach); Olga Barbato (Angelina); David Kissell (Phil Chomsky); Gloria Parker (Water Glass Virtuoso); Bob & Etta Rollins (Balloon Act); Bob Weil (Herbie Jayson); David Kieserman (Ralph, Club Owner); Mark Hardwick (Blind Xylophonist); Alba Ballard (Bird Lady); Maurice Shrog (Hypnotist); Belle Berger (Lady in Trance); Herschel Rosen (Lady in Trance's Husband); Joe Franklin (Himself); Cecilia Amerling (Fan in Dressing Room); Maggie Ranone (Lou's Daughter); Charles D'Amodio (Lou's Son); Joie Gallo (Angelina's Assistant); Carl Pistilli (Tommy's Brother); Lucy Iacono (Tommy's Mother); Julia Barbuto (Tropical Fish Lady); Nicholas Pantano (Greeter at Party 1); Rocco Pantano (Greeter at Party 2); Tony Turca (Rocco); Gilda Torterello (Annie); Ronald Maccone (Vincent); Antoinette Raffone (Vincent's Wife); Michael Baldalucco (Money Ripper

1); Richard Lanzano (Money Ripper 2); Dom Matteo (Carmine); Camille Saviola (Lady at Party 1); Sheila Bond (Lady at Party 2); Betty Rosotti (Lady at Party 3); Howard Cosell (Himself); John Doumanian (Waldorf Manager); Gary Reynolds (Waldorf Manager's Friend); Diane Zolten (Fan at Waldorf 1); William Paulson (Fan at Waldorf 2); George Axler (Fan at Waldorf 3); Leo Steiner (Deli Owner).

Production Credits Director: Woody Allen; Producer: Robert Greenhut; Screenplay: Woody Allen; Photography: Gordon Willis; Executive Producer: Charles H. Joffe; Production Design: Mel Bourne; Editor: Susan E. Morse; Costume Design: Jeffrey Kurland; Music: Dick Hyman; Associate Producer: Michael Peyser.

19. THE PURPLE ROSE OF CAIRO (1985) Mia Farrow (Cecilia); Jeff Daniels (Gil Shepherd); Danny Aiello (Monk); Irving Metzman (Theater Manager); Stephanie Farrow (Cecilia's Sister); David Kieserman (Diner Boss); Elaine Grollman, Victoria Zussin, Mark Hammond, Wade Barnes, Joseph G. Graham, Don Quigley, Maurice Brenner (Diner Patrons); Paul Herman, Rick Petrucelli, Peter Castellotti (Penny Pitchers); Milton Seaman, Mimi Weddell (Ticket Buyers); Tom Degidon (Ticket Taker); Mary Hedahl (Popcorn Seller); Dianne Wiest (Emma); Margaret Thompson, George Hamlin, Helen Hanft, Leo Postrel, Helen Miller, George Martin, Crystal Field (Movie Audience); Ken Chapin, Robert Trebor (Reporters); Benjamin Rayson, Jean Shevlin, Albert S. Bennett, Martha Sherrill, Gretchen MacLane, Edwin Bordo (Moviegoers); Andrew Murphy (Policeman 1); Thomas Kubiak (Policeman 2); Alexander Cohen (Raoul Hirsh); John Rothman (Mr. Hirsh's Lawyer); Raymond Serra (Hollywood Executive); George J. Manos (Press Agent); Sydney Blake (*Variety* Reporter); Michael Tucker (Gil's Agent); Peter Von Berg (Drugstore Customer); David Weber (Photo Double); Glenne Headley, Willie Tjan, Lela Ivey, Drinda La Lumia (Hookers); Loretta Tupper (Music Store Owner); the cast of *The Purple Rose of Cairo:* Jeff Daniels (Tom Baxter); Edward Herrmann (Henry); John Wood (Jason); Deborah Rush (Rita); Van Johnson (Larry); Zoe Caldwell (The Countess); Eugene Anthony (Arturo); Ebb Miller (Bandleader); Karen Akers (Kitty Haynes); Annie Joe Edwards (Delilah); Milo O'Shea (Father Donnelly); Peter McRobbie (The Communist); Camille Saviola (Olga); David Tice (Waiter); James Lynch (Maître D').

Production Credits Director: Woody Allen; Producer: Robert Greenhut; Screenplay: Woody Allen; Photography: Gordon Willis; Production Designer: Stuart Wurtzel; Editor: Susan E. Morse; Original Music: Dick Hyman; Executive Producer: Charles H. Joffe; Associate Producers: Michael Peyser, Gail Sicilia; Costume Designer: Jeffrey Kurland.

20. HANNAH AND HER SISTERS (1986) Mia Farrow (Hannah); Woody Allen (Mickey Sachs); Barbara Hershey (Lee); Carrie Fisher (April Knox); Michael Caine (Elliot); Dianne Wiest (Holly); Maureen O'Sullivan (Norma); Lloyd Nolan (Evan); Max von Sydow (Frederick); Sam Waterston (David Tolchin); Julie Kavner (Gail); Lewis Black (Paul); Julia Louis-Dreyfus (Mary); Christian Clemenson (Larry); J. T. Walsh (Ed Smythe); John Turturro (Writer); Rusty Magee (Ron); Allen Decheser, Artie Decheser (Hannah's Twins); Ira Wheeler (Dr. Abel); Richard Jenkins (Dr. Wilkes); Tracy Kennedy (Brunch Guest); Fred Melamed (Dr. Grey); Benno Schmidt (Dr. Smith); Joanna Gleason (Carol); Tony Roberts (Norman); Maria Chiara (Manon Lescaut); Daniel Stern (Dusty); Stephen Defluitter (Dr. Brooks); The 39 Steps (Rock Band); Bobby Short (Himself); Rob Scott (Drummer); Beverly Peer (Bass Player); Daisy Previn, Moses Farrow (Hannah's Children); Paul Bates (Theater Manager); Carrotte, Mary Pappas (Theater Executives); Bernie Leighton (Audition Pianist); Ken Costigan (Father Flynn); Helen Miller (Mickey's Mother); Leo Postrel (Mickey's Father); Susan Gordon-Clark (Hostess); William Sturgis (Elliot's Analyst); Daniel Haber (Krishna); Verna O. Hobson (Mavis); John Doumanian, Fletcher Previn, Irwin Tenenbaum, Amy Greenhill, Dickson Shaw, Marje Sheridan, Mary Beth Hurt (Thanksgiving Guests); Ivan Kronenfeld (Lee's Husband).

Production Credits Director: Woody Allen; Producer: Robert Greenhut; Screenplay:

Woody Allen; Photography: Carlo Di Palma; Executive Producer: Jack Rollins and Charles H. Joffe; Art Direction–Set Direction: Stuart Wartzel and Carol Joffe; Editor: Susan E. Morse; Costume Designer: Jeffrey Kurland; Associate Producer: Gail Sicilia.

21. RADIO DAYS (1987) Julie Kavner (Mother—Tess); Wallace Shawn (Masked Avenger); Michael Tucker (Father—Martin); Josh Mostel (Abe); Dianne Wiest (Bea); Mia Farrow (Sally White); Danny Aiello (Rocco); Jeff Daniels (Biff Baxter); Tony Roberts ("Silver Dollar" Emcee); Diane Keaton (New Year's Eve Singer—Monica Charles); Mike Starr, Paul Herman (Burglars); Don Pardo ("Guess That Tune" Host); Martin Rosenblatt (Mr. Needleman); Helen Miller (Mrs. Needleman); Danielle Ferland (Child Star); Julie Kurnitz (Irene); David Warrilow (Roger); Michael Murray ("Avenger" Crook); William Flanagan ("Avenger" Announcer); Seth Green (Little Joe); Renee Lippin (Ceil); William Magerman (Grandpa—Nathan); Leah Carrey (Grandma); Joy Newman (Ruthie); Hy Anzell (Mr. Waldbaum); Judith Malina (Mrs. Waldbaum); Fletcher Farrow Previn (Andrew); Oliver Block (Nick); Maurice Toueg (Dave); Sal Tuminello (Burt); Rebecca Nickels (Evelyn Goorwitz); Mindy Morgenstern (Show and Tell Teacher); David Mosberg (Arnold); Ross Morgenstern (Ross); Kenneth Mars (Rabbi Baumel); Andrew Clark (Sidney Manulis); Lee Erwin (Roller Rink Organist); Roger Hammer (Richard); Terry Lee Swarts, Margaret Thomson (Nightclub Customers); Denise Dummont (Latin Singer); Dimitri Vassilopoulos (Porfirio); Larry David (Communist Neighbor); Rebecca Schaeffer (Communist's Daughter); Belle Berger (Mrs. Silverman); Guy Le Bow (Bill Kern); Brian Mannain (Kirby Kyle); Stan Burns (Ventriloquist); Todd Field (Crooner); Peter Lombard (Abercrombie Host); Martin Sherman (Mr. Abercrombie); Crystal Field, Maurice Shrog (Abercrombie Couple); Marc Colner (Whiz Kid); Robert Bennett (Teacher with Carrot) [Note: In the film, this character is a woman]; Joel Eidelsberg (Mr. Zipsky); Jimmy Sabat (Chester); Peter Castellotti (Mr. Davis); Gina DeAngelis (Rocco's Mother); Shelley Delaney (Chekhov Actress); Dwight Weist (Pearl Harbor Announcer); Ken Levinsky, Ray Marchica (USO Musicians); J. R. Horne (Biff Announcer); Kuno Spunholz (German); Henry Yuk (Japanese); Sydney A. Blake (Miss Gordon); Kitty Carlisle Hart (Radio Singer); Robert Joy (Fred); Henry Cowen (Principal); Philip Shultz (Whistler); Mercedes Ruehl, Bruce Jarchow (Admen); Greg Gerard (Songwriter); David Cale (Director); Ira Wheeler (Sponsor); Hannah Rabinowitz (Sponsor's Wife—Doris); Edward S. Kotkin (Diction Teacher); Ruby Payne, Jaqui Safra (Diction Students); Paul Berman (*Gay White Way* Announcer); Richard Portnow (Sy Simon); Barbara Gallo, Jane Jarvis, Liz Vochecowizc (Dance Palace Musicians); Ivan Kronenfeld (On-the-Spot Newsman); Frank O'Brien (Fireman); Yolanda Childress (Polly's Mother); Artie Butler (New Year's Eve Singer); Gregg Almquist, Jackson Beck, Wendell Craig, W. H. Macy, Ken Roberts, Norman Rose, Robert Tate, Kenneth Walsh (Radio Voices); Woody Allen (Narrator).
Production Credits Director: Woody Allen; Producer: Robert Greenhut; Screenplay: Woody Allen; Director of Photography: Carlo Di Palma; Production Designer: Santo Loquasto; Editor: Susan E. Morse; Art Direction-Set Direction: Santo Loquasto; Carol Joffee, Les Bloom, and George DeTitta, Jr.; Musical Supervision: Dick Hyman; Associate Producers: Ezra Swerdlow, Gail Sicilia; Costume Designer: Jeffrey Kurland; Executive Producers: Jack Rollins and Charles H. Joffe.

22. SEPTEMBER (1987) Denholm Elliott (Howard); Dianne Wiest (Stephanie); Mia Farrow (Lane); Elaine Stritch (Diane); Sam Waterston (Peter); Jack Warden (Lloyd); Ira Wheeler (Mr. Raines); Jane Cecil (Mrs. Raines); Rosemary Murphy (Mrs. Mason).
Production Credits Director: Woody Allen; Producer: Robert Greenhut; Screenplay: Woody Allen; Director of Photography: Carlo Di Palma; Production Designer: Santo Loquasto; Editor: Susan E. Morse; Executive Producers: Jack Rollins and Charles H. Joffe; Costume Designer: Jeffrey Kurland.

23. ANOTHER WOMAN (1988) Gena Rowlands (Marion Post); Mia Farrow (Hope); Ian Holm (Dr. Kenneth Post); Blythe Danner (Lydia); Gene Hackman (Larry Lewis); Betty Buckley (Kathy); Martha Plimpton (Laura); John Houseman (Marion's Father); Sandy Dennis (Claire); David Ogden Stiers (Young Marion's Father); Philip Bosco (Sam); Harris Yulin (Paul); Frances Conroy (Lynn); Fred Melamed (Patient's Voice); Kenneth Welsh (Donald); Bruce Jay Friedman (Mark); Bernie Leighton (Piano Player); Jack Gelber, John Schenck (Birthday Party Guests); Noel Behn, Gretchen Dahm, Janet Frank, Dana Ivey, Fred Melamed, Alice Spivak (Engagement Party Guests); Mary Laslo (Clara); Carol Schultz (Young Clara); Dax Munna (Little Paul); Heather Sullivan (Little Marion); Margaret Marx (Young Marion); Jennifer Lynn McComb (Young Claire); Caroline McGee (Marion's Mother); Stephen Mailer (Young Paul); Jacques Levy (Jack); Dee Dee Friedman (Waitress); Josh Hamilton (Laura's Boyfriend); Kathryn Grody (Cynthia Franks); John Madden Towey (Waiter); Michael Kirby (Psychiatrist); Fred Sweda (Tom Banks); Jill Whitaker (Eleanor Banks).
Production Credits Director: Woody Allen; Producer: Robert Greenhut; Screenplay: Woody Allen; Photography: Sven Nykvist; Editor: Susan E. Morse; Production Designer: Santo Loquasto; Costume Designer: Jeffrey Kurland; Executive Producers: Jack Rollins and Charles H. Joffe; Associate Producers: Thomas Reilly, Helen Robin.

24. OEDIPUS WRECKS (in **NEW YORK STORIES**) (1989) Woody Allen (Sheldon); Marvin Chatinover (Psychiatrist); Mae Questel (Mother); Mia Farrow (Lisa); Molly Regan (Sheldon's Secretary); Ira Wheeler (Mr. Bates); Joan Bud (Board Member); Jessie Keosian (Aunt Ceil); Michael Rizzo (Waiter); George Schindler (Shandu the Magician); Bridget Ryan (Rita); Larry David (Theater Manager); Paul Herman (Detective Flynn); Herschel Rosen (Store Clerk); Lola André, Martin Rosenblatt, Helen Hanft, Annie-Joe, Ernst Muller, Adele French, Selma Hirsch, Briz, Lou Ruggiero, Elana Cooper (Citizens); Andrew MacMillan (Newscaster); Jodi Long, Nancy Giles (TV Interviewers); Mayor Ed Koch (Himself); Mike Starr, Richard Grund (Hardhats); Julie Kavner (Treva).
Production Credits Director: Woody Allen; Producer: Robert Greenhut; Screenplay: Woody Allen; Photography: Sven Nykvist; Editor: Susan E. Morse; Production Designer: Santo Loquasto; Executive Producers: Jack Rollins and Charles H. Joffe; Costumes: Jeffrey Kurland.

25. CRIMES AND MISDEMEANORS (1989) Bill Bernstein (Testimonial Speaker); Martin Landau (Judah Rosenthal); Claire Bloom (Miriam Rosenthal); Stephanie Roth (Sharon Rosenthal); Greg Edelman (Chris); George Mano (Photographer); Anjelica Huston (Dolores Paley); Woody Allen (Cliff Stern); Jenny Nichols (Jenny); Joanna Gleason (Wendy Stern); Alan Alda (Lester); Daryl Hannah (Lisa Crosby); Sam Waterston (Ben); Zina Jasper (Carol); Dolores Sutton (Judah's secretary); Joel S. Fogel, Donna Castellano, Thomas P. Crow (TV Producers); Mia Farrow (Halley Reed); Martin Bergmann (Professor Louis Levy); Caroline Aaron (Barbara); Kenny Vance (Murray); Jerry Orbach (Jack Rosenthal); Jerry Zaks (Man on Campus); Barry Finkel, Steve Maidment (TV Writers); Nadia Sanford (Alva); Chester Malinowski (Hit Man); Stanley Reichman (Chris's Father); Rebecca Schull (Chris's Mother); David S. Howard (Sol Rosenthal); Garret Simowitz (Young Judah); Frances Conroy (House Owner); Anna Berger (Aunt May); Sol Frieder, Justin Zaremby, Marvin Terban, Hy Anzell, Sylvia Kauders (Seder Guests); Victor Argo (Detective); Lenore Loveman, Nora Ephron, Sunny Keyser, Merv Bloch, Nancy Arden, Thomas L. Bolster, Myla Pitt, Robin Bartlett (Wedding Guests); Grace Zimmerman (Bride); Randy Aaron Fink (Groom); Rabbi Joel Zion (Rabbi).
Production Credits Director: Woody Allen; Producer: Robert Greenhut; Screenplay: Woody Allen; Photography: Sven Nykvist; Editor: Susan E. Morse; Production Designer: Santo Loquasto; Costume Designer: Jeffrey Kurland; Executive Producers: Jack Rollins and Charles H. Joffe.

26. ALICE (1990) Joe Mantegna (Joe Ruffalo); Mia Farrow (Alice Johnson Tait); William Hurt (Doug); June Squib (Hilda); Marceline Hugot (Monica); Dylan O'Sullivan Farrow (Kate); Matt Williamson (Dennis); Julie Kavner (Decorator); Billy Taylor (Trainer); Holland Taylor (Helen); Michael-Vaughn Sullivan (Hairstylist); Robin Bartlett (Nina); Linda Wallem (Penny); Gina Gallagher (Joe's Daughter—Shanna); Patience Moore (Schoolteacher); Diane Cheng (Dr. Yang's Assistant); Kim Chan (Dr. Yang's Patient); Keye Luke (Dr. Yang); Linda Bridges (Saleslady); Anthony Cortino (Dog Groomer); Cybill Shepherd (Nancy Brill); Alec Baldwin (Ed); Katja Schumann (Circus Equestrian); Vanessa Thomas (Circus Aerialist); Blythe Danner (Dorothy); Gwen Verdon (Alice's Mother); Patrick O'Neal (Alice's Father); Kristy Graves (Alice at 18 Yrs.); Laurie Nayber (Young Dorothy); Rachel Miner (Alice at 12 Yrs.); Amy Louise Barrett (Mrs. Keyes); Caroline Aaron (Sue); Alexi Henry (Kimberly); James Toback (Professor); Bernadette Peters (Muse); Elle Macpherson (Model); Ira Wheeler, Lisa Marie (Office Xmas Party Guests); Diane Salinger (Carol); Alfred Cherry (Vicki's Analyst); David Spielberg (Ken); Bob Balaban (Sid Moscowitz); Peggy Miley (Dorothy's Maid); George Manos, Kim Weston-Moran, Peter Tolan, Kenneth Edelson, Marvin Terban, James McDaniel, Roy Attaway (Dorothy's Xmas Party Guests); Jodi Long, Suzann O'Neill, Don Snell, Robert Polenz (Park Avenue Couples).
Production Credits Director: Woody Allen; Producer: Robert Greenhut; Screenplay: Woody Allen; Photography: Carlo Di Palma; Editor: Susan E. Morse; Production Designer: Santo Loquasto; Costume Designer: Jeffrey Kurland; Production Manager: Joseph Hartwick; Co-Producers: Helen Robin, Joseph Hartwick; Associate Producers: Thomas Reilly, Jane Read Martin; Executive Producers: Jack Rollins and Charles H. Joffe.

27. SCENES FROM A MALL (1991) Bette Midler (Deborah Feingold-Fifer); Woody Allen (Nick Fifer); Bill Irwin (Mime); Daren Firestone (Sam); Rebecca Nickels (Jennifer); Paul Mazursky (Dr. Hans Clava); Gregory Moore, Michael Brown, Jonathan Guss, David Frye (Barbershop Quartet); Joseph Warren, Brian Warren, Darrell Maison (Joe Cool & the Coolers—Rap Group); Marc Shaiman (Pianist); Augustin Bustamante, Leonel Cruz, Telmo Hernandez, Steve Ortiz, Ramon Ponce, Fernando Quinones (El Mariachi Bustamante); Joan Delaney (Woman Interviewer); Amanda Bruce (Woman Interviewee); Betsy Mazursky (Information Woman); Jack Brodsky (Pharmacist); Glen Alterman (Owner Museum Shop); Marilyn Pasekof (Woman at Bookstore); Patrick Farrelly (Santa); Hideheko Takada (Sushi Chef); Tichina Arnold (Ticket Seller); Wanakee Legardy (Dress Shop Saleswoman); Carol Harris (Waitress Nuvo Najavo); Vira Colorado, Billy Graham (Security Guards); Chin Long Zhang (Chinese Acrobat); Kamarr (Magician); Kathy Kamarr (Magician's Assistant); Robert Garrett (Bartender); Fabio Lanzoni (Handsome Man); Steven Dominic Prestianni (Male Sikh); Heather Golden (Female Sikh); Jose Rafael Arango (Bus Boy); Bobby Caravella (Man in Parking Garage); Laura Baler (Chocolate Candy Girl); James Duane Polk (Man on Movie Line); Penny Gaston, Minna Rose, Stewart Russell, Joe Viviani (Pharmacy Persons); Larry Sherman, Shiro Dishi, Ron Barry-Barry (Men on Carphones); Michael Greene, Stuart Pappé (Motorcyclists); Andre Phillipe (Taxi Driver); Phillip Nozaki, Donnie Kelber (Kids in Van); Rene Victor, Ann Lochart, Pam Hayden (ADR Voices).
Production Credits Director: Paul Mazursky; Producer: Paul Mazursky; Screenplay: Roger L. Simon and Paul Mazursky; Photography: Fred Murphy; Production Design: Pato Guzman; Editor: Stuart Pappé; Costume Designer: Albert Wolsky; Music: Marc Shaiman; Co-Producers: Pato Guzman and Patrick McCormick; Associate Producer: Stuart Pappé.

28. SHADOWS AND FOG (1992) Woody Allen (Kleinman); Mia Farrow (Irmy); John Malkovich (Clown); Madonna (Marie); Michael Kirby (Killer); Donald Pleasence (Doctor); Lily Tomlin (Prostitute); Jodie Foster (Prostitute); Kathy Bates (Prostitute); Anne Lange (Prostitute); John Cusack (Student Jack); Kate Nelligan (Eve); Fred Gwynne (Hacker's Follower); Julie Kavner (Alma); Kenneth Mars (Armstead the Magician); David Ogden

Stiers (Hacker); Wallace Shawn (Simon Carr); Philip Bosco (Mr. Paulsen); Josef Sommer (Priest); Camille Saviola (Landlady); Robert Silver (Hacker's Follower); Charles Cragin (Spiro); Robert Joy (Spiro's Assistant); W. H. Macy (Cop with Spiro); James Rebhorn (Vigilante); Victor Argo (Vigilante); Daniel Von Bargen (Vigilante); Kurtwood Smith (Vogel's Follower); Eszter Balint (Woman with Baby); Rebecca Gibson (Baby).

Production Credits Director: Woody Allen; Producers: Jack Rollins and Charles H. Joffe; Screenplay: Woody Allen; Director of Photography: Carlo Di Palma; Editor: Susan E. Morse; Music: Kurt Weill; Production Design: Santo Loquasto; Art Direction: Speed Hopkins; Set Decoration: George DeTitta Jr., Amy Marshall; Costume Design: Jeffrey Kurland; Dolby Sound: James Sabat; Associate Producer/Assistant Director: Thomas Reilly; Casting: Juliet Taylor.

Appendix 2

Woody's Favorites
Actors and Actresses Woody Has Used in
More Than One Film

It's a big help to know people so that
you can write to their strengths.
Woody Allen

When it comes to actors, Woody Allen recognizes a good one when he finds one,
and when he does, he sticks with those who have delivered the goods, and rewards them
by hiring them again.

Over the years, Woody has used a coterie of actors and actresses in more than one
role, and this feature takes a look at some of these multifarious and multitalented thes-
pians, and lists the films in which they've appeared and the roles they've played.

Caroline Aaron

Crimes and Misdemeanors (Barbara)
Alice (Sue)

Danny Aiello

The Front (Danny La Gattuta)
Annie Hall (Man in junk-food establishment—cut from final version)
The Purple Rose of Cairo (Monk)
Radio Days (Rocco)
The Floating Light Bulb (play) (Max Pollack)

Hy Anzell

Bananas (Patient)
Annie Hall (Joey Nichols)
Radio Days (Mr. Waldbaum)
Crimes and Misdemeanors (Seder Guest)

Wade Barnes

Stardust Memories (UFO Follower)
The Purple Rose of Cairo (Diner Patron)

Robin Bartlett

Crimes and Misdemeanors (Wedding Guest)
Alice (Nina)

Ken Chapin

Stardust Memories (Sandy's Father)
Zelig (On-Screen Interviewer)
The Purple Rose of Cairo (Reporter)
Radio Days (Interviewer—cut from final version))

Martin Chatinover

Zelig (Glandular Diagnosis Doctor)
Radio Days (Mr. Globus—cut from final version)

Howard Cosell

> *Bananas* (Himself)
> *Sleeper* (Himself)
> *Broadway Danny Rose* (Himself)

Jeff Daniels

> *The Purple Rose of Cairo* (Gil Shepherd)
> *Radio Days* (Biff Baxter)

Blythe Danner

> *Another Woman* (Lydia)
> *Alice* (Dorothy)

Gina DeAngelis

> *Broadway Danny Rose* (Johnny's Mother—Mrs. Rispoli)
> *Radio Days* (Rocco's Mother)

John Doumanian

> *Annie Hall* (Coke Fiend)
> *Manhattan* (Porsche Owner 2)
> *Stardust Memories* (Armenian Fan)
> *Zelig* (Greek Waiter)
> *Broadway Danny Rose* (Waldorf Manager)
> *Hannah and Her Sisters* (Thanksgiving Guest)
> *Radio Days* (Polly Phelps Man—cut from final version)

Mia Farrow

> *A Midsummer Night's Sex Comedy* (Ariel)
> *Zelig* (Eudora Fletcher)
> *Broadway Danny Rose* (Tina Vitale)
> *The Purple Rose of Cairo* (Cecilia)
> *Hannah and Her Sisters* (Hannah)
> *Radio Days* (Sally White)
> *September* (Lane)
> *Another Woman* (Hope)
> *Oedipus Wrecks* (Lisa)
> *Crimes and Misdemeanors* (Halley Reed)
> *Alice* (Alice Tait)
> *Shadows and Fog* (Irmy)

Stephanie Farrow

> *Zelig* (Sister Meryl)
> *The Purple Rose of Cairo* (Cecilia's Sister)

Joanna Gleason

> *Hannah and Her Sisters* (Carol)
> *Crimes and Misdemeanors* (Wendy Stern)

Mark Gordon

> *Don't Drink the Water* (Merik)
> *Take the Money and Run* (Vince)

George Hamlin

> *Zelig* (Experimental Drugs Doctor)
> *Radio Days* (The Bigot—cut from final version)

Mark Hammond

The Purple Rose of Cairo (Diner Patron)
Radio Days (Mr. Brooks—cut from final version)

Helen Hanft

Manhattan (Party Guest)
Stardust Memories (Vivian Orkin)
The Purple Rose of Cairo (Movie Audience Member)
Oedipus Wrecks (Citizen)

Jessica Harper

Love and Death (Natasha)
Stardust Memories (Daisy)

Paul Herman

Radio Days (Burglar)
Oedipus Wrecks (Detective Flynn)

Julie Kavner

Hannah and Her Sisters (Gail)
Radio Days (Mother)
Oedipus Wrecks (Treva)
Shadows and Fog (Alma)

Diane Keaton

Sleeper (Luna)
Love and Death (Sonia)
Annie Hall (Annie Hall)
Interiors (Renata)
Manhattan (Mary Wilke)
Radio Days (Monica Charles)

Ivan Kronenfeld

Hannah and Her Sisters (Lee's Husband)
Radio Days (On-the-Spot Newsman)

Jerry Lacy

Play It Again, Sam (Humphrey Bogart)
Play It Again, Sam (play) (Humphrey Bogart)

Louise Lasser

What's New, Pussycat? (The Nutcracker)
What's Up, Tiger Lily? (vocal dubbing)
Take the Money and Run (Kay Lewis)
Bananas (Nancy)
Everything You Always Wanted to Know About Sex* (*But Were Afraid to Ask)
  (Gina; Female Spider—in unfilmed segment)
Stardust Memories (Secretary)

Bernie Leighton

Hannah and Her Sisters (Audition Pianist)
Another Woman (Piano Player)

Renee Lippin

Stardust Memories (Sandy's Press Agent)
Radio Days (Ceil)

William Magerman

Annie Hall (Alvy's deaf uncle—cut from final version)
Stardust Memories (Extra)
Radio Days (Grandpa)

Janet Margolin

Take the Money and Run (Louise)
Annie Hall (Robin)

Fred Melamed

Hannah and Her Sisters (Dr. Grey)
Another Woman (Patient's Voice; Engagement Party Guest)

Michael Murphy

The Front (Alfred Miller)
Manhattan (Yale)

Joan Newman

Annie Hall (Alvy's Mom)
Stardust Memories (Sandy's Mother)

Tony Roberts

Play It Again, Sam (Dick Christie)
Annie Hall (Rob)
Stardust Memories (Tony)
A Midsummer Night's Sex Comedy (Dr. Maxwell Jordan)
Hannah and Her Sisters (Norman)
Radio Days ("Silver Dollar" Emcee)

Jack Rollins

Stardust Memories (Studio Executive)
Broadway Danny Rose (Himself)

Martin Rosenblatt

Annie Hall (Alvy's Uncle)
Radio Days (Mr. Needleman)
Oedipus Wrecks (Citizen)

John Rothman

Stardust Memories (Jack Abel)
Zelig (Paul Deghuee)
The Purple Rose of Cairo (Mr. Hirsh's Lawyer)
Radio Days (Effects Man—cut from final version)

Jaqui Safra

Stardust Memories (Sam)
Radio Days (Diction Student)

Raymond Serra

Manhattan (Pizzeria Waiter)
The Purple Rose of Cairo (Hollywood Executive)

Wallace Shawn

Manhattan (Jeremiah)
Radio Days (Masked Avenger)

Kuno Spunholz

> *Zelig* (Oswald Poli)
> *Radio Days* (German)

Mike Starr

> *Radio Days* (Burglar)
> *Oedipus Wrecks* (Hardhat)

Daniel Stern

> *Stardust Memories* (Actor)
> *Hannah and Her Sisters* (Dusty)

David Ogden Stiers

> *Another Woman* (Young Marion's Father)
> *Shadows and Fog* (Hacker)

Victor Truro

> *Manhattan* (Party Guest)
> *Stardust Memories* (Hostility Psychoanalyst)

Michael Tucker

> *The Purple Rose of Cairo* (Gil's Agent)
> *Radio Days* (Father—Martin)

Kenny Vance

> *Manhattan* (Television Producer)
> *Stardust Memories* (New Studio Executive)
> *Crimes and Misdemeanors* (Murray)

Dimitri Vassilopoulos

> *Stardust Memories* (Cabaret Patron)
> *Zelig* (Martinez)
> *Radio Days* (Porfirio)

Sam Waterston

> *Interiors* (Mike)
> *Hannah and Her Sisters* (David Tolchin)
> *September* (Peter)
> *Crimes and Misdemeanors* (Ben)

Dwight Weist

> *Zelig* (Hearst Metrotone Announcer)
> *Radio Days* (Pearl Harbor Announcer)

Dianne Wiest

> *The Purple Rose of Cairo* (Emma)
> *Hannah and Her Sisters* (Holly)
> *Radio Days* (Bea)
> *September* (Stephanie)

Appendix 3

Through Woody's Ears
The Music in Woody Allen's Life and Films

I would like, in the course of my life, to do . . . a musical.
Woody Allen

Music is feeling, then, not sound.
Wallace Stevens, from "Peter Quince at the Clavier"

[Woody's] talent as a scorer of movies is widely overlooked, or is so taken for granted that it passes unremarked. Music is such an integral part of Woody's presentation of a film, and his use of tunes from 1900 to 1950 so pronounced, that it is possible to recognize a Woody Allen film from the score alone.
Eric Lax, *Woody Allen: A Biography*

Jazz is a perfect music for him. It hates authority. It is a quirky, individual style requiring great discipline to play right. It is all the things that fit his comic character.
Eric Lax, quoted in *Time*, October 23, 1989

It's the best life I can think of if you're a really talented musician because communication in music is so emotional in every way.
Woody Allen, quoted in *Time*, October 23, 1989

Woody Allen's use of music in his films has always been one of the sweeter pleasures of his work. He seems to have a knack for picking the right song for the right moment. It was clear that we should begin to pay serious attention to the music in Woody's films when we first heard the opening passages of George Gershwin's "Rhapsody in Blue" at the beginning of *Manhattan*.

For his first three films, Woody counted on the talents of film scorers such as Marvin Hamlisch and Mundell Lowe. Then, in 1973, with *Sleeper*, Woody performed with the Preservation Hall Jazz Band and the New Orleans Funeral Ragtime Orchestra for the film's score. (Woody plays a twelve-key Rampone clarinet made in Italy around 1890. He uses a wide-open mouthpiece and a Rico Royale No. 5 reed (which is very hard. According to *Time* magazine, "Benny Goodman once borrowed Woody's clarinet for a sit-in and had to shave the reed down with a kitchen knife before he could get a toot out of it").

Following *Sleeper*, Woody turned to the music of Sergei Prokofiev for *Love and Death*. He had originally wanted to use Stravinsky, but editor Ralph Rosenblum talked him out of it and instead suggested Prokofiev. Rosenblum argued that Stravinsky was too strong and Prokofiev the better choice. He was right. The music in *Love and Death* fits the film perfectly.

In 1977's *Annie Hall* Woody for the first time used classic American popular songs to add layers of texture to a film. Diane Keaton sang "Seems Like Old Times" and "It Had to Be You." They worked.

For his next film, *Interiors*, he used only recorded music, which befitted the somber and stately tone of the film, but then, in 1979, came *Manhattan*. Woody employed no fewer than thirteen George Gershwin songs in that film, and the score was acclaimed as being another "character" in the film, such was its impact.

He followed *Manhattan* with *Stardust Memories*, again turning to the great catalogue of American popular music. For that film, Woody tapped everyone from Glenn Miller and Hoagy Carmichael to Benny Goodman and his clarinet idol, Sidney Bechet.

Then, for *A Midsummer Night's Sex Comedy,* Woody again drew from classical music, this time the light and airy music of Felix Mendelssohn, again a perfect choice for the pastoral feel of the film.

After *Midsummer* came *Zelig,* a unique musical experience. There were more than a dozen songs from the 1920s and 1930s, as well as original period songs about Leonard Zelig composed by Dick Hyman.

For *Broadway Danny Rose* Woody depended on the talents of Dick Hyman, who arranged Nick Apollo Forte's two original songs used in the film.

The Purple Rose of Cairo again used original music by Dick Hyman, as well as three standards.

Then, in 1986, *Hannah and Her Sisters* was released, and you would almost think it was *Manhattan* all over again. The selection of songs in *Hannah* was perfect. Each piece added layers of meaning to the different storylines, from the beginning strands of "You Made Me Love You" to the closing "Isn't It Romantic?" And we also got to hear Carrie Fisher do a very sweet rendition of "The Way You Look Tonight." The music in *Hannah and Her Sisters* was, and is, quite memorable.

And then Woody went wild. His 1987 autobiographical memoir, *Radio Days,* contains no fewer than *forty-three* songs. (Including Dick Hyman's unforgettable laxative jingle "Re-Lax." Once you hear it, you'll be able to sing it immediately, and will never forget it.) Woody and company ably captured the ambience and warmth of World War II Brooklyn, and succeeded in conveying just how important the music—and the radio—was to people of that era. Much delightful music from that period is, unfortunately, pretty much ignored today.

The music of *September* can be summed up in one name: Art Tatum. Actually, only a couple of Tatum pieces are played during the film, but the songs so communicate just the right mood that their essence permeates the late summer feel of the film.

In *Another Woman* Woody used the work of Erik Satie, Edgard Varèse, and Gustav Mahler for the first time, as well as more of Cole Porter, Jerome Kern, Dorothy Fields, and Erroll Garner.

The score of *Oedipus Wrecks* contributed enormously to the comic tone of the film. Case in point: "Sing, Sing, Sing" plays on the soundtrack as Sheldon's mother and aunt amble down the hallway to his office. The choice of this song was inspired. And the use of "I Want a Girl (Just Like the Girl That Married Dear Old Dad)" as the closing song is the perfect thematic coda.

In *Crimes and Misdemeanors* Woody drew upon Irving Berlin and Franz Schubert, in addition to using "Happy Birthday to You" and the work of Xavier Cugat. The musical selections in *Crimes* are eclectic, appropriate, and very entertaining.

Woody's 1990 release, *Alice,* finds him turning to none other than the Great One, Jackie Gleason himself, for no fewer than four selections. Woody also used "The Way You Look Tonight" again (he used it in *Hannah*), and the Castilians' "La Cumparsita" (which he previously used in *Radio Days*).

For his most recent film, *Shadows and Fog,* Woody relied solely on the music of Kurt Weill.

Take the Money and Run (1969)
Music by Marvin Hamlisch.

Bananas (1971)
Music by Marvin Hamlisch.

Everything You Always Wanted to Know About Sex* (*But Were Afraid to Ask) (1972)
Music by Mundell Lowe. (Note: Thierry de Navacelle, in his 1987 book about the filming

of *Radio Days, Woody Allen on Location,* states that "[Dick Hyman] started with Woody on *Everything You Always Wanted to Know About Sex* [in] 1972." The screen credits for *Sex* said, "Music Composed and Conducted by Mundell Lowe," and there is no mention of Hyman anywhere else in the credits.)

Sleeper (1973)
Music by Woody Allen, with the Preservation Hall Jazz Band and the New Orleans Funeral Ragtime Orchestra.

Love and Death (1975)
Music by Sergei Prokofiev.

Annie Hall (1977)
Songs
• "Seems Like Old Times"; Music by Carmen Lombardo; Lyrics by John Jacob Loeb.
• "It Had to Be You"; Music by Isham Jones; Lyrics by Gus Kahn.
Recorded music
• "A Hard Way to Go"; Performed by Tim Weisberg.
• Christmas Medley; Performed by the Do-Re-Mi Children's Chorus.
• "Sleepy Lagoon"; Performed by Tommy Dorsey.

Interiors (1978)
Recorded music
• "Keepin' Out of Mischief Now"; Performed by Tommy Dorsey.
• "Wolverine Blues"; Performed by the World's Greatest Jazz Band.

Manhattan (1979)
Music by George Gershwin.
George Gershwin songs and compositions performed by the New York Philharmonic, conducted by Zubin Mehta
• "Rhapsody in Blue"
• "Love Is Sweeping the Country"
• "Land of the Gay Caballero"
• "Sweet and Low Down"
• "I've Got a Crush on You"
• "Do-Do-Do"
• " 'Swonderful"
• "Oh, Lady Be Good"
• "Strike Up the Band"
• "Embraceable You"
George Gershwin songs performed by the Buffalo Philharmonic, conducted by Michael Tilson Thomas
• "Someone to Watch Over Me"
• "He Loves and She Loves"
• "But Not for Me"

Stardust Memories (1980)
Piano music arranged and performed by Dick Hyman: "Hebrew School Rag" (music by Dick Hyman), "Just One of Those Things" (music by Cole Porter), "Easy to Love" (music by Cole Porter).
Songs and classical compositions
• "Tropical Mood Meringue"; Music Written and Performed by Sidney Bechet.
• "I'll See You in My Dreams"; Performed by Django Reinhardt; Music by Isham Jones and Gus Jones.

- "Tickletoe"; Performed by Lester Young with Count Basie & His Orchestra; Music by Lester Young.
- "Three Little Words"; Performed by Jazz Heaven Orchestra; Music by Bert Kalmer and Harry Rubin.
- "Brazil"; Sung by Marie Lane; Music by Ary Barroso, Lyrics by S. K. Russell.
- "Palesteena"; Performed by the Original Dixieland Jazz Band; Music by J. Rusell Robinson and Con Conrad.
- "Body and Soul"; Performed by Django Reinhardt; Music by Edward Hyman, Robert Sour, John W. Gree, and Frank Eyton.
- "Night on Bald Mountain"; Performed by the Vienna State Opera Orchestra; Music by Moussorgsky.
- "If Dreams Come True"; Performed by Chick Webb; Music by I. Mills, E. Sampson, and B. Goodman.
- "One O'Clock Jump"; Performed by Jazz Heaven Orchestra; Music by Count Basie.
- "Sugar"; Music by Maceo Pinkard and Sidney Milton.
- "Sweet Georgia Brown"; Music by Ben Bernie, Kenneth Casey, and Maceo Pinkard.
- "Moonlight Serenade"; Written and Performed by Glenn Miller.
- "Stardust"; Performed by Louis Armstrong; Music by Hoagy Carmichael; Lyrics by Mitchell Parish.

A Midsummer Night's Sex Comedy (1982)
Music by Felix Mendelssohn

Zelig (1983)
Music composed and adapted by Dick Hyman.
Original songs by Dick Hyman
- "Leonard the Lizard"
- "Doin' the Chameleon"
- "Chameleon Days"
- "You May Be Six People, But I Love You"
- "Reptile Eyes"
- "The Changing Man Concerto"

Additional songs
- "I've Got a Feeling I'm Falling" by Harry Link, Billy Rose, and Thomas (Fats) Waller; Sung by Roz Harris.
- "I'm Sitting on Top of the World" by Ray Henderson, Samuel M. Lewis, and Joe Young; Sung by Norman Brooks.
- "Ain't We Got Fun" by Raymond B. Egan, Gus Kahn, and Richard Whiting; Performed by the Charleston City All Stars.
- "Sunny Side Up" by Lew Brown, B. G. DeSylva, and Ray Henderson; Performed by the Charleston City All Stars.
- "I'll Get By" by Fred E. Ahlert and Roy Turk; Performed by the Ben Bernie Orchestra.
- "I Love My Baby, My Baby Loves Me" by Bud Green and Harry Wilson; Performed by the Charleston City All Stars.
- "Runnin' Wild" by A. H. Gibbs, Joe Grey, and Leo Wood; Performed by the Charleston City All Stars.
- "A Sailboat in the Moonlight" by John Loeb and Carmen Lombardo; Performed by the Guy Lombardo Orchestra.
- "Charleston" by James P. Johnson and Cecil Mack; Performed by Dick Hyman.
- "Chicago, That Toddlin' Town" by Fred Fisher; Performed by Dick Hyman.
- "Five Foot Two, Eyes of Blue" by Ray Henderson, Samuel M. Lewis, and Joe Young; Performed by Dick Hyman.
- "Anchors Aweigh" by George D. Lottman, Alfred H. Miles, Domenico Sanino, and Charles A. Zimmerman; Performed by Dick Hyman.

Broadway Danny Rose (1984)
Music supervisor: Dick Hyman.
Songs
- "Agita"; Written and Performed by Nick Apollo Forte.
- "My Bambina"; Written and Performed by Nick Apollo Forte.

The Purple Rose of Cairo (1985)
Original music by Dick Hyman.
Songs
- "Cheek to Cheek" by Irving Berlin; Vocal by Fred Astaire.
- "I Love My Baby, My Baby Loves Me" by Bud Green and Harry Warren.
- "Alabamy Bound" by Ray Henderson, B. G. DeSylva, and Bud Green.

Hannah and Her Sisters (1986)
Segment from the opera *Manon Lescaut* by Puccini performed by the Orchestra of the Regio Theater, conducted by Angelo Campori.
Songs and classical compositions
- "You Made Me Love You" by Joseph McCarthy and James V. Monaco; Performed by Harry James.
- "I've Heard That Song Before" by Sammy Cahn and Julie Styne; Performed by Harry James.
- "Bewitched" by Richard Rodgers and Lorenz Hart.
- "Just You, Just Me" by Raymond Klages and Jesse Greer.
- "Where or When" by Richard Rodgers and Lorenz Hart.
- "Concerto for Two Violins and Orchestra" by J. S. Bach; Performed by the Sofia Soloists Chamber Orchestra; Conducted by Vassil Kazandjiev.
- "Back to the Apple" by Frank Foster and Count Basie; Performed by Count Basie & His Orchestra.
- "The Trot" by Benny Carter; Performed by Count Basie and His Orchestra.
- "I Remember You" by Johnny Mercer and Victor Schertzinger; Performed by Dave Brubeck.
- *Madame Butterfly* by Puccini; Performed by Rome Opera Chorus & Orchestra; Conducted by Sir John Barbirolli.
- "Concerto for Harpsichord in F Minor" by J. S. Bach; Performed by Leonhardt Gustav.
- "You Are Too Beautiful" by Richard Rodgers and Lorenz Hart.
- "If I Had You" by Jimmy Campbell, Reg Connelly, and Ted Shapiro; Performed by Roy Eldridge.
- "I'm in Love Again" by Cole Porter.
- "I'm Old-Fashioned" by Jerome Kern and Johnny Mercer.
- "The Way You Look Tonight" by Jerome Kern and Dorothy Fields.
- "It Could Happen to You" by Johnny Burke and James Van Heusen.
- "Polkadots and Moonbeams" by Johnny Burke and James Van Heusen.
- "Avalon" by Vincent Rose, Al Jolson, and B. G. DeSylva.
- "Isn't It Romantic?" by Richard Rodgers and Lorenz Hart.

Radio Days (1987)
Musical supervision: Dick Hyman.
Songs and classical compositions
- "The Flight of the Bumblebee" by N. A. Rimsky-Korsakov; Performed by Harry James.
- "Dancing in the Dark" by Arthur Schwartz and Howard Dietz.
- "Chinatown, My Chinatown" by William Jerome and Jean Schwartz.
- "Let's All Sing Like the Birdies Sing" by Roger Hargreaves, Stanley J. Damerell, and Tolchard Evans.
- "I Double Dare You" by Jimmy Eaton and Terry Shand; Performed by Larry Clinton.

- "You're Getting to Be a Habit with Me" by Harry Warren and Al Dubin.
- "September Song" by Kurt Weill and Maxwell Anderson.
- "Body and Soul" by John W. Green, Edward Heyman, Robert Sour, and Frank Eyton; Performed by Benny Goodman.
- "In the Mood" by Joe Garland; Performed by Glenn Miller.
- "Radio Show Themes" by Dick Hyman.
- "Carioca" by Vincent Youmans, Gus Kahn, and Edward Eliscu.
- "Tico, Tico" by Zequinha Abreu, Aloysio Oliviera, and Erwin Drake.
- "La Cumparsita" by Matos Rodriguez; Performed by the Castilians.
- "Frenesi" by A. Dominguez; Performed by Artie Shaw.
- "All or Nothing at All" by Jack Lawrence and Arthur Altman.
- "The Donkey Serenade" by Herbert Stothart, Rudolf Friml, Bob Wright, and Chet Forrest; Performed by Allan Jones.
- "South American Way" by Al Dubin and Jimmy McHugh; Performed by Carmen Miranda.
- "Mairzy Doats" by Milton Drake, Al Hoffman, and Jerry Livingston; Performed by the Merry Macs.
- "If You Are But a Dream" by Moe Jaffe, Jack Fulton, and Nat Bonx; Performed by Frank Sinatra.
- "Begin the Beguine" by Cole Porter.
- "Opus One" by Sy Oliver; Performed by Tommy Dorsey.
- "You and I" by Meredith Willson; Performed by Tommy Dorsey.
- "Paper Doll" by Johnny S. Black; Performed by the Mills Brothers.
- "Pistol Packin' Mama" by Al Dexter; Performed by Bing Crosby and the Andrews Sisters.
- "If I Didn't Care" by Jack Lawrence; Performed by the Ink Spots.
- "Schloff Mein Kind" by Emil Decameron.
- "I Don't Want to Walk Without You" by Julie Styne and Frank Loesser.
- "Remember Pearl Harbor" by Sammy Kaye and Don Reid; Performed by Sammy Kaye.
- "Babalu" by Margarita Lecuona and S. K. Russell; Performed by Xavier Cugat.
- "They're Either Too Young or Too Old" by Arthur Schwartz and Frank Loesser; Performed by Kitty Carlisle Hart.
- "That Old Feeling" by Lew Brown and Sammy Fain; Performed by Guy Lombardo.
- "Re-Lax Jingle" by Dick Hyman; Performed by Mia Farrow.
- "Lullaby of Broadway" by Al Dubin and Harry Warren; Performed by Richard Himber.
- "American Patrol" by F. W. Meacham; Performed by Glenn Miller.
- "Take the 'A' Train" by Billy Strayhorn; Performed by Duke Ellington.
- "(There'll Be Blue Birds Over) The White Cliffs of Dover" by Walter Kent and Nat Burton; Performed by Glenn Miller.
- "Goodbye" by Gordon Jenkins; Performed by Benny Goodman.
- "I'm Gettin' Sentimental over You" by Ned Washington and George Bassman; Performed by Tommy Dorsey.
- "You'll Never Know" by Harry Warren and Mack Gordon.
- "One, Two, Three, Kick" by Xavier Cugat and Al Stillman; Performed by Xavier Cugat.
- "Just One of Those Things" by Cole Porter.
- "You'd Be So Nice to Come Home To" by Cole Porter.
- "Night and Day" by Cole Porter.

September (1987)
Songs
- "On a Slow Boat to China" by Frank Loesser; Performed by Bernie Leighton.
- "Out of Nowhere" by John Green and Edward Heyman; Performed by Ambrose & His Orchestra.

- "Just One More Chance" by Sam Coslow and Arthur Johnston; Performed by Ambrose & His Orchestra.
- "My Ideal" by Leo Rubin, Richard A. Whiting, and Newell Chase; Performed by Art Tatum, Ben Webster, Red Callender, and Bill Douglass.
- "What'll I Do" by Irving Berlin; Performed by Bernie Leighton.
- "Who" by Jerome Kern, Otto Harbach, and Oscar Hammerstein II; Performed by Bernie Leighton.
- "I'm Confessin' (That I Love You)" by Al J. Neiburg, Doc Dougherty, and Ellis Reynolds; Performed by Bernie Leighton.
- "Moonglow" by Will Hudson, Eddie DeLange, and Irving Mills; Performed by Bernie Leighton.
- "When Day Is Done" by Robert Kaischer and B. G. DeSylva; Performed by Bernie Leighton.
- "Night and Day" by Cole Porter; Performed by Art Tatum, Ben Webster, Red Callender, and Bill Douglass.

Another Woman (1988)
Songs and classical compositions
- "Gymnopédie no. 3" by Erik Satie; Performed by the Orchestre de la Societé Concerts du Conservatoire; Conducted by Louis Auriacombe.
- "The Bilbao Song" by Kurt Weill and Bert Brecht.
- "Unaccompanied Cello Suite in D Major" by Johann Sebastian Bach; Performed by Yo-Yo Ma.
- "Ecuatorial" by Edgard Varèse; Performed by Ensemble Intercontemporain.
- "Perdido" by Juan Tizol; Performed by the Dave Brubeck Quartet.
- "You'd Be So Nice to Come Home To" by Cole Porter; Performed by Jim Hall.
- "Lovely to Look At" by Dorothy Fields and Jimmy McHugh; Performed by Bernie Leighton.
- "A Fine Romance" by Jerome Kern and Dorothy Fields; Performed by Erroll Garner.
- "Make Believe" by Oscar Hammerstein II and Jerome Kern; Performed by Erroll Garner.
- "Symphony no. 4 in G Major" by Gustav Mahler; Performed by the New York Philharmonic; Conducted by Leonard Bernstein.
- "Smiles" by Will Callahan and Lee S. Roberts; Performed by Teddy Wilson.
- "On the Sunny Side of the Street" by Jimmy McHugh and Dorothy Fields; Performed by Teddy Wilson.
- "Sonata for Cello and Piano no. 2" (BMV 1028) by Johann Sebastian Bach; Performed by Mischa Maisky and Martha Argerich.
- "Roses Of Picardy" by Fred E. Weatherly and Haydn Wood; Performed by Frankie Carle.
- "Sonata for Cello and Piano no. 3" (BMV 1029) by Johann Sebastian Bach; Performed by Mischa Maisky and Martha Argerich.

Oedipus Wrecks (1989)
Songs
- "I Want a Girl (Just Like the Girl That Married Dear Old Dad)" by William Dillon and Harry Van Tilner; Performed by Frankie Carle.
- "Mother" by Howard Johnson and Theodore Morse; Performed by Bernie Leighton.
- "Sing, Sing, Sing" by Louis Prima; Performed by Benny Goodman.
- "In a Persian Market" by Albert Ketelby; Performed by Wilbur de Paris. ("In a Persian Market" was also used in Woody's 1981 play, *The Floating Light Bulb,* during the scene in which Paul performs for Jerry Wexler, and at the end of the play after Enid throws Max out of the apartment.)
- "I'll Be Seeing You" by Sammy Fain and Irving Kahal; Performed by Liberace.
- "I've Found a New Baby" by Jack Palmer and Spencer Williams; Performed by Wilbur de Paris.

- "All the Things You Are" by Jerome Kern and Oscar Hammerstein II; Performed by David Rose & His Orchestra.
- "June in January" by Ralph Rainger and Leo Rubin; Performed by David Rose & His Orchestra.

Crimes and Misdemeanors (1989)
Songs and classical compositions
- "Rosalie" by Cole Porter; Performed by the Jazz Band.
- "Dancing on the Ceiling" by Richard Rodgers and Lorenz Hart; Performed by Bernie Leighton.
- "Taking a Chance on Love" by Vernon Duke, John La Touche, and Ted Fetter.
- "I Know That You Know" by Vincent Youman, Anne Caldwell O'Dea, and Otto A. Harbach.
- "English Suite no. 2 in A Minor" by Johann Sebastian Bach; Performed by Alicia de Laroccha.
- "Home Cooking" by Hilton Ruiz; Performed by the Hilton Ruiz Quartet.
- "Happy Birthday to You" by Mildred J. Hill and Patty S. Hill.
- "Sweet Georgia Brown" by Ben Bernie, Maceo Pinkard, and Kenneth Casey; Performed by Coleman Hawkins.
- "I've Got You" by Frank Loesser and Jacques Press.
- "This Year's Kisses" by Irving Berlin; Performed by Ozzie Nelson & His Orchestra.
- "All I Do Is Dream of You" by Nacio Herb Brown and Arthur Freed.
- "Quartet no. 15 in G Major" (Op. 161, D.887) by Franz Schubert; Performed by the Julliard Quartet.
- "Murder He Says" by Frank Loesser and Jimmy McHugh; Performed by Betty Hutton.
- "Beautiful Love" by Victor Young, Wayne King, Egbert Van Alstyne, and Haven Gillespie.
- "Great Day" by Vincent Youmans, William Rose, and Edward Eliscu; Performed by Bernie Leighton.
- "Star Eyes" by Don Raye and Gene DePaul; Performed by Lee Musiker.
- "Because" by Guy D'Hardelot and Edward Teschmaker; Performed by Lee Musiker.
- "Crazy Rhythm" by Irving Caesar, R. Wolfe Kahn, and Joseph Meyer; Performed by the Wedding Band.
- "I'll See You Again" by Noël Coward; Performed by the Wedding Band.
- "Cuban Mambo" by Xavier Cugat, Rafael Angulo, and Jack Wiseman; Performed by the Wedding Band.
- "Polkadots and Moonbeams" by Johnny Burke and Jimmy Van Heusen; Performed by the Wedding Band.
- "I'll Be Seeing You" by Sammy Fain and Irving Kahal; Performed by Liberace.

Alice (1990)
Songs
- "Limehouse Blues" by Philip Braham and Douglas Farber; Performed by Jackie Gleason.
- "Breezin' Along with the Breeze" by Dizzy Gillespie, Seymour Simons, and Richard A. Whiting; Performed by Jackie Gleason.
- "I Dream Too Much" by Dorothy Fields and Jerome Kern; Performed by Paul Weston & His Orchestra.
- "Limehouse Blues" by Philip Braham and Douglas Farber; Performed by Ambrose & His Orchestra.
- "Moonglow" by Will Hudson, Eddie DeLange, and Irving Mills; Performed by Artie Shaw & His Orchestra.
- "La Cumparsita" by Matos Rodriguez; Performed by the Castilians.
- "The Courier" and "World Music" by Linda Hudes; Performed by the Big Apple Circus Band.

- "Caravan" by Edward Kennedy Ellington, Irving Mills, and Juan Tizol; Performed by Erroll Garner.
- "I Remember You" by Johnny Mercer and Victor Schertzinger; Performed by Jackie Gleason.
- "Moonlight Becomes You" by Johnny Burke and James Van Heusen; Performed by Jackie Gleason.
- "The Way You Look Tonight" by Jerome Kern and Dorothy Fields; Performed by Erroll Garner.
- "Alice Blue Gown" by Joseph McCarthy, Jr. and Harry Tierney; Performed by Wayne King & His Orchestra.
- "Concerto no. 1 in A Minor for Violin and Orchestra" (BMV 1041) by Johann Sebastian Bach; Performed by the English Chamber Orchestra; Conducted by Pinchas Zuckerman.
- "Darn That Dream" by Edgar DeLange and Jimmy Van Heusen; Performed by Thelonius Monk.
- "Southern Comfort" by Danny Alguire, Frank Thomas, and Ward Kimball; Performed by the Firehouse Five Plus Two.
- "Mack the Knife" by Kurt Weill, Marc Blitzstein, and Berthold Brecht.
- "Flight of the Foo Birds" by Neal Hefti; Performed by Count Basie.
- "Will You Still Be Mine?" by Matt Dennis and Thomas M. Adair; Performed by Erroll Garner.
- "O Tannenbaum"/"We Wish You a Merry Christmas"; Performed by Liberace.

Shadows and Fog (1992)
Music by Kurt Weill from *The Threepenny Opera*.

Appendix 4

Woody and the Oscars

I'm not making films because I want to be in the movie business.
I'm making them because I want to say something.
Woody Allen

What interests me is solely the work itself. I didn't enter the film business
and then ask myself, "What can I buy? What can I option?"
I have ideas I want to express.
Woody Allen

There are two things that bother me about [the Academy Awards]. They're
political and bought and negotiated for—although many worthy people
have deservedly won—and the whole concept of awards is silly. I cannot abide
by the judgment of other people, because if you accept it when they say you
deserve an award, then you have to accept it when they say you don't. Also,
it's hard not to get a slightly skewed feeling about the Academy Awards
because apart from the ads and the campaigning and the studio loyalties,
it's a popularity contest really, because if the picture is not seen well or
didn't do very well, its chances are hurt.
Woody Allen, from a 1974 interview

They came to my office. My secretary called up and said, "What do you want
to do with them?" Well, I'm certainly not going to put Oscars in my house!
Woody Allen, from an interview with Tom Shales in *Esquire*, April 1987

Nominations and Wins
(• • • = WIN)

1965
MUSIC (Song): "What's New, Pussycat?" (Burt Bacharach and Hal David) from *What's New, Pussycat?* (Lost to "The Shadow of Your Smile" from *The Sandpiper*)

1966
=0= (*What's Up, Tiger Lily?*)

1967
MUSIC (Song): "The Look of Love" (Burt Bacharach and Hal David) from *Casino Royale* (Lost to "Talk to the Animals" from *Dr. Doolittle*)

1968
=0=

1969
=0= (*Don't Drink the Water* and *Take the Money and Run*)

1970
=0=

1971
=0= (*Bananas*)

1972

=0=(*Play It Again, Sam* and *Everything You Always Wanted to Know About Sex** (**But Were Afraid to Ask*)

1973

=0=(*Sleeper*)

1974

=0=

1975

=0=(*Love and Death*)

1976

WRITING (Screenplay Written Directly for the Screen): *The Front* (Walter Bernstein) (Lost to *Network* by Paddy Chayefsky)

1977

• • • PICTURE: *Annie Hall*

ACTOR: Woody Allen; *Annie Hall* (Lost to Richard Dreyfuss in *The Goodbye Girl*)

• • • ACTRESS: Diane Keaton; *Annie Hall*

• • • DIRECTOR: Woody Allen; *Annie Hall*

• • • WRITING (Screenplay Written Directly for the Screen): Woody Allen and Marshall Brickman; *Annie Hall*

1978

ACTRESS: Geraldine Page; *Interiors* (Lost to Jane Fonda in *Coming Home*)

SUPPORTING ACTRESS: Maureen Stapleton; *Interiors* (Lost to Maggie Smith in *California Suite*)

DIRECTOR: Woody Allen; *Interiors* (Lost to Michael Cimino for *The Deer Hunter*)

WRITING (Screenplay Written Directly for the Screen): Woody Allen; *Interiors* (Lost to *Coming Home* by Waldo Salt and Robert C. Jones)

ART DIRECTION: Mel Bourne; Daniel Robert; *Interiors* (Lost to *Heaven Can Wait;* Paul Sylbert and Edwin O'Donovan; George Gaines)

1979

SUPPORTING ACTRESS: Mariel Hemingway; *Manhattan* (Lost to Meryl Streep in *Kramer vs. Kramer*)

WRITING (Screenplay Written Directly for the Screen): Woody Allen and Marshall Brickman; *Manhattan* (Lost to *Breaking Away* by Steve Tesich)

1980

=0=(*Stardust Memories*)

1981

=0=

1982

=0=(*A Midsummer Night's Sex Comedy*)

1983

CINEMATOGRAPHY: Gordon Willis; *Zelig* (Lost to Sven Nykvist for *Fanny & Alexander*)

COSTUME DESIGN: Santo Loquasto; *Zelig* (Lost to Marik Vos for *Fanny & Alexander*)

1984

DIRECTOR: Woody Allen; *Broadway Danny Rose* (Lost to Milos Forman for *Amadeus*)

WRITING (Screenplay Written Directly for the Screen): Woody Allen; *Broadway Danny Rose* (Lost to Robert Benton for *Places in the Heart*)

1985
WRITING (Screenplay Written Directly for the Screen): Woody Allen; *The Purple Rose of Cairo* (Lost to Earl W. Wallace and William Kelley for *Witness*)

1986
PICTURE: *Hannah and Her Sisters* (Lost to *Platoon*)
• • • SUPPORTING ACTOR: Michael Caine; *Hannah and Her Sisters*
• • • SUPPORTING ACTRESS: Dianne Wiest; *Hannah and Her Sisters*
DIRECTOR: Woody Allen; *Hannah and Her Sisters* (Lost to Oliver Stone for *Platoon*)
• • • WRITING (Screenplay Written Directly for the Screen): Woody Allen; *Hannah and Her Sisters*
ART DIRECTION–SET DECORATION: Stuart Wartzel; Carol Joffe; *Hannah and Her Sisters* (Lost to Gianni Quaranta and Brian Ackland-Snow; Brian Savegar and Elio Altramura for *A Room with a View*)
FILM EDITING: Susan E. Morse; *Hannah and Her Sisters* (Lost to Claire Simpson for *Platoon*)

1987
WRITING (Screenplay Written Directly for the Screen): Woody Allen; *Radio Days* (Lost to John Patrick Shanley for *Moonstruck*)
ART DIRECTION–SET DECORATION: Santo Loquasto; Carol Joffe, Les Bloom, and George DeTitta, Jr.; *Radio Days* (Lost to Bruno Cesari for *The Last Emperor*)

=0= (*September*)

1988
=0= (*Another Woman*)

1989
DIRECTOR: Woody Allen, *Crimes and Misdemeanors* (lost to Oliver Stone for *Born on the Fourth of July*)
WRITING (Best Original Screenplay): Woody Allen; *Crimes and Misdemeanors* (lost to Ronald Bass and Barry Morrow for *Rain Man*)

1990
WRITING (Best Original Screenplay): Woody Allen, *Alice* (lost to Tom Schulman for *Dead Poets Society*)

Appendix 5

Woody, the Actor
The Directors Woody Has Worked For

> I'm not really much of an actor, but I have a personality that is, for better or worse, identifiable to an audience.
> **Woody Allen**

Donner, Guest, Ross, Ritt, Godard, and Mazursky

Woody Allen has appeared in films he did not direct. Those films are listed below, along with brief profiles of the directors who have directed Woody Allen. (For complete details on the specific films in which Woody appeared [except for *King Lear,* which was only a cameo], see Chapter 5.)

1. *What's New, Pussycat?* (1965); Directed by Clive Donner.
   CLIVE DONNER is a British director who was born in 1926, entered the film business in 1942, and has been directing since the midfifties. Donner holds the distinction of being the first director to direct Woody Allen.

2. *Casino Royale* (1967); Woody Allen's segment directed by Val Guest (segments of the films also directed by John Huston, Ken Hughes, Robert Parrish, and Joseph McGrath).
   VAL GUEST is a British writer-producer-director born in 1911. He wrote many comedy screenplays in the thirties for Will Hay, Arthur Haskey, the Crazy Gang, and others. He directed the Woody Allen segment of *Casino Royale* in 1967.

3. *Play it Again, Sam* (1972); Directed by Herbert Ross.
   HERBERT ROSS is a prolific director who has "specialized" in the romantic comedy, particularly the work of Neil Simon. Ross had hits with 1977's *The Goodbye Girl* and 1989's *Steel Magnolias.*

4. *The Front* (1976); Directed by Martin Ritt.
   MARTIN RITT is a first-rate director who has made many memorable films, including *Sounder, Norma Rae,* and *Nuts. The Front* was based on his and his colleagues' experience of being blacklisted in the 1950s.

5. *King Lear* (1987); Directed by Jean-Luc Godard.
   JEAN-LUC GODARD is a French director of surrealistic, "new wave" films. Writing about Godard's work, critic John Simon once said, "Since Godard's films have nothing to say, perhaps we could have ninety minutes of silence instead of each of them."
   This scathing critique notwithstanding, Woody Allen obviously has found something in Godard's work he likes, since he agreed to appear in the director's (universally panned) 1987 film of the Shakespeare classic, *King Lear.* Woody's role amounted to nothing more than a walk-on: he was a soliloquizing film editor by the name of "Mr. Alien."
   This appearance by Woody was his first work for another director since *The Front.*

6. *Scenes from a Mall* (1991); Directed by Paul Mazursky.
   PAUL MAZURSKY has specialized in films that take hard, realistic (yet humorous) looks at marriage and modern relationships. His 1978 film, *Unmarried Woman,* is harrowing in its depiction of the effects of divorce. My personal favorite of Mazursky's films is his wonderful 1986 comedy, *Down and Out in Beverly Hills.*
   After Woody worked in *Scenes from a Mall,* he said that he would like to cast

Mazursky in one of his films. (Mazursky is also an actor. In addition to appearing in his own *Enemies: A Love Story* in 1989, and as Dr. Hans Clava in his own *Scenes from a Mall,* he has appeared as an actor in *Alex in Wonderland* in 1970, *A Star Is Born* in 1976, *A Man, A Woman, and a Bank* in 1979, *Into the Night* in 1984, and *Scenes from the Class Struggle in Beverly Hills,* also in 1989.)

Appendix 6

The Uncollected Nonfiction

Woody Allen has occasionally written nonfiction pieces for a variety of publications, and the list below highlights a few of the more notable articles.

"What's Nude Pussycat?" (U1), "The Girls of *Casino Royale*" (U4), and "Everything You've Always Wanted to Know About Sex You'll Find in My New Movie" (U7) are humorous statements on the films *What's New, Pussycat?*, *Casino Royale*, and *Everything You Always Wanted to Know About Sex*, details of which you will find in Chapter 5.

U1. "What's Nude Pussycat?"; *Playboy*, August 1965.

U2. "Quoi de Neuf, Pussycat?"; *L'Avant-Scène*, Paris, Numéro 59, 1966.

U3. "Attention! See Europe with the King of the International Set (me)"; *Esquire*, February 1966.

U4. "The Girls of *Casino Royale*"; *Playboy*, February 1967.

U5. "How Bogart Made Me the Superb Lover I Am Today"; *Life*, March 1969.

U6. "Woody, the Would-Be Critic"; *New York Times*, May 2, 1971.

U7. "Everything You've Always Wanted to Know About Sex You'll Find in My New Movie"; *Playboy*, September 1972.

U8. "On *Love and Death*"; *Esquire*, July 19, 1975.

U9. "Annie Hall"; *L'Avant-Scène*, Paris, December 15, 1977.

U10. Random Reflections of a Second-Rate Mind"; *Tikkun* magazine, January/February 1990.

Annotated Bibliography

Herein are books on Woody Allen and his work, and also on related subjects.

Of most titles a mini-review is offered that will, I trust, act as a guide to and a starting point for further study of the Woody Allen world.

The opinions expressed here are based on my reviews and on my evaluation of each book's importance in helping us learn more about Woody and his work.

Some of these titles succeed, some don't.

All have value, though, and I can think of worse ways to spend time than reading through this eclectic collection of critique, commentary, and trivia.

. . . but we need the eggs: The Magic of Woody Allen by Diane Jacobs (New York: St. Martin's Press, 1982).

    . . . but we need the eggs covers Woody and his career from the early nightclub years through 1981's *The Floating Light Bulb,* and offers readable, perceptive, and entertaining commentary. A lengthy interview with Woody (excerpted throughout the book) adds to the appeal of this well-thought-out study. His career and creative output are examined thematically, with appropriate excerpts from the films and essays illustrating and buttressing important points. . . . *but we need the eggs* also offers an index, a filmography, a photo section, and a book and play bibliography (although the book bibliography lists only Woody's three essay collections). Highly recommended.

Diane Keaton: The Story of the Real Annie Hall by Jonathan Moor (New York: St. Martin's Press, 1989).

    A well-done, very current biography of Diane Keaton that pays particular attention to her involvement with Woody. Woody's influence on Diane and her career is acknowledged not only in the title of the book, but also in two informative chapters, "Woody," and "Oh, Yeah, Woody's Girl?" The book has a photo section, an index, and a filmography and list of theatrical performances. A general bibliography lists books important to the Keaton fan, and there's an articles bibliography.

Everything You Always Wanted to Know About Woody Allen: The Ultimate Quiz Book by Frank Weimann (New York: Shapolsky Publishers, 1991).

    This was the third quiz book published about Woody's work, and it is the worst of the lot. This book seems to have been slapped together with very little effort, and was apparently published simply to cash in on Woody's popularity. Author Weimann makes the same mistake the other quiz book authors did: he uses the multiple-choice quiz format and he attempts to be as witty as Woody with the "incorrect" choices. Here is an example from Weimann's *Sleeper* quiz:

> 23. Miles was afraid he'd see something "weird and futuristic" like:
>   a) the body of a crab with the head of a social worker.
>   b) the face of a fish with the voice of Rona Barrett.
>   c) the head of a city official with the brains of an imbecile.
>   d) none of the above.

It's always a tipoff that a quiz author is floundering when he or she resorts to a "none of the above" or an "all of the above" choice. This is not to say that Weimann did not do his research. He did, and it's obvious that he is a true Woody fan. It's just that his quizzes are badly constructed (as well as badly edited—I found typos that should have been caught) and, for me, most of the entertainment value of the book was lost. One smart move, though, was organizing the quizzes by film. But the problems with the book outweigh the pluses.

The Films of Woody Allen by Robert Benayoun (New York: Harmony Books, 1986).
This is a superb study of Woody and his work that was originally published in French as *Woody Allen: Au-Dèla du Language*. Like Douglas Brode's book, it is over-sized and photo-packed, but unlike Professor Brode, Benayoun chooses to examine Woody's films thematically, rather than on a chapter-by-chapter/film-by-film basis. Benayoun, a noted and respected French film critic, focuses on the duality of "Woody Allen," positing that Woody "the director" and Woody "the actor" are two quite different animals, and that each aspect of the man has matured in different ways with each new work. Benayoun's book contains over two hundred photos, three "Q & A" interviews with Woody himself, a filmography, a play bibliography, a look at Woody Allen's use of music, a biographical section, and a general bibliography. The book is current through *Radio Days*. Recommended.

The Films of Woody Allen by Giannalberto Bendazzi (Ravette, 1987).
A book in Italian about Woody and his work. Published only in Italy.

The Films of Woody Allen by Douglas Brode (New York: Citadel Press, 1991).
This is one of the best volumes ever written about Woody Allen's work. Douglas Brode is a professor of film and a film critic, and his insights are astute and impor-tant. The underlying thesis of his study of Woody's work is "the paradox principle," which states that "[Woody's] best moments, comic or otherwise, are those in which the image and words contradict one another." A simple concept, but one which elucidates much of the subtext in Woody's work. Professor Brode inspects each of Woody's films, focusing on Woody's employment of the paradox principle, and pays particular attention to Woody's contrapuntal use of food and death as primary themes and images in his work. The book has close to four hundred photos, but no bibliography or index. Douglas Brode's *The Films of Woody Allen* (not to be confused with Robert Benayoun's book of the same name) is must reading for the serious Woody Allen fan. Highly recommended. (See my interview with Douglas Brode in Chapter 3.)

Fun with Woody: The Complete Woody Allen Quiz Book by Graham Flashner (New York: Henry Holt and Company, 1987).
This is the best of the three quiz books published on Woody's work. The book has over five hundred questions, and the quizzes are complete through *Radio Days*. The book also contains miscellaneous quizzes, plus quotes by Woody and unique pho-tos scattered throughout. A well-organized, very well-constructed quiz book. *This one* is a lot of fun. Recommended.

I Dream of Woody by Dee Burton (New York: William Morrow & Co., 1984).
This book must take the prize as the most bizarre book ever published about Woody Allen. Dee Burton collected, compiled, analyzed, and annotated people's dreams about Woody, noting especially how a person's (dream) perception of Woody was due in a large part to the latter's public persona. An interesting idea, but ultimately a boring book.

Loser Take All by Maurice Yacowar (New York: Frederick Ungar, 1979; expanded edition, 1991).
Maurice Yacowar's *Loser Take All* is a definitive and an authoritative full-length critical study of Woody Allen's work. This is a *very* comprehensive resource that offers penetrating insights into the Woody Allen persona. The book has twenty-nine chapters, broken into five parts: "The Public Face of Woody Allen"; "Woody in the Theater"; "Woody the Writer"; "Woody's Films: Guilt-Edged Cinema"; and "Through the Eighties." Each chapter is thoroughly footnoted, and the book carries two photo sections, a very comprehensive index, an excellent filmography and

discography, and superb primary and secondary bibliographies. The bibliographies, in fact, are the most complete and wide-ranging ever published. *Loser Take All* is not for every Woody fan: this volume and Nancy Pogel's book constitute almost a graduate-level study of Woody's work. But it is an enlightening and educational experience, and on second thought, perhaps it is a book that *should* be for every Woody fan. Recommended.

Love, Sex, Death and the Meaning of Life by Bill Hirsch (New York: McGraw-Hill, 1981).
This is another excellent appraisal of Woody's work. Written by an associate professor of English and film at Brooklyn College, Hirsch explores Woody's influences, from the urban Jewish modernist literary milieu to the high culture of Tolstoy and Ingmar Bergman. The book has eight chapters. *Love, Sex, Death and the Meaning of Life* was published in 1981, and in the last chapter Hirsch offers a particularly precognitive prediction:

> The comedian's progress: 1990 will almost surely indicate a record of experiment and achievement that bears only the faintest traces of the original Allen schlemiel but that will continue to surprise and delight and occasionally to infuriate us.

Hirsch's book is current through *Stardust Memories,* and includes an index, a bibliography, and a filmography, but no photos. Recommended.

Mia Farrow: Flower Child, Madonna, Muse by Sam Rubin and Richard Taylor (New York: St. Martin's Press, 1989).
This is an interesting and entertaining biography of Woody's long-time other half and includes a great deal of material of interest to Woody fans. Two entire chapters (out of eleven) deal solely with her relationship (both personal and professional) with Woody Allen. The book has an index and a photo section. (Speaking of photos, I think the front-cover photo of Mia is one of the nicest ever taken, and that on the back one of the worst. Go figure.)

Mia: The Life of Mia Farrow by Edward Z. Epstein and Joe Morella (New York: Delacorte Press, 1991).
This is an up-to-the minute bio of Mia that spends not much more than a chapter (Chapter 15) on her relationship with Woody. It is well researched, though, and very informative if you're looking for info on the varied and sometimes tumultuous life of Mia Farrow.

The Movies of Woody Allen: A Short, Neurotic Quiz Book by David Wild (New York: Perigee Books, 1987).
This quiz book isn't bad, although the construction and layout of the book leave much to be desired. Wild offers six hundred questions, scattered through only twelve quizzes. You'll find fill-ins, and multiple-choice, matching, and true-false questions spanning many films in each quiz. I'm sure the author thought the variety and mix would be entertaining, but sometimes it's just confusing. Overall, though, the research is good. As with Frank Weimann's book, I don't like the "incorrect" choices in the multiple-choice questions not being drawn from Woody's material.

Non-Being and Somethingness by Stuart Hample (New York: Random House, 1978).
This was a collection of Stuart Hample's comic strips based on Woody Allen's jokes. The book featured an introduction by R. Buckminster Fuller.

On Being Funny: Woody Allen and Comedy by Eric Lax (New York: Charterhouse Press, 1975).

This was one of the first two books ever published about Woody Allen (the other was *Woody Allen: Clown Prince of Humor*) and it must still be considered one of the best. Eric Lax and Woody Allen have been friends for decades, and this book was written with Woody's approval and participation, as was Lax's later authorized biography. *On Being Funny* focuses on the early years, and includes unique material, such as the transcript of Larry Gelbart and Woody Allen's parody of Ingmar Bergman's *Wild Strawberries* called *Strange Strawberries*. *On Being Funny* has twelve chapters, all of which are titled by either a Woody Allen quote, or a paraphrase of something said by someone having something to do with Woody (such as Ralph Rosenblum). They are:

1. "Nothing you do here can affect your career in any way."
2. "I had to struggle to keep alive in that kind of company."
3. "I could have made it twice as funny and half as successful."
4. "I don't find any of this fun."
5. "We need one with a little more gorgiositude."
6. "I want to make it funny and pretty and the two are opposite."
7. "Like digging a grave at a cemetery—over and over again."
8. "You have to end like a house afire."
9. "What I'm trying to do is grow."
10. "Feeding the monster."
11. "It's not that I'm afraid to die, I just don't want to be there when it happens."
12. "People tell me there are a lot of guys like me, which doesn't explain why I'm lonely."

The book includes a photo section, and a very complete index. *On Being Funny* is long out of print (Lax utilized about twenty-five pages from it in *Woody Allen: A Biography*), but many libraries still have it. It is a fascinating look at the early years of Woody Allen's career, and an entertaining read. Recommended.

On Being Funny: Woody Allen and Comedy by Eric Lax (New York: Manor Books, paperback edition, 1977).

The paperback edition of Lax's Charterhouse book.

The Other Side of the Moon: A Biography of David Niven by Sheridan Morley (New York: Harper & Row, 1985).

This one is included because of some interesting information about the making of *Casino Royale*. If you're a Niven fan, you'll read it cover to cover. If not, just look up *Casino Royale* in the index and read about Woody's participation in that film.

When the Shooting Stops . . . the Cutting Begins by Ralph Rosenblum and Robert Karen (New York: Viking Press, 1979).

Ralph Rosenblum was Woody Allen's editor for *Take the Money and Run, Bananas, Sleeper, Love and Death, Annie Hall,* and *Interiors.* This book is his somewhat solipsistic career autobiography which will be of interest to Woody fans mainly for his comments about working on those six Woody Allen films. Of particular interest is Chapter 19, "*Annie Hall:* It Wasn't the Film He Set Out to Make," which gives details on the *original* version of Woody's masterpiece. Long out of print, *When the Shooting Stops* might be reposing in a library somewhere, so you may need a book-search service to locate it for you. (A search service found the book for me—for $35.00. Be prepared to pay two, three, or even more times the original price for a "found" book.) Recommended, though, for the *Annie Hall* info not found anywhere else.

Woody Allen by Gilles Cèbe (Paris: Henri Veyrier, 1981).
A book in French about Woody and his work. Published only in France.

Woody Allen by C. Dureau (PAC, 1985).
Another book in French about Woody and his work. Published only in France.

Woody Allen by Michel Lebrun (PAC, 1979).
Still another book in French about Woody and his work. Published only in France.

Woody Allen by Nancy Pogel (Boston: G. K. Hall & Co., 1987).
This book is easily the most scholarly book ever written about Woody's work. It was part of Twayne Publishers' Filmmaker series, and was written by Nancy Pogel, a professor of American thought and language at Michigan State University who also teaches in its Film Thematic Program. This is serious stuff. Pogel's book has eleven chapters. The book also contains a brief chronology, a section of notes and references, a selected bibliography, a filmography, an index, and photos scattered throughout. For a serious, scholarly appraisal of Woody's work, you won't get much better (or deeper) than this. In his profile of Woody in the December 1991 issue of *Playboy,* Mordecai Richler called Pogel's book "pretentious," and cited a couple of the more abstruse quotes from the text. I concur that the book may be dense and complex, but I don't agree that it's out of pretense that Pogel presents her material in this manner. I think that she's very sincere, and that Richler just can't be bothered with esoteric critique. This is an important book that takes a serious and sober look at the development of an American artist. Recommended (for serious film buffs and scholars, or those of you who want to become serious film buffs or scholars).

Woody Allen: Au-Dèla du Language by Robert Benayoun (Paris: Editions Herscher, 1985).
This was the original French language edition of Benayoun's book *The Films of Woody Allen.* (See my review of that title.)

Woody Allen: A Biography by Lee Guthrie (New York: Drake Publishers, 1978).
Nancy Pogel said this of Guthrie's book in her own *Woody Allen:* "This unauthorized and untrustworthy biography was taken off the market shortly after publication when Allen sued Guthrie and Drake Publishers because Guthrie appropriated materials from Allen, from Eric Lax, and from other secondary sources without attribution." If this is true (and I have no reason to doubt that it is), this would seem to be strange behavior by Guthrie. Before her Woody book was published, she had written a biography of Cary Grant, and had been a working newspaper reporter and magazine editor. She should have known better. The "recall" of this title makes it a rare Woody Allen collectible. It's a fairly innocuous book, and one that seems as unreliable as Pogel asserts. (The few items of fact that I checked from Guthrie's book seemed accurate enough. I think the whole problem with the book was Guthrie's unattributed use of material.) If you're interested in perusing this book, you'll have to track it down at a library, or through a book-search service.

Woody Allen: A Biography by Eric Lax (New York: Alfred A. Knopf, 1991).
This volume is the first authorized biography of Woody Allen, and the fact that Woody approved it is evident on every page. *Woody Allen: A Biography* is in six parts:

Introduction: "The Digger Ant's Vacation"
Part One: "Snared in the Web of Escape"
Part Two: "The Heart of Show Business"
Part Three: "Ladies and Gentlemen, Woody Allen!"
Part Four: "Hold the Dolce Vita, S'il Vous Plaît"
Part Five: "The Million-Dollar Finesses"

There are over thirty thousand of Woody Allen's words in this tome, and many of his remarks appear here for the first time. Eric Lax, the author of a previous book about Woody, is a personal friend of the very private director and, thus, had total access to Woody's sets, scripts, cutting room, and even Woody himself. Lax is a fan, as well as a friend, and so you won't find much here that even borders on the negative. But Lax does provide the reader with comprehensive material and accurate details about Woody's life and work. The book contains two photo sections and a very comprehensive index, but no bibliography, filmography, or discography. Highly recommended.

Woody Allen, The Clown Prince of American Humor by Bill Adler and Jeffrey Feinman (New York: Pinnacle Books, 1975).
This was one of the first books published about Woody and it contained some charming and entertaining material. The book had six chapters. Woody's early years are adequately covered, and his later essays are cogently critiqued. Probably the most perceptive chapter in the book is Chapter 5. Adler and Feinman walk you through the imagined practical technique of writing like Woody Allen. Of course, it's meant as an instructive device, since what they can't add to the recipe are the sensibility and genius of Woody himself, but the technique does enlighten the reader as to the various influences on Woody's comedic methodology. *Clown Prince* is now more than fifteen years out of date, but I recommend it for some of its unique features. No index, filmography, discography, or bibliography, but there is an extensive photo section.

The Woody Allen Companion by Stephen J. Spignesi (Kansas City: Andrews and McMeel, 1992).
This volume.

The Woody Allen Encyclopedia by Mark A. Altman (Las Vegas: Pioneer Books, 1992).
This is an oversized trade paperback written by a Woody Allen fan for Woody Allen fans. (And by that I mean it is definitely not an academic probe of Woody, but an informal, humorous survey.) The book contains several informative essays—serious and comedic—about different facets of Woody's work, as well as a humorous "sequels" parody. Altman offers details on *Interiors 2; Return to Manhattan;* and *Sleeper 2: Judgement Day.* Contributors and participants include Thomas Doherty, David Dean Salter, Mitch Rubinstein, Ezra Swerdlow, and Julie Kavner. The heart of the book is a limited encyclopedic concordance to the people, places, and things of Woody's films. Author Altman told me he was very displeased with the publisher's version of this book (asserting it's his first draft rather than final text) and has asked to have his name removed from the book. Caveat emptor.

Woody Allen: His Films and Career by Douglas Brode (New York: Citadel Press, 1985).
This was the original title and edition of what was reissued in an expanded and revised edition in 1991 as *The Films of Woody Allen.* (See that title above.)

Woody Allen: An Illustrated Biography by Myles Palmer (New York: Proteus, 1980).
This book is a general-interest biographical overview of Woody and his career, and contains some rare photos not found elsewhere. Interesting, but out of print.

Woody Allen—Mel Brooks by Robert Benayoun, Vincent Canby, Peter W. Jansen, Bert Koetter, Christa Maerker, Hans Gunther Pflaum, and Hans Helmut Prinzler (Munich: Carl Hanser Verlag, 1980).
A book in German about Woody and Mel Brooks. Published only in Germany.

Woody Allen: New Yorker by Graham McCann (New York: Polity Press, 1990).

A comprehensive critical study of Woody's work written by a Cambridge University professor. The book explores Woody's work through *Oedipus Wrecks,* and examines the nightclub routines and essays as well. McCann is obviously a fan, but the volume erroneously claims to be "the first detailed study of Woody Allen's life and work."

Woody Allen on Location by Thierry de Navacelle (New York: William Morrow & Co., 1987).

This is a day-by-day diary of the making of *Radio Days.* (See the feature on the book at the end of the *Radio Days* section in Chapter 5.) It is an informative but emotionless work that suffers from an overload of minutiae and a paucity of comment by Woody. Worth a peek, though, if you're curious about what it's like on a Woody Allen set.

About the Author

Stephen Spignesi, a full-time writer, is the author of three books about Stephen King: *The Stephen King Quiz Book* (New York: NAL/Signet, 1990); *The Complete Stephen King Encyclopedia* (Chicago: Contemporary Books, 1992); and *The Second Stephen King Quiz Book* (New York: NAL/Signet, 1992). Stephen's first book was the highly regarded 1987 "Andy Griffith Show" encyclopedia, *Mayberry, My Hometown* (Ann Arbor: Popular Culture, Ink), which was recently released in paperback. Spignesi lives in New Haven, Connecticut, with his wife, Pam.